The Anglicized and Illustrated Dictionary of Interior Design

Josette H. Rabun
Catherine L. Kendall

Line Drawings by Julie L. Rabun

PEARSON

Boston   Columbus   Indianapolis   New York   San Francisco   Upper Saddle River
Amsterdam   Cape Town   Dubai   London   Madrid   Milan   Munich   Paris   Montréal   Toronto
Delhi   Mexico City   São Paulo   Sydney   Hong Kong   Seoul   Singapore   Taipei   Tokyo

Editorial Director: Vern Anthony
Acquisitions Editor: Sara Eilert
Assistant Editor: Laura Weaver
Editorial Assistant: Doug Greive
Director of Marketing: David Gesell
Senior Marketing Coordinator: Alicia Wozniak
Marketing Manager: Harper Coles
Marketing Assistant: Les Roberts
Associate Managing Editor: Alexandrina Benedicto Wolf
Production Project Manager: Alicia Ritchey

Operations Specialist: Deidra Skahill
Art Director: Jayne Conte
Cover Designer: Bruce Kenselaar
Cover Art: Julie Rabun
Lead Media Project Manager: Karen Bretz
Full-Service Project Management: Element LLC
Composition: MPS Limited
Printer/Binder: Edwards Brothers Malloy
Cover Printer: Lehigh-Phoenix Color/Hagerstown
Text Font: 11/12.5 Kepler Std Light Semicondensed

Credits and acknowledgments borrowed from other sources and reproduced, with permission, in this textbook appear on the appropriate page within text.

Many of the designations by manufacturers and sellers to distinguish their products are claimed as trademarks. Where those designations appear in this book, and the publisher was aware of a trademark claim, the designations have been printed in initial caps or all caps.

Library of Congress Cataloging-in-Publication Data

Rabun, Josette H.
  The anglicized and illustrated dictionary of interior design/Josette H. Rabun, Catherine L. Kendall, Julie L. Rabun.
    pages cm
  ISBN 978-0-13-092538-1
1.   Decoration and ornament—Dictionaries.   2.   Interior decoration—Dictionaries   I.   Title.
  NK1165.R33 2013
  747.03—dc23
                                                                                    2012008177

10 9 8 7 6 5 4 3 2 1

ISBN 10: 0-13-092538-1
ISBN 13: 978-0-13-092538-1

Contents

Preface   iv

Guide to Pronunciation   v

Dictionary of Words   1–312

Appendix   313–354

    Architects, Artists, and Designers   315–340

    Case Piece   341

    Chair Vocabulary   342

    Door Design   343

    Wall Design   344

    Architectural Orders   345–346

    Feet   347

    Joints   348

    Legs   349

    Moldings   350

    Motifs/Ornaments   351–353

    Pediments   354

Preface

The Anglicized and Illustrated Dictionary of Interior Design includes traditional, historic, and modern day terminology ranging from pre-classical to present day. Since the inception of the interior design profession, the world of design as a whole has expanded to include many cultures and languages. Where necessary, the words are anglicized within the dictionary to facilitate correct pronunciation, which allows the professional designer, student, or layperson to become more competent. In addition to the anglicized entries, a pronunciation guide is provided to facilitate understanding. This invaluable tool emphasizes the importance of correct pronunciation in the field of interior design, where foreign language terms are abundant. Contemporary communication incorporates a worldwide dialogue, necessitating a better understanding of diverse vocabulary.

The dictionary has over 1,200 drawings that further enrich the definitions. Designers regularly depend upon visual resources as a part of the identification process. In order to increase comprehension, the authors have painstakingly identified key terms that are further defined with an illustration.

Also included are modern terms not found in other interior design dictionaries that prove to be invaluable to both interior designers and those in related fields. Technical terminology, such as electrical, plumbing, heating, ventilation and cooling, as well as terms specific to architecture and engineering building systems, are not included because these terms are usually found in books specific to those disciplines.

The Anglicized and Illustrated Dictionary of Interior Design should function as a working tool for interior designers as well as those in related fields. The scope of the words, articulated with precise anglicized definitions that include illustrations where appropriate, will prove to be an invaluable resource to the professional and amateur alike.

ACKNOWLEDGMENTS

The authors and illustrator would like to thank our family, friends, colleagues, and students for their limitless encouragement, support, and patience throughout this long process. As with any large-scale project, there are a great number of individuals who facilitated completion. However, we would like to offer special thanks to Dr. Daniel F. Pigg for his contributions as an outside editor, and Dr. Robbie G. Blakemore for her willingness to allow a number of illustrations from her text to be reprinted in this book.

Guide to Pronunciation

Adapted from Merriam-Webster Online Dictionary

Vowels	Used in	Example	Consonants	Used in	Example
a	relax, past	rihLAKS- relax	b	baby, bone	BAYbee- baby
ay	date, same	DAYT- date	ch	chubby, checker	CHUbee- chubby
ah	father, far	FAHthur- father	d	bidder, do, did, done	BIdur- bidder
aw	chainsaw, thaw	CHAYNsaw- chainsaw	f	stuff, rough, fluff	STUF- stuff
e	federal, pet	FEDurul- federal	g	got, big, rag	GAHT- got
ee	meander, bleed, feed, speed	meeANdur- meander	h	headwind, hat, hold	HEDwind- headwind
i	swish, trip, snip	SWISH- swish	j	journey, join, jab, nudge	JURnee- journey
iy	frightful, side, buy	FRIYTful- frightful	k	carrot, cake, kite, ache, book	KEruht- carrot
oh	boneless, know, beau	BOHNles- boneless	l	valley, cool, flash	VAlee, valley
oi	destroy, annoy	diSTROI- destroy	m	mammal, dam, move	MAmul- mammal
oo	reunion, rule, fool	reeYOONyun- reunion	n	never, pan	NEHVur- never
ow	flout, noun, sound	FLOWT- flout	ng	something, sang, sink	SUMthing- something
u	monotony, ton, fun, abut	muNAHtunee- monotony	p	plus, lip, trapper	PLUS- plus
uu	wood, would, book	WUUD- would	r	rambunctious, race, terror	ramBUNKshus- rambunctious
y	young, cue, yet	YUNG- young	s	citation, salad, less, city	siyTAYshun- citation
			sh	machine, mash, mission, special	muSHEEN- machine
			t	later, untie, latter	LAYtur- later
			th	thing, ether, thoughtful	THING- thing
			v	volume, invite	VAHLyoom- volume
			w	away, willing, wander	uWAY- away
			wh	while, whale, when	WHIYL- while
			z	raise, zone, breeze	RAYZ- raise
			zh	revision, garage	reeVIHzhun- revision

á la Reine (AH LAH RAYN)

A French flat upholstered chair back.

Aalto stacking stools

See *Alvar Aalto stacking stools. See Alvar Aalto, 1898–1976, in the Architects, Artists, and Designers Appendix.*

abaca (AH ba kah)

A strong fiber known technically as Manila hemp and used for cordage, carpet, matting, and wall covering.

abachi (ah BAH chee)

A wood. See also *ayous.*

abacus (AA be kus)

1) The block that forms the uppermost member of the capital of a column and divides the capital from the entablature. 2) A small table or sideboard of the Hellenistic or late Roman period used to show plates. 3) In architecture the slab that forms the uppermost portion of the capital of a column.

abacus

abattant (AH bet ahnt)

French term for a drop leaf or hinged panel of a table as in secrétaire à abattant. See also *secrétaire à abattant.*

abbey (Aa bee)

A monastery or convent. See also *monastery.*

ablaq (ah BLAHK)

Alternating colors or shades of different materials, such as red and white or black or white in Arab architecture or alternating light and dark in the Byzantine. This technique is also found in the masonry architecture of Spain and Europe.

abattant

aboudikrou (AH boo dee kroh)

A wood found in Africa that resembles mahogany or sapele. See *sapele.*

abstract art or abstract design

An art expression conveying emotions through nontraditional forms and color.

Abstract Expressionism

An art movement using rapid renderings of shapes and free use of color to express the subconscious. Known as "action painting" in England.

abulation fountain (ah BYOO lay shun FOWN ten)

Fountain located outside of a mosque used for ritual cleaning.

acacia (AH kay sha)

A durable, strong light brown hardwood from Australia and Africa, similar to the American locust, and often used by Eastern nations during the ancient times for religious and sacred buildings. Today, it is used for architectural and ecclesiastical woodwork and for furniture. See also *blackwood.*

Académie des Beaux Arts (ah KA de mee DAY BOHZ ART)

A French art school founded in 1816 after the dissolution of the Academy of Architecture.

acajou moé (AH ka joh MOH ay)

French term for mahogany or any of the many related trees, imported into France from the time of the Regence. See also *mahogany, Age of Mahogany,* and *primavera.*

acajou mouchetë (AH ka joh MOO chet)

French word for a mahogany popular in the late Louis XVI period and also used in England as a fiddle back mahogany since it resembled wood on the finest violins and other stringed instruments.

acanthus or akanthos (ah KAN thuhs)

A motif of Egyptian origin designed with formalized leaves used in Greek and Roman architecture on Corinthian capitals for enrichment on molding and surfaces. See *illustration in the Motifs/Ornaments Appendix.*

accolade (AA koh layd)
An ornamental treatment composed of two ogee curves meeting in the middle to form a richly decorated molding for use over a door, window, or arch.

accolade

accotoir or accoudoir (A koh twar/A koh dwar)
French term for the wood arm support or elbow rest that extends from the frame of the chair seat to the base of the arm. See also *arm stump*.

accouplement (Ah KOO ple mohntt)
A pair of columns or pilasters placed close together, in pairs.

aceitillo (ah SAY tee yoh)
A fine grain West Indian hardwood, resembling satinwood in color and appearance and used for furniture.

acerra (AH ser ah)
Roman term for a short legged lidded incense box with projections on the lid, or "horns."

achech (u CHEK)
Half lion and half bird fantasy animal found in ancient Egyptian art. See also *hieracosphinx*.

acorn
A turned ornament shaped like an acorn and used on late 16th-century to late 18-century furniture for decoration.

acorn

acorn chair
The name given to a 17th-century Jacobean oak chair with acorn-shaped pendants decorating the cross rail of the back.

acorn turning
A term for Elizabethan and Jacobean table and chair bulbous elements called cup and cover.

acrolith (AA kroh lith)
A classical Greek statute or sculptural figure which has heads, legs, arms, and feet carved of marble, while the wooden body is sheathed in gold.

acropolis (AH krop oh lis)
An elevated stronghold or group of buildings of ancient Greek cities usually with a temple of patron divinity that also served as a civic symbol.

acroteria, acroterion, or akroter (AH kroh ter ee yah)
A pedestal for statutes and other ornament placed on the lower parts and apex of a pediment.

acroteria, acroterion, or akroter

Act of Parliament clock

An inexpensive clock with an enameled glazed face and elegant shaped mahogany band introduced in the mid18th century to early 19th century in England and found in coffee houses or public spaces to definite time when the mail coaches began running. Often referred to as Act of Parliament clock because of the act introduced by Parliament in 1797 that imposed a tax on all clocks of five shillings; the act was repealed the following year. See also *coaching inn clock*.

Act of Parliament clock

Act of Settlement of 1701

In England the act provided the pass of the Stuart line of monarchy to the Hanoverian line since there were no heirs from the union of William III and the future Queen Anne; thus the first Hanoverian monarch, George I (great grandson of James I), a German who could not speak English, became king.

Action Office

First new generation of furniture along the lines of psychological needs of the workers designed by George Propst, along with George Nelson.

Adam brothers

John, Robert, James, and William, architects/designers of Scottish decent, influenced English design during the middle and late 18th century by designing important buildings and interiors in a restrained, classical manner referred to as the neoclassical style.

Adam Style c. 1760–1765 to 1792

Elegant neoclassical style created by the Adam brothers in England around 1760–1790. The lead architect/designer of the period was Robert Adam. *See Robert Adam, 1728–1792, in the Architects, Artists, and Designers Appendix.*

Adam Style

Adamesque (AA dem esk)

English Neoclassical work that resembles the work of the Adam brothers.

adaptation

Changing the design of a building or interior for a new use.

addorsed (AH dorst)

Placing objects back to back.

Adelphi (AH del fy)

A Greek term for brothers and the trademark name of the Adam Brothers of England in the latter part of the 18th century. See also *Adam brothers.*

Adirondack Style (aa du RAHN dak STIYL)

An American style of furniture and

Adirondack Style

interiors developed in the Adirondack Mountains using tree branches.

adobe

Spanish word for the sun dried brick often used in Mexico and the southwestern United States.

adobe

adze (AADZ)

An axe used in wood carving with cutting edge at right angles to the handle.

aedicule, pl. aedicula (EH dik yool)

A miniature shelter or canopied niche consisting of an entablature with a pediment supported by a pair of columns or pilasters; a door or window frame resembling such a structure.

aedicule with ears

The ends of the entablature projecting slightly beyond the columns or pilasters.

aedicule

aegicranes (Eh ji kraynz)

The heads and skulls of goats or rams used as a decorative motif on altars, friezes, etc. in classical Greek and Roman sculpture and on furniture by Neoclassical designers of the late 18th and early 19th centuries.

aeolic (EE oh lik)

A variant of the Ionic, the architectural order.

aegicranes

Aeron chair

An ergonomic chair made largely of recycled material, a product of Herman Miller, designed in 1994 by Don Chadwick and Bill Stumpf. See *Don Chadwick 1936–*, and *Bill Stumpf, 1936–2006, in the Architects, Artists, and Designers Appendix.*

Aeron chair

Aesthetic movement

A British art and design movement of the 19th century formed to rid themselves of the rigid Victorian design in favor of a free expression, with a predominant theme of "Art for Art's Sake."

afara (AH fa rah)

A tropical African wood of light yellow with dark grey markings used in cabinet making. See also *korina and limba.*

affronted, affronté (AH fron ted, AH fron tay)

Animals and/or figures facing each other and used as decorative features over doors and in pediments.

affronted, affronté

agate ware or agateware (AA get WAYR)

An 18th-century pottery resembling agate or quartz produced in England by Wedgwood and other potteries.

Age of Enlightenment

An 18th-century neoclassicism revival to inform society and advance knowledge; a time where architects could study classical architecture through first-hand examination of extant remains of Roman antiquities, view monuments of the Renaissance, visit site excavations of classical cites, and interact with influential architects.

Age of Mahogany

An English period spanning from approximately 1710 to 1765 when mahogany was the prominent wood favored by designers and patrons. Many pieces produced in this wood were Georgian and Chippendale furniture. See also *acajou moe and primavera.*

Age of Oak

An English period spanning from 1500 to 1660, the English Renaissance, when oak was predominately used for furniture and interior treatment. This period includes the Tudor, Elizabethan, Jacobean, and Cromwellian periods.

Age of Reason

See *Age of Enlightenment.*

Age of Revivals

The 19th century was a time of revival for the Classic, Renaissance, Rococo, and Gothic, each style following and overlapping one another in interior, furniture design, and building.

Age of Satinwood

An elegant period in England spanning about 1755 to 1800 when cabinetmakers favored the light, radiant wood for furniture. The Adam brothers, Hepplewhite, and Sheraton used it in their work. See also *satinwood.* See *George Seddon, 1727–1801, in the Architects, Artists, and Designers Appendix.*

Age of Walnut

A period in England from early 1600s to 1730 covering the Restoration, Stuart, William and Mary, and Queen Anne that predominantly used walnut in furniture and interiors.

agora (ah GOR ah)

An ancient Greek open public meeting place or marketplace.

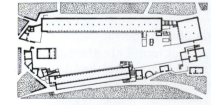

agora

agraffe, agrafe, agraffe
(AH grahf)
The keystone of an arch especially when carved with a human face or cartouche.

aigrette (ay GRET)
French term often interpreted in furniture and interiors as a decorative feather or plume. See also *egret*.

aisle
A passageway in a building between sections or seats, as found in a theater or church.

ajouré (ah joo RAY)
A French term for a design created by piercing holes in wood, ceramics, metals, etc.. as often found on an ajouré bowl with a decorated pierced design. See also *pierced work*.

akanthos (AH kan thus)
See *acanthus*.

Akari lamp (ah KA ree LAMPS)
See *Isamu Noguchi Akari lamp*. See *Isamu Noguchi, 1904–1988, in the Architects, Artists, and Designers Appendix*.

ako (AY koh)
See *chen chen*.

akroter (AH kroh ter)
See *acroter*.

agraffe, agrafe, agraffe

aigrette

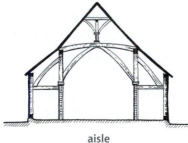

aisle

akume (u KOO mu)
A hard, durable wood that is resistant to fungi and wood borer insects, but could warp and splint. See also *bubinga*.

ala, pl. alae (AY lah)
Small rooms or recesses opening off the atrium in the ancient Roman house. See also *atrium*.

alabaster (AA lah bast er)
A fine-grained, slightly translucent stone of very pure gypsum with a smooth mild-white surface used for ornament and sculpture.

alabastron (AA lah bas tron)
A Greek vase.

alacena (AHL sen ah)
A Spanish term for a cupboard built into the wall and enclosed by doors.

Alcazar (ahl KAH zahr)
A Moorish or Spanish castle built in the middle of the 14th century; the word is derived from Arabic meaning "castle."

alcove (AAL kohv)
Initially a Spanish concept of private area separated from a main area by recessing a small room attached to a larger one, or as a small space adjacent to a larger room to accommodate a bed, piano, etc.

alcove cupboard
An 18th-century English alcove or corner cupboard formed as a part of the paneling in a room. See also *buffet, coin, corner cupboard, encoignure,* and *quoin*.

alcove bed
A late 18th-century or early 19th-century French bed highly decorated on the exposed side since it was to be placed in an alcove. See also *lit á la Polonaise*.

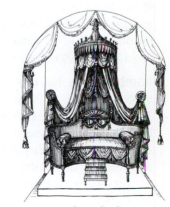

alcove bed

5

alder (AL der)

A pale brown European and American wood aging to a darker golden brown that is often used in plywood due to its strength or used for country or provincial furniture.

alençon lace (AA loh soh LAYS)

A French decorative fabric or needle-point lace often referred to as the Queen of Laces.

Alexander Calder mobile

A mobile designed by Alexander Calder (1898–1976) as a visual art type of kinetic sculpture to take advantage of the principle of equilibrium. See *Alexander Calder, 1898–1976, in the Architects, Artists, and Designers Appendix.*

alfiz (AAL fihz)

A horseshoe arch typical of Moorish architecture.

Alhambra Granda (aal HAAM bru)

A Spanish-Muslim citadel or palace with exquisite geometric patterns, intricate arabesques, and Arabic characters, begun in 1248 and enlarged in 1279 and 1306. See also *Moresque.*

Alhambra vases (aal HAAM bru VAYS ez)

Tall amphora shaped vases of luster earthen ware made in the 11th century in the Hispano-Mauresque style and decorated with arabesques and Arabic inscriptions.

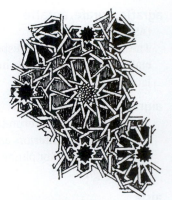

Alexender Calder mobile

alfiz

Alhambra Granada

Alhambresque (aal HAAM bres kay)

Fanciful ornamentation that resembles the style used at Alhambra. See also *stalactite.*

allegory (AA le gor ee)

A figurative representation such as a symbol for a king or queen or an American eagle symbolizing the power of the Continental Congress in America.

alloy (AAL oi)

Two or more metals mixed to create a new metal with some characteristics of the original and some new qualities of the blend. See also *bronze.*

almery (AJ mur ee)

In a medieval structure a cupboard that was set into the wall thickness; later the cupboard was used to contain the portion of food set aside for pensioners and servants. See also *ambry.*

almon (AHL mun)

A wood found in the Philippine with color variation from tan to a soft reddish tone with an interrupted stripe figure.

almond (AHL mund)

A two-pointed oval-shaped pendant of cut glass or crystal used to embellish a chandelier.

almoner's cupboard (AHL mun erz CU berd)

An English Renaissance cupboard that was crudely constructed.

alpaca (AHL pa kah)

A woven fabric usually made from long, fine, and usually dark wool from Peruvian sheep -llama series or the cloth could be of alpaca wool or a mixture of sheep wool, cotton, or silk.

Alhambresque

allegory

agraffe, agrafe, agraffe
(AH grahf)
The keystone of an arch especially when carved with a human face or cartouche.

aigrette (ay GRET)
French term often interpreted in furniture and interiors as a decorative feather or plume. See also *egret*.

aisle
A passageway in a building between sections or seats, as found in a theater or church.

ajouré (ah joo RAY)
A French term for a design created by piercing holes in wood, ceramics, metals, etc.. as often found on an ajouré bowl with a decorated pierced design. See also *pierced work*.

akanthos (AH kan thus)
See *acanthus*.

Akari lamp (ah KA ree LAMPS)
See *Isamu Noguchi Akari lamp*. See *Isamu Noguchi, 1904–1988, in the Architects, Artists, and Designers Appendix*.

ako (AY koh)
See *chen chen*.

akroter (AH kroh ter)
See *acroter*.

agraffe, agrafe, agraffe

aigrette

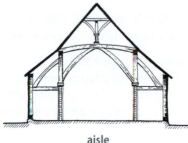
aisle

akume (u KOO mu)
A hard, durable wood that is resistant to fungi and wood borer insects, but could warp and splint. See also *bubinga*.

ala, pl. alae (AY lah)
Small rooms or recesses opening off the atrium in the ancient Roman house. See also *atrium*.

alabaster (AA lah bast er)
A fine-grained, slightly translucent stone of very pure gypsum with a smooth mild-white surface used for ornament and sculpture.

alabastron (AA lah bas tron)
A Greek vase.

alacena (AHL sen ah)
A Spanish term for a cupboard built into the wall and enclosed by doors.

Alcazar (ahl KAH zahr)
A Moorish or Spanish castle built in the middle of the 14th century; the word is derived from Arabic meaning "castle."

alcove (AAL kohv)
Initially a Spanish concept of private area separated from a main area by recessing a small room attached to a larger one, or as a small space adjacent to a larger room to accommodate a bed, piano, etc.

alcove cupboard
An 18th-century English alcove or corner cupboard formed as a part of the paneling in a room. See also *buffet, coin, corner cupboard, encoignure,* and *quoin*.

alcove bed
A late 18th-century or early 19th-century French bed highly decorated on the exposed side since it was to be placed in an alcove. See also *lit á la Polonaise*.

alcove bed

5

alder (AL der)

A pale brown European and American wood aging to a darker golden brown that is often used in plywood due to its strength or used for country or provincial furniture.

alençon lace (AA loh soh LAYS)

A French decorative fabric or needle-point lace often referred to as the Queen of Laces.

Alexander Calder mobile

A mobile designed by Alexander Calder (1898–1976) as a visual art type of kinetic sculpture to take advantage of the principle of equilibrium. See *Alexander Calder, 1898–1976, in the Architects, Artists, and Designers Appendix.*

alfiz (AAL fihz)

A horseshoe arch typical of Moorish architecture.

Alhambra Granda (aal HAAM bru)

A Spanish-Muslim citadel or palace with exquisite geometric patterns, intricate arabesques, and Arabic characters, begun in 1248 and enlarged in 1279 and 1306. See also *Moresque.*

Alhambra vases (aal HAAM bru VAYS ez)

Tall amphora shaped vases of luster earthen ware made in the 11th century in the Hispano-Mauresque style and decorated with arabesques and Arabic inscriptions.

Alexender Calder mobile

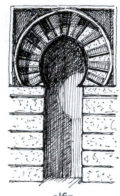

alfiz

Alhambra Granada

Alhambresque (aal HAAM bres kay)

Fanciful ornamentation that resembles the style used at Alhambra. See also *stalactite.*

allegory (AA le gor ee)

A figurative representation such as a symbol for a king or queen or an American eagle symbolizing the power of the Continental Congress in America.

alloy (AAL oi)

Two or more metals mixed to create a new metal with some characteristics of the original and some new qualities of the blend. See also *bronze.*

almery (AJ mur ee)

In a medieval structure a cupboard that was set into the wall thickness; later the cupboard was used to contain the portion of food set aside for pensioners and servants. See also *ambry.*

almon (AHL mun)

A wood found in the Philippine with color variation from tan to a soft reddish tone with an interrupted stripe figure.

almond (AHL mund)

A two-pointed oval-shaped pendant of cut glass or crystal used to embellish a chandelier.

almoner's cupboard (AHL mun erz CU berd)

An English Renaissance cupboard that was crudely constructed.

alpaca (AHL pa kah)

A woven fabric usually made from long, fine, and usually dark wool from Peruvian sheep -llama series or the cloth could be of alpaca wool or a mixture of sheep wool, cotton, or silk.

Alhambresque

allegory

altar

A table or elevated surface upon which sacrificial or religious ceremonies may be enacted.

altar table

An English name for an elevated table, slab, or communion table used for religious rites, sacrifices or offerings.

altar table

altarpiece

A painting, sculpture, or decorative screen often found above the back of an altar.

alto-relievo

alto-relievo (AHL toh re LEE voh)

A French Renaissance sculptural relief work in which the carved area projects more than half their thickness beyond the main surface. See also *haut-relief* and *high relief.*

alure or allure (AH loor)

A passage way around the roof of a church or along the parapets of a castle.

Alvar Aalto paimio chair

A well-known classic chair designed in 1931–32 by Alvar Aalto, Finnish designer, named for the town in southwestern Finland, where Aalto built a sanatorium. The slanted back of the chair supposedly helped the patient with tuberculosis breathe better. See *Alvar Aalto, 1898–1976, in the Architects, Artists, and Designers Appendix.*

alure or allure

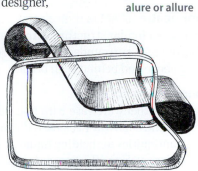

Alvar Aalto paimio chair

Alvar Aalto stacking stool

A simple stool originally made of birch with three legs designed by Alvar Aalto in the 1930s. It is referred to as the Vilpuri stool. See *Alvar Aalto, 1898–1976, in the Architects, Artists, and Designers Appendix.*

Alvar Aalto stacking stool

amaranth (AA mer anth)

A dark purplish wood used since the 19th-century which turns brown when exposed to light and used for contemporary furniture. Often referred to as "Purpleheart." See also *purpleheart* and *violet wood.*

amberina glass (AAM bur een u GLAS)

An ornamental two-colored glass (amber to deep red) made in America during the late 19th century.

ambo, pl. ambores (AHM boh)

A raised stand used in medieval Italian churches for reading the scriptures and speaking to congregations and later replaced by the pulpit.

amboyna (AAM boi nah)

A French term for an East Indian wood with rich golden brown to orange color, highly mottled with burls and bird eye's figures. It was used in the late 18th century as a veneer and decoration banding.

ambry (AAM bree)

See *aumbry* and *almery.*

ambulantes (aam byoo LAHNT)

A French term used to define a small or occasional portable table used for serving purposes. See also *rafraichissoir, servante,* and *serviteur fidèle.*

ambulantes

ambulatory (aam byoo la TOR ee)

The aisle or passageway around the apse in a church.

ambulatory

American Chippendale

A style of furniture made in the mid to late 18th century by American colonial craftsmen based on Queen Anne, Georgian, and Chippendale designs. See *Thomas Chippendale II, 1718–1779, in the Architects, Artists, and Designers Appendix.*

American Colonial

The American style of furniture and decorative arts that prevailed from 1630 to 1789 before and at the time of the American Revolution. See also *colonial*.

American Eagle period

A style synonymous with the early part of the American Federal period in the late 1800s to early 1900s, in which the eagle was a popular motif due to the continental Congress decree to adopt the eagle as a symbol of power.

American Eagle period

American Empire mirror

See *Constitution mirror*.

American Empire period

A design style of furnishing and interiors popular in the United States from 1820 to 1840 based on French Empire and later Sheraton designs. The lead designer of the period was Duncan Phyfe, who used acanthus leaves, pineapples, cornucopias, and stencil gliding as decorative motifs and techniques. See also *butcher furniture*. See *Duncan Phyfe, 1768–1854, in the Architects, Artists, and Designers Appendix.*

American Federal period

An American style influenced by the Adam brothers, Hepplewhite, and Sheraton, and the introduction of the first professional architects and designers in the United States, who under the influence of both Jefferson and Washington used classical designs for federal buildings. See also *Federal Style*.

American Queene Anne furniture

A dominant 18th-century furniture style in America based on Queen Anne style in England, characterized by its solid walnut wood with curving lines, especially the cabriole leg. See also *American Chippendale*.

amorino

amorino, pl. amorini (AH mor ee noh)

Italian term for a winged cherub or cupid used extensively during the Renaissance. See also *cherub* and *putti*.

amphiprostyle (AAM fi proh stiyl)

In classical architecture buildings with a porch or portico on both the front and back.

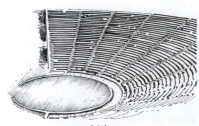

amphitheatre

amphithalomos (AAM fi thal e mohs)

In a Greek house a bedroom especially for unmarried daughters.

amphitheatre (AAM fa thee ah ter)

An oval or circular structure with a central stage or arena surrounded by tiers of seats rising above and behind each other.

amphora (AAM for ah)

A green earthenware vase with two side handles and a narrow neck used during the Greek antiquities for holding liquid or solid provisions, such as oil, wine, or food.

amphora

anaglyph (AA nah glif)
A type of carving embellished by low relief.

anaglypha (AA nah glif ah)
A vase or vessel carved with raised ornamentation.

anaglypta (AA nah glip tah)
A Greek term for a composition ornament made in gesso and plaster compounds and applied to walls and ceilings to simulate a carved, bas relief effect. See also *composition ornament,* *carton-pierre,* and *pastigilia.*

anaglypha

ananas bed (aa NAAN ahs BED)
A bed with exquisitely detailed pineapple finials presented to Marie Amelie by her father, King Louis Philippe, to commemorate the couple's first meeting in Martinique.

ancon, pl. ancones (AANG kahn)
Architectural term for a scroll-shaped bracket or console supporting a cornice or entablature. See also *console.*

andirons (AAN diyr enz)
Metal supports used in pairs to hold logs in a fireplace. Chenets is the French word for andirons. See also *brand dogs,* *chenets,* and *fire dogs.*

andron (AAN dron)
Greek term for men's quarters in a Greek classical house, usually a dining room.

andronitis (AAN driy tis)
Greek term for the owner's family suite in a classical Greek house.

ananas bed

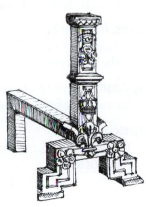
andirons

androsphinx (AAN droh sfinks)
An Egyptian art sculptured lion with a human head similar to the Giza sphinx. See also *sphinx.*

angel bed
An 18th-century English name for a bed with a canopy that extends to the floor and only partially over the bed, similar to the French lit d' ange or lit à la duchesse. See also *canopy bed, half tester bed, lit d' ange,* or *lit à la duchesse.*

angle chair
See *corner chair or roundabout chair.*

Anglo-Japanese
English furniture or art pieces inspired by Japan.

anigre' (AHN ee gray)
A wood with light fine grain.

animal couchant foot (AA ni mel KOO shant FUUT)
A foot resembling an animal lying down found in ancient Egypt, Greek, and Roman furniture, also used during the 19th century during the Empire period.

ankh (AANK)
An Egyptian symbolic motif symbolizing life.

ankle
Near the bottom of a furniture leg before it spreads out against the foot.

annealing (AH neel ing)
The gradual cooling of hot glass to render it less brittle.

androsphinx

angel bed

abcdefghijklmnopqrstuvwxyz

9

annulet (AAN yoo litt)

A small, narrow molding called a fillet and found encircling the lower part of the Doric capital.

Ant chair

See *Arne Jacobsen ant chair*. See *Arne Jacobsen, 1902–1971, in the Architects, Artists, and Designers Appendix*.

anta, pl. antae (AHN tah)

The extended side walls in the form of a pilaster between which columns may be located, usually found on a classical structure or interior.

anta

Antebellum period

A period in the United States existing between the Revolutionary War of 1789 and the beginning of the American Civil War in 1860 when the United States was rebuilding itself after the war with England.

antechamber (AAM tee chaym ber)

An outer room where guests wait before entering the chamber room.

antefix or antifixae (AAN tee fiks)

An upright conventionalized spreading leaf or fanlike ornament used in antique Greek and/or Roman decoration to conceal the open end of a row of tiles.

antefix

antepagmenta or antepagment

(AAN te pag men tah)

The decorative dressings made of stone or stucco to enrich the door jambs or windows.

anthemion, pl. anthemia (AAN them EE ah)

A Greek and Roman decoration based on the honeysuckle or palm leaf pattern, often referred to as the honeysuckle ornament, and used to enhance moldings, particularly during the French Empire period. See *illustration in the Motifs/Ornaments Appendix*.

anthropometrics (AAN thro poh meh trihks)

Science or study of measurement and proportion of the human form, with particularly reference to stature, weight, and height.

anthropomorphic (AAN throh poh mor fik)

A combination of human form and animal for a decorative motif.

antic, antic work

A form of decorative work consisting of incongruous animal and human figures with scrolls, foliage, etc. to decorate molding determination and other parts of medieval architecture.

antic, antic work

antimacassar (AAN tee mah kaa suhr)

A protective device used in the early 18th century to prevent the soiling of upholstered chair backs caused by macassar oil hair dressing, also called a tidy. See also *Macassar* and *tidy*.

antique

The accepted term for a work of art, piece of furniture or a decorative art object that is at least 100 years old.

antiquity

A work of art, piece of furniture or decorative art or craft of ancient times (classical era or older).

antis, in (AAN tis)

Columns are said to be in antis when placed between a pier or pilaster at the thickened end of a projecting wall. See also *in antis*.

apadana (AA pah dah na)

An audience hall in Persia that had a half-dome ceiling.

apex (AY peks)

The highest peak or tip of any structure in architecture or construction.

apophyge (AA pah fu gee)
A molding with a slight concave curve or sweep at the top and bottom of the shaft of a column where the shaft springs from the base or capital.

appareil en épi (AH pah ray AHN epee)
An architectural term used by the French for the way bricks are laid in an herringbone pattern.

appartement or appartment (AH part ment)
A French term appearing in the 15th century for a series of rooms in linear order where a person can progress from the most public room to the most private one.

appartement de commodité (AH part ment DEH koh MAH di tay)
A French term for ceremonial rooms usually located on the garden side and arranged in linear order for the purpose of receiving important people.

appartement de parade (AH part ment DEH pah RAYD)
French for a group of rooms used for entertainment and reception of visitors.

appartement de société (AH part ment DEH soh SIY eh tay)
A French term for a suite of small rooms with less formal décor where people of similar status socialize and dine.

appartement des bains (AH part ment DAY BAAN)
French term for rooms used for bathing.

applewood
A fruit wood, very hard and reddish brown, used for provincial styles of furniture and occasionally for large boards.

applied molding
Popular 17th-century English moldings of geometrical form enriched with carved ornament, applied to surfaces to give the effect of paneling, also called Jacobean ornament.

appliqué (AA plee kay)
French word for a decorative ornament applied to a surface; also a wall bracket or sconce. Also, a French term for a fabric with a shaped-cutout with pieces of contrasting color sewn and/or pasted onto the fabric back of another material. See also *girandole* and *sconce*.

appliqué

apron
A horizontal flat piece of trim under a chair seat, frieze of a table, bottom frame of a case piece or window sill, usually enhanced with ornament.

apse (APS)
The semicircular or angular extension usually in the east end of a Christian church or basilica. See also *nave* and *transcept*.

apse

apsidal (AAP si dul)
A small apse on the aisle side of a Christian church or basilica.

apsis gradata
(AAP sis GRAH dah tah)
The Italian word for the chair occupied by the bishop in early Christian basilicas that was raised above the ordinary stalls by several steps.

aqueduct (AA kwe dukt)
An architectural structure with high arches supporting a water channel.

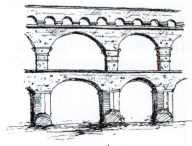
aqueduct

aquatint (AH kwah tint)
A method of etching on copper which renders a transparent effect similar to watercolor. One of the greatest aquatinters of the late 18th century and early 19th century was Goya. See also *engraving*.

arabesque (AA rah behsk)
Decorative scroll and leaf pattern, classical in origin, with stems rising from a root or other motif, used as a design on vertical panels. See *illustration in the Motifs/Ornaments Appendix*.

arbor (AHR bur)
A light open framework, often a lattice, used as a support for vines or as a shady garden shelter. See also *trelliswork*.

arbor-vitae (AHR bur VEE tay)
An evergreen tree native to North America, excellent wood for furniture.

Arc de Triumphe (AHRK du REE ahmf)
A monumental structure in the shape of one or more arched passages, usually built to commemorate a victory in war or to honor a king or general. See also *triumphal arch*.

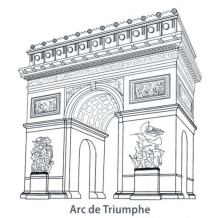

Arc de Triumphe

arc, pl. arcae (AHR kuh)
Spanish Renaissance storage chest used chiefly for storing treasures. See also *coffer*.

arca ferrata (AHR kuh fer AH tah)
A very heavy strong Roman chest used to place valuables bound with iron or bronze bands. See also *coffer*.

arcade (AHR kayd)
A series of adjoining arches supported by pillars or columns usually forming a part of the architectural treatment on the façade of the building. See also *Florentine arch*.

arcade

arcaded back (AHR kay ded BAHK)
A furniture back, usually a chair or bed back, with top rail cut to resemble one or more arches with pillars.

arcaded panel (AHR kay ded PAAN ul)
Typical English Renaissance panel decoration consisting of two stubby columns with arches in low relief, also used on chests in the French Renaissance.

arcaded panel

arcading (AHR kay ding)
A series of columns with their entablatures or arches that are represented in relief to decorate panels or fill open frames, especially in the 17th century.

arch
An architectural structure

arcading

that spans an opening, supported from the sides only, and consists of wedge-shaped blocks called voussoirs. See also *extrados, interrupted arch, intrados, keystone,* and *voussoirs*.

arch brick

Wedge-shaped bricks or curved pointed structure members used in the construction of the arch. See also *voussoir*.

arch order

A classical architectural system of framing arches with engagaed columns or pilasters and entablatures.

arch rib

See *rib arch*.

archaic (AHR kay ik)

Primitive, ancient, antiquated.

archebane-couchette (AHRCH bayn KOO shet)

A 16th-century Italian word for a bench or coffer with a back, sides, and arms. Same as *English settle*. See also *settle*.

arched molding

A half-round undecorated convex molding often used in pairs.

arched stretcher

An arched or hooped stretcher found between the legs of chairs, tables, or case pieces during the latter 17th-century English Restoration period. Originally it could be found in Spain. See also *hooped* or *rising stretcher*.

arched stretcher

Architect's period

Furniture and decoration of 18th century England designed by well-known architects, such as Sir Christopher Wren, William Kent, etc., who employed classical architectural features and motifs. See *William Kent, 1685–1748,* and *Sir Christopher Wren, 1632–1723, in the Architects, Artists, and Designers Appendix.*

architect's table

An 18th-century specialized combination of drawing table and desk referred to as an artist's table or architect's table made to serve the needs of draftsmen, artists, and architects. See also *table à l'architecte*.

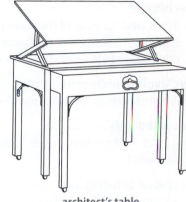

architect's table

architectonic (AHRK ih tek tahn ik)

Architectural features employed in furniture design or in structures, such as pilasters, cornices, and friezes.

Architectural Style (60-20 B.C.E.)

Second phase of the Pompeii painted interiors from 60 to 20 B.C.E. See also *Pompeii*.

architectural terra cotta

Hard burned glazed or unglazed clay building units, usually larger in size than brick, used in building construction; plain or ornamental, machine-extruded or hand-molded.

architecture

The art and science of building and in keeping with principles of design, both aesthetically and functionally, especially edifices that contribute to human health and pleasure.

Architecture françoise (AHR ki tek chur FRAHN swahz)

Four volumes written in the 17th-century by Jacques François Blondel (1705–1774), a traditionalist, who demonstrated classicism as a source of traditionalism. See *Jacques François Blondel, 1705–1774, in the Architects, Artists, and Designers Appendix.*

architrave (AHR ki trayv)
The lowest member of the three principal divisions of a classical entablature; also a molding used to surround a door or window opening. See also *epistyle*.

archivolt or archivoite (AHR ki volt)
A continuous ornamental molding found on the face of an arch.

arcuated (AHR kyoo ay tid)
A term used to characterize arched or arch-like form, distinct from trabeated.

arcuated construction (AHR kyoo ay tid KAHN struk shun)
A term applied to construction using arches for its support.

ardish (AR dish)
A style of decoration in East India where bits of colored glass are embedded in the ceiling or in the wall plaster to give a sparkling effect.

arena
An enclosed circular or oval-shaped public space used for public entertainment, such as musical performances, shows, or sporting events.

Arfe or Arphe family
Famous German silversmiths of the 15th and 16th centuries whose work influenced the Plateresco architectural ornament of the Spanish Renaissance. See also *Plateresco*.

Argand lamp
A lamp designed by Arni Argand, Geneva, Switzerland, in 1783 which was the first scientifically constructed oil lamp with an adjustable wick and provisions for the introduction of air inside the wick as well as around the outside.

Argand lamp

Argyle chair
See *Charles Rennie Mackinstosh Argyle chair*. See *Charles Rennie Mackintosh, 1868–1928, in the Architects, Artists, and Designers Appendix*.

arkwright
An early English or late Gothic term for a cabinetmaker; construction resembles carpentry more than cabinetry.

arm chair or armchair
Chair with arm supports and called an "armed" or "arming chair" to distinguish it from the single or side chair; armchairs became popular in the late 17th century. See also *cacqueteuse*.

arm pad
A upholstered cushion pad found on the arm of a chair and referred to in France as manchettes since the arm pad was extensively used on French furniture especially Louis XV and Louis XVI styles. See also *manchette*.

arm rest or arm rail
A specific support used for resting the arm.

arm stump or arm support
A term for the vertical part of the chair that supports the front of the arm; often it is carved, turned, or shaped.

Armand Rateau chaise lounge (ahr MAHND RAAT oh SHEZ LOWNJ)
A doe-legged chaise that was the zenith of Art Deco design in the 1920s; designed by Armand Rateau. See *Armand-Albert Rateau, 1882–1938, in the Architects, Artists, and Designers Appendix*.

Armand Rateau chaise lounge

armario (ahr MAHR ee oh)
A large Spanish Renaissance cupboard generally with upper and lower sections enclosed with two doors, similar to the Italian armadio and to the French armoire.

armarium, pl. armaria
(ahr MAYR ee um)

A cabinet, probably used by the treasure-loving Romans for the display of family treasures.

armoir, armoire, or en armoire
(AHR MWAHR)

French term for a large upright cupboard or wardrobe with a door or doors used originally for storing armor and later for clothes. See also *garderobe*, *kas*, and *wardrobe*.

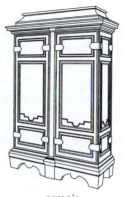

armoir

armoire à deux corps
(ahr MWAHR ah du kop)

A French Renaissance two-piece cupboard enclosed with doors and architectural features, such as a pediment, extremely fashionable during the late 16th-century. See *beaufait* and *cabinet à deux*.

armorial (ahr MOR ee ul)

A coat of arms denoting the status and allegiance of a person or family.

armure (AHRM yur)

A nonreversible cloth made with a raised satin pattern that consists of small, isolated conventional motifs arranged to form an overall design. The original fabric cloth with small interlaced design was prevalent during the crusades (11th and 12th centuries).

armoire á deux corps

armorial

Arne Jacobsen ant chair

A light, stable, and stackable modern chair designed by Arne Jacobsen in 1952 and produced by Fritz Hansen for the Danish pharmaceutical firm Novo Nordis. The name Ant was based on its similarity to an ant with its head raised. Originally it had three plastic legs, but the newer version has four tubular steel legs. It is a classic design that has proven to remain popular. See *Arne Jacobsen, 1902–1971, in the Architects, Artists, and Designers Appendix*.

Arne Jacobsen ant chair

Arne Jacobsen egg chair

A molded fiberglass frame chair with a crepe pure wool upholstery, designed by Arne Jacobsen in 1958 for the Radisson SAS hotel in Copenhagen and manufactured by Fritz Hansen. A very popular chair. See *Arne Jacobsen, 1902–1971, in the Architects, Artists, and Designers Appendix*.

Arne Jacobsen egg chair

Arne Jacobsen swan chair

A molded shell of synthetic material covered by fabric in a wide range of colors sitting on an aluminum swivel base, designed by Arne Jacobsen in 1958 for the Radisson SAS Royal Hotel in Cophengan and produced by Fritz Hansen. See *Arne Jacobsen, 1902–1971, in the Architects, Artists, and Designers Appendix*.

arqueta (AHR ke tah)

A Spanish term for a very small chest used as a receptacle for holding jewels, usually highly ornamented. The fondness of table boxes in Spain was an old Moorish legacy.

Arne Jacobsen swan chair

abcdefghijklmnopqrstuvwxyz

arras or arras tapestry (AH rahs)
An English tapestry of heavy texture with precious metals woven into the design, originating in the Arras, France tapestry weaving center in the 14th and 15th centuries. See also *Mortlake Tapestry Works* and *tapestry*.

arris, pl. arrises (AA ris)
The sharp edge formed by the coming together of two surfaces at an angle, such as the angle formed by the two sides of a brick.

arrow
A decorative theme of a slender shaft with a triangular pointed tip at one end and a "feathered" end at the back used as a motif in the revivals of classic styles, starting with the Renaissance and continuing through the Directoire, Empire, and Biedermeier periods. See also *Biedemeier, Directoire, and Empire.* See *illustration in the Motifs/Ornaments Appendix.*

arrow spindle

arrow back chair
Modern term for a type of American Windsor chair having three or more arrow-shaped spindles to the back and very popular during the second quarter of the 19th-century. See also *Windsor chair.*

arrow spindle
A flattened decorative spindle with arrow tip found on chair backs of Sheraton, American Federal, and some American Windsor.

Art Deco
Term for a French decorative style of the 1920s and 1930s popular in Europe and America coined in the 1960s and derived from the title of the 1925 Paris Word Fair, *L 'Exposition Internationale des Dècoratifs et Industriels Modernes.*

Art Deco

Art Moderne (AHRT mah DERN)
A term used to refer to a later phase of the Art Deco, a decorative streamline look and inspired by American industrial design style called streamlining (Zephyr trains, cars, and buses).

Art Moderne

Art Nouveau (AHRT NOO voh)
A French term for the "new art" style just before and after 1900 characterized by flowing curves and nature inspired elements; more prevalent in the decorative arts.

Art Workers' Guild
A group of artists and designers founded in 1884 who admired Ruskin and Morris and established the guild to provide an important platform for public discussion as an alternative to the Royal Institute of British Architects and the Royal Academy. See *William Morris, 1834–1896, and John Ruskin, 1819–1900, in the Architects, Artists, and Designers Appendix.*

Art Nouveau

arte povera (ART POH vay rah)
A form of decorating furniture in the 18th-century using hand-colored engraved prints similar to French découpage applied to wooden furniture in imitation of the court furniture of the period, referred to as "poor man's art". See also dé*coupage.*

artesonado (ahr TAY soh nah doh)
Moorish ornately carved woods used for ceilings, paneling, and doors, usually made of Spanish cedar and left in a natural state except in public buildings where it would often be gilded or painted.

Arthur Mackmurdo ebonized carved chair

A carved mahogany side chair designed by Arthur Mackmurdo in 1882, pre-dates the Art Nouveau period by ten years, and considered to be the first manifestation of the Art Nouveau movement. See *Arthur Mackmurdo, 1851–1942, in the Architects, Artists, and Designers Appendix.*

artifact

A stone, bone, metal or clay object of great antiquity made by humans, especially prehistoric objects.

artisan

One who is a skilled worker in a trade, such as a cabinetmaker, textile designer, weaver, etc.

artists' table

Tables introduced in the 18th century for the use of architects, artists and draftsman with folding or retractable leaves and adjustable tops.

Arts and Crafts movement

An aesthetic movement of the late 19th century, primarily in England and to some extent in America, led by the teachings of William Morris, the leader of the movement, and John Ruskin, in an effort to improve the quality of life through a return to the principles and methods of the hand craftsmanship in design and the industrial arts. See *William Morris, 1834–1896, and John Ruskin, 1819–1900, in the Architects, Artists, and Designers Appendix.*

Arthur Mackmurdo ebonized carved chair

Arts and Crafts movement

aryballos (AA rib a las)

A small round or globe-shaped Greek vase used to carry oil or perfume. See also *lagynos* and *oinochoe.*

ash

A tree native to England that is grayish-white to pale yellow, strong with great elasticity and used for country-made furniture, in particular the seats of Windsor chairs.

ash, English

A strong, flexible native English wood used in the 18th century for making inexpensive country furniture. See also *olive wood.*

ashlar (AASH ler)

Building stones cut in square or rectangular blocks and used for construction of a building.

asiatic base (AY zhee aa tik BAYS)

The base of the column where a double scotia is separated by a thick or double torus with scotia being the concave part and torus the convex molding.

aspen

An American wood belonging to the poplar family, very light-colored and easy-to-work, similar to the European white poplar.

aspidistra stand (AA pid i strah STAND)

A late 19th-century plant stand standing on three or four legs made of wood or terra-cotta with an opening on the top especially to hold the plant, aspidistra lurida.

assembly

Event in the English country house where persons of both sexes would assemble for such activities as balls, supper, cards, tea drinking, dancing, etc.

Assyrian (AH seer ee an)

An ancient Mesopotamian civilization art form located in the region of the Tigris and Euphrates rivers. See also *Babylonia* and *Mesopotamia.*

aster carvings

Three sunflower decorative carvings on the central panel of Connecticut chest during the 17th and 18th centuries. See also *Connecticut chest.*

astragal (AAS trih gil)

A small molding that is half-round or beaded in the shape of a torus and used to cover the joints on the edge of case pieces or between adjacent doors or windows. See *illustration in the Moldings Appendix*.

astral lamp (AAS trawl LAMP)

An early 19th-century oil lamp, a type of Argand lamp, with the burner set on a swinging tubular arm and made so the flattened, ringed cistern holding the oil does not throw a shadow; also called sinumbra lamp. See also *Argand lamp*.

astral lamp

ataurique (aa TAWR eek)

Surfaces with carved designs found in plasterwork or stucco wall decoration. Commonly used in Spanish Moorish architecture.

atélier (ah TEL yay)

French term for a workshop where artwork or handicrafts are done by a designer, artist, or artisan.

athénienne (AH the nee-en)

A round tripod table or stand introduced late in the reign of Louis XVI and designed in the form of an antique tripod copied from those found at Pompeii. See also *tripod table*.

athénienne

atlas, pl. atlantes (AAT les)

A full, male figure, a variant of a caryatid, used in place of a column to support an entablature. See also *caryatid*.

atlas

atrio (AH tree oh)

The enclosed courtyard of a Spanish Colonial church used for burial grounds and outdoor services.

atrium, pl. atria (AY tree um)

In a Roman house, the principal room or courtyard; later it became the forecourt of a Christian basilica, and today it is an open space in a building or building complex. See also *patio*.

atrium corinthium (AY tree um KOR in thee um)

An atrium supported by rows of columns and an opening in the ceiling, or an atrium with the peristyle.

atrium displuviatum (AY tree um dis ploov ee AY tum)

An atrium where the roof angles away from the opening so water does not drain from the roof.

atrium testudinatum (AY tree um test ood in AY tum)

A completely roofed atrium with no impluvium or compluvium.

atrium tetrastylum (AY tree um tet rah sti LUM)

An atrium supported by four columns, one column at each corner of the impluvium.

atrium tuscanicum (AY tree um tus KAN ee um)

An Etruscan or Roman atrium with an opening supported by parallel beams, not by columns, that in turn support rafters, allowing a covered walkway between the rooms and the open atrium.

attached column

See *engaged column*.

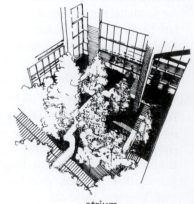

atrium

attic

In classical architecture, a position above the cornice or entablature of an interior or exterior façade.

attic base

Typically on Ionic and Corinthian columns the base consists of a pair of torus moldings flanked by a scotia (concave) molding.

Attic Style

A classical style, pure in form and elegant in style, associated with Athens.

aubergine (AW ber zheen)

The French word for an eggplant, a purple-black color; also Chinese enamel or glaze derived from manganese.

Aubusson (AH boo sahn)

A French carpet woven with a flat weave with no pile, like a tapestry, and named for the French tapestry works in Aubusson which dates back to the 15th century.

auditorium

A large room, hall enclosure, theater, or building used for public meetings or performances.

auger flame (AW ger FLAYM)

Term for a finial with an elongated spiral twist resembling a carpenter's auger and placed on American Chippendale furniture and American tallboys or hoods of long case clocks.

aula (A wlah)

The German term applies to a large hall, while in ancient architecture, it referred to a court or hall, especially an open court attached to a house.

attic

auger flame

aumbry (AAM bree)

Latin word for chest or small cupboard used in churches to hold sacred books, vessels, linens, and/or utensils of the Eucharist. It also could be the name for a storage place or wardrobe. See also *ambry*.

aureole (OR ee ohl)

A painted halo around the head of a sacred figure in the form of a circular, elliptic, or quadrangular shape, also called mandorla or vesica piscis. See also *mandorla*.

Austrian drape

A shirred shade or curtain made of light weight vertical panels and when raised, the material gathers in a series of parallel cords. See also *Roman shade*.

avant-garde (ah VANHNT GAHRD)

Experimental concepts especially in the arts usually developed by the intelligentsia or a group active in the new techniques of a given field.

aventurine lacquer (ah VEN chur een LAAK ur)

An 18th-century French lacquer finish that imitated the color and quality of mineral aventurine, also called "nashiji" where it florished during the Muromachi period (1338–1573) and became more and more intense over the centuries.

avodire (AA voh di ray)

A blond wood with strong, dark brown vertical streaking, a fine texture, and illustrious quality, often used for veneering purposes on modern furniture.

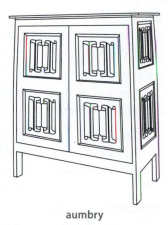

aumbry

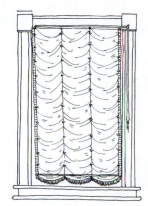

Austrian drape

axial
A straight line where objects are arranged on both sides with respect to symmetry.

axial planning
A room, building, or plan that is longitudinal along an axis or a layout that is symmetrical about an axis.

Axminister
A hand-woven wool carpet with a cut pile and a variety of patterns and colors, named after the town of Axminister, England where in the mid-18th century a carpet factory was started.

ayacahuite (iy e ke WEE tay)
A pinewood found in Mexico and Central America often used for furniture and given a painted or lacquered finish with the common name of Mexican White Pine in the family: Pinaceae.

ayous (AY yoos)
A soft, lightweight wood from the west coast of Africa, similar to primavera and somewhat like mahogany, used in veneers. See also *abachi.*

azulejos (AH sool ay hohs)
Spanish term for earthenware tiles manufactured in Spain and Portugal, usually painted with floral patterns or scenes of bullfights, sporting or social events. Term is derived from the word azul meaning blue, typically painted in blue and white.

b cupboard

A piece of furniture, consisting of a settle and a cupboard, primarily found in medieval era farmhouses.

bab

A reference to a gate or door in Muslim architecture.

baby cage

Another name for a baby walker, appearing in various forms since the 14th and 15th century, morphing to the familiar round or square frame in the 17th century.

Babylonia (baa bul OH nee u)

The ancient empire of Mesopotamia that flourished from 2025 to 538 BCE until it was conquered by the Persians; known for the architectural accomplishment of stepped temple structures, called ziggurats. See also *ziggurat*.

Baccarat (BAH ku rah)

French factory located in Northern France, best known for tableware and paperweights of various colors. A highly regarded French crystal, primarily used for lighting and table décor.

bachelor's chest

Small 18th-century chest of drawers with a hinged top that when opened forms a writing surface.

back arch

A concealed arch that carries the inner part of a wall while the outer facing material is carried by a lintel.

baby cage

bachelor's chest

back filling

The filling inside the outer curve of an arch or the rough masonry used behind a building material facing.

back hearth or inner hearth

The section of a hearth that is incorporated into the fire box area.

back post

Stiles or posts of a chairback that continue down to form the rear legs of a chair.

back splat

See *splat*.

back stool

A medieval stool with triangular seat and three legs, one of which extended upward to form a primitive back containing a shoulder height rail.

back-cut veneer

Veneer with a striped figure created by a process similar to half-round slicing.

backgammon board and table

Specialized tables used for playing backgammon. They first appeared in the 17th century, with many fine examples produced in France and England.

backplate

The decorative metal plate used as a backing on furniture hardware pulls or pendants. Backplates often have a stamped design.

backstamp

The printed device commonly used on the back of English ceramics that supplies information such as date, pattern name, and maker.

backup

The part of a masonry wall found behind the exterior facing.

back stool

bacon cupboard

A settle or long bench, original to the Middle Ages, containing a paneled backrest that doubles as a cupboard for storing bacon and incorporating drawers under the seat.

bag table

A serving or sewing table popular in the 18th and 19th centuries, characterized by a cloth sack or bag beneath drawers. Typical in England and America. See also *pouch table*.

Bagnell (BAAG nul)

Queen Anne style clock manufacturer located in Boston during the beginning of the 18th century. Usually composed of brass or wood with the outer casings made of mahogany or maple.

baguette (baa GET)

A petit, rounded bead molding.

bahut (BAY)

In architecture, the rounded upper course of a wall or parapet or the low wall topping a cornice to carry the roof structure. In furniture, a French term for a medieval chest or coffer with a rounded top, used while traveling. See also *cassone*.

bai yan (BIY YAHN)

A Chinese apothecary or medicine cabinet containing numerous small drawers.

baigneuse (bay NOO zay)

A daybed resembling a tub, in which the back ascended downward to form the sides and the sides pointed from the back of the seat to the front. Common during the French Empire period.

bail

A curved metal loop or ring used to form a furniture handle.

bacon cupboard

bail handle

A type of furniture hardware, introduced in the English William and Mary period, characterized by an arched metal loop hung between two bolt heads that pierce a drawer front. Commonly made of brass.

bailey

The courtyard or area between the outer walls and the keep of a castle.

baked finish

Paint or varnish that has been baked at a temperature over 150°F to produce a tough, durable finish.

balconet (baal ku NET)

A shallow ornamental railing used outside a window that mimics the appearance of a balcony. Also known as a balconette.

balcony

A platform extending from a building, often cantilevered or supported from below and enclosed by a banister or railing. Also a projecting platform within an auditorium, used for seating over the main floor.

baldachino (bahl de kee noh)

A canopy used above alters or thrones, often supported by columns and occasionally embellished. The most recognizable example is Bernini's baldachino in St. Peter's Cathedral in Rome. Also known as a baldachin, baldaquin, or ciborium.

balconet

balcony

baldachino

baldaquin bed (bahl de KAAN BED)

A French reference for a canopy or tester bed, commonly found in late 18th-century France and England.

balistraria (baal u STRAYR ee u)

A narrow slit in the wall of a fortification through which an archer's arrows can be launched.

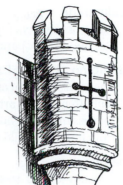

balistraria

ball and claw foot

A furniture foot constructed of a bird's claw grasping a ball. Presumed to be an ancient Chinese design suspected to mean world power, the ball and claw foot is commonly seen on English, European and Dutch furniture of the 17th and 18th centuries. See *illustration for claw and ball foot in the Feet Appendix.*

ball and ring

A 17th-century turning, commonly found in English and American furniture, that resembles a simplified bead and reel turning. See also *bead and reel.*

ball and steeple finial

A wood turning celebrated in 18th-century American furniture. The lowest aspect of the ball and steeple finial was the sphere-shaped ball mounted upon a succession of rings, sized according to scale, which constructed a peak that resembled a steeple.

ball chair

See *Eero Aarnio globe or ball chair.* See *Eero Aarnio, 1932-,* in the *Architects, Artists, and Designers Appendix.*

ball flower

A sphere-shaped ornament consisting of a ball encased within three or four cup shaped petals of a flower, popular during the late 13th and 14th centuries.

ball foot

A turned furniture foot, spherical or nearly spherical in shape, commonly used in the 17th century.

ball leg tip

A small metal cup or ferrule that covers the bottom of a ball-shaped foot. Leg tips are generally made of brass and are often used to attach casters to the legs of furniture.

ball turning

A turning containing a sequence of small balls, prominent during the 17th century. See also *knob turning.*

balloon back chair

A chair style introduced by Hepplewhite in the early 19th-century noted for its rounded back that mimics the shape of a hot air balloon. Also prevalent during the Victorian era.

balloon clock

A late 18th-century and early 19th-century clock characterized by its unique hot air balloon shaped case.

balloon curtains

A window treatment characterized by billowing panels of fabric, shirred or gathered at regular intervals, to create exaggerated poufs or balloons.

balloon frame

An early 19th-century lightweight frame construction innovation that uses long pieces of lumber to extend the exterior wall height of a structure, e.g., from wall base to roof.

balloon shade

A shirred or gathered fabric window shade that pulls up into soft, billowing folds and terminates in a scalloped edge.

balloon back chair

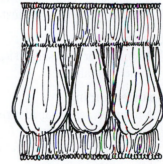

balloon curtains

23

ballroom chair

A small, slight and easily transportable armless chair often characterized by an arcaded back of delicate spindles and turned wooden legs. Popular during the 19th and 20th centuries.

balneum *pl. balnea* (baal NOOM)

A small Roman bath often attached to a private house.

baluster, banister

One of a number of short vertical posts or columns supporting a stair's handrail, often turned in a vase-like shape.

ballroom chair

baluster and bobbin

Decorative turning, also known as a baluster and ring, typically combining an alternating series of vase-shaped balusters and bobbins or rings. Commonly found on early American Windsor chairs.

baluster and ring

See *baluster-and-bobbin*.

baluster and spindle

See *spindle-and-baluster*.

baluster back

A chairback, commonly used on a Windsor chair, containing a series of baluster-shaped back splats.

baluster leg

A rounded or vase-shaped leg commonly found on chairs and tables.

baluster turning

A rounded, vase-shaped turning, commonly used on 16th and 17th-century furniture, pulled from components of an architectural balustrade.

balustra

A dense hardwood native to South Africa that is light tobacco brown in color.

baluster

Balustrade

A row of balusters topped by a rail, serving as a low parapet or barrier.

Bambino (baam BEE noh)

The representation of Christ as an infant often used in art of the early Italian Renaissance. Also literally translated from Italian as child or baby.

bamboo

A woody jointed grass, native to tropical areas, popularly translated into wood turnings during 17th and 18th-century England and America. Now used as a sustainable flooring option because of its fast growth. See also *bamboo furniture, bamboo shades, bamboo-turned chair,* and *bamboo ware*.

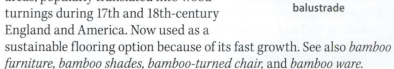

balustrade

bamboo furniture

Furniture constructed from bamboo, popular during the Victorian era. Its striking jointed appearance was also commonly replicated in wood by British cabinetmakers in the late 18th and early 19th centuries.

bamboo shades

A window treatment constructed of thin strips of bamboo that can be maneuvered up or down.

bamboo-turned

A wood turning, popularly used during the 17th and 18th centuries in England and America, that mimics the jointed look of bamboo. See also *bamboo-turned chair*.

bamboo-turned chair

A chair with turnings that look like stylized bamboo to reflect the Chinese taste favored by Englishmen and Americans of the 17th and 18th centuries. Generally constructed from light hardwoods, such as maple, and gilded or painted a light color.

bamboo-turned chair

bamboo ware

A dark cane-colored stoneware imitating bamboo introduced by Josiah Wedgwood in 1770.

banc à ciel (BAHN AH see EL)

French for a bench with a canopy seen during the Gothic era.

banc à dos (BAHN AH DOO)

French for a bench with a back common in the Gothic era.

banchetta (bahn KET u)

Italian for little bench. The term banquette is derived from this Italian word.

banco (bahn KOH)

Italian for bench.

bancone (bahn KOHN ay)

A 15th-century Italian writing table with an oblong flat surface that extended well beyond the frieze which contained two framed drawers and rested on runner feet.

band pattern

A linear pattern of the same width that uses one or more motifs in repetition to extend the length.

band or fillet

A common reference for a flat molding used in architecture and cabinetmaking.

banded column

A column containing a lower drum with greater diameter than the actual shaft. Common during the French Renaissance period.

banderole (BAHN dur oh lay)

A common Renaissance decoration that depicts a carved or painted decorative ribbon, often filled with inscriptions.

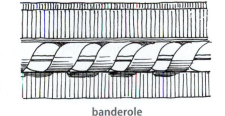

banderole

banding

Narrow strips of veneer used as a border or decorative inlay on the top surface of a chest or table, or a drawer front. See also *cross banding*.

bandy leg

American Colonial term for a cabriolet leg, a furniture leg that bows outward at the knee. See also *cabriolet leg*.

banister

1) The handrail of a staircase. 2) Another name for baluster.

banister-back chair

A chairback common in England and America during the late 17th and early 18th centuries, characterized by vertical split banisters or spindles within the back. See also *brewster chair* and *carver chair*.

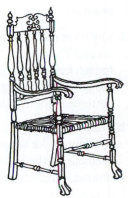

banister-back chair

banjo clock

American clock, named for its contoured resemblance to the instrument. Patented in 1802 by Simon Willard.

bank

A long seat or bench from the Middle Ages. Also known as a banc. See also *banquette*.

Bank of England chair

A popular 19th-century English Regency chair with arms rising from front posts and continuing around the back in a constant curve, similar to the tub chair. Usually incorporating cabriole legs and a serpentine-shaped front seat rail.

banner screen

Popular adjustable fire screen of the 18th century, consisting of an upright pole carrying a framed shield of tapestry or needlework. See also *cheval screen, pole screen,* and *horse screen*.

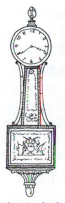

banjo clock

abcdefghijklmnopqrstuvwxyz

banqueta
A low, generally upholstered, Spanish stool.

banquette (bahn KET)
French for an upholstered stool or settee.

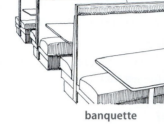
banquette

banquette de billiard (bahn KET du bee YAAR)
French for a bench specifically designed for viewing billiards. An added back and high seat create better viewing and differentiate it from the traditional banquette.

bantam work
A technique for lacquering, unique to Holland and England, commonly used during the 17th century. Design was generally incised into a black ground. Originated from the Dutch Java province of Bantam.

banuyo (baan YOO yoh)
A wood indigenous to the Philippines and Indonesia used for furniture and cabinetwork. It is easily worked and known for its durability, fine grain, and golden brown color.

baptistry
A detached portion of the church designated for baptism, until the 10th century.

bar back
A term used in the 18th century by George Hepplewhite for a shield shaped chair back containing concave curved bars that arch upward to meet the yoke rail. See also *shield back*.

bar foot
A furniture foot, similar to a runner foot, that has a bar connecting the front and rear legs.

baptistry

bar tracery
A design created by intertwining stone bars within a Gothic window arch.

barbeaux (BAHR boh)
A French term for cornflowers. It refers to the common decoration of ceramics with sprigs and cornflowers in 18th and 19th-century France and England. The design is reported to have stemmed from a Sevres designer working for Maria Antoinette in 1782.

barberry or berbery
A hard, close-grained, yellow colored wood that has been used since the 17th century for inlaying.

barber's chair
An 18th-century English corner chair, occasionally seen with an extended headrest, used for shaving. The chair developed into its familiar form with an adjustable head, back and footrest, in the 19th-century.

barber's chair

barbican (BAAR bi kun)
A tower placed at a gateway or bridge, used as an outer defense mechanism.

Barbizon School
A mid 19th-century school of French landscape painters, including Millet, Rousseau, Corot, and Diaz, who romanticized peasant life in their work.

barbican

Barcelona chair

See *Mies van der Rohe Barcelona chair. See Ludwig Mies van der Rohe, 1886–1969, in the Architects, Artists, and Designers Appendix.*

barefaced tenon

A joinery term used for a tenon that has a shoulder only on one side. Commonly used in the construction of wood doors.

barefaced tongue joint

A joinery term used for a tongue that is rabbeted only in one side of the board.

barège (BAHR uj)

A sheer fabric generally of wool combined with silk or cotton that resembles gauze.

bargeboard

A decorative board that follows the roofline, concealing the roof rafters in Victorian architecture.

bargello (bahr JEL oh)

A zigzag needlework pattern, seen in 17th-century upholstery. Named after the Bargello Museum in Florence, Italy which houses two chairs in its collection incorporating the stitch work. Now called flame stitch.

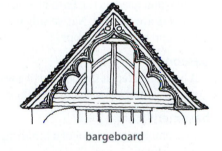

bargeboard

barjeer/ barjier (bahr JEER/bar JEER)

Term used in the late 18th century by George Hepplewhite for a bergère or armchair.

barley sugar twist

See *barley twist.*

barley twist

A decorative spiral turning resembling a stick of barley sugar or double rope, commonly used on English furniture legs and stretchers of the mid-late 17th century. Also known as barley sugar twist.

Barocco (bah ROH koh)

See *Baroque.*

barometer cases

An elegant wooden case, commonly seen in the 18th century, made to house a barometer, a popular household accessory of the time period.

Baroque table

Baroque (bah ROHK)

A term referring to the style of art, decoration, and design of 17th-century Italy. Large scale, bold detail, and sweeping curves are unique to the style. Baroque is an Italian term, named for the 15th-century Italian architect Barrochio who was influential in the style.

barquette molding (bahr KET)

A small convex molding constructed with bead or olive berry ornaments.

barré (bahr RAY)

Textile term for a fabric containing a horizontal barred or striped effect.

barred door

A term used with antique furniture to describe a glass cabinet, bookcase, or secretaire door with glass panes set in wood fretwork.

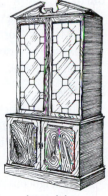

barred door

barrel chair

A mid 19th-century chair, developed in England, that resembled rural chairs made of wine barrels. The upholstered armless chair has a curved back and round seat.

barrel-back chair

See *Frank L. Wright barrel-back chair.* See *L. Wright, 1867–1959, in the Architects, Artists, and Designers Appendix.*

barrel-shaped seat

See *garden seat.*

barrel vault

A semicircular masonry vault that receives support from parallel walls. Also called a tunnel vault.

barrier-free design

See *accessible design.*

barrow

An ancient tomb constructed to mimic an actual burial vault.

bartizan (BAHR tu zun)

An overhanging turret projecting from the walls of a Medieval fortification, designed to allow expansive exterior views and protection to guards. See also *guerite.*

basalt ware

An unglazed black stoneware developed by Wedgewood in the late 18th century, made to resemble the volcanic mineral basalt. See also *basalt.*

basalt/basaltes

An dark igneous rock often used for carving statues in ancient Egypt. Basalt also is a reference used in ceramics for a black porcelain. See also *basalt ware.*

barrel chair

barrel vault

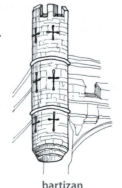

bartizan

Basculant chair

See *Le Corbusier basculant chair.* See *Le Corbusier, 1887–1965, in the Architects, Artists, and Designers Appendix.*

base

The lowest part of a column or piece of furniture. Generally wider than the parts above. See also *plinth, pedestal,* and *stylobate.*

base molding

A type of trim molding used at the base of a wall. In furniture, the lowest supporting member of case pieces.

base rail

A rail found at the lower edge of the carcass on a case piece or directly above the legs on a chair or sofa.

base wood

The wood used as the base of a piece of furniture onto which beautiful veneers are applied. Native softwoods are commonly used in America. Oak and beech in Europe.

baseboard

A board located at the bottom of a wall. It is typically embellished with moldings and leans against the floor.

basement

In architecture, a level of a building below the main story.

bases

A valence used on the lower part of a bed during the 17th and 18th centuries.

basilica plan

Originally a Roman hall of justice or commercial exchange with a large central nave and side aisles. The plan later formed the basis of the early Christian church with an apse added at the end of the nave.

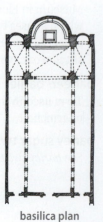

basilica plan

basin and ewer
A matching bowl and pitcher used for washing hands during and after meals before utensils such as forks were introduced.

basin stand
A washstand designed to hold a hand basin, common in 18th-century England. Also called a bason stand.

basket-handle arch
A low crowned elliptical arch whose width is much greater than its height.

basket chair
See *croquet chair*.

basket stand
A late 18th-century table with two tiers, generally circular in form and surrounded by galleries, supported by a tripod base.

basketweave
A brick pattern or closely woven textile that mirrors a checkerboard or the texture of basket work.

bason stand
See *basin stand*.

bas-relief (BAH-ree LEEF)
French for the Italian *basso-relievo,* meaning low relief. A carving technique in which the design only slightly protrudes from the surface.

basses
The lower part of a 17th-century English or French bedstead. Also the textile cover for the base, closely resembling a dust ruffle.

basin and ewer

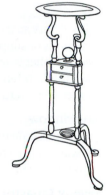

basin stand

basket stand

basset table (BAA set TAY bul)
An 18th-century Queen Anne card table, specifically designed for playing the popular English card game, five-handed basset.

bassinet
A oblong baby bed or cradle, initially basketlike in shape.

basso rilievo (bah SOH-ree-EEV-oh)
Also seen as baso-rilievo. See also *bas-relief*.

basswood
A soft, creamy white wood, with little to no figure, from the linden tree. Often used for carving, millwork and boxes.

bast fibers
Durable fibers from stalky plant such as hemp, jute, and flax.

bastion
A projecting part of a fortification wall. Also known as a bulwark.

bat
In masonry, a cut piece of a brick such as half bat or quarter bat.

bat printed
Same as transfer printed. See *transfer printing*.

batement light
A window light of a multi-light window with vertical sides, but with a sill that is angled or not horizontal, typically found in Gothc tracery.

bathroom
An ancient Greek bench.

bathtub
A tub used for bathing.

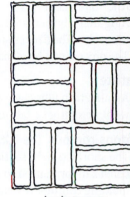

basketweave

batement light

batik (bah TEEK)

A figured fabric created by outlining a design in hot wax and dipping it into a dye. The dye resists the wax, which is removed to reveal the design. The process can be repeated to give a striking multi-colored effect.

batiste

An airy, thin fabric woven of cotton, silk, linen, wool, or synthetic fabrics.

bâtons-rompus (be TOHN rohm Poo)

The short, straight sections of molding, usually convex in form, used to create the chevron molding commonly found in Romanesque architecture.

bat's wing brasses

A bailed drawer handle common in the Queen Anne Style, known for its shape that resembles a conventionalized bat with outstretched wings.

batten

A narrow strip of wood used to cover a joint between other boards. Or, a strip of wood used to diagonally brace one or more parallel boards.

battered

A structure with an inward slope, such as a wall.

batting

Sheets or rolls of cotton used for stuffing and padding upholstered items.

battlement

The crenellated parapet found at the top of a wall, generally seen on castles or forts. Originally designed for defense, later added as an architectural decoration. See also *crenellation*.

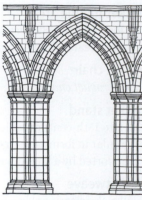

battered

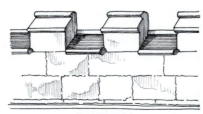

battlement

Bauhaus (BOW hows)

A German school of architecture and design founded by Walter Gropius in 1919 that was influential in the development of modernism. Although short lived (1919 to 1932), the school's functional aesthetic for the industrial age sustained famous allies such as Lászó Moholy-Nagy, Johannes Itten, Marcel Breuer, Paul Klee, and Wassily Kandinsky.

baxian zhou (bahsh EE en JOH)

A raised square Chinese dining table named for the legendary Eight Chinese Immortals, hence reflecting the importance of the communal act of eating. Also seen as ba xian zhou.

bay

The empty space found between columns or supports. Also a building section that is separated or defined from the whole, often by arches, columns or other architectural features.

bay window

A composition of windows, set at an angle, within a protruding bay that rises from the ground.

Bayeux Tapestry (baa YUU TAP us tree)

A famous French tapestry of the Romanesque period that commemorates the Norman victory in England.

baywood

A fine grained wood also known as Honduras mahogany. See also *mahogany*.

bead

A molding consisting of carved spheres or beads. See *illustration in the Moldings Appendix*.

bead and butt

A flush framed panel with bead molding that runs on the edges that adjoin the stiles. Also known as bead butt or bead butt work.

bay

bay window

bead and reel

A carved bead molding containing alternating round and oval disc shaped forms.

bead curtains

A semitransparent device, made of individual strings of beads, used in door openings, windows, arches, or as a room divider.

bead flush

A small, almost circular molding that borders a panel.

bead molding

A convex molding carved with small cylindrical forms that resembles a string of beads or pearls. Also known as beading. See *illustration in the Moldings Appendix.*

beaded drawer

A drawer with a small half-round or quarter round molding running the perimeter of its edges. Commonly used during the 18th century in England. See also *cock beading.*

beading

See *bead molding.*

beak head

An elaborate decorative molding, popular during the Norman period, containing animal heads with downward pointing beaks. Commonly seen in doorways.

beaker

A tall drinking glass with a wide mouth and slight flaring sides.

beam

A long piece of timber or metal used as a horizontal support for roofs or ceilings.

beamed ceiling

A ceiling created by exposing or mimicking the beams found on the underside of the floor above.

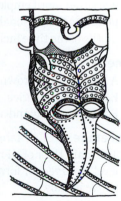

beak head

bearer strip

See *bearing rail.*

bearing partition

See *bearing wall.*

bearing rail

The horizontal member that carries a drawer in a cabinet, chest, or other piece of furniture.

bearing wall

A vertical weight supporting wall, also known as a bearing partition.

bear's paw foot

A late 17th or early 18th-century furniture foot, distinguished by a carved furry paw, occasionally mingled with a ball. Sometimes seen in the designs of Thomas Chippendale.

Beau Brummel table

Beau Brummel table (BOH BRUM ul TAY bul)

A late 18th-century Englishman's dressing table with an intricate system of adjustable mirrors, candlestands, shelves and drawers, named after a famous dandy of the time.

beaufait (boh FAY)

Early spelling of buffet. Also seen as beaufatt or beaufet. See also *buffet.*

Beauvais (boh VAY)

Famous French tapestry and textile factory started under the reign of Louis XIV, but perhaps most famous for the work of Francois Boucher, who designed tapestries under the reign of Louis XV. The factory also became famous for producing pastoral pile rugs in pastel colors during the late 18th century.

beaufait

Beaux-Arts (BOHZ-ahr)

A 19th-century style of architecture cultivated by the École des Beaux-Arts in Paris, known for use of historic forms, rich detail, and monumental scale.

bed bolt

Commonly covered by a decorative brass plate in the American Federal Style, a sunken bolt and nut used to attach a bed rail to the headboard or footboard.

bed chair

An early 18th-century chair that converted into a bed, invented by the Dutch. Styled with cabriole legs and Dutch feet, the chair was often made of nut wood or maple inlaid with tulipwood.

bed chamber

A compartment designed for sleeping and resting.

bed frame

A modern term used for a steel frame designed to support a box spring and mattress. Used alone or bolted to a headboard, the frame is generally set on casters.

bed molding

A small molding found directly under the corona and above the frieze of a cornice.

bed of estate

A elaborate canopied bed used by the most important members of a Medieval household.

bed rails

The long, horizontal members, generally made of wood, used to connect the headboard and footboard of a bed. When united by slats, they support the mattress set.

bed steps

A set of short steps, common in 18th-century England and America, designed to make high beds more accessible.

bed steps

bed stock

Term used for the supporting framework of many 16th-century English and Continental beds.

bedding

Coverings, such as sheets and blankets, used for a bed.

bedrest

A pillow incorporating arms and a back.

bedroom chair

A small side chair designed for use in a bedroom. Often designed in the late 18th century and early 19th century by Thomas Sheraton, the bedroom chair was generally constructed from a stained or japanned beech frame with rush seat.

bedside cupboard

An 18th-century bedside cupboard containing a doored compartment used for a chamber pot. See also *pot cupboard*.

bedstead

The supporting frame of a bed.

bee

A stylized motif employed during the early 19th-century French Empire period as the personal symbol of Napoleon Bonaparte. Other popular motifs of the time included laurel wreaths, the letter N, stars, and eagles.

beech

A light reddish brown, densely textured hardwood, indigenous to Europe and America, used extensively for provincial furniture of France and England since the 17th century.

bel étage (BEL AY tahj)

The main floor of a French château, generally one floor above ground level, reserved for formal reception rooms. Also known as a *piano nobile* in Italy.

bell

In architecture, the part of a capital between the necking and abacus.

bell cote

A cupola or other small roof structure designed to house bells.

bell turning

A late 17th-century bell-shaped turning popular on furniture legs and supports of the William and Mary Style.

Belleek (bah LEEK)

An Irish ceramics factory, established around 1863, known for a fine, translucent, ivory colored china with characteristic iridescent glaze.

bell cote

bellflower or husk

Popular 18th-century decorative motif often used on the legs of a table, characterized by conventional bell-shaped flowers, inlaid one below the other in vertical strings. See also *catkins* and *husk ornament*. See *illustration in the Motifs/Ornaments Appendix.*

bellfry

A bell tower or steeple designed to hold bells, often found as part of church architecture.

bellows

An instrument used as a fireplace accessory that expands to take in air and when contracted expels it. Often highly decorated, carved or embellished.

belt course

A slightly projecting band of brick, stone, tile or shingles generally found between floor levels. Also know as a string course. See also *string course.*

Belter chair

See *John Henry Belter chair.* See *John Henry Belter, 1804–1864, in the Architects, Artists, and Designers Appendix.*

bellfrey

belvedere

Literally translated from Italian as beautiful view. An open sided and fenestrated projection, such as a cupola, found on the upper most part of a building. Designed for viewing or cooling, belvederes were commonly seen in Italian Renaissance architecture.

bench

An elongated stool for two or more people. See also *carreau.*

bench tables

See *settle.*

benetier

A container for holy water.

benge (BENJ)

An African wood known for its rich brown colored ground with dark contrasting figure. Commonly used for cabinetwork, furniture components, and decorative veneers.

bentwood furniture

Furniture made by stream bending wood into curvilinear forms. Made famous by Austrian designer, Michael Thonet in 1857, the process was also used by 20th-century modern designers such as Charles Eames and Alvar Aalto.

benetier

bentwood rocker

See *Michael Thonet bentwood rocker.* See *Michael Thonet bentwood rocker.* See *Michael Thonet, 1796–1871, in the Architects, Artists, and Designers Appendix.*

Berber

Originally a simple, geometric, hand knotted wool rug made by the Berber tribes of North Africa. Today, a coarse pebble textured carpet with the natural, undyed look of wool.

bergère (bur ZHAYR)

An upholstered armchair with enclosed sides and cushioned seat, developed in France during the Louis XV period, but also popular during the Louis XVI period. The name was often corrupted in 18th-century England into barjier, burjair, or barjair.

bergère

bergeries (BAYR je ree)

French for a painting, tapestry, or textile containing a pastoral scene. See also *toile de jouy.*

Bessemer process

A 19th-century process developed by Henry Bessemer for refining iron by blasting compressed air through it.

beton brut (bay TOHN BRUUT)

French for an architectural style known for using reinforced concrete construction. See also *brutalism.*

betty lamp

An early American lamp with a small teapot like spout with an enclosed wick and a shallow, covered basin filled with oil, grease, or tallow for fuel. Generally hung from a hook or chain.

bevel

The rim of a surface that has been cut at an angle. See also *chamfer.*

beveled glass

A decorative angled glass edge produced by grinding and polishing. Often used for mirrors, doors, and windows.

beveled siding

See *clapboard.*

bezant

Medieval for a gold coin. Also, a decorative disc-shaped motif often seen in Byzantine architecture and heraldry.

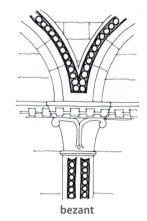

bezant

bianco-sopra-bianco (bee AHN koh SOH prah bee AHN koh)

Italian for the white tin glaze on a pale blue or grayish white ground, used on majolica pottery during the 16th and 18th centuries. Also used by English delftware manufacturers in the 18th century.

bibelots (BIB u loh)

French term for late 19th-century small trinkets, knickknacks, or art objects created for display on étagères or whatnots.

Bibendum chair (bi BEN dum CHAYR)

See *Eileen Gray Bibendum chair. See Eileen Gray, 1878–1976, in the Architects, Artists, and Designers Appendix.*

bible box

A 17th-century box with lid, originally designed to store important papers as well as the family Bible. Later, often constructed with a hinged sloping lid that served as a writing surface or reading stand when closed. Also known as a writing til in France and a slope or writing box in England.

bible box

bible or chancel chair

An early to mid 17th-century chair with hinged seat compartment used for storing a bible. Otherwise the chair is styled similarly to a wainscot chair. See also *chancel chair, panel-back chair,* and *scrowled chair.*

bibliothèque (bib LEE oh tek)

French for a library or large bookcase. Also a room found in a Roman house which housed scrolls and other items for the owner.

bibliothèque

bidet (bi DAY)

French for a bathroom fixture designed for washing gentalia.

Biedermeier (BEED ur mi yur)

An early to mid 19th-century German style modeled after the French Empire, but with middle class sensibilities. Named after the popular cartoon character "Papa Biedermeier," furniture of the style used local woods, painted details of black and gold, and classical motifs such as columns, lyres, wreaths, and plumes to mimic French forms. The style was also popular in Austria and Northern Italy.

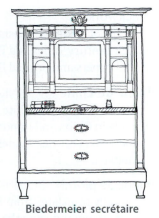

Biedermeier secrétaire

bifore window (biy FOHR win DOH)

A double lancet window divided by a colonnette, popular in Italian Renaissance architecture.

bifrons

A two-faced god of mythology representing transitions such as past and future, often seen in doorways and gated entrances of ancient Roman architecture.

bilbao mirror, bilboa mirror (bil BOW MEER or)

A mirror, originating in Bilboa, with a frame of marble and wood and a pair of slender columns running vertically up the sides.

bifrons

billet

A Norman architectural ornament comprised of regularly spaced, horizontal log-shaped elements. Originating from the old French word billette, a diminutive log.

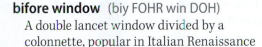

billet

binding

A reference used by upholsterers for the different types of laces or braids that are used to increase the strength of drapery borders.

biotechnical design

See *ergonomic design*.

birch

A strong, light, fine grained wood used for furniture, cabinetry, doors, and trims. The even texture and grain make it easy to work with and enable it to mimic more costly woods such as mahogany and walnut.

birdcage clock

See *lantern clock*.

birdcage support

An 18th-century English and American support used under a tilt-top tabletop, resembling a birdcage composed of turned colonettes.

birdcage support

bird's beak or crow's bill molding

A molding whose section resembles the beak of a bird. See *illustration in the Moldings Appendix*.

bird's eye

Small dots or spots, generally found in maple, that resemble a bird's eye.

bird's eye perspective

An architectural drawing showing a panoramic aerial view of an architectural exterior or interior similar to what would be seen by a bird.

biscuit

See *bisque*.

biscuit tufting

A form of tufting that produces regularly spaced squares on an upholstered piece. See also *tufting*.

bisected vault

A derivative of a barrel vault with only one impost, whose crown abuts the opposite wall.

bisected vault

bisellium (BIY se Lee um)

An ancient Roman seat of honor for two people.

bishop's sleeve curtains

A window treatment whose side panels are cinched or poufed to create a billowing effect.

bisque

A French term for porcelain or pottery that has been fired, but not glazed. First appearing in France during the 18th century.

bistro table

A small circular table with a pedestal base footed of iron and tabletop of marble, metal, or more recently plastic laminate. Typical of French outdoor cafes.

black gum

See *tupelo*.

black walnut

See *walnut, black*.

blackamoor

A decorative figure of a black African or other dark skinned person, such as a Moor, used during the Italian Renaissance and again in the Victorian period.

blackwood

A hardwood native to Australia and Tasmania, often painted or stained to mimic ebony, such as in the 19th-century American Victorian pieces of John Henry Belter. Similar to acacia. See also *acacia*.

blackamoor

blackwork

A type of embroidery using black or silver thread, popular during 16th-century Tudor and Elizabethan England. The style inspired many wall papers and printed linings of the time.

blanc-de-chine (BLAHNK-DU SHEEN)

French for Chinese white. A popular clear-glazed white porcelain made in China and imported to Europe during the late 17th century and 18th centuries. Widely copied by many manufacturers, including Meissen.

blanc de plomb (BLAHNK du plohm)

Literally translates from French as white lead. In furniture, a finish made popular during the time of Louis XV when white painted furniture was ordered for the Petit Trianon.

blanket chest

A colonial American chest (17th and 18th centuries) with a hinged top and one or two drawers below. Also known as a mule chest. See also *Connecticut chest* and *Hadley chest*.

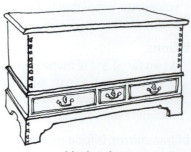

blanket chest

blind

A window treatment used to control light and air, generally of slats of fabric, wood, metal, or plastic. They may work by rolling or folding up or on a roller. See also *Austrian shade* and *Roman shade*.

blind arcade

An arcade of decorative arches applied to a wall so that they have no openings or glazing. Commonly seen in Romanesque architecture.

blind arcade

blind arch

An arch set against a wall and hence has no opening.

blind-fronted

A contemporary term used to describe a bureau bookcase or bureau cabinet containing paneled doors on the top section.

blind header

In masonry, a brick header that is concealed inside a wall in order to bond adjacent tiers of brick. Also, a brick or other masonry unit laid to give the appearance of a whole unit when it is actually not.

blind tracery

Tracery that adjoins a wall and hence is not pierced through.

blind window

A decorative window containing the general outline and respective moldings of a window, but with no opening or glazing.

blister figure

A wood grain effect created by irregular contours of annual growth rings. Also known as a quilted figure.

block and turned

A square furniture leg that is turned below the point receiving heightened structural tension.

block flooring

See *parquet*.

block foot

A cube-shaped foot popular in mid 18th-century English and American furniture. Favored by Thomas Chippendale since it often appeared on the end of a Marlborough leg. See also *marlborough foot* and *cube foot*. See *illustration in the Feet Appendix*.

block print

A method of printing textiles, originating in ancient China, using carved wooden blocks coated with dye to produce patterns. The technique is widely used throughout East Asia.

blockfront

A case piece that is divided into three parts, the center one extending past the two on either side. Commonly seen in 18th and 19th-century English and American bookcases, chests, cabinets, presses, and wardrobes. See also *breakfront*.

blockfront

blond woods

General term given to woods with a light golden or beige color such as aspen, holley, and birch. Also known as blonde woods.

blunt arch

A blunt pointed arch pulled from two centers within the span. Also known as a drop arch.

blunt arrow leg

A leg with ball tip found on 18th-century American Windsor chairs.

boasting

The crude preliminary shaping of stone by a carver or sculptor.

board and batten

External siding or interior paneling composed of wide vertical boards alternating with thin wooden strips, called battens.

boat bed

A bed of the French Empire period with raised ends of equal height that terminated in an outward scroll. Also called a *lit en bateau*.

boat-shaped table

A table with a top that curves inward at the ends of the long sides, remaining straight on the short sides. Commonly used in conference and dining rooms.

bobbin turning

A turned leg or stretcher, popular in the mid-to-late 17th century, containing repeating small bulbs similar to bobbins. Also commonly seen on the stretchers of late 18th-century Windsor chairs. See *illustration in the Legs Appendix*.

abcdefghijklmnopqrstuvwxyz

bobeche, bobache (boo BESH, boo BASH)
A collar or disk set at the candle socket base of a candlestick, chandelier, or sconce, to catch melting wax or hold suspended pendants.

bocage (boh KAHJ)
The use of decorative trees, branches, leaves or foliage in the background of pottery or porcelain figures. Also used in relation to the same in tapestries.

bochka (BOHK kah)
Literally translated from Russian as barrel. A traditional Russian roof in the form of a half cylinder with a curved pointed top, resembling an onion dome in section.

bocote (boh COH tay)
A hard, dense tropical hardwood known for its dark, dramatic striping. Indigenous to Mexico, South America, and Central America, it is prized by cabinetmakers and woodturners, as well as commonly used for flooring and veneer. Also known as Mexican rosewood.

body
The clay or other material used in making pottery or porcelain, as set apart from the glaze and other finishes.

bodying in
A term used in woodworking, for the filling of coarse wood grains to allow for a smoother finish.

bofet (boh FAY)
An early spelling of buffet.

boffet chair (boh FET CHAYR)
A Byzantine turned spindle-back chair with two front legs and one back leg, thought to have been introduced into Europe by the Normans.

bog oak, black oak
An oak bogwood that is very dark in color due to its burial beneath peat bogs in East Anglia, a region of eastern England. Used for turnings and inlay work since the 16th and 17th centuries.

bois de bout (BWAH duh boh)
French for end grained wood, i.e. a wood that has been cut at a right angle to the grain, thus giving a darker appearance.

bois de fil (BWAH du fee)
French for wood cut following the lines of the grain. See also *fil de bois*.

bois de rose (BWAH du rohz)
A yellowish-brown wood with pinkish tinge popularly used for veneer work on 18th and early 19th-century French furniture. Indigenous to Central and South America. See also *tulip wood*.

bois de violette (BWAH du VEE oh let)
French for kingwood. See *kingwood*.

bois de zebre (BWAH du zi BRAH)
French for wood of zebra. See *bossona*.

boiserie (BWAH seh ree)
French word for woodwork, particularly carved wooden wall panels of 18th-century French Rococo Style interiors.

bolection molding (boh LEK shun MOHL ding)
A molding projecting far past the wall plane or panel to which it is applied. Often used to conceal a joint between surfaces of different levels. Also called balection, belection, bellexion, bilection, and bolexion. See *illustration in the Moldings Appendix*.

boiserie

bolster
In interiors, a long narrow, often cylindrical pillow or cushion popular in the late 18th and early 19th centuries. In architecture, a short timber capping a post to increase the bearing surface and reduce a beam's span.

bolster arm
A cylindrical arm of an upholstered chair that mimics a bolster. Often found on mid 19-century lounge chairs

bolster top

The turned top rail of a chair with a cylinder-shaped central section.

bolt-head ornament

Circular disks used as furniture embellishment in the 19th century, mimicking metal ornaments found on Greek and Roman doors.

bolster top

Bombay furniture

Reference to furniture from India after the fall of the Mogul Empire (1740). A composite of French and Portuguese styles overlaid with rich Indian carving.

bombé (bohm BAY)

French for "blown out." General reference for furniture with a bulging, convex shape. First appeared during the Louis XIV period on commodes, chest, and bureaus, and later in Holland, England, and America.

bombé chest

bonader (boh NOH dur)

Swedish and Swedish-American wall hangings of the 18th century containing peasant scenes.

bonbonierre (bohn BOHN yayr)

A small decorative box used for storing sweetmeats or comfits, a sugar coated candy made from fruit and nuts or seeds, originating from the French term bonbon meaning sweetmeat.

bond

A masonry term, for the arrangement of bricks, blocks, or other masonry units in a set pattern for strength, stability, and/or aesthetics. See also *checkerboard bond*, *common bond*, *English bond*, *Flemish bond*, *running bond,* and *stretcher bond.*

bond course

A masonry term for the course or row of bricks that overlaps another.

bone china

A translucent white china, produced in England since the 1800s, whose name originated from the addition of bone ash into the kaolin.

bonheur-du-jour (bohn UR-DOO JOR)

A popular lady's writing desk of mid 18th-century France, set on tall, slender legs, with a raised back often forming a small cabinet. The desk was sometimes fitted to house toilet accessories, while the back or cabinet served as display space for ornaments and trinkets.

bonnet scroll

A term sometimes used in America for a swan neck or scrolled pediment.

bonheur-du-jour

bonnet top

An American term for a segmental arch or broken segmental arch used as a pediment on tallboys, secretaires, and cabinetry. Termed as "domed" or "hooded" in England. See also *hood* and *hooded top.*

bonnetière (bohn e TEE ayr)

An 18th-century French cabinet, whose size and shape allowed easy storage of the hats and bonnets unique to the regions of Normandy and Brittany.

book box

See *bible box.*

book match

See *book-matched veneer.*

book table

An 18th-century pedestal table with a rectangular, circular, or hexagonal shape, fitted with exposed or doored bookshelves on all sides.

bonnetière

bookcase

A furniture piece designed with shelves to hold books. Primarily an architectural design until the 17th century, the bookcase later developed into a freestanding unit with glazed doors. In the mid-late 18th century a two-part unit, otherwise known as the secretary, secretaire or secretaire bookcase, became fashionable. This new form had glazed doors above and a solid cupboard or drawers below. See also *secretary*.

book-matched veneer

A veneer matching technique using consecutive slices of veneer and turning one piece over, like a page in a book, to join the adjacent piece.

bookrest

A portable and adjustable framework used to hold a book or manuscript for reading. Popular in 18th and 19th-century libraries, it was also known as a reading stand.

bookstand

A low, open bookshelved unit with castors, common to the 18th and 19th centuries.

boot-rack

A set of horizontal bars, fitted in the lower part of a wardrobe, designed to store boots and shoes. In the 19th century, it developed into an open rack similar to contemporary shoe racks, but fitted with drawers at the base for storing brushes and shoe black.

bootjack

A board with a V-shaped cutout, used for the easy removal of boots. Often seen built-in to the end board of some early American chests.

borax

Slang for cheap, showy, and poorly constructed furniture.

border

A decorative strip, ornament, or motif that edges an object.

border pattern

A continous running motif or ornament often used to design decorative borders, bands, and panel frames.

Børge Mogensen Spanish chair (BOHRJ moh GEN sun SPAAN ish CHAYR)

A mid 20th-century modern chair by Danish designer Børge Mogensen, constructed with an oak frame, leather seat and back, and broad wooden armrests. The chair was inspired by traditional rustic hunting furniture of Spain's Islamic influenced region of Andalusia. See *Børge Mogensen, 1914–1972, in the Architects, Artists, and Designers Appendix.*

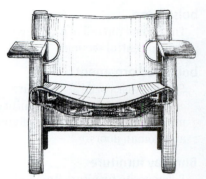

Børge Mogensen Spanish chair

Børge Mogensen model 1789 spoke-back sofa

A slat back sofa designed in 1945 originally for the Cabinetmaker's Guild Exhibition by Scandinavian designer Børge Mogensen. It was commercially produced by Fredericia A/S in 1963 and featured a beech wood frame that allowed one arm to be lowered for use as a daybed. See *Børge Mogensen, 1914–1972, in the Architects, Artists, and Designers Appendix.*

Børge Mogensen model 1789 spoke-back sofa

borne (BORN)

A French round or oval sofa with a central pillar or rail serving as a back, popular in the center of public rooms within a Victorian home. Also called a born.

borne

Borneo cedar

See *yellow seraya*.

borning room

A room, common to Colonial New England homes, where babies were born and often kept during infancy. Generally located near a kitchen or keeping room due to their warmth.

boss

In architecture, a projecting ornament placed at the intersections of beams, moldings, or ribs of vaults. Common motifs include the head of an angel, a flower, foliage, or a hanging pendant. On furniture, a small round or oval ornament commonly seen in 17th and 18th-century English and American work.

boss

bosse (BAHS)

An often figured, pinkish to reddish brown African wood, commonly used as veneer for furniture, interior doors, and paneling. Also called African cedar or cedar mahogany. See also *piqua*.

bossona (boh SOHN uh)

A reddish-brown hardwood with black and brown streaks, similar to rosewood. Commonly found in Brazil, Paraguay, Uruguay, and Venezuela, bossona is commonly used in design for cabinetmaking, furniture, flooring. See also *bois de zebre*, *goncalo alves*, and *zebrawood*.

Boston chair

An 18th-century American chair with curved back spindles designed to fit the human form and a large crest rail ending with shoulders on both sides.

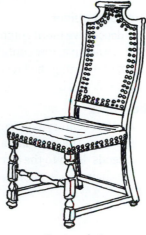

Boston chair

Boston rocker

A 19th-century American rocking chair, developed in New England and characterized by a tall spindled back, wide top rail, a seat that curves down at the front and up at the back, and arms that follow the seat's curve. Commonly painted black and ornamented with painted details.

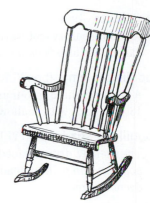

Boston rocker

boteh (BOH tuh)

A tear drop motif frequently seen in Persian rugs. Commonly known in the West as a paisley.

bottle-end glazing

The bull's eye effect created by using bottle bottoms to glaze the doors of English and continental cabinets and cupboards of the 16th and 17th centuries. See also *crown glass*.

bottle turning

A bottle-shaped turning, originating in Holland, but commonly found on the legs of 17th-century William and Mary furniture.

bouchon (BOO shahn)

An 18th-century removable cover for the marble top of a bouillotte table. Composed of a cork pad with wool fabric on one side and leather on the other, the cover created a level surface between the table's top and brass gallery.

boudoir (boo DWAHR)

A woman's private apartment or room used for retreat from court life during the Louis XV period. From the French word *bouder*, meaning "to pout."

boudoir chair (boo DWAHR CHAYR)

A small, fully upholstered chair, commonly Louis XV (rococo) in style, designed for a lady's bedroom or dressing room.

abcdefghijklmnopqrstuvwxyz

bouillotte (boo YET)
An 18th-century foot warmer from France. Also a small table with gallery. See also *bouillotte table*.

bouillotte lamp (boo YET LAMP)
A portable, three or four armed, candlestick-like lamp of the late 18th century, with shallow shade. Originally used on a *bouillette table*.

bouillotte shade (boo YET SHAYD)
The shallow, drum-shaped shade of a *bouillotte lamp*. Often made of tôle, a decorated metal.

bouillotte table (boo YET TAY bul)
A small 18th-century French table, characterized by its round shape, and marble top with brass or bronze gallery. Two small drawers and candle slides were often designed within the table's apron. Originally designed for playing bouillette, a popular card game of the time.

bouillotte table

bouleuterion (boo loo TEER ee ahn)
Ancient Greek building used for government business.

Boulle work (BOOL WURK)
A method of metal and tortoiseshell inlay developed by André Charles Boulle during the Louis XIV period. The technique involved gluing a sheet of brass, German silver, or pewter to a sheet of tortoiseshell and then cutting out a delicate scrolled design. The brass pieces could then be set into the tortoiseshell ground (première partie) or the tortoiseshell into the brass ground (contrepartie). Boulle work continued to be used during the Régence period. See also *première partie* or *contre-partie marquetry*. See *André Charles Boulle, 1642–1732, in the Architects, Artists, and Designers Appendix*.

boultine (BAAL teen)
A small convex molding originally set below the abacus in a Tuscan and Roman Doric capital. In section, equaling one fourth of a circle. Commonly known as quarter round.

Bourbon period
The part of the French Renaissance, dating from 1589 to about 1730, relating to the reigns of the Bourbon monarchs, including Henry IV, Louis XIII, and Louis XIV. Also incorporates the Régence.

Bourbon Restoration
The restoration of the Bourbon monarchy to the French throne in 1824, after the fall of Napoleon. See also *French Restoration period*.

bousillage (boo ZEE ahj)
French for posts on sill. A type of construction, commonly used by 18th-century French settlers in America, utilizing a mixture of clay and grass as a filler between vertical posts. Other fibrous materials such as Spanish moss or hair were often mixed within the mud as well. See also *pierrotage*.

bow
One of the first porcelain factories in England. Founded in 1744, the factory first produced imitations of popular imported Oriental porcelains, but was most known for their soft-paste porcelain, containing bone ash.

bow and quiver

bow and quiver
A decorative motif composed of an achery bow and an arrow container called the quiver, popular during the French Neoclassic period of Louis XVI.

bow back
An 18th-century Windsor chair popular in America. The chair has a bowed frame that extends down to the arms or to the seat of the chair.

bow back Windsor chair

bow front, bowfront, or swell front

A furniture front containing a convex curve or swell to the front. Popular with 18th-century English designs of the Adam brothers and George Hepplewhite, the front is commonly found on case pieces such as chests, commodes, and sideboards.

bow front chest

bow top

The top rail of a chair formed in a continuous, unbroken curve or the front edge of a desk designed in the same manner.

bow window

A large window that projects outward from a wall in a curved or semicircular fashion. Also known as a compass window.

bowfat (BOH fat)

A cupboard, similar to a buffet, used to store dining and drinking wares in an 18th-century American home.

bowl stand

See *washstand*.

bowtell (BOH tel)

A decorative roll molding, commonly used in Gothic architecture. Also known as a boutell, boltel, boultine, or bowtel. See also *boultine*.

box

A container, often having a lid, used for storing various items. Also known as letter box. See also *bible box, casket, desk box,* and *knife box*.

box bed

An old fashioned bed with framed paneling on three sides and the top, and curtains or shutters that can be drawn on the open side for privacy. A common cottage piece seen in Northern England and Scotland until the mid 19th century. Also called a box bedstead. Later the term was occasionally used for a bed that folds up against a wall. See also *lit clos*.

box chair

A contemporary term for a paneled armchair with a high back and hinged storage compartment beneath the seat.

box joint

A wood joint with a series of interlocking, tapered fingers. See also *finger joint*.

box match

A decorative veneer technique similar to a diamond match, but set at an angle to produce a sequence of radiating squares that flow from the center.

box pleating

Fabric that has been collected into folds. The folds are then pressed or stitched to create box shapes. Box pleating is often seen in draperies.

box seat

A box shaped seat cushion with welting defining the edges. Also known as a box cushion.

box settle

A chest or settle with a box below the hinged seat. Popular in England's Tudor and Elizabethan periods, as well as America's 17th and 18th-century provincial furniture.

box spring

A bedspring consisting of spiral springs contained in a cloth covered, box-like frame. Used with a mattress to prolong durability.

box stool

A 17th-century stool with a hinged top that functions as the seat.

box stretcher

A stretcher system for a table, chair, or cabinet, that forms a square or rectangular arrangement between the legs.

box stretcher

43

boxed heart

A sawn timber or board that fully encloses the log's heart or pith within its four faces.

boxwood

A fine, even textured, light cream or yellow colored wood with a lustrous finish when polished. Seen in inlay and border work of 16th-century oak and walnut pieces and the satinwood furniture of the 18th century. Boxwood is also used for carving and turning small objects such as handles, chess pieces, and rulers. It is indigenous to Europe, northwest Africa, and southwest Asia. Also known as common box or European box.

brace

A part used to add strength or reinforce. Generally found within under-framing, like a corner block or stretcher on furniture or a cross brace between beams or joists in construction.

braced back

The reinforced back of a Windsor chair, created by two spindles extending from the chair's seat back extension to the top rail. Also known as a fiddle-braced back.

bracket

In architecture, a structural element used to support a projecting part of a building, such as a cornice. The same term stands for a furniture support member that runs from the legs to the body, an ornamental shelf designed to hang on a wall, or a decorative detail found under the overhanging edge of a stair tread.

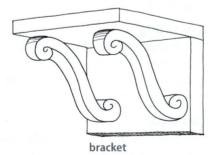

bracket

bracket candlestick

A decorative wall sconce with projecting candlestick.

bracket clock

Originally, a small weight-driven clock that had to be mounted on a bracket so that its weights could hang freely. Later, the term was applied to spring-driven table clocks of the 17th and 18th centuries.

bracket cornice

An interior treatment composed of an ornamental wooden cornice, supported by brackets that mimics a corbel table.

bracket foot

A short furniture foot with straight corner edge and curved inner edges, popular on 18th-century English and American case pieces. See *illustration in the Feet Appendix*.

bracketed stair

A staircase with brackets applied to the exposed sides, under the tread nosing, to add architectural detail.

bracketed stair

brad

A small, tapered nail with a slight ridge replacing the head, commonly used for finish work.

braid

A narrow fabric band, of varying widths and weaves, used to trim, bind, or edge.

braided rug

A round or oval rug, generally associated with Colonial American interiors, made from twisted strips of cloth that are braided and then sewn together. See also *rag rug*.

brand dog

See *andiron, chenette*, and *fire dogs*.

bras

See *chandelier d' applique*.

brass

An alloy made of copper and zinc.

brass, antiqued

A darkened finish produced when brass oxidizes. May be mimicked through chemical application

brass, polished

A bright mirror-like finish produced by polishing brass.

brasses

General term for hardware made from brass.

brattishing, brandishing, bretisement (BRAAT ish ing, BRAAND ish ing, bre TIYZ ment)

A decorative cresting found on screens, panels, parapets, or cornices of 18th-century Tudor architecture. The ornamentation often contains leaf or flower forms.

brazier (BRAH zee-ay)

A device used, until the 19th century, as an early portable heater. A simple design comprised of a legged pan to hold hot coals. The term also refers to an individual who works with brass.

Brazilian rosewood

A Brazilian wood, characterized by streaks that range from dark purple to dark brown. See also *rosewood, Brazilian.*

Brazilwood

A bright orange-red colored wood from Brazil, known for its strength and ability to take a high shine. Used primarily for cabinetwork, parquet flooring, and bows for stringed instruments. Seen in inlay work of the 17th century. Also known as bahia wood, Brazilette, para wood, pernambuco wood, and Brazilian ironwood.

breakfront

A case piece that is divided into three parts, the center one extending past the two on either side. Also noted as break front.

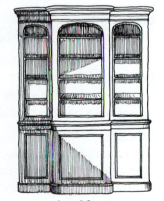
breakfront

breakfront desk

A two-piece unit with a bookcase that sits on top of a projecting desk base, similar to a stepback cupboard.

breeze bricks

A brick made of pan breeze and Portland cement, often used in the construction of a clay brick wall because it easily holds nails.

breton (bre TOHN)

The provincial style found in Brittany, a cultural region in northwest France.

Brewster chair

A 17th-century American chair, made in the colony of New England and named after Elder Brewster, a prominent early settler of the area. It is a turned chair with heavy posts, a rush seat, and vertically spindled back, often set in a double row. See also *bannister-back chair* and *carver chair.*

Brewster chair

bric-à-brac (BRIK AH BRAAK)

A general term given to miscellaneous decorative objects. Thought to stem from the French phrase "de bric et de broc" which translates to by "hook or by crook."

brick

A small clay rectangle baked hard by the sun or a kiln, commonly used as a building material. Standard size is 8 3/4" × 4 1/4".

brick, adobe

A brick composed of clay and straw, roughly molded in a form and dried in the sun. Commonly used in hot dry climates.

brick arch

See *voussoir.*

brick, building

See *brick, common.*

brick, clinker

A brick that has been fired longer to fuse materials within the clay and make a harder product that is prominently used as pavers.

brick, common

A brick made with no attempt to control color or set texture. Also called a building brick.

brick, economy

A cored, modular brick with nominal size of 4"d × 4"h × 8"l and actual size of 3-5/8"d × 3-5/8"h × 7-5/8"l. Creates a 4" course.

brick, engineered

A semivitreous brick that is denser and stronger than an ordinary face brick with a nominal size of 4" × 3-1/5" × 8" and an actual size of 3-5/8" × 2-13/16" × 7-5/8".

brick, facing

Brick used for exterior facing, designed with special consideration given to color and texture.

brick, fire

A brick made to withstand high temperatures, used especially in fireplaces and as a furnace lining. Often yellow or beige in color, fire bricks come in two standard sizes; 4-1/2" × 3" × 9" and 9" × 4-1/2" × 2-1/2". Also comes as a thinner "split" that measures 9" × 4-1/2" × 1-1/4" used for fireplace inserts and wood stove liners.

brick, gauged

A brick that has been sized to specific dimensions by molding, cutting, or rubbing.

brick, Norman

A solid clay brick with nominal dimensions of 3"d × 2-1/2"h × 12"l and actual dimensions of 2-5/8"d × 2-1/4"h × 11-5/8"l. Also commonly made as a slightly higher brick called a jumbo Norman brick.

brick, Roman

A long, thin brick, used for facing, that is usually yellow-brown in color and has a nominal size of 4"d × 2"h × 12"l and an actual size of 3-5/8"d × 1-5/8"h × 11-5/8"l.

brick, salmon

A soft, under-fired brick named for its reddish orange tint. It is commonly used as a filler to provide rigidity and insulation in timber-framed houses. Also called a chuff or place brick.

bridal chest

A chest, often beautifully ornamented, specifically designed for the storage and accumulation of clothing (the trousseau) and household items in preparation for marriage. Also known as a hope chest or dower chest.

brise-soleil (BREEZ soh LAY)

French for sun breaker. A permanent sun-shading device, popularized by Le Corbusier, that extends from the outside of a building. Louvers are often incorporated to keep out the high angled summer sun, yet let the low angled winter sun reach the building's façade.

Britannia metal (bri TAAN ee u MET ul)

An inexpensive alternative to silver, used in the production of many household objects during the 18th century.

British Colonial

Furniture and architecture created in the 18th and early 19th centuries, within British colonies such as the West Indies, South Africa, and India. Inspired by English Georgian counterparts, but interpreted by native craftsmen into simplified designs, full of native details and charm.

broadcloth

A lustrous plain or rib woven textile, generally made of cotton, silk, or rayon.

broadloom

A carpet woven on a wide loom, in widths from 9 to 18 feet, in order to create a seamless installation.

brocade

A woven silk textile designed with raised figures that resemble embroidery. Commonly used in the 17th and 18th centuries through present day as upholstery, draperies, and bed hangings. Also known as bracado.

brocade, carpet

A carpet with a raised design that appears embossed, formed by heavy twisted yarns on a straight fiber ground.

brocatelle (broh KAH tel)

A heavy silk and linen fabric, with a raised design on a plain or twill background, originally designed to mimic tooled leather. Also a variegated yellow marble with flecks of white and gray, indigenous to France and Italy. Sometimes seen as brocatel or brocadella.

brocatelle violette (broh KAH tel vee OH let)

A variety of French brocatelle marble with a purple undertone, heavily used in 18th and 19th-century French designs such as the Petit Trianon at Versailles and the Paris Opera House.

broché (BROH shee)

A fabric woven with a patterning weft, alongside the primary weft, in order to attain a raised design similar to brocade. Generally produced of cotton or silk.

broken arch

An elliptical arch whose sides do not join at the apex, similar to a broken pediment. Commonly seen over doors and windows. See also *broken pediment*.

broken front

A piece of furniture with planes of varying projection found on the front. Many 18th and 19th-century bookcases, wardrobes, and presses were designed with projecting central sections and flanking sides. See also *breakfront*.

broken pediment

A straight, rounded, or scrolled pediment whose sides do not meet in the center. The open space is instead often filled with a decorative device such as a finial or urn and is commonly seen capping windows, doors, and case pieces. See also *gooseneck* or *swan neck pediment*. See *illustrations in the Pediments Appendix*.

broken scroll or swan neck

A broken pediment with two opposed S curves with scrolled upper ends forming the raking lines, usually featuring a small central pedestal, sometimes topped with a vase, pineapple or finial at its center. See *illustrations in the Pediments Appendix*.

broken triangle

A broken straight sided pediment forming a triangular shape. See *illustrations in the Pediments Appendix*.

bronze

A compound made of copper and tin, used for furniture and sculpture since ancient times. See also *patina*.

bronze d'ameublement (BRAHNZ dahm OO blum awnt)

Decorative bronze hardware such as handles, escutcheons, pulls, etc. First seen on French furniture of the early 18th century.

bronze-doré (BRAHNZ dohr AY)

French for gilt bronze, a finish created to imitate gold.

bronze furniture

Furniture made of bronze, commonly used since the ancient Greeks and Romans, and again in the late Renaissance and Empire periods of France.

bronzeur (BRAHNZ ur)

A French reference to an individual who works with bronze. Bronze workers were divided into two guilds: the fondeurs and the doreurs. The first were responsible for casting and finishing the metal, the second for chasing and gilding it.

brown oak

A deep brown English wood used mainly for cabinetmaking. The wood gets its brown color from fungi caused by the damp soil.

brownstone

A sandstone that is soft brown to reddish brown in color and used for building. It is also the name for middle to late 19th-century row houses, found in cities of the northern United States, that are faced with brownstone.

abcdefghijklmnopqrstuvwxyz

brûlete parfum (broo LET pahr FUM)

French for perfume burner. Historically an urn-shaped container, designed to hold charcoal, that was drizzled with perfume to freshen a space. Also called a brûle-parfum.

Bruno Mathsson miranda chair

A birch framed easychair created by Bruno Mathson in 1941, constructed with arms of laminated beech and a seat and back of plaited webbing. See *Bruno Mathsson, 1907–1988, in the Architects, Artists, and Designers Appendix.*

Bruno Mathsson miranda chair

Brussels carpet

An English carpet, first introduced in the 18th century and distinguished by its multiple colors that run with the warp yarns, level loop, and cotton backing. Popular during the English Regency and American Federal periods.

brutalism

A style of modern architecture, seen from the 1950s to the mid 1970s, characterized by massive stark forms, usually of exposed concrete.

bubinga (boo BEEN gah)

A West African hardwood known for its reddish-brown ground with uniformly spaced purple stripes, primarily used for cabinetwork, furniture and paneling. Also known as African rosewood, essingang, or buvenga. See also *akume*.

bucket armchair

An English Regency armchair with a concave rounded back, often cained, and scrolled arms that start mid seat rail and curve upward to form the chair's top rail.

buckle back chair

A Victorian chair with a back resembling a belt buckle, a variation of the balloon back with a straight cross rail set within the back.

bucranium (bu KRAYN ee um)

A sculptured representation of a bull or ox skull, often seen on Roman Ionic and Corinthian friezes. Also called a bucrane.

bucranium

Buen Retiro (BWAYN ru TEE roh)

18th-century Spanish porcelain manufactured at the royal residence of Buen Retiro, outside Madrid. Founded by Charles III of Naples who, upon inheriting the Spanish throne, brought the ceramic artists and potters of Capo di Monte with him.

buffet

French for a sideboard or cupboard. Developed during the 16th century in France and England as a server and a place for storing dishes. Also known as beaufete or buffette.

buffet à deux corps

A large buffet of two parts with the upper section set back from the front and sides, popular during the 18th century in France.

buhl work (BYOOL WURK)

A 19th-century English term for Boulle work. See also *Boulle work*.

building block

A hollow concrete unit used in construction. May also be formed of clay.

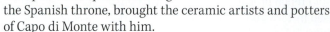

buffet à deux corps

building board

A board used as sheathing for walls, partitions, and ceilings; composed of heavy paper adhered to a plaster core. Available in standard 4" × 8" × 1/2" sheets. Also known as wallboard. See also *drywall* and *gypsum board*.

built-in furniture

Furniture such as beds, bookcases, cabinets, chests, etc. built as an integral part of the structure.

bulb bowl

A bowl for growing bulbs, often designed with three feet.

bulbous form

A common Renaissance wood turning, resembling a large melon, often seen as furniture supports for English, French, Italian, and Dutch work. Also called a melon bulb. See also *cup and cover turning* and *melon turning*. See *illustration in the Legs Appendix*.

bullion (BUUL yon)

Heavy corded trim used on upholstery and window treatments, originally containing gold or silver thread.

bull nose, bullnose edge

A rounded convex edge found on wood, stone, glass, tile, and other materials.

bull nose

bull-nosed step

A step, usually at the base of a flight of stairs, with a projecting, rounded end whose width extends beyond the others.

bull's eye

A glazed or louvered opening that is oval or round in form, used for air circulation or adding natural light. Also the circular figure found in crown glass, commonly used in the glazing of Edwardian Cottage Style furniture doors. Known in France as oeil-de-bouef. See also *crown glass* and *oeil-de-bouef*.

bull's eye mirror

A round decorative mirror, generally with a convex glass and carved wooden frame. See also *girandole*.

bull's eye mirror

bull's head

See *bucranium*.

bulto (BOOL toh)

A carved wooden, polychromed sculpture, generally religious in nature, often seen in New Mexico.

bun foot or Flemish foot

A foot that resembles a flattened ball or bun, commonly seen on furniture of the late 17th century. See *illustration in the Feet Appendix*.

bundle

Package of wallpaper, generally in single, double, or triple rolls.

bunk

Originally the sleeping berth of a ship's cabin. Later applied to the same in railway sleeping cars of Great Britain and Europe.

bunk bed

A bed unit with one bed frame stacked upon another, generally equipped with a built-in ladder or set of steps for easy access. The design maximizes floor space, allowing two people to sleep in a small area.

buon fresco (BWAHN FRAYskoh)

An ancient technique in which paintings are created on wet plaster. A true fresco that locks pigments into the surface that reached its height during the Italian Renaissance.

bureau (BYOOR oh)

Originally a piece of fabric draped over a table when used for writing. Sheraton defined it as a "common desk with drawers." In England, it is now a reference to any piece of furniture containing a desk and drawers. In America, it has become synonymous with a chest of drawers.

bureau

bureau à caissons latéreaux

A Louis XVI writing table with a central drawer flanked by two or three narrow drawers. Similar to a modern pedestal desk, the design provided ample knee space to the user. Literally translated as a bureau with lateral compartments.

bureau à cylindre (BYOOR oh AH si LAHN drah)

A French cylinder-top desk, popular during the Louis XV and Louis XVI periods. Occasionally seen in Scandinavia and Germany. Also called a bureau a rideau. See also *cylinder top.*

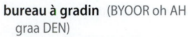

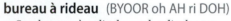
bureau à cylindre

bureau à gradin (BYOOR oh AH graa DEN)

A French writing table with a tier, or several tiers, of small drawers or compartments built at the back of the desktop.

bureau à rideau (BYOOR oh AH ri DOH)

See *bureau à cylindre* and *cylinder top.*

bureau bedstead

A bed designed to fold into a unit resembling a bureau.

bureau bookcase

An 18th-century term used by Chippendale for a bureau cabinet.

bureau cabinet

A desk topped with a tall cupboard containing glazed, paneled, or mirrored doors. See also bureau bookcase.

bureau commode

A Louis XIV desk with drawers below.

bureau dressing table

An 18th-century table characterized by a desk set on tall cabriole legs, drawers beneath the writing surface, and a hinged mirror mounted to the top.

Bureau du Roi (BYOOR oh doo RAH)

The cylinder-top writing desk of Louis XV, designed Jean-Francois Oeben in 1760 and finished by Jean Henri Reisener in 1769.

bureau en dos d'âne (BYOOR oh on doh DAHN)

French for donkey's back bureau. A small Louis XV slant front desk on tall cabriole legs. Also known as a bureau en dos d'âne. See also *bureau en pente.*

bureau en pente (BYOOR oh on PENT)

A French slant front desk, first seen in the Louis XV period and generally raised on cabriole legs. Also known as a *bureau en dos d'âne.*

bureau Mazarin (BYOOR oh mah ZAH ran)

A 17th-century French writing desk named for Cardinal Mazarin, the French regent from 1642 to 1661. The desk is characterized by a pedestal of three drawers on either side, each raised on sets of four legs with X or H shaped cross bracing.

bureau plat (BYOOR oh PLAT)

A large, flat, basically rectangular, writing table with a series of drawers (usually three) set side-by-side within the apron. Created by Andre Charles Boulle during the reign of Louis XIV.

bureau plat

bureau table

A late 18th-century kneehole table, designed and named by John Goddard of Newport, Rhode Island.

bureau toilet

A French bureau designed for a lady and fitted with compartments for storing toiletries. See also *bureau dressing table.*

burgher (BUR gur)

A wealthy middle class or bourgeoisie citizen, a member of the merchant class.

burgomaster chair

See *roundabout chair*.

Burgundian Style

A provincial furniture style of the French Renaissance, native to the Rhone Valley area and noted for its massive construction and high relief carving, often full of allegorical figures. Hugues Sambin, an architect from Dijon, was considered the primary arbiter of the design. See also *cabinet à deux corps*.

burjar/ burjair (BUR yar/ BURCH ayr)

A term used by Chippendale for a bergère. See *bergère*.

burl

A knot or irregular growth pattern found in the wood of a tree, sliced in cross section to produce beautiful decorative veneer with a curly mottled pattern. Commonly found in walnut, maple, and ash trees.

burnt work

Line drawings burned onto wood by a heated metal stylus.

buro table

A term for an early American bureau on legs, commonly incorporating drawers.

burr

See burl.

bust

A sculpture representative of the upper portion of a human body, showing only the head, shoulders, and upper chest.

butcher furniture

A term used by Duncan Phyfe for the heavy furniture he created, after 1820, in the popular Second Empire and Late Empire styles of France. See also *American Empire, Second Empire,* or *Late Empire.*

butler

A rare informal label for a late 18th-century American cellaret or wine cooler.

butler finish

A distinctive silver finish produced by buffing the surface with fine abrasives.

butler's desk

A type of drop-front desk that when closed resembles a chest of drawers. When the upper drawer is partially pulled out, the face drops down to create a writing surface and the back half is fitted with small doors, drawers, and pigeon holes.

butler's sideboard

A unique 18th-century American sideboard containing a central drawer, with hinged face, fitted as a writing surface with desk compartments. Similar to a butler's desk. See also *butler's desk*.

butler's tray table

A small, portable side table incorporating a top with hinged edges, designed with cut out hand holds, that lift to form a tray.

butsudan (butt su DAAN)

A Buddhist shrine, in the form of a doored cabinet, often seen in Japanese homes. Literally translates as Buddha's House.

butt

The portion of a tree stump, with unique graining, used for making decorative veneers.

butt hinge

A common type of door hinge composed of two leaves and a visible pin joint.

butt joint

A simple wood joint formed by fastening two pieces of wood at a right angle, set with glue, nails, or screws. See *illustration in the Joints Appendix.*

butt match

A form of veneer matching produced by laying consecutively cut pieces end to end to form a continuous strip. Also called an end match.

butter cupboard

A European cabinet, designed with ventilation, used for storing bread.

butterfly

A decorative motif, original to the Orient, commonly seen in the Second Empire period of mid to late 19th-century France.

butterfly table

An 18th-century American drop leaf table with leaves supported by swinging brackets resembling butterfly wings

butterfly table

butterfly wedge

A butterfly-shaped cleat used to fasten boards together.

butternut

An American wood also known as white walnut because of its resemblance to black walnut, although not as strong. The wood is tan to brown in color and has a coarse grain and a soft texture that takes finishes well. Commonly used for paneling, cabinetry, furniture and carvings. Also known as oil nut.

buttoning

An upholstery method introduced in the latter half of the 18th century, known for its buttoned quilted effect created by pulling strong thread through the upholstery cover and stuffing and tying it off to the frame or webbing. Threads are then hidden on the outside by self upholstered buttons.

buttonwood

Trade name for the cross grained, reddish-brown wood of the American Plane tree, sometimes used for making chairs.

buttwood veneer

Veneer obtained from the area of a tree where the roots and trunk meet, commonly producing a curly mottled figure.

buttress

An exterior architectural support commonly found in Gothic era cathedrals, tied into masonry walls in order to disburse the structure's load bearing weight.

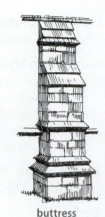

buttress

byobu (biy OH boo)

A traditional Japanese folding screen used for dividing rooms, generally adorned with decorative painting and calligraphy

Byzantine (BI zun teen)

A reference to the ornate architectural and artistic style of the Byzantine Empire, centered in Constantinople, the seat of the Roman Empire from 476 to 1200. Architecture and interiors of the style were characterized by soaring spaces, domes, intricate marble columns and inlay, and sumptuous mosaics. Furniture of the style was entirely ecclesiastical or royal in nature, covered with rich, ornate carvings and inlays of gold, glass, and stone. Byzantine is also a reference to a three-sided corner chair originating from the Orient and later seen in Italy.

Byzantine chair

cabaret fledermaus (kaa bu ray fle DUR mows)
See *Josef Hoffmann cabaret fledermaus*. See *Josef Hoffmann, 1870–1956, in the Architects, Artists, and Designers Appendix*.

cabbage rose
A Victorian rose design motif used on wallpaper, carpet, fabric, china, etc., to compliment the color schemes in Victorian houses.

cabin bed
See *captain's bed*.

cabinet
A private room used for study or conducting business; also a type of furniture with shelves, drawers, and/or compartments. See also *étagère*.

cabinet à deux corps (KAAB u nit AH DU KOR)
A French antique two-piece cabinet with doors above and below that housed shelves behind the doors. See also *armoire à deux* and *Burgundian Style*.

cabinet bed
See *Murphy bed*.

cabinet interieur (KAAB u nit in TEER eur)
Inner room to the petit appartement du roi used by the sovereignty as a part of the official bedchamber where court ceremonies took place.

cabinet particulier (KAAB u nit pahr TIK you leay)
A small room intended for use by one or more persons to discuss personal issues.

cabinet pulls
See *specific types of cabinet pulls*.

cabinet-secrétaire (KAAB u nit se KRU tayr)
An 18th-century French term for a desk with a cabinet above the work surface. See also *secrétaire*.

cabinet-vitrine (KAAB u nit vi TREEN)
A French word for a glass-paneled cabinet popular in the late 17th and early 18th centuries for displaying rare articles, such as porcelain from China, objects d'art, and other precious merchandise. See also *vitrine*.

cabinetmaker
A specialized artisan who makes fine furniture.

cabinetwork or cabinetmaking
The practice of making fine furniture and interior woodwork, as distinguished from construction work or carpentry.

cable molding
A type molding designed to look like a twisted rope and used for decorative moldings of the Romanesque period in England, France, and Spain, also adapted for 18th-century furniture by Thomas Sheraton. See also *rope molding* and *torsade*. See *illustration in the Moldings Appendix*.

cable fluting
A convex circular molding formed in the flutes of a column with the cables usually rising about one-third of the distance up the shaft. See also *fluting*.

cabochon (kaa BOO shohn)
A French word to define a round or oval convex ornament with a plain center, suggesting a gem or polished stone, also a square or diamond geometrical-shaped stone inserted into a floor to formalize the design. See *illustration in the Motifs/Ornaments Appendix*.

cabriole chair
An armchair with an upholstered back, usually oval or cartouche shaped, made in the mid 18th century in England during Chippendale's French period and described by Sheraton in *The Cabinet*. See also *cabriole leg* and *Louis XV Style*.

cabriole leg (kaab REE ohl LEG)
A French term used to designate a form of sinuous tapering leg, curved outwards at the knee, in toward the ankle, and out again at the foot. See also *bandy leg* and *hock leg*. See *illustration in the Legs Appendix*.

cabriole seat
A term used to describe an upholstered chair seat with a rounded shape.

cabriolet (kaab REE oh lay)
A fashionable French chair or armchair, especially prevalent during the Louis XV period; characterized by its concave back designed to fit the human body for more comfort. See also *chaise en cabriolet*.

cache pot (KAASH PAHT)
French term used to describe a container or flowerpot made of china, wood, or porcelain.

cacqueteuse (kaak KU uuz)
A conversational chair with a high, narrow back and curved arms from the early French Renaissance. Same as caquetoire. See also *chaise de femme*.

cadeira de sola (kah DAY ru DEE SOH la)
A 17th-century Spanish/Portuguese chair, much like the ladder-back chair. Same as Majorca chair.

caduceus (KAH doo see-us)
A symbolic wand or staff associated with Mercury and the Greek god Hermes; characterized by two serpents entwined around it with two wings at the top, used today as the symbol of the medical profession.

caduceus

caen stone (KAHN STOHN)
A yellowish color limestone from Caen in Normandy, often used in medieval English buildings.

café curtains
Short opaque or translucent curtains used especially for covering the lower part and sometimes the upper portion of the window, hung from a series of sliding rings on a rod.

caffoy (kaaf FOI)
A plush early 18th-century fabric used for draperies and hangings in English state rooms.

cage cup
Roman glass cup from around the mid-third and mid-fourth century C.E., made of the similar glass as the cameo vessel; purpose and meaning is debatable with many believing the cup represented use as a lamp. See also *diatreta*.

caisson ceiling (KAY sahnz SEE ling)
A classical Chinese architectural feature in the form of a sunken coffer, bordered by a square, a polygon, or a circle; usually decorated with distinctive designs; dating back 2,000 years to the Han Dynasty. Also, can be a watertight chamber used in construction below water. See also *coffer* and *lacunaria*.

calamander (kahl AH mahn dur)
A wood, mottled with brown and black streaks, imported from Ceylon and used for banding and veneering in 18th-century furniture. See also *coromandel wood*.

calathus, pl. calathi (KAHL ah thohs)
A vase-shaped basket core of the Corinthian capital; also represented in Greek painting and sculpture as a symbol of abundance and fruitfulness.

calcimine (KAL se miyn)
A white water-based painting mixture containing zinc oxide, glue, and coloring; used as a wash for walls and ceilings.

caldarium (KAHL dah ree-um)
An ancient Roman chamber for hot steam baths. Same as calidarium.

Calder mobile
See *Alexander Calder mobile*. See *Alexander Calder, 1898–1976, in the Architects, Artists, and Designers Appendix*.

calendering (KAAL un dur ing)
A mechanical finishing process in which paper or cloth is pressed into sheets through heated cylinders to produce a smooth, glazed, or polish finish.

calf's tongue molding, calves' tongue molding
A molding featuring pointed tongue-shaped forms all pointing in the same direction or toward a common center around an arch.

calico
A plain woven cotton cloth originally produced and imported from India.

calligraphy

An artistic, stylized, or highly ornamental form of decorative writing.

cama (KAH mah)

A Spanish term for a bed or bedstead.

camber (KAAM ber)

A beveled edge where two surfaces meet at an angle different than 90 degrees.

cambric (KAAM brik)

An original plain-weave linen or cotton fabric made in Cambrai, France; the coarser versions are used for linings as opposed to the softer, loosely woven cotton, which are sheer.

came

Lead strips, medieval in origin yet still current, used to frame the pieces of glass in leaded or stained glass windows.

camel back (KA mul BAK)

A shield-back chair of late Chippendale or Hepplewhite Style, with a serpentine curved top rail. See also *shield back*.

camel-back sofa

An upholstered sofa of the mid 18th century with a serpentine back that rises to a hump in the center.

camel's hair

A very soft, light tan to brownish cloth made of hair from a camel, often mixed with wool or other fiber, used for making rugs.

cameo

A stone or imitation of stone carved in relief, used for decoration in the 18th century on English furniture. See also *carving*.

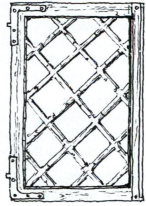

came

camel-back sofa

cameo back

Hand-carved, upholstered oval back and seat in fine fabric, popular during Louis XVI as the Colquette chair, in England during the Adamesque period, and during Sheraton Style. See also *oval back*.

cameo glass

Luxury glass art from ancient Rome and revived in the mid 19th century, which was equal to the French Art Nouveau, characterized by carving through layers of different colored glass to produce white opaque figures and motifs over a dark undercoat.

camera (KAAM e ru)

An Italian word for the owner's bedchamber at the piano nobile level where the most treasured possessions were kept.

camlet, camblet, or chamlet (KAHM lay, KAHM blay, SHAHM lay)

A 14th-century French fabric, originating in Asia, made of camel's hair, silk, and wool; imported in the 17th century and manufactured in England.

campagnola (KAHM pagn yo lah)

Provincial furniture made in the outlying districts of Italy, characterized by its simple manner.

campaign chest

A chest of drawers designed primarily for military use, often collapsible for moving, characterized by two or three drawers with one drawer fitted with a secretaire for composing letters and with sunken brass handles for ease in transporting.

campaign chest

campanario (KAHM pahn a ree-oh)

A Spanish word for a belfry, church tower, or bell tower.

campaniform (kaam PAAN i fohrm)

A word meaning bell-shaped.

campanile (kahm pah NEE lee)

A freestanding bell tower, constructed especially in Italy in connection with a church or a town hall.

Campeachy chair (kahm PAY chay CHAYR)

A chair made out of logwood from Campeache, Mexico, and used by Thomas Jefferson in his home at Monticello. It has an X-shaped stretcher base with a sling seat made of reinforced leather, finished with nailhead trim.

campo santo (KAHM poh SAHN toh)

Spanish or Italian term for a cemetery or burial place.

canale, pl. canali (KAH nah lay)

A Spanish term for a duct or spout in which rainwater is discharged.

canapé (kaan AH pay)

A French sofa with open or closed arms, usually designed en suite with bergère and fauteuil. See also *sofa*.

canapé a corbeille (kaan AH pay AH KOHR bay)

A French word for a kidney-shaped settee or sofa with a gracefully sweeping curve around the front, forming semi-circular ends that resemble a round basket; corbeille is the name of a French wide basket or breadbasket.

canapés de l'amitié (kaan AH payz du lah MEE tee)

French word for a 19th-century French Revival Style settee for two or three people.

candelabra (plural for candelabrum) (kaan di LAH bru)

A large decorative candlestick which has multi-branched candleholders, usually placed on a table or stand.

campanile

Campeachy chair

canapés de l'amitié

candelabro (kaan di LAH broh)

An 11th-century single candleholder for table and floor that was exceedingly tall; found especially in northern Spain.

candelabrum (kaan di LAH brum)

A French term for a candleholder that holds one or more candles and is usually placed on a table. See also *candelabra* and *chandelier*.

candle board

A small ledge or sliding shelf fitted below the writing service of a desk or table top, which was used to hold a candlestick, principally a device used during the period of 18th-century English furniture.

candle box

A tall, hinged hanging box with a rectangular or cylindrical shape, made of wood or tin and pierced with holes, in which candles are kept.

candle brackets

A picket or spike for candles or other light, placed on the wall or at the base of the upper part of a secretary to hold a candle or candles.

candle screen

An 18th-century small adjustable table shield on a table or writing desk to keep the glare of the candle from shining on the face.

candle slides

See *candle board*.

candlestand

A lightweight, portable table; usually pedestal, tripod, or four legged; used to accommodate candles, lamps, vases, or small objects.

candlestick holder

A holder, often decorated, made of wood, china, metal, or pottery, with a socket or spike for holding a candle.

candelabrum

C and S scroll

A spiraled and convoluted line, resembling a rolled piece of paper, used in decorative design, such as acanthus leaves, cabriole legs, volutes, and even furniture feet as seen in a C scroll foot. See *illustrations in the Feet and Legs Appendices*.

cane

Stems from specific palms, grasses, or plants used to weave or plait into a mesh that is yielding, making the chair more comfortable to sit or lean against; popular as elegant seating and chair-back material during the Louis XIV, XV and XVI periods in France; also during the 17th and 18th centuries in Holland, England, and America.

caned-back chair

A decorative and comfortable chair with the seat and a portion of the back of cane, a distinctive feature, with the woven pattern set into a round or oval frame radiating out from the center, very popular during the late 18th and 19th centuries.

canephora, pl. canephores (KAH ne for ah)

A sculptured maiden, similar to a caryatid, but with a basket on her head; originally used in place of columns or caryatids, also used as support on furniture or as decoration, particularly during the French and Italian Renaissance.

canné (kaan NAY)

French word for cane or caning, as in chaise cannée or caned seat.

cannellated (kaan UL lay tud)

See *fluting*.

canopeum (KAAN oh pee-um)

A medieval Latin word for a cloth covering put over a bed to provide shelter from insects.

canopic (KAAN oh pik)

A vessel used by ancient Egyptians to hold the viscera of the embalmed body.

canopy

A draped covering over a bed or throne that was suspended from the ceiling in the medieval period; later the covering was draped from a frame supported by posts. In architectural terms, the canopy is a projection above a door or window. See also *baldochino, canapé, causeuse,* and *tester*.

canopy bed

See *angel bed, half-tester bed, lit d'ange,* and *lit à la duchesse*.

canopy chair

A 16th-century chair, originating in France, where the chairs were known as "sentry" chairs with high backs and sides, usually made of cane or wicker. See also *porter's chair*.

canted (KAANT ud)

A square corner that is cut at a slanted angle, often found on case furniture; synonymous with chamfer and splay. See also *bevel, chamfer,* and *splay*.

canted

canteen

Small case with compartments for flasks, bottles, or cutlery. See also *cordial case*.

canterbury (KAAN tur bur eez)

A decorative wooden stand having compartments and divisions to hold music or magazines, popular in England from 1790 to 1890.

canterbury

cantilever
A form of construction with a horizontal projecting beam beyond the supporting wall or columns used structurally for the support of balconies, eaves, and other extensions.

canton (KAHN tohn)
An Italian term for a decorated corner of a building with projecting masonry, a pilaster, or some other feature.

Canton China
Chinese blue and white china brought to American beginning in the 17th century.

Canton enamel
Painted enamel named for the principal place of manufacturer, similar to the Famille rose porcelain, with silver and gold covered with a background layer of enamel (often white), then fired and fired again.

cantonniere (kahn TOHN yayr)
French word for a narrow embroidered window band, referred to as a valance and used on French State beds during the 16th and 17th centuries. See also *lambrequin* and *valance*.

Cape Cod cottage
A traditional house originating in New England in the 17th century; characterized by its simple style with little ornamentation, a story and a half with a steep pitched roof, large chimney, and low, broad frame.

capilla mayor (KAH pee ya MIY yor)
A Spanish term for a sanctuary that contains the high altar.

capital
The top element or crowning feature of a column placed over the shaft and under the entablature. See *Composite, Corinthian, Doric, Ionic,* and *Tuscan.* See *illustration for Composite Order in the Architectural Orders Appendix.*

capo di monte (KAH poh DEE MON tay)
An Italian porcelain founded in 1743 in Naples by the Capodimonte porcelain factory; one of the finest porcelain products in the world. See also *Buen Retiro.*

cantilever

capomo (KAH poh moh)
Semi-hard, very handsome wood, which is both durable and workable, with blonde on the outside and reddening nearer the heart; used for cabinets, floors, tables, handles, and guitars.

capsa, pl. capsae (KAAP su)
Cylindrical case or box used to store books or other things.

captain's bed
A platform bed with drawers and a mattress on top; also referred to as a chest bed or cabin bed.

captain's chair
A low-backed wooden armchair with a barrel back and bent arms with turned spindles as supports and a shaped seat with turned legs; also called a firehouse Windsor chair. See also *firehouse Windsor chair.*

captain's chair

captain's chest
A sturdy wooden chest, usually oak, made for the 19th-century sea captain to store personal belongings.

caqueteuse (KAY ku tuuz)
See *caquetoire.*

caquetoire (KAY kut wahr)
An early 16th-century French Renaissance term meaning to "gossip" or "chatter" that refers to a small, light chair with a tall, narrow carved back, a trapezoid seat (wide at the front and narrow at the back), curved inward arms, and legs close together at the back and wider apart at the front, all joined by a perimeter stretcher, designed to accommodate ladies' wide skirts. Same as caqueteuse. See also *fauteuil.*

carcase or carcass (KAHR kus)
The basic, boxlike structure of a piece of furniture, without veneer or other materials. See also *frame.*

caquetoire

cardo maximus (KAHR doh MAAKS i mus)

The main street in Roman city planning designed to be a North-South street in Roman cities, military camps, and colonies; this street is also the center of economic life with shops and vendors.

card cut

Ornamental latticework or Chinese-style fretwork carved in low relief, featured as decoration on Chippendale furniture, especially found on furniture with Chinese characteristics.

card tables

A table made to fold used for gaming, introduced toward the end of the 17th and 18th centuries and very popular in the William and Mary and Queen Anne periods; characterized as a square, circular, tripod, or pedestal with depressions at the corners for candlesticks, and even deeper depressions for counters or money. See also *game table* and *flip-top table*.

carding

The act or process of opening, cleaning, and straightening raw fibers before spinning them into yarn.

carillon (KAAR i lun)

A set of at least 23 chromatically tuned bells housed in a free-standing bell tower, or the belfry of a church on which music can be played. See also *campanile*.

Carlton table or Carlton House table

A fashionable 18th-century writing table, referred to by Sheraton as a "ladies' drawing and writing table," which had a raised back and sides with small drawers, pigeonholes, and compartments for writing accessories; usually made of mahogany or satinwood with inlay. See also *writing table*.

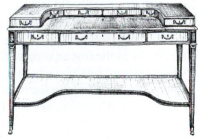
Carlton House table

Carolean Style (kaar u LEE un STIYL)

An English style of furniture and interior design spanning the years of 1660–1688 during the time of Charles II and often referred to as Restoration Style. See also *Restoration Style*.

Carolingian architecture (kaar u LIN jeeun AHR ki tek chur)

Architecture and art in the French and German Romanesque Style from the 8th to 10th centuries during the Empire of Charlemagne.

carpanthian elm burl
(kahr PAAN theeun ELM BURL)

Well-known and beautiful light-brown to brick-red veneer wood with small burl patterns packed close together; from a species of elm in the Carpathian Mountains in Europe. See also *burl*.

Carolean Style

Carpenter's Gothic or Carpenter Gothic, Rural Gothic

A United States architectural style of the 19th century that improvises upon authentic Gothic, but with little awareness of the original Gothic approach, the style built by carpenters was freed to emphasize charm and quaintness with its turrets, spires, pointed arches, and gingerbread motifs.

Carpenter's Gothic

carreau, pl. carreaux (kaar OH)

A French term for a square tile or brick; also a soft thick cushion used on chairs or a couch; known as a squab cushion. See also *bench* and *squab*.

carreaux d'octagones (kaar OH d'ahk tu GUN)

A floor design used during the 18th century in England when black diamonds (also known as cabochons) were inserted at the junctures of larger intersecting slabs of lighter colored stones.

abcdefghijklmnopqrstuvwxyz

carrel or carol (KAAR ul)

A niche, stall, or small recess in a library stack for private study, having originated in the Middle English period around the 13th century at Westminster Abbey, where the term is used in reference to a niche in the north cloister for a monk to sit, read, or study.

carriage or carriage piece

A beam used to support the stair system and stair treads.

carrousel (kaa ROO zel)

A military dressage or military drill with an equine demonstration, used for a display by Louis XV in 1662 when the Place du Carrousel was so named.

cartapesta (KAHR te pay stah)

Italian term defining the art of using paper to create sculptural art, originating in Italy during the 17th century, also called paper-mache.

cartel clock (KAHR tel KLOK)

A hanging wall clock of French origin, during both the Louis XV and Louis XVI periods; characterized by fanciful designs with a wooden or ormolu frame. See also *regulateur* and *regulator*.

Carter's Grove

A Georgian mansion, located about 7 miles east of Williamsburg, designed and built by David Minitree in 1755 for one of Virginia's most influential early families, Carter Burwell. It was added to the Colonial Williamsburg Foundation in 1969, then sold to CNET founder Halsey Minor for a private residence in 2007. The brick house with Flemish bond has a grand central hall, which opens into four rooms, two with antechambers. The house is also flanked by a kitchen and service building.

cartibulum (KAHR tee boo lum)

An ancient Roman oblong marble table or sideboard placed near the impluvium.

carton-pierre (KAHR tun PEE yar)

A type of composition of glue, whiting, paper pulp, and chalk, formed to imitate stone, wood, or metal; introduced by Robert Adam for interior architectural embellishment, such as lightweight ornament used where plaster is too heavy. See also *anaglypta, composition, gesso*, and *pastigilia*.

cartonnage (KAHR ton ahj)

Egyptian funerary masks made by building up layers of papyrus stiffened with gesso (plaster), then reinforced with linen and molded for the mummy mask.

cartonnier (KAHR tohn yay)

French word for a matching paper-case with small drawers used to hold papers, which stood at the end of a bureau-plat (flat desk); often it was decorated with tooled leather.

cartoon

A preliminary sketch or mock-up of a design used for a pattern to be copied in another medium.

cartouche (kahr TOOSH)

A French term for a sculpted ornamental panel or tablet usually of oval shape with the edges curled; the tablet is sometimes carved with arms with initials or an inscription. See *illustration in the Motifs/Ornaments Appendix*.

cartouche back (kahr TOOSH BAK)

An upholstered chair or sofa with a cartouche-shaped back, which often contains a coat of arms or inscription.

carved rug

A rug with a pattern created by cutting the pile to different levels, making shadows or sculptural effects.

Carver chair (KAHR vur CHAYR)

A 17th-century American turned chair with a wood or rush seat and turned legs that rise vertically above the seat as support for the back, while the front legs also rise to support the arm spindles; named for John Carver, the first governor of Plymouth Colony. See also *banister-back chair* or *Brewster chair*.

Carver chair

carving

A form of cutting into the wood surface to create a pattern by gouging, chipping, or scratching, whether wholly or partially.

carving, cameo type

A low-relief carving resembling a cameo stone used for decoration on English furniture, particularly Sheraton and early Empire styles.

caryatid, pl. caryatides (KAAR ee-a tid)

A female form used in a support position, as a column. In furniture design it was usually a decorative support; it was also used to support an entablature of a mantle, etc. See also *atlas*.

cascade (kaas KAYD)

A vertical fabric treatment that is a long, evenly folded piece of drapery, falling from the top and folded to look like zigzags; the reverse side of the material is visible at intervals, so a lining in a another color is often used. See also *jabot*.

case

A receptacle, such as a cabinet, used to provide storage space; also means the shell of a chest of drawers or other storage pieces.

case clock

A clock housed in some form of receptacle.

cased glass

A type of glass with two or more layers of different colors, in which the outer layer is cut so decorative patterns show through.

casegoods or case piece

Furniture used for storage, applied generally to bookcases, chests, cabinets, drawer units, and other objects without upholstery; also referred to as architectural furniture. See also *carcase* or *carcass*.

casement cloth

A lightweight curtain fabric, usually sheer drapery cloth, made of cotton, linen, silk, mohair, wool, nylon, rayon, or a mixture of these fibers.

caryatid

casement window

A window in which the sash is hinged at the side so it opens outwards or inwards.

casework

Custom designed or manufactured furniture with dimensions enabling it to be attached to walls; often referred to as cabinetwork.

casement window

cashmere

A soft wool textile made from Indian goat hair spun into yarn.

cashmeres work

A form of furniture decoration from the province of Kashmire, India, during the 18th and 19th centuries where small pieces of mirrors created a carved geometric pattern on a surface or panel, often called a "mirror-mosaic."

casing

Finished frame or final trim of wood or metal around the top, and both sides of a window or door opening.

casket

A small portable box or chest made of precious woods or metal inlays, carvings, and paints, used to hold trinkets, jewels, papers, and other valuable items.

cassapanca (kah sah PAYN kah)

An Italian Renaissance chest with a wooden seat, arms, and a paneled back with the seat hinged so the lower portion could be used for storage space.

cassapanca

cassette (KAH set)

A French term for a coffret, casket, or small box.

cassettoncino (KAH set ohn chee noh)
Small Italian chiffonier or lowboy chest with three drawers.

cassolet or cassolette (kaas oh LAY / kaas oh LET)
A French term for a small box or vase with perforated cover to emit incense or perfume.

cassone, pl. cassoni (kah SOH neh)
An Italian Renaissance, elaborately carved storage chest, which may be inlaid or carved, prepared with gesso ground, then painted and gilded. See also *bahut, bridal chest, cedar chest, hope chest,* and *wedding chest.*

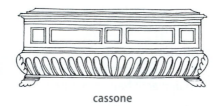
cassone

cassone nuziale (kah SOH ne NOO zee-ah lay)
Italian term for a Renaissance dower chest that usually bears the coat of arms of the two families joined together in marriage.

cassonetta (KAA soh ne tah)
Italian word for a small box.

cassoon (KAA soon)
See *coffered panel.*

cast
A reproduction of a sculpture made of plaster of Paris using a mold.

cast aluminum
Aluminum that has gone through one of several processes known as casting to produce different types of products that looks like cast iron.

cast glass
An ancient Egyptian technique in which molten glass is directed into a mold where it solidifies; still used today.

cast iron
An important building material in the 19th century, which contains 3.5 percent carbon, was first made in the late 18th century in England; also used by the Victorians for decorative work and for their love of factory methods producing cheap goods made out of iron alloy formed in a mold.

cast iron

casters or castors
Small wheels on swivels attached to the feet of chairs, stands, tables, or other pieces of furniture to facilitate moving without lifting.

Castle chair
See *Wendell Castle chair.* See *Wendell Castle, 1932–, in the Architects, Artists, and Designers Appendix.*

cat
A trivet stand used during the 18th century for warming plates in front of the fire; the stand is well ringed with sockets for plates of various sizes.

catacombs (KAAT ah kohmz)
Underground passageways in Rome used as cemeteries; also used by the early Christians for religious worship services and as hiding places from the Romans.

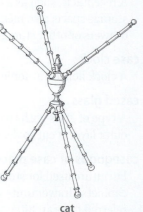
cat

catenary (KAA te naar ee)
See *festoon* and *swag.*

catenary arch (KAA te naar ee ARCH)
An arch that takes the form of the curve of a hanging chain. See also *arch.*

catenary curve (KAA te naar ee KURV)

A curve that a cable or chain assumes when supported at the ends and allowed to hang by its own weight.

Catenary group (KAA te naar ee GROOP)

In 1963 George Nelson, with Herman Miller, developed a flexible, resilient seating group upholstered and suspended from steel cables hanging downward in a catenary curve design.

cathedra (kah THEE drah)

The Roman chair similar to the Greek klismos but much heavier in proportion; also the chair for a bishop from which the term cathedral is derived. See also *klismos*.

cathedra supina (kah THEE drah)

A Roman chair similar to the cathedra but with the back fixed at an easy angle more suitable for comfort and relaxation.

cathedral

The principal church in a diocese, specifically the bishop's church or a church that is the seat of the bishop.

cathedral ceiling

A high-pitched, sloping ceiling that is slanted toward the central ridge beam.

cathedral glass

Unpolished monochromatic glass that is translucent and may be colored and usually textured on one side; derived from medieval European cathedrals from the 10th century onward in which windows of stained glass were a feature.

cathedral shape

Shape of pointed arch tracery from the late 18th and 19th centuries (Gothic revival) in England and America found on the backs of chairs and on the bases of some chests of drawers.

catkins (KAAT kinz)

An 18th-century decorative motif consisting of a slender axis with many apetalous flowers along its side similar to the bellflower or husk ornament and used as a pendant or to represent a chain of stylized bell-shaped flowers. See also *bellflower* and *husk ornament*.

catshead

A common architectural element found on multi-storied mills, agricultural buildings, and factories, characterized by a small extension protruding from the gable end of a larger roof, used to protect the ropes and pulleys for lifting equipment. Also, styles such as Queen Anne have architectural features such as catshead for nonfunctional features.

catshead

Caucasian rugs (KAH kay zhen RUGZ)

An oriental rug in which the oldest identifiable group is the so-called Kuba dragon appearing around the mid 17th century. Designs are mainly produced in Kuba, Shirvan, Dagestan, Darabagh, and Kazark but varying by location. Rugs are characterized by endless repeat of typical animal and floral forms and also in geometric designs; colors are jewel-like, especially red, blue, white, and sometimes yellow.

caulicoli or caulcole or cauliculus (KOWL ee koh lee / KOWL koh lay / KOWL ee ke les)

A term used to describe the stalks rising out of the lower leafage of the Corinthian column and terminating in leaves that support the volutes.

causeuse (KAW zuuz)

A small settee or sofa for two persons, similar to a marquise. See also *canapé, marquise chair*, and *tête-à-tête*.

cavetto (KAH ve toh)

Concave, quarter-round molding used predominantly on cornices with other moldings, decoratively on furniture, and on mantels. Also, on the cornice of the Doric order of the theatre of Marcellus, forming the crowning feature. See *illustration in the Moldings Appendix*.

cavity wall

An architectural feature where a wall consists of two separate walls of masonry, separated by an air space, and joined by wall-ties.

cavo-relievo or cavo-rilievo (KAH voh-REE yay voh)
A relief sculpture in which the highest point of the carving in the project does not rise beyond the original surface. See also *intaglio rilevato*.

Caxton chair
A 19th-century chair made with a flat caned seat and turned iron legs with stretchers, splayed slightly back with a top and center rail; used in church and parish halls, schools, or concert halls; and sometimes in residential settings.

Caxton chair

cedar
A durable wood with a characteristic fragrance used for lining drawers, boxes, closets, and chests to protect against moths.

cedar chest
An American household long, low chest made from cedar or lined with cedar; used for storage of woolens, blankets, etc. See also *cassone* and *hope chest*.

cedar, red
A wood mainly used for shingles or lining drawers, chests, etc.

celadon (se lah DAHN)
One of the most beautiful Chinese porcelains with a gray-blue to green glaze.

celature (SEL ah chur)
The art of decorating metal surfaces by engraving, chasing, or embossing.

cella (CHEH lah)
In classical architecture, the inner chamber of a temple or a shop facing the street in ancient Rome; also called naos. See also *naos*.

cellar
A medieval undercroft, often brick-lined and vaulted, which was used for storage; while in modern times the undercroft is at street level, open to the sides, but covered by the building above.

cellaret (SEL ur aht)
An 18th-century portable cabinet or case lined with lead and fitted for storing wine bottles. See also *garde du vin* and *sarcophagus*.

cellarette (SEL ur et)
Same usage as a cellaret; a case or sideboard for holding bottles of wine or liquor or a cabinet for storing bottles of wine or liquor.

cellarette

Celtic cross (KEL tik KRAHS)
A form of a Latin cross with a ring around the intersection of the bars.

cement
A powdered substance made by grinding calcined limestone and clay to mix with water and sand to make mortar or mixed with water, sand, and gravel to make concrete.

cenaculum, pl. cenacula (chen u KOO loom)
A derivative of the Latin word cena, meaning "meal," known as the dining area or "upper room" often located on the second floor of the Roman home.

Celtic cross

cenotaph (SE ne taaf)
A monument erected to honor the dead whose remains are elsewhere or cannot be recovered.

centaur (SEN tor)
A Greek mythological term for a figure having the head, arms, and trunk of a man combined with a horse's body and legs; in other words, half human and half horse.

centaur

center drawer guide

A wooden track down the center of a drawer that fits into a metal guide, runs the length of the drawer, and helps with opening and closing.

center table

A large table, which can be many different shapes, which stands in the center of a room or hallway to be used for any purpose.

centering

A temporary timber construction used as scaffolding in the construction of vaults or domes; when the masonry has set, it is removed.

center-hall plan

An American Colonial house with two rooms symmetrically located on each side of a centrally located hallway; the stair in the hallway leads to the loft above. See also *hall-and-parlour house*.

centralized plan

A plan that in form radiates from or around a center point.

Century Guild, The

An English guild formed by A. J. Mackmurdo and others in 1882 during the Craft Revival movement. See *Arthur H. Mackmurdo, 1851–1942, in the Architects, Artists, and Designers Appendix*.

ceramics

An art of molding, modeling, and baking in clay to produce products of porcelain, tile, earthen ware, etc.

ceramic color glaze

A vitreous substance, layered or coated, which has been fired and fused to a clay object in order to color, decorate, strengthen, or waterproof it.

certosina (sur toh SEE nah)

An Italian technique used to inlay bone, ivory, or light-colored wood against a dark background in geometric marquetry patterns. See also *inlay, intarsio, mosaic, marquetry*, and *pietra dura*.

Cesca chair (CHES kah CHAYR)

See *Marcel Breuer Cesca chair*. See *Marcel Breuer, 1902–1981, in the Architects, Artists, and Designers Appendix*.

chacmool (CHAHK mool)

A pre-Columbian Mesoamerican figure found from El Salvador to Michoacán, with the best examples from Chichenltza and Tula. The figure is characterized by its typical half-reclining position supporting himself on his elbows, with head turned to one side.

chaffeuse (SHAF feuz)

A low French, armless chair with a tall, narrow back, placed by the fireside with the chair seat so low that the knees of the person seated were slightly higher than the lap so mothers could cradle the baby between the knees while nursing or changing it.

chaiere (SHA ee-yar)

A 13th-century French term for boxlike chair with a back, usually carved, along with carving on the arms. The special seat for one in authority during the Gothic period was called a chayere. See also *chaire* and *chayere*.

chaines (CHAYNZ)

A 17th-century French domestic wall decoration consisting of vertical bands of rusticated masonry that divided the façades into panels or bays.

chair and a half

A low, wide, upholstered 18th-century English armchair, often referred to as the drunkard's chair. See also *drunkard's chair*.

chair bed

An 18th-century English chair that could be converted into a bed by lowering the back and extending the seat.

chair of estate

A medieval upholstered chair used by women that required the use of a footstool; characterized by its low seat and tall, narrow back.

chair parts

See *illustrations in the Appendix*.

chair rail or rail dado

Horizontal molding placed about 30" up the wall at the top of a dado or placed without the dado and referred to as a dado cap, used to protect the wall from being scraped by chair backs.

chair table or chair-table

An armchair with a circular or rectangular back hinged to swing over to a horizontal position where it rests on the arms of the chair to form a table.

chaire (SHAYR)

French word from the early Renaissance for a raised seat for the pope, bishop, lord, or head of a family, characterized by its boxlike structure, and a tall, heavily carved back with carved arms. See also *chaire* and *chayere*.

chaire à haut dossier (SHAYR AH OH DOH see-ay)

A large, high-backed French leather or tapestry chair designed for domestic use during the 16th-century French Renaissance.

chaise (SHEZ)

A French term identifying a form of daybed or sofa with an upholstered back for reclining; divided into two or three parts, with two parts being a bergère and a large stool, and the third part being two armchairs with a stool between.

chaise à accoudoir (SHEZ AH Ak oo dwar)

See *cockfight chair* and *fumeuse*.

chaise à bras (SHEZ AH BRAHZ)

French Renaissance armchair.

chaise à capucine (SHEZ AH CHAH pyoo keen)

French low slipper chair.

chaise à porteurs (SHEZ AH POR turz)

French term for a Porter's hall chair.

chaise à vertugadin (SHEZ AH VUR too gah din)

French Renaissance chair without arms, used by ladies when wearing crinolines or voluminous skirts.

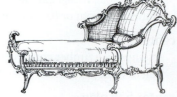

chair table

chaise brisée (SHEZ BRE zay)

A form of French chaise often referred to as the "broken duchess" since it consisted of two parts: the chair and an elongated separate footstool that was often attached; the secondary piece had a footboard.

chaise longue (SHEZ LAHNG)

French term for a long upholstered chair designed for reclining. See also *couch, duchesse,* and *peche mortel.*

chaise longue

chaise percée (SHEZ PUR see)

French term for a chair or enclosed box at sitting height with an opening cut in the top and placed over a pewter or earthenware chamber pot, having the appearance of a throne, in vogue during the Louis XIV, XV, or XVI period. It was sometimes called a close stool or necessary stool. See also *close stool.*

chaise volante (SHEZ voh LAHNT)

A lightweight chair, which could be easily moved, often with casters, appearing during the Empire period.

chaitya (CHAYT yah)

A Buddhist or Hindu prayer hall or hall of worship in the form of a basilic, including a stupa. The hall also has a horseshoe-shaped window called a chaitya window.

chalice (CHAAL is)

The cup or goblet used as part of the church sacrament to hold wine.

chalit (CHAA lit)

French word for a bedstead.

chamber horse

An English exercise chair popular with the wealthy from 1790 to 1820, designed to simulate the trotting of a horse, which was considered good exercise to remain fit, hence when the weather was not fit to ride outside, one could ride inside. The chair was made of mahogany and leather.

chamber horse

chambre à coucher (SHAM bruh AH koo SHAY)
French word for a room within a house where there is a bed for sleeping.

chambre de parade (SHAM bruh DEH pah RAHD)
A part of the appartment de parade where the aristocracy had a very public life and received a very important person; room was highly decorated with the finest pieces of furniture, etc.

chamfer (CHAAM fur)
A flat surface formed by smoothing off the angle made where two surfaces meet; a beveled edge connecting two surfaces. See also *arris edge, beveled, canted,* and *splay.*

champlevé (SHAM pleev)
A decorative enameling technique in which the pattern is grooved into a metal base and the grooves are filled with colored glass or enamel, then fired.

chancel (CHAAN sul)
French term describing the sanctuary area of a church or cathedral, usually the whole continuation of the nave east of the crossing in a cruciform church.

chandelier (SHAAN de leer)
A French term used since the 17th and 18th centuries for a hanging light fixture with branches for candles or electric lamps. See also *candelabrum.*

chandelier d'applique (SHAAN del eer D'AP lee kay)
French wall brackets with candleholders or branches usually held by a human figure, a satyr, or masks. See also *bras.*

chandelier

channel
A simple, continuously furrowed or grooved molding cut into a surface as a decorative accent, sometimes running vertically up and down the shaft of a column and sometimes filled with reed-shaped convex mold. See also *fillet* and *fluting.*

channel back
An upholstered chair or sofa with a tight back having deep vertical channels to provide definition and usually more cushioning.

chantry chapel (CHAAN tree CHAAP ul)
An English subchapel dedicated for the purpose of changing masses for the dead.

chanyi chair (CHAHN yee CHAYR)
A classical Chinese meditation chair with a wide, spacious seat for sitting with the legs drawn up in a cross-legged position. See also *zuiwengyi.*

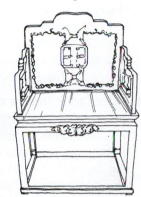
chanyi chair

chaplet (CHAAP let)
Architecturally, the term describes a small molding, carved into beads, pearls, olives, etc. It can also mean a wreath or garland for the head, and several other definitions not related to architecture.

chapter house
A building or room in which the chapter of a church or religious residence holds meetings; also in which a fraternity or sorority assembles.

char-pai (SHAHR-pay)
A Pakistani and/or Indian portable string cot that comes in many colors and sizes and is used primarily for sleeping, but it can be used for several other functions, such as a seat, temporary fence, sunscreen, carrying goods, a stretcher for the sick, or for birth and death ceremonies.

Charles Eames LCW chair
A molded birch plywood chair designed by Charles and Ray Eames, produced by Herman Miller in 1946, recognized by *Time* magazine as "The Best Design of the 20th Century" for its charm and comfort. See *Charles Eames, 1907–1978, in the Architects, Artists, and Designers Appendix.*

Charles Eames LCW chair

Charles Eames DAR dining arm chair

A Charles Eames fiberglass chair reinforced with plastic, presented at the Museum of Modern Art in 1948 for the "Low Cost Furniture" competition in New York, featuring a shell that conformed to the body's shape. See *Charles Eames, 1907–1978, in the Architects, Artists, and Designers Appendix.*

Charles Eames DAR dining arm chair

Charles Eames lounge chair

A plywood and leather lounge chair and ottoman released in 1956 after years of development by designers Charles and Ray Eames for Herman Miller furniture company, characterized for decades as a classic design with comfort, and a distinquished 20th-century design. See *Charles Eames, 1907–1978, in the Architects, Artists, and Designers Appendix.*

Charles Eames lounge chair

Charles Eames Time Life stools

Solid walnut stools designed by Ray Eames in 1960 for the Time-Life Building in Rockefeller Center New York City, manufactured by Herman Miller Company. See *Ray Kaiser Eames, 1912–1988, in the Architects, Artists, and Designers Appendix.*

Charles Eames Time Life stools

Charles Locke Eastlake desk

A walnut desk designed by Charles Eastlake, a British architect and writer, characterized by a simpler style than the earlier Victorian style. See *Charles Locke Eastlake, 1836–1906, in the Architects, Artists, and Designers Appendix.*

Charles Locke Eastlake desk

Charles of London sofa

A 20th-century upholstered sofa with low armrests and an upholstered platform.

Charles Rennie Mackintosh argyle chair

Oak chair with black stain finish designed by Charles Rennie Mackintosh in 1898–99, one of Mackintosh's first private commissions of furniture for the Luncheon Room of Catherine Crantston's tea room on Argyle Street in Glasgow, now reconstructed and known as the Willow Tea Rooms. See *Charles Rennie Mackintosh, 1868–1928, in the Architects, Artists, and Designers Appendix.*

Charles Rennie Mackintosh a chair

Charles Rennie Mackintosh Hill House chair

A tall, narrow chair designed by Charles Rennie Mackintosh in 1904 for the blue room at Hill House in Helensburgh, Scotland, constructed of black-lacquered ashwood with an upholstered seat. See *Charles Rennie Mackintosh, 1868–1928, in the Architects, Artists, and Designers Appendix.*

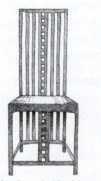

Charles Rennie Mackintosh Hill House chair

Charles Voysey two hearts chair

An early 20th-century oak chair designed by Charles Francis Annesley Voysey, with a rush seat and two hearts conveying a deeper meaning of warmth, comfort, and love; also symbolic decorations supporting the Arts and Crafts movement of simplicity and function and opposing the Victorian Style. See *Charles Francis Annesley Voysey, 1857–1941, in the Architects, Artists, and Designers Appendix.*

Charles Voysey two hearts chair

Charles X period

French period from 1824 to 1830, which was part of the Restoration with a mixture of styles from late Empire Style, Louis XVI, and Rococo with Renaissance details.

chashitsu (CHAH sheet soo)

A small elegant pavilion or room in which Japanese tea ceremonies occur.

chasing (CHAY sing)

Embossing, engraving, or incising metal to create a pattern. See also *ormulu*.

chateau, pl. chateaux (SHAA toh)

A French luxurious country house or stately residence some distance from the city.

chattra, pl. chatri (CHAAT tru)

An umbrella-shaped dome or finial that crowns a stupa in Hindu architecture.

chauffeuse (SHOH fuuz)

A French Renaissance term for a low-seated fireside chair, derived from the word chauffer, meaning "to warm."

chayers a dorseret (SHAY urz AH DOR sur et)

A 14th-century French chair, carved of oak or chestnut, elaborately gilded with highlights of color, a bulky seat and throne-like construction, abandoned by the end of the 15th century for the more comfortable chaise. See also *canopy chair*.

check

Architecturally, a small uneven crack that appears in lumber, perpendicular to the annual rings, but radiating away from the heart of the trunk.

checker, chequer

Decoration using alternately colored squares or contrasting tones, found in furniture or inlaid ornament after c. 1550. Same as checkerboard.

checkerboard bond

An arrangement of masonry units in a pattern, flat or on edge, as a purely decorative or ornamental feature; often referred to as a basket weave. See also *bond*.

checkerboard match

Small squares of veneer arranged so that the grain lines alternate in direction, then the pattern is repeated to produce a checkerboard effect.

cheek

An architectural term meaning the upright face of one side of an opening.

cheekpieces

Wings or fins designed in 18th-century England for tall easy chairs, such as wing chairs, to protect the head of the person seated from drafts or fireside heat.

cheesebox seat

A rounded or bell-shaped chair seat, usually of rush, with a thin strip of wood around the edge.

chef d'oeuvre (SHEF DUHvr)

French word for masterpiece.

cheffonier (SHEF ohn yay)

See *chiffonier*.

chen chen (CHEN CHEN)

An African wood with a ribbon stripe, relatively soft and lightweight, used for architectural woodworking projects due to its interesting grain pattern. See also *ako*.

chêne (CHEN)

A French word for oak.

chenets (SHE nay)

A French word for andirons, while the English version is fire dogs. See also *andirons, brand dogs,* and *fire dogs*.

chequer-work

A pattern formed by alternating colors or texture in different ways to resemble a chessboard; commonly found in stone, brick, or tile pavements during the 16th and 17th centuries.

cherrywood

A fruit wood of reddish color used in the 17th and 18th centuries for cabinetmaking because of its strength and resistance to warping; also used for marquetry and inlays. See also *American cherry*.

cherub, pl. cherubim or cherubs (CHAYR ub)

Architecturally, the term is used in reference to a winged baby or child, particularly during the Italian and French Renaissance; also called an amorino. The English wood carver, Grinling Gibbons, often used the winged head alone. See also *amorino* and *putti*.

cherub head

A winged celestial being depicted as a angel or as a chubby-faced child with child's head only; appearing in Renaissance architecture, furniture, and in churches. See also *têtes d'anges*.

chess table

An 18th-century game table that incorporated squares laid out in a checkered pattern with 64 squares in an eight-by-eight grid designed for two players.

chest

A form of receptacle of considerable size with a hinged lid, utilized for storage; during the 17th century drawers were added to the chest design. See also *bahut*.

chest bed

See *captain's bed*.

chest of drawers

A piece of furniture fitted with a set of drawers within a frame, used for storage, usually of clothing.

chest-on-chest

A chest of drawers in two parts, one set on top of the other, usually with the top chest being slightly smaller and surmounted by cornices or pediments; typically English and American in origin of the 18th and 19th centuries and very similar to the tallboy or highboy. See also *highboy* and *tallboy*.

chest-on-stand

A tall double chest of drawers, technically known as a highboy with the lower section being a lowboy; common in England during the late 1600s. See also *highboy* and *tallboy*.

Chesterfield chair

A stuffed and tufted low club chair typically made of leather.

Chesterfield settee

A large, overstuffed sofa with upholstered arms, deeply padded often with buttons, named for the Earl of Chesterfield in the late 19th century, brought to Canada from England in 1903, then into northern California.

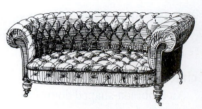

Chesterfield settee

chestnut

A soft wood, native to Europe and England, with a moderately soft grayish-brown and sometimes white appearance, resembling oak; its coarse grain and strongly marked rings makes it unsuitable for fine detail, so it is used more for turned work, veneer, inlay, or carving. Wormy chestnut was very popular for paneling.

cheval glass (SHE vahl GLAS)

A full-length mirror held by a cheval or horse of two vertical columns with a mechanism for adjusting the glass; hence it is literally a "horse mirror." See also *horse dressing glass, pier glass, psyche,* and *swing glass*.

cheval screen (SHE vahl SKREEN)

A fire screen that is mounted on two bracketed feet. See also *banner screen* and *horse screen*.

cheval glass

cheveret (SHE vu ray)

A small 18th-century English lady's writing table with a single drawer under the writing surface and slender legs joined at the bottom of a shelf. See also *sheveret*.

chevet (she VAY)

A French term that refers to a grouping of chapels around the east end of the church or chancel; also the term is used in reference to the head of a bed or bolster or a bedside table. See also *table de chevet*.

chevron

A Romanesque molding resembling an inverted V and forming a zigzag design, supposed to represent the rafters in the gable of a house. See also *dancette* and *zig-zag*. See *illustration in the Motifs/Ornaments Appendix*.

chiaroscuro (KAAR oh skoo roh)

An Italian term implying exaggerated shading or the strong contrast of light and dark areas in a painting or picture. See also *clare-obscure* and *grisaille*.

Chicago window

A tripartite window introduced by Louis Sullivan at the Carson, Pirie, Scott store in Chicago, 1899–1904, and characterized by a fixed wide center glass pane flanked on one or both sides by double-hung sash windows for light and ventilation.

Ch'ien Lung porcelain (chee-EN LOONG POR se len)

Porcelain from the Ch'ing Dynasty reign of Emperor Ch'ien Lun in China.

chiffonier (shi FAHN yay)

French term for a narrow, high chest of drawers sometimes with an attached mirror. See also *chest of drawers, cupboard*, and *semainier*.

chiffonière (shi FAHN ee-ar)

Same as chiffonier. It can be a small table with two or three drawers and enclosed shelving, used to hold yarn.

chiffonier

chifforobe (SHI fo rohb)

A tall closet-like piece that came into existence in America by combining the wardrobe section for hanging clothes with drawers on the other side for storage. Alternate spellings include chiffarobe and chifferobe.

chigai-dana (CHEE giy DAH nah)

A Japanese term for shelves built into a wall, which were first a feature of the Shoin Style of domestic architecture during the Kamakura period (1192–1333).

chigi (CHEE gee)

A distinctive Shinto architectural feature of scissors-shaped finials located on the ridge where poles appear to extend from the gable, intersecting at the ridge and continuing upward to form an X-shape; exclusively used today on Shinto buildings to distinguish them from other religious structures.

chih (CHEE)

Chinese architectural term for stone or bronze bases found on a podium to support columns.

chimera (KIY meer ah)

A mythological animal, originating with the Greeks and Romans, with the head of a lion, part goat, with a dragon tail, eagle's wings, etc., used as a leg or furniture support during the Renaissance and Empire periods and also again in 19th-century designs.

chimera

chimneypiece

The ornamental structure of stone, marble, or wood surrounding a fireplace and the chimney breast above it. See also *ledge* and *mantelpiece*.

chimneypiece

Ch'in Dynasty (CHEN DIY nest ee)
The first ruling dynasty of China, which ruled from 221 B.C.E. to 206 B.C.E., by conquering the warring feudal states of the late Chou period.

Ch'ing Dynasty (CHENG DIY nest ee)
The last ruling dynasty of China from 1644 to 1912, also known as the Qing Dynasty (pronounced Ch'ing) or the Manchu Dynasty. See also *Manchu Dynasty* and *Qing Dynasty*.

china
European name for the first porcelain imported from the Orient. See also *creamware, ironware, porcelain, Queensware,* and *Staffordshire.*

china cabinet
A cabinet with a glass front and sides for the display of china, introduced in the late 17th and early 18th centuries when collecting Oriental china was fashionable. Same as china closet or china case.

china clay
Kaolin, a soft white clay; an essential ingredient in the manufacture of porcelain and china. See also *kaolin.*

China silk
A sheer plain woven fabric, which is almost transparent and often dyed various colors.

china stone
An English term for petuntse, which is an essential ingredient of true porcelain, known in China in its raw form as tzu-shih. See also *petuntse.*

Chinese bracket foot or Chinese foot
Known as a bracket foot and favored by Chippendale in the mid 18th century. See also *bracket foot.*

Chinese fret or key design
Similar to the Greek fret design, but made of square-sectioned timber, forming square and rectangular patterns with diagonals adding triangular shapes. Used by Chippendale in his Chinese work; also used on balustrades, gates, friezes, and railings; chinoiserie-inspired.

Chinese Chippendale
See *Chippendale Chinese chair.* See *Thomas Chippendale II, 1718–1779, in the Architects, Artists, and Designers Appendix.*

Chinese lacquer
A type of red lacquer on a black background, often with gold and silver.

Chinese manner chair
A low Chinese meditation chair, containing cushions, sometimes with a high back to support the head and a large seat where the legs can be crossed in front of the body.

Chinese room
A room with wallpaper or traditional hand-painted designs of landscapes, birds, flowers, and legendary figures often created by European wallpaper designers incorporating Chinese art elements and furnished with imported Chinese furniture or Chippendale adaptations.

Chinese rugs
A Chinese rug differs entirely from other Oriental rugs in color and design, usually featuring a plainer background, narrow border, and central medallion. Finer antique Chinese rugs have blue and tan, with some having cherry, apricot, and yellow, using the colors to enhance motifs of dragons, peonies, floral motifs, clouds, and waves.

Chinese wallpaper
Beautiful hand-painted wallpaper designs based on classical Chinese themes were introduced into Europe in the late 17th century with panels that covered the entire room without repeating the designs. By the 18th century, Chinese paper with floral and natural designs were in vogue. They were eventually replaced with oriental scenes with corresponding figures. Chinese wallpaper became so popular in France and England that artisans began imitating the wallpaper; also at that time chinoiserie was reaching its peak, and Chinese rooms filled with Chinese motifs, wallpaper, and furniture were fashionable.

chinoiserie (sheen WAH zur ee)
Decorative elements derived from Chinese traditional design and interpreted by Western designers with the source of inspiration being the Orient in such motifs as lacquer, textiles, carving of Chinese fretwork on pagodas, latticework, printing, ceramics, silver, etc. The fashion of Chinese art became known in the 17th century but continued to grow in popularity in the 18th century in France, England, Germany, and Italy, and even continued into the 19th century.

chintz (CHINTZ)

A printed and glazed cotton fabric with floral designs, usually in bright colors; originally a painted or stained calico from India, used in Europe for bedcovers and draperies, especially toile de Jouy, which was manufactured from 1700 to 1843 at Juoy, near Paris. An unglazed calico is called cretonne.

chip carving

A technique in which a shallow, low-relief pattern, usually geometric, on furniture is accomplished by chipping out the pattern.

Chippendale Chinese chair

An 18th-century Chippendale adaptation for furniture designed in the Chinese taste, influenced by chinoiserie, Chinese motifs, and Sir William Chambers's work. See *Thomas Chippendale II, 1718–1779,* and *Sir William Chambers, 1723–1796, in the Architects, Artists, and Designers Appendix.*

Chippendale Chinese chair

Chippendale furniture styles

The term used in the late 19th and early 20th centuries to describe the popular furniture designed by Thomas Chippendale and his contemporaries in the 1750s and 1760s. See *Thomas Chippendale II, 1718–1779, in the Architects, Artists, and Designers Appendix.*

Chippendale ladder-back chair

A popular mahogany Chippendale chair from 1750 to 1790, characterized by three shaped, pierced cross rails topped with a serpentine fret-pierced crest rail. See *Thomas Chippendale II, 1718–1779, in the Architects, Artists, and Designers Appendix.*

Chippendale ladder-back chair

Chippendale ribband-back chair

A Chippendale chair back characterized by interlacing ribbons connecting the stiles. See *Thomas Chippendale II, 1718–1779, in the Architects, Artists, and Designers Appendix.*

chipping

A crack, flaw, or defect found in wood, stone, or glass caused by the removal of a small piece.

chochin (CHOH chin)

Japanese paper lantern used to light the outside of a building, characterized by a spiral-shaped coil of thin, fine bamboo covered with Japanese paper and with rings fitted to the top and bottom so it can collapse and fold flat when not in use.

Chippendale ribband-back chair

choir

The area of a church reserved for singers; part of the chancel, usually having stalls or seats.

choir stall chair

A medieval chair, characterized by a box shape and high paneled back with solid arms and a box beneath the seat, found in church choirs.

chos-n (CHOH sun)

One of the last and longest-lived imperial dynasties in Korea, better known as the Yi, that carried out sweeping land reforms and produced an abundance of epistles, ranging from royal public edicts to private letters. See also *Yi.*

Chou Dynasty (CHOO DIY nest ee)

Chou Dynasty, referred to as the Zhou Dynasty, 1045–256 B.C.E., lasted longer than any other dynasty in Chinese history.

chryselephantine (KRIS el e fan teen)

A combination of ivory and gold used for statuary on ancient Greek objects where the exposed body, face, and hands were ivory and the clothing or drapery was gold.

ch'uang (CHWANG)
Chinese term for a long bed, couch, or platform designed for resting upon.

chu-che (CHOO-CHAY)
The upturned roof on a structure in China.

church-going chair
A 16th- and 17th-century wood chair with a leather or fabric seat; characterized by its portability, light weight, and ability to fold; usually the back of the chair was made up of a colonnade motif of spiral colonettes.

churn molding
A zigzag molding that enriched Norman architecture.

churrigueresco (CHUR ee gayr es koh)
Late Spanish Baroque design of 1650 to 1780 in architecture and decoration, characterized by elaborate ornamentation and curved lines; influenced by the architect Churriguera.

chute or chutes (SHOOT / SHOOTZ)
French term for the decorative bronze pieces, usually gilded, that protect and ornately decorate the exposed angles and legs on commodes, tables, desks, and other fine furniture.

ciborium (se BOR ee-um)
A vaulted canopy of wood, stone, etc., supported by four columns, usually placed over an altar; also it could refer to a goblet-shaped vessel for holding Eucharistic bread. See also *baldacchino*.

ciel de lit (SEE-el DE LEE)
French word for a bed canopy or bed tester. See also *plafond*.

cimborio (sim BOR ee-oh)
In Spanish, the term means a lantern admitting light over a crossing tower or elevated structure above a main roof.

cincture (SINK chur)
A convex molding at the top and bottom of a classical column, dividing it from the base and capital.

cinquecento (CHINK we chenk oh)
An Italian word for the 16th century in Italy, which is one of the most highly developed periods of the Italian Renaissance.

cinquefoil (SINK foi-ul)
A Gothic motif in the form of a five-lobed-shaped curve, used in some furniture and as a motif on Gothic tracery. See *illustration in the Motifs/Ornaments Appendix*.

circassian walnut (SUR kaa shee-un WAHL nut)
A handsome, expensive brown wood with a curly grain, found near the Black Sea; sometimes called Black Sea walnut. It is used for furniture, veneer, and paneling.

circlehead or round top window
A variety of window units characterized by one or more curved frame members and used over window or door openings.

cire perdue (SEER PUR doo)
French term for "lost wax" casting, a sculptural process of making a model in plaster coated with wax; then the model is coated with perforated plaster or clay, and when heated, the mold will lose the wax as it runs out of the holes. Molten lead is poured into the space occupied by the wax and the sculptor breaks the mold, removes the plaster core, and continues to polish the metal product.

ciselé velvet (CHE sel' vel vet)
A velvet comprised of both tufted pile and loop pile with a pattern formed by the contrast of the cut and uncut loops.

ciseleur (SEE se lur)
A French word that defines a craftsman who ornaments bronze and other metals by chiseling; an engraver or chaser of metal ornaments.

cist (SIST)
An ancient Roman box or container used for storing sacred utensils.

cista (SIS tah)
A Latin term for a trunk or chest used by Romans for storing jewels, etc.

cistern (SIS turn)

A large receptacle, usually a silver vessel, used to cool wine at the dining table; also a receptacle or cellarette for storing water.

citadel (sit e del)

A stronghold or fortified place; a commanding position in or near a city.

City Beautiful movement

A reform movement of the 1890s and 1900s in North American architecture and urban planning for the intent to improve urban infrastructure by using beautification and monumental grandeur with classical design; originally closely associated with Chicago, Detroit, and Washington, D.C.

cladding

An aesthetic or protective surface such as a wall finish, including use of vinyl, siding, wood, metal, glass, ceramic, etc.

clap table

An 18th-century English console table supported on brackets, usually with a pier looking glass set over it.

clapboard

A narrow long board used for exterior horizontal siding with one edge of the board thicker than the other, hence the board overlaps the one below. See also *beveled siding, lap siding*, and *weatherboard*.

clapboard house

A North American house found in New England typically around the 17th century where clapboard was used as the siding. Clapboard was also used on houses as a protective cover in late Gothic and early Renaissance England; it was eventually brought to Canada and other parts of the New World.

clare-obscure (KLAYR-ub SKYOOR)

A technique of painting characterized by strong differentiations between light and dark and bold contrasts; originating during the Renaissance as a drawing technique. See also *chiaroscuro*.

classic

Works of sculpture, architecture, arts, and literary arts having the characteristics of ancient Greece or Rome, which was of the highest standard and acknowledged as excellent; influence of the classical antiquity of the Greeks and Romans can be seen in the 18th and 19th centuries, which was called the Neoclassic period.

classical

Same as classic.

Classical Revival

An early 19th-century architectural movement in England and the United States, which derived its inspiration from a revived interest in Greek and Roman classical forms and motifs.

Classical Revival

clathri (claath REE)

A lattice of bars used for the gratings on windows or cages for animals.

clathri

clavated (KLAY vay ted)

A type of turning used for early Spanish Renaissance furniture legs and stretchers shaped like a club, growing gradually thicker at the top.

clavecin (KLAAV se)

A French musical instrument invented in 1759 by Jean-Baptiste Thilaie Delaborde, a French Jesuit priest. See also *clavichord* and *pianoforte*.

clavicembalo (KLAA vee chemb ah loh)

A term derived from the Latin clavis or key and cymbalum, another term that was designated in the Middle Ages for musical instruments with ropes in which the ropes are made to play by means of a keyboard, similar to an organ.

clavichord (KLAAV i kord)

An early 17th-century stringed musical instrument with or without legs, ancestor of the modern piano, known in England during the Carolean, William and Mary, and Queen Anne periods. See also *clavecin* and *pianoforte*.

claw and ball foot

A type of carved foot in the form of a bird's claw grasping a sphere or gripping a ball; supposedly a derivation from the Orient representing the dragon's claw clutching a sacred jewel; used with the cabriole leg especially during the first half of the 18th century in England during the Georgian period. See also *talon and ball foot*. See *illustration in the Feet Appendix*.

cleat (KLEET)

A wood or iron strip attached to a surface as a means of strengthening or supporting the surface.

clef pandante (KLEF PAHN dahnt)

French architectural term for boss. See also *boss*.

clepsydra (KLEP se drah)

An ancient device that measured time by the gradual or regulated flow of water; also called a water clock.

clerestory

Windows or openings placed in the upper part of wall or in the highest story, especially above a roof, located to bring light into the central area of a building. Same as clere-story, clearstory, or clear-story.

cloak pin

A Roman or Celtic open ring brooch used as a clothing fastener; also referred to as a holdback.

cloche (KLOHSH)

A bell-shaped transparent glass cover fitted over a wood base used chiefly outdoors to protect plants against frost; also the term means a woman's close-fitting, bell-shaped hat made of felt or cloth.

clock

See specific clocks for definitions.

cloison (KLWAH zun)

A term for partition, specifically a dividing band used in the divisions between sections in cloisonné work or in stained-glass window tracery.

clerestory

cloisonné (KLWAH zu nay)

A type of decorative enamelwork in which metal filaments are fused to outline a pattern using a gold, silver, or copper setting that is filled in with enamel paste.

cloister (KLOI stur)

A covered walkway with a roof or vaulted passage connecting monasteries and the church to the chapter house or other buildings in the monastery; a feature of medieval architecture.

clos (KLO)

A French word for an enclosed vineyard.

cloister

close chair

A chair-shaped latrine with a removable chamber pot beneath the hinged lid, sometimes called a close stool chair; used in domestic settings before the toilet or water closet became a standard part of the structure. Same as close stool chair.

close stool chair

See *close chair, necessary stool*, and *night close*.

closed stringer

A type of stairway where the stringer is attached to the wall, while the other side is harboring a banister and rungs.

closer

The last stone, tile, or brick in a horizontal course or a piece of brick finishing a course.

closet

The last room, but highly decorated, in the preferred order of rooms where the most serious business was held by the most important persons; used extensively during the Louis's reigns.

closing ring

A metal device in the shape of a ring that is fastened to a door; used to pull it shut.

closure

A brick that is cut or trimmed three-quarter length used to finish a course at the end or used at corners to obtain proper bonding.

clothes press

A wardrobe, chest, or a piece of furniture designed for storing clothes, usually with wide drawers and a cabinet, sometimes with hanging space.

cloven foot

A furniture foot in the form of a cleft rear hoof of a deer, introduced in early 18th-century France; originally derived from the Romans. See also *doe's foot*, *hoof foot*, and *pied de biche*. See *illustration for peid de biche in the Feet Appendix*.

club chair

A large, plush upholstered easy chair with arms varying from high to low, with wide to thin upholstery, which is usually buttoned leather; the style is based on club chairs popular and fashionable in gentleman's clubs of England, particularly during the Victorian period.

club foot

A round, pad-shaped foot found on a cabriole leg; used in 18th-century English furniture. See also *pad foot*. See *illustration in the Feet Appendix*.

clustered or cluster column leg

A column for a furniture leg comprised of several small shafts around a large one, giving the appearance of a cluster column; often used in the Gothic taste by Chippendale during the 18th century. See *illustration in the Legs Appendix*.

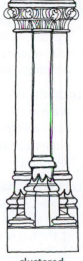

closing ring

clustered column

A column with three or more shafts clustered together to form a single support; commonly seen in Gothic Style architecture. Same as compound column.

coaching inn clock

A mid 18th-century clock introduced when mail coaches began to run to a certain timetable; characterized by a hanging, weight-driven, plain design with a large wooden dial printed in bold black Roman numerals. See also *Act of Parliament clock* and *Parliament clock*.

coal scuttle

A coal container, usually a metal bucket, shaped with a wide lip to permit pouring coal on the fire. See also *pipkin*.

coat of arms

A term applied to heraldic design, which consists of a shield and certain accessories unique to a person, family, state, or institution; commonly called armorial bearings, armorial devices, heraldic devices, or arms. Originally used by feudal lords and knights in the mid 12th century on battlefields to identify the enemy from the allied soldiers, expanding to social classes and families by the 13th century, and finally to a variety of institutions or families in the 21st century. See also *armorial* and *heraldic symbols*.

coated glass

A term for a one-way mirror; a mirror on one side and a pane on the other, which allows vision from one direction only.

cobbler's bench

A bench for a shoemaker with a seat, last holder, and compartments for pegs and tools.

cochlea (KOH klee ah)

An architectural term for a spiral staircase.

clustered column

cochlea

cock bead molding

A small astragal molding used for the edges of drawer fronts to protect the veneer; used from 1730s to the end of the 18th century in England and America. See also *single arch molding*. See *illustration in the Moldings Appendix*.

cockade   (kah KAYD)

A decorative knot of ribbons, such as a rosette, usually worn on the hat as a badge during the French Revolution.

cockfight chair

A special 18th-century English chair with a curved yoke and a small shelf at the top of the rail used for reading, writing, or viewing sports, especially at cockfights where the gentleman straddled the seat facing the back and kept score on the adjustable easel. See also *fumeuse, straddle chair, voyelle,* and *voyeuse.*

cockfight chair

cockleshell

A shell similar to that of a cockle that was used as a carved decorative feature on furniture knees, cresting, and pendants of chairs and furniture in the early 18th-century English and French period designs. See also *scallop shell, shell, rocaille,* or *rococo.* See *illustration in the Motifs/Ornaments Appendix.*

cocktail table

See *coffee table.*

coco wood

A sound, environmentally responsible wood with a unique grain pattern of either natural light-tan color or a medium honey-brown, made from the stem fiber of the coconut palm and best suited for flooring, furniture, kitchen cabinets, and other products.

cocobolo   (kohk oh BOH loh)

A Central American hardwood, which is typically orange or reddish-brown with a figuring of darker irregular traces weaving through the wood; only the heartwood is used for modern furniture and fancy cabinetwork.

coconut chair

See *George Nelson coconut chair.* See *George Nelson, 1908–1986, in the Architects, Artists, and Designers Appendix.*

coffee table

A term used in relation to a low, light occasional table used in front of a sofa or couch.

coffer

A medieval chest used for storage and for transporting valuables; see coffered ceiling for an illustration of a structural grid used on the ceiling with recessed geometric panels. See also *arca ferrata, jewel box,* and *lacunaria.*

coffer

coffered ceiling

A ceiling or suspended grid with recessed geometric panels developed in the Italian Renaissance. See also *lacunaria* and *soffit.*

coffered paneling

A sunken panel located in a ceiling, soffit, or vault below the level of the surrounding framework, usually in the shape of a square, rectangle, or octagon, and often highly decorated or ornamented.

coffered ceiling

coffre (KAH fur)

French term for a chest or box used to hold valuables; or architectur-ally, a sunken panel in the shape of a square, rectangle, or octagon in a soffit, vault, or ceiling. See also *coffer*.

coffre fort (KAH fur FORT)

A French word for a box or chest usually made of metal with iron straps and a lock to secure valuables stored within.

coffret (KAH fret)

A French term for a small chest or box, similar to a coffre or coffre fort.

cogging (KAHG ing)

The tenon from a wooden beam designed to fit into the grooved out beam to form a joint; cogging is joining two beams with tenons.

cognac chair (KOHN yak CHAYR)

See *Eero Aarnio cognac chair*. See *Eero Aarnio, 1932– , in the Architects, Artists, and Designers Appendix*.

Cogswell chair

A 20th-century brand of an upholstered easy chair with open armrests, a sloping back, an upholstered seat and back with a low upholstered platform.

coiffeuse (KWAH fooz)

A typical 18th-century French dressing table that has a dressing mirror, derived from its use in dressing hair. See also *poudreuse*.

coign (KOIN)

See *quoin*.

coin

An 18th-century English triangular corner cupboard. See also *corner cupboard, encoignure*, and *squinch*.

coir (KOIR)

Doormats made from coconut husk; roughly textured rugs.

collage

A technique of creating a composition or picture made of pieces of paper, cloth, wallpaper, and other materials glued to a canvas or a surface; derived from the French word for gluing. See also *montage*.

collar

A molding in the form of a ring or band on a table or chair leg.

collar beam

A horizontal timber or a tie beam in a roof truss that connects the two opposite rafters at a point below the ridge, usually in the upper half of the rafter length.

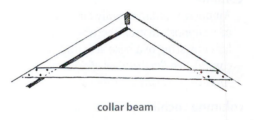

collar beam

Colonial American period

The Colonial period in America from the earliest settlement to the Revolution; the American interior decoration and furniture, a blending of several European influences with the new provincial setting found in the thirteen British colonies.

Colonial Revival Style

A nationalistic architectural style expressing American patriotism through its return to classical architecture, garden design, and inte-rior design in the United States, popular in the late 19th century through the mid 20th century.

colonnade

A row of columns, arranged side by side, usually supporting an entablature and forming a corri-dor or passageway. See also *stoa*.

colonnade

colonnette (KAH lu net)

A miniature or small thin column used ornamentally or as a support on furniture or also in architecture. Same as colonna and colonnate.

colossal order

An architectural order that spans two or more stories.

colossus (ke LAH ses)

A gigantic statue of huge proportions of a human (or god).

column

An upright pillar, usually circular in plan, that acts as a support; in architecture, a supporting pillar consisting of a base, a cylindrical shaft, and a capital. See *illustrations of types of columns in the Architectural Orders Appendix*.

columna cochlis (KAH lum nah KAWK lis)

A large monumental column with a spiral staircase around its center line.

columna rostrata (KAH lum nah RO strah tah)

A monumental Tuscan column with its shaft embellished with prows or beaks of antique Roman warships, originally to honor naval victories.

columnar leg

A column-like support for chairs or tables. See *illustration in the Legs Appendix*.

comb-back Windsor chair

A type of Windsor chair in which several spindles extend above the back, topped with an additional rail resembling a comb fashionable in the 18th century. See also *comb-back writing chair, three-back Windsor chair*, and *Windsor chair*.

comb-back writing chair

A writing-arm Windsor chair.

column

comb-back Windsor chair

comb-back writing chair

combination stair

A T-shaped stair popular in the 19th century in which access to the first landing is provided by the formal front stair and by the supplemental service stair to a common intermediate landing.

commerce table

A folding card table with an X-shaped underframe and an oval top, named after the game Commerce, a card game played in the 18th and 19th centuries.

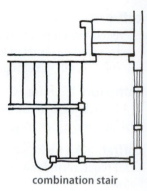
combination stair

commesso (KOH me soh)

A 16th-century Florentine mosaic technique often used to fashion pictures with thin, cut-to-shape pieces of brightly colored semiprecious stones, used mainly for table tops and small wall panels.

commode

A type of chest or cabinet, usually low, with legs of different lengths and two or more drawers; or it may have doors, which were introduced in the late 17th century.

commode

commode desserte (kah MOHD day ZART)

An 18th-century French oblong sideboard or commode with a drawer in the center and flanked by open shelves on either end that are quarter-circle rounded.

commode en console (kah MOHD EN KON sohl)

A French term for an 18th-century commode, usually with a single drawer and attached to the wall.

commode en tombeau (kah MOHD EN TOM boh)

A French Louis XV low cabinet or chest of drawers at the height of the dado rail, further characterized by short legs and deep drawers, very heavy in appearance with the lowest drawer only inches off the floor.

commode step

The bottom step or a flight of steps with the end being curved.

common bond

Brick pattern laid with five rows of stretchers, one row of headers, five rows of stretchers, one row of headers, repeated.

common rafters

One of a series of rafters that extends from the plate of the roof to the ridge board to support the roofing of the building.

Commonwealth

The time in England when the republic ruled not only England, but also Ireland and Scotland, from 1649 to 1660, with Oliver Cromwell as leader of the puritanical period, a very severe system of government. Same as Cromwellian period.

comodini (KOH moh dee nee)

Italian term for a bedside table with a single door and a small drawer above.

companion chair

A popular mid to late 19th-century chair consisting of three upholstered curved chairs, joined in the center so they appear to radiate from a central point; each chair designed to accommodate two persons, similar to a tête-à-tête. See also *tête-à-tête*.

companion chair

compartmented ceiling

A paneled ceiling divided into grids and usually surrounded by moldings.

compass seat

A term for a rounded chair seat, introduced in the early 18th century, often referred to as a pincushion seat or chair.

compluvium (kahm PLOO vee um)

A roof opening in a Roman residence above the atrium through which rainwater could fall into the cistern located under the floor, referred to as the impluvium. See also *impluvium*.

compluvium

compo, also composition

A paper-mache or plaster material made of glue, whiting, paper pulp, and chalk to imitate wood, stone, metal, etc., and used for making lightweight interior architectural embellishments for a ceiling, a panel, a frame, or even a piece of furniture; particularly in the 18th century. See also *anaglypta*, *carton-pierre*, *gesso*, *pastiglia*, and *stucco*.

Composite Order

One of the architectural orders used by the Romans with the capital composed of both Corinthian and Ionic orders; Corinthian acanthus leaves and the Ionic volute. See *illustration in the Architectural Orders Appendix.*

composition ornament

A mixture of whiting, resin, and size to make plaster, molded into shapes, often carved and applied to a surface as an architectural embellishment or motif. See also *composition* or *carton-pierre*.

compound column

See *clustered column*.

concave

The reverse of convex; instead the object is curved in or sunken.

concertina side table (KAHN sur tee nah SIYD TAY bul)

An English card table from the 18th and 19th centuries constructed so the rear portion can pull out, the sides follow in a concertina action, with locking slide and storage compartment.

concertina side table

concha (KAHN chah)

A Spanish or Latin American word meaning "something shaped like a shell," a shell-shaped structure or a shell motif.

confessional

A rather large, upholstered French chair with wings; also the term refers to the enclosure where a priest hears a confession.

confidante or confidente

(KAHN fah dahnt; KAHN fee dent)
A French term for a sofa or settee with small attached angled seats at either end and with upholstered divisions or arms separating them from the main section.

confidante

confortable (KAHN for tah blu)

An all-upholstered early French Renaissance chair, before the design of the bergère.

congé (CON jay)

An architectural term for a molding with a concave profile, similar to cavetto and commonly referred to as quarter round.

Connecticut chest

An early American oak or pine chest with one or more drawers standing on four legs, often painted and decorated with split spindles, moldings, and panels featuring Tudor roses, so called because many have been found in the Connecticut valley. See also *Hadley chest* and *Wethersfield chest*.

conodial vault (KOH noh dee-al VAULT)

See *fan vault*.

console

A French term for a decorative bracket, usually of scroll form, used to support a cornice or shelf. See also *ancon* and *bracket*.

console

console desserti or console desserte (KAHN sohl DEZ ur tee)

A French term for a small serving table similar to a sideboard.

console leg

A basic furniture foot named for its resemblance to a bracket; includes both plain and scrolled with a curved outside edge; used by both Hepplewhite and Sheraton. See also *bracket foot*.

console mirror

The mirror placed over a pier table. See also *petticoat mirror*.

console servante (KAHN sohl SUR vahnt)

A French table with a marble top and a shelf below used for serving; similar to the French console dessert used in the Louis XVI period.

console table

A French small side table, usually fixed to a wall with one or two front legs for support, placed between windows with a mirror above it. See also *pier table*.

console table

Constitution mirror

An American mirror from the late 18th or early 19th centuries, adopted after the Constitution, characterized by a row of balls for decoration on the head or cornice of the frame, usually the frame is of walnut or mahogany and is partly gilded; also referred to as tabernacle mirror. See also *American Empire mirror* and *trumeau mirror*.

Consulate Style (KAHN su let STIY ul)

French period of government from 1799 to 1804 during the Napoleonic era; sometimes referred to as the Directoire Style.

contador (KAHN tah dor)

A large Portugese cabinet-on-stand with drawers, often hand carved or decorated with inlay ornament that is either geometrical or semi-abstract.

Contemporary Style

A style conforming to the present or recent times; a period that is relevant to the present; a descriptive term current in the 1950s and 1960s for furniture industrially produced from modern materials and completely different from traditional or antique styles.

contour chair

An upholstered or molded chair shaped to fit the form or contours of the human body especially to reduce fatigue and discomfort.

contre-parti (KAHN tre-PAHR tee)

A French term used to describe a form of Boulle work in which the brass forms the groundwork, and the tortoiseshell is less dominant. See also *Boulle work*.

contract furniture

Furniture designed especially for use by the many people in the workplace or in public areas that must withstand heavy usage; usually sold only to the trade and not in retail stores.

convenance (KAHN ven ahns)

An 18th-century Louis XV space planning theory that dealt with functional relationships among certain aspects of the position of rooms, the size of the room, ornamentation, and character, as well as dictating the arrangement that differentiated public from private.

convento (kohn VEN toh)

Italian/Spanish word for a convent for nuns or a monastery for monks that adjoins a church.

conversation chair

A term often used in reference to many other chairs over several centuries, e.g., the 16th-century caqueteuse or the 18th-century cockfight or roundabout chair, or the 19th-century "vis-a-vis" or "dos-a-dos." The chair is not as low, making it more comfortable than a lounge or easy chair. See also *cockfight chair, roundabout chair*, and *voyeuse*.

conversation chair

conversation pit

A sunken portion of a living area formally known in the 1960s and 1970s as the "conversation pit" with chairs, sofas, and other furniture so people could gather to talk, usually around a fireplace.

convertible sofa

A sofa that can be changed from a sofa to a bed; often referred to as a sleeper sofa or sofa bed.

convex

A surface that curves or rounds outward like the exterior of a sphere; opposite of the word concave.

convolute

A material that is rolled, coiled, fluted, or wound in the shape of a spiral or a scroll; described as convoluted.

cope

The technique of joining two molded strips to make tight-fitting inside corner joints or to fit the contours of an abutting joint.

coping

The capping on the upper part of an exterior wall to protect the wall from rain coming from the top, and also to enhance the beauty of the architecture.

Coptic

The native Christian in Egypt from the 4th to the 7th centuries, an ethno religious group.

Coptic cloth

A fine, dense cotton cloth with a plain weave, produced by Christian descendants of ancient Egyptians during the 4th to the 7th centuries.

Coptic textile

A 4th to 7th-century woven textile made of linen and designed in Egypt by the Coptic Christians.

coquillage (KOH kee-ahj)

A French term for a shell-like pattern with birds, flowers, and other carved ornaments, derived from the French word coquille meaning a shell; used during the French Rococo period to decorate mirrors, seat rails on chairs, aprons of cabinets, and commodes, etc.

coquillage

coquille (KOH kwee)

French for the motif shell. See also *shell motif*. See *illustration of a shell motif in the Motifs/Ornaments Appendix*.

coquina (koh kee NAH)

A soft, whitish, and porous limestone, made up of shells, fragments of shells, and coral; used as a building material.

corbeil or corbeille (KOR bay)

A sculptured basket of fruit or flowers used in architectural design, especially on a column capital.

corbel

An projecting architectural element or bracket that extends beyond the surface of the wall to support a beam. See also *bracket*.

corbel table

An architectural element consisting of a continuous row of corbels providing support for the cornice; originating in the 11th century on churches with decorated scrolls, rods, or geometrical shapes. See also *bracket cornice*.

corbel vault

A structure having the form of a vault using the architectural technique of corbelling to span a space and strong enough to support the weight from above.

corbelled arch (KOR beld ARCH)

An arch-like construction of masonry courses that uses the corbelling technique to span a space.

corbie-stepped gable
(KOR bee-STEPT GAY bul)

A stair-step pattern at the top of a triangular gable-end building with the top of the parapet projecting above the roofline and the stone wall stacked in a step-type design as a decoration and as a way to finish the brick courses; found in England, Switzerland, Sweden, Denmark, and Germany from the 15th century onwards. Same as crow-stepped gable.

corbie-stepped gable

corbu chair or Corbusier chair

See *Michael Thonet Le Corbusier chair*. See *Michael Thonet, 1796–1871, in the Architects, Artists, and Designers Appendix*.

Cordovan leather or cordwain

An equine leather, originally prepared from goatskin, but now made from the fibrous flat muscle beneath the hide on the rump of the horse, prepared by the Moors in Cordova, Spain.

core

Porous internal plywood with alternating layers of wood slices and a surface of finished wood-grain veneer.

Corinthian Order

The most elaborate of the three Greek orders of architecture, distinguished by its carved acanthus leaves and four volutes; adapted and developed by the Romans, whose most popular order became the Corinthian. See *illustration in the Architectural Orders Appendix*.

Corinthianesque (ke RIN three-in esk)

A type of column with bracketed capitals, fanciful scrolls, and heraldic escutcheons used in the early Renaissance, Spanish plateresque period.

corner basin stand

A washstand found in the bedchambers of wealthy English families at the end of the 18th century; also found in publications by Sheraton, Hepplewhite, and others.

corner basin stand

corner block

A reinforced triangular block glued and/or nailed or screwed into the inner angles or corner of chair frames, etc., as a means to reinforce the joints and add inner strength.

corner chair

A chair made with a square seat with back splats on two sides and three legs with the fourth leg being located in the middle of the front; design intended for the corner of a room. See also *roundabout chair, smoker's chair,* and *writing chair.*

corner cupboard

A triangular cupboard designed to fit in the corner of a room with the front being diagonal or curved; some smaller ones were hung, while larger cupboards were an integral part of the furnishings; found throughout the 18th century in England and America. See also *alcove cupboard, buffet,* and *coin.*

corner table

A table designed to be square or triangular that fits into a corner of a room or with couches and chairs; found in many different periods or styles.

cornice

The projecting uppermost molding or crowning portion of a classic entablature or any projecting element at the top of cabinets, bookcases, and other pieces of furniture.

cornish (KOR nish)

See *cornice.*

cornucopia (korn e KOH pee-ah)

A term meaning horn of plenty used decoratively as a twisted horn filled with overflowing fruits and flowers; symbolizing prosperity and abundance; popular during many historical styles, but especially a favorite stencil motif in 19th-century America.

corner cupboard

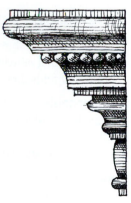

cornice

cornucopia sofa

A sofa so named due to its scrolled arms carved to resemble a cornucopia, with the sofa back and legs often repeating this motif; designs from various stylistic periods, such as the English Regency, Empire Style, American Federal and Empire furniture.

coro (KOR oh)

Italian term for the choir of a Renaissance church.

corolitic (KOR oh li tick)

A word meaning decoration with branches sculpted with foliage.

coromandel lacquer

Lacquerwork composed of polychrome designs on a black background and used for Louis XV case pieces by first applying the lacquer very thickly and in successive layers, then incising design motifs or engraving.

coromandel screen

An ebony folding screen coated in dark lacquer, carved, often painted gold or other colors, and decorated with scenes of Chinese life or landscapes decorated with scenes of Chinese life, landscapes, European hunting scenes, and jade and other precious stones; often had European hunting scenes. Originally made in China during the Qing Dynasty, Kangxi period (1661–1720), then transported to Europe in the late 17th and early 18th centuries.

coromandel wood

A hard, variegated ebony wood with grey to brown mottling or with black and yellow stripes resembling rosewood; from the Coromandel coast of India and used for banding and veneering on furniture during the late 18th century. Same as calamander wood. See also *ebony.*

corona

The vertical projection in the upper part of a cornice, situated below the cymatium, with the undersurface recessed to allow the water to drip away from the wall.

corona

corona lucis (KOR oh nah loo SEES)
Architectural word for a chandelier suspended from the roof or vault of a church with one or more concentric hoops, arranged pyramidically, to hold tapers, which are lighted on special solemn occasions.

corona lucis

cortile (kor TEE lay)
An open inner courtyard surrounded by an arcade and enclosed by the walls of a large dwelling; characteristic of the Italian Renaissance palaces or palazzos in Florence and Rome.

cosmati (KOHZ mah tee)
Type of decorative geometric mosaic technique of cut work formed from marble inlays of small triangles and rectangles of colored stones and glass mosaics separated by large plain bands or sections on the floors, walls, and furniture, usually in churches and tombs, during the 12th and 13th centuries by the Cosmati family from Rome, seven members of architects, sculptors, and workers from four generations.

cortile

costumer (KAHS too mur)
An umbrella holder. See also *hatrack* and *umbrella stand*.

cottage furniture
A softwood furniture painted white, gray, lilac, or pale blue that was mass produced during the mid 19th century, featured in *The Architecture of Country Houses* by A. J. Downing (1850) and recommended for rural surroundings.

cottage orne (KAH tij ORN)
A rustic cottage, often with a thatched roof, weatherboarding with rough-hewn columns, originating in the Picturesque movement of the 18th century and early 19th century; meant for the farm laborer or middle class, but many were built in England for the gentry on a large scale.

cottage piano
An 18th- and 19th-century small upright piano with a keyboard projecting from the case; behind the keyboard was a fretwork panel with a pleated silk curtain. Similar to the upright piano, the first ones had a tall case.

cottage-set curtain
A double set of curtains covering upper and lower; one hanging above the other; usually the top pair overlaps the bottom pair and the upper tier is sometimes ruffled on the edges and often tied back to allow light.

couch (KOWCH)
A long seat usually upholstered with supports and cushions, similar to a sofa. A French invention during the early 17th century that developed into a daybed or chaise longue. Americans often confuse a couch with a sofa or settee; since the 18th century, however, it has been considered a daybed. See also *chaise longue, daybed, uchess, rest beds*, and *sofa*.

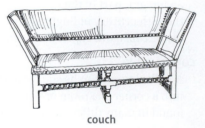

couch

couchette (KOO shet)
A daybed that converts from a seat into a bed; also a narrow bed on a train that folds down from the wall.

counter-table
A medieval table used for counting money with a hinged lid at one end allowing access to a shallow space; today it is a table or surface for the display of goods and is taller than a standard table.

counterpane
A bedspread or coverlet placed on a bed, more specifically a quilt woven of cotton with raised figures; also referred to as a Marseilles quilt.

Country Chippendale

A style of Thomas Chippendale chairs, produced in the countryside during the mid 18th century, usually made of painted pine with simplified versions of the original Chippendale splats and shaped top rail, but still skillfully made.

Country French

Furniture designs found in country homes of France in Normandy, Provence, and Bordeaux, made with no right or wrong rules but with warmth and comfort; a style that never goes out but will remain for years to come even in American furniture with a country French style embedded in the early American look. See also *French Provincial*.

country made

Simple and plain furniture made by the country cabinetmakers; showing plain decorative styles. Same as provincial furniture.

coupled columns

One or two columns grouped or arranged in pairs; in classical orders, usually spaced half a diameter apart.

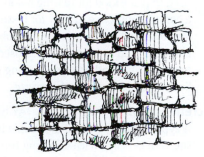

coupled columns

cours d'honneur (KOR DAH nur)

French term for courtyard of a grand house or palace, often enclosed and located in front of the main house.

course rubble

Masonry of rough brick or stones set in mortar, not laid in regular courses.

course rubble

court cupboard

A cupboard with three shelves for display and one enclosed level for storage; introduced into England from France in the late 16th century for use in the great hall; sometimes called a buffet. See also *buffet, cupboard, plate cupboard,* and *sideboard.*

court cupboard

court furniture

Style of furniture, very formal and elegant, created for royalty and the lavish styles of the courts.

courting chair

A love seat or small sofa. See also *causeuse, double chair, settee, sofa, tête âtête,* and *two-chair-back settee.*

courting mirror

A small mirror (about 17.5″ × 12″) from the 18th to early 19th centuries with a wood frame border and often reverse painted on glass reserves, commonly given to young women by their suitors. Due to the high price of mirror glass, young women held them in high regard.

cove

A concave molding used to connect a wall to a ceiling; also an architectural word for a large concave molding used in a cornice or under the eaves. See *illustration in the Moldings Appendix.*

coved ceiling

An architectural feature created when a concave surface forms part of the ceiling at its edge by curving to eliminate the sharp right angle where the wall and the ceiling meet. See also *cove.*

coved ceiling

coved cupboard

An early American cupboard with a projection on the top.

coved skirting

An architectural term, also referred to as skirting board or mopboard, to describe a molding used to conceal the joint formed by an interior wall and the floor. See also *skirting.*

Cowhorn chair

See *Hans Wegner Cowhorn chair*. See *Hans Wegner, 1914–2007, in the Architects, Artists, and Designers Appendix*.

cracking

A means of producing fine cracks or patterns of cracks under the surface of a material, such as pottery, porcelain, glass, etc. Same as crackling; see also *crazing*.

crackle glaze

A deliberate creation of fine cracks in the glaze of glass or porcelain by immersing the molten object into cold water and refiring to seal the cracks.

cradle or crib

A child's bed made in many styles and variations, mounted on rockers or a swinging arrangement, with or without a hood, originating in the earliest times but almost replaced by the modern crib.

Craftsman furniture

Mission Style furniture made of oak in the early 20th century by Gustav Stickley and published in his magazine entitled *The Craftsman*. See also *Mission Style*. See *Gustav Stickley, 1858–1942, in the Architects, Artists, and Designers Appendix*.

Craftsman, The

A magazine published in the United States in 1903 by Gustav Stickley depicting the Arts and Crafts movement and the Mission Style architecture and furniture by Stickley.

Craftsman movement

An American design and furniture style developed in the late 19th century based on Arts and Crafts in Britain with prominent craftsmen designers Gustav Stickley, Greene brothers, Frank Lloyd Wright, etc.

cramoisy (KRAAM oiz ee)

An archaic word for crimson cloth from the Medieval and Renaissance periods.

Cranbrook Academy of Art

An American Design School located in Bloomfield Hills, Michigan, established by George Gough Booth in 1927, with Eliel Saarinen, the first president, introducing workshops in architecture, painting, and sculpture; many of the outstanding designers of the 20th century were affiliated with the academy, such as Charles and Ray Eames and Harry Bertoia.

craquelure

Fine cracks all over the surface of oil paintings; caused by shrinkage, varnish, and paint film movement.

crayon engraving

See *intaglio* or *intaglio engraving*.

crazing (KRAY zing)

Fine line cracks in the glaze of ceramic ware or glass, also appearing on paintings.

creamware

A lead-glazed, ivory-colored earthenware, popular between 1740 and 1756, perfected by Staffordshire during this time. See also *earthenware, ironstone*, and *Queen's ware*

creche (KRESH)

A miniature nativity scene with figures, set with stable and animals made from various materials, such as plaster, wood, china, etc.

crédence (KRAY dahns)

A medieval storage piece elevated on legs used to place food for tasting before serving, a common practice in Italy for testing food for poisoning before serving the nobility; characterized by its open and closed shelves for preparing food or for displaying plates. See also *bofet, buffet*, and *desserte*.

crédence

credence table (KRAY dahns TAY bul)

A type of oak or walnut side table from the 17th century with a folding top where dishes were placed prior to service at the table; then used in the 19th century as a small table near the altar for bread and wine.

credenza (kri DEN zah)

An Italian sideboard, cupboard, or crédence with great variety in design; a popular 15th-century design during the Renaissance. See also *buffet, crédence,* and *sideboard.*

credenza

crémaillère (KRE mah yur)

A French word for a fireplace hearth swinging crane.

cremo (KREE moh)

Italian creamy white marble with veining similar to Calcutta gold.

crenel (KRE nel)

One of a series of embrasures or indentations between two merlons in a battlement or crenellated wall.

crenellation

crenellation or crenelated (KRE ne lay shun / KRE ne lay ted)

Top of the castle walls during the medieval period, characterized by alternating indentations or embrasures with raised portions or merlons. See also *battlement.*

crepidoma (KRE peed oh mah)

The stepped base of a Greek temple on which colonnades are placed, with the highest step being the stylobate.

crescent stretcher

An arched or hooped stretcher that curves upwards, often used on American Windsor chairs to reinforce the legs.

crest or cresting

A decorative carving on the topmost part of a piece of furniture, especially along the top rail of a chair; also the pierced ornament at the ridge or edge of a roof.

crest

crest rail

The top horizontal rail of a chair back, often elaborately carved and shaped, particularly during the 16th and 17th centuries.

cretonne (KREE ton)

A heavy, unglazed cotton, printed fabric, similar to chintz but with larger and less detailed designs; useful for draperies, slip-covering, and upholstery.

crewel embroidery

Embroidery using varicolored worsted wool or crewel yarn in floral designs, often combined with animal figures, on unbleached linen used primarily for bed hangings during the 17th and 18th centuries in England.

crib

A child's bed with enclosed sides and legs to raise the bed off the floor.

cricket

A low, wooden English stool, also found in America, characterized by proportions that are one-third that of a standard stool.

cricket table

A plain circular table with three legs and a shaped apron of the Jacobean period in England.

crinoline stretcher

See *crescent stretcher.*

criosphinx (KREE ohs finks)

In Egyptian mythology, a sculptural form that represents the body of a lion on the head of a ram or a man.

criss-cross curtains

See *Priscilla curtains.*

cristallo (KRIS tah loh)

An Italian Renaissance glass made totally clear without the slight yellow or greenish color, made from iron oxide with a small addition of manganese; developed in Venice where glass manufacturing secrets were kept.

crocket

Gothic ornament designed with a curled leaf or bud used originally as a decoration on the sides of pinnacles on Gothic turrets and sub-sequently on furniture designs as finials on chairs; also used on cathedrals in imitation of a bishop's crozier, which symbolized his func-tion as a shepherd protecting his sheep.

crocket

crocket capital

A series of crockets used to decorate the capital of a column.

crocking

Rubbing off excess dye from a printed or dyed fabric; also the transfer of excess dye to another surface, such as a piece of cloth, furniture, etc.

cromlech (KRAM lek)

A Brythonic word referring to a prehistoric monument structure encircling a mound. Today the term is virtually obsolete.

crocket capital

Cromwellian chair

A mid 17th-century chair named after Oliver Cromwell and made during the Puritan period; characterized by its sturdy and squarish design with a seat and back of leather, garnished with brass-headed nails and bobbin turnings applied especially to legs and stretchers; this is the only decoration because luxury and orna-ment were shunned during the austere climate of the Puritans. Made in England and in urban colonial America.

Cromwellian period (1649–1660)

See *Commonwealth*.

croquet chair

A popular Victorian chair made from plaited twigs or woven wicker with padded cushions or buttoned upholstery, used outside in the garden or in the house; sometimes referred to as a basket chair.

cross fire

A figure extending across the grain of wood giving a mottled, fiddle-back, raindrop, or finger-roll effect that adds greatly to the beauty as the transverse pattern appears highlighted on the wood.

cross grain

Wood or fabric in which the fibers deviate from the parallel to the diagonal; having an irregular or diagonal grain as opposed to a parallel grain.

cross-hatching or crosshatching

Two or more sets of intersecting parallel lines creating a pattern or producing the effect of shade.

cross-rail

The horizontal slat or connecting element between the back posts on a chair.

cross section

A cut through something at right angles to its axis in order to view a building, room, or object.

cross stretcher

Intersecting X-stretcher used to connect and support the legs of a chair or other pieces of furniture such as tables and case pieces. See also *X-stretcher*.

cross vault

A vault formed by two or more barrel vaults intersecting at right angles; also may be called a groin or cross vaulting.

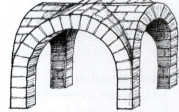

cross vault

crossbanding or cross banding

A term used when a narrow border of veneer is inserted on the surface of furniture, wainscoting, etc., so that the wood veneer is at right angles to the grain of the adjacent wood. See also *banding*.

crossette (KRAH set)

Projection at a corner of a door or window architrave at the lintel level; these extensions beyond the trim are known as earpieces, elbows, knees, lugs, or shouldered architrave.

crossing

The area, which is nearly square, at the intersection of the nave, chancel, and transepts in medieval or cathedral church design.

crotch or crutch

A term used to describe where something forks or splits into two or more branches at the base of an object (such as a tree trunk), almost like a V-shape.

crotch veneer

A piece of wood cut from the intersection of a branch of the trunk or the fork of a tree; highly valued for its figure and/or curly effect for wood veneer.

crown

A decorative motif carved, painted, or embroidered, found in French, Italian, Flemish, and English work as a symbol of royalty.

crown bed

A cloth covering, supported on poles or suspended, usually over a bed. See also *baldaquin*.

crown glass

A form of window glass made by the process of whirling or spinning a glass bubble in order to form a flat dish with a lump or button left in the center by the rod of the glass blower. See also *bottle-end glazing*, *bull's eye*, and *oeil-de-bouef*.

crown molding

A mold crowning an architectural element, particularly the fillets and cymas placed above the fascia in a classical cornice or the highest moldings on a door, window, or cabinet.

crown plate

In crown post construction, a longitudinal structural member at the apex of the roof supporting the ends of the rafters.

crown post

Any upright or vertical member of a roof truss, such as a king post. See also *king post*.

crow's bill

An architectural molding from the Gothic period with carved bird's head or beaks. See also *bird's beak molding*. See *illustration of bird's beak in the Molding Appendix*.

crow-stepped gable

See *corbie-stepped gable*.

cruciform (KROO si form)

A floor plan in the shape of a Latin cross.

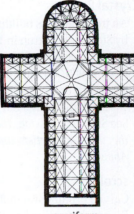

cruciform

cruck construction

A technique used for roof construction in medieval times using a pair (crucks) joined at the ridge and combining the functions of upright post and rafter or embedded into the wall head; the crucks take the full weight of the roof and serve as support for the walls of the building. Referred to as blades in some parts of England.

cruck construction

crypt (KRIPT)

An underground chamber or space, especially found in a church or cathedral, often used for burial of martyrs or saints and sometimes containing chapels.

cryptoporticus (KRIP toh por ti kus)

A covered passageway in Ancient Roman architecture, usually designed to provide shade or a cool place for walking.

crystal

A transparent clear quartz that resembles ice, cut and faceted to sparkle and reflect light; often imitation of crystal will be found in glass.

Crystal Palace

An iron and glass building designed by Sir Joseph Paxton in 1851 for the Great Exhibition of London, encompassing 900,000 square feet of sheet glass with the largest pane 49″ × 10″ in a hall nearly 1,851 feet long. See Sir *Joseph Paxton, 1803–1865, in the Architects, Artists, and Designers Appendix*.

Crystal Palace

C-scroll

Carved ornamental motif in the shape of a C or inverted C used in France during the late 16th and 17th centuries and later in England, chiefly on furniture; also used for legs. See *illustration in the Legs and Motifs/Ornaments Appendices*.

cuadrangulo (KWAH drang oo lah)

Spanish term for quadrangle meaning a square or space surrounded by buildings forming a courtyard.

cube chair or grand confort chair

See *Le Corbusier grand confort chair*. See *Le Corbusier, 1887–1965, in the Architects, Artists, and Designers Appendix*.

cube foot

A square or cube-shaped basic furniture foot; even though it appeared from 1600 to 1800, its popularity occurred in the mid 18th-century English and American furniture, especially in Chippendale-style furniture, where it appeared on the end of the straight Marlborough leg and became known as the Marlborough foot. See also *block foot*. See *illustration in the Feet Appendix*.

cubiculum (kyoo BIK yoo lum)

A Roman bedroom or room for sleeping in a Roman house.

Cubism

An modern art movement in painting and sculpture, lasting from 1907 to 1914, based largely on geometric pattern and abstract design, led by Picasso, Braque, and Gris.

cuisine (KWE zeen)

French for kitchen.

cul-de-lampe (KUL-de-lahm pay)

A pendant ornament or a kind of bracket-corbel of wood, metal, or stone, supporting a lantern or lamp, and shaped like a pyramid or cone; usually highly decorated with carving or painting.

culina (Koo lee nah)

A term that refers to a kitchen in an ancient Roman house, or domus.

cuneiform (KYOO nee ah form)

A type of writing made by using wedge-shaped marks on clay tablets; used in Sumeria, Babylonia, and Assyria.

cup and cover turning

A carved, melon-shaped, bulbous form resembling a bulb or cup with a lid or cover, found on table legs or bedposts of Elizabethan and Jacobean furniture. See also *bulbous form* and *melon bulb*. See *illustration in the Legs Appendix*.

cup-turned leg

A turned leg resembling an inverted cup that was prevalent during the 17th and early 18th centuries, characteristic of the William and Mary Style in England; also know as the bell and trumpet leg.

cupboard

A cabinet for storage, known under various names and often spelled in different ways such as coppeboard or copborde; also designed with low or high legs, with drawers or with shelves, some behind closed doors.

cupboard

cupid's bow crest

A term used to describe a curved cresting composed of a double ogee curve with ears or spiral volutes on the ends, named for the resemblance to a Cupid's bow; typical of the top rail of a Chippendale chair back.

cupola (KYOO pu lu)

A small dome rising above a roof on a circular base with openings for ventilation.

curio cabinet

A cabinet, usually of glass, to showcase collectibles, china, or other decorative objects, designed to be any size from large pieces of furniture to small; dating back to 16th century Flemish designs, and even more popular during the Victorian era. See also *whatnot*.

curled hair

Curled horse hair used for upholstery filling or padding for mattresses, pillows, or chairs; known for its durability and toughness.

curly

Woods, such as maple, walnut, birch, etc., with curves in the grain; often prized and not to be confused with markings such as bird's eye, blister, or wavy.

curricule chair (KOR ik oo lay CHAYR)

See *curule chair*.

curtail step

The lowest step of a flight of stairs terminating with a curved end.

curtain

Cloth that hangs in a window, doorway, or around a bed for privacy; a moveable drape or screen in a theater; or something that acts as a barrier, screen, or cover to separate, protect, or conceal something.

curtain wall

An outer enclosing wall of a building that is nonstructural but only serves as a cladding and merely keeps out the weather.

curtibulum (KOR tee boo lum)

Table placed in the middle of a Greek and Roman atrium to represent the hearth.

curule (KOR oo lay)

Ancient Roman seat composed of an interlaced X-form base and intended for use by persons of higher rank. See also *sella curulis*.

curule

curule chair

A 17th-century chair designed after the ancient Roman sella curulis with its curved legs, curved seat, and X-shaped base. Other types of curule chairs in addition to the Roman curules are the Renaissance folding chairs, as well as popular chairs in the Regency and Empire periods. Same as curricule chair. See also *faldistorium, sella curulis*, and *X-shaped chair*.

curule legs

Heavy, curved, X-shaped legs used in the Roman Republic and later in the Renaissance period, continuing into the Regency and French Empire.

curvilinear

A design consisting of curved lines, as in the flowing tracery of the Gothic period, and also in the design of furniture of the Rococo and Art Nouveau Styles.

cushion freize

A convex frieze found beneath a cornice in some Classical orders; also found on cabinets in the late 17th and 18th centuries.

cusped arch

In architecture the arch composed of small arches; the intersection of lobed or scalloped forms that appeared on early Islamic work and more commonly in Moorish architecture, then adopted by European Gothic architecture. See also *arch*.

abcdefghijklmnopqrstuvwxyz

cusp or cusping

The point marking the intersection of two ornamental arcs (as from the intrados of a Gothic arch).

cut-card latticework

Open designs cut from wood; often applied to a seat rail or a stretcher; sometimes used on Chinese Chippendale furniture, particularly the chairs.

cyclopean (SIY kloh peen)

Large, irregular blocks of stone used for construction; so named because only a giant or cyclops could lift such heavy stones.

cyclostyle (SIY kloh stiy ul)

An architectural term describing a structure composed of a circular group of columns without a core.

cylinder front

A quarter-round fall front on a desk designed to pivot, made during the late 18th century in England and France. See also *fall front*.

cylinder-top desk

A desk where the top swings into place to cover the writing surface but is not flexible; whereas the roll-top desk has a top that is flexible and rolls into place.

cusp

cylinder-top desk

cylinder wash hand table

A mechanical table designed in the 1790s by Thomas Sheraton, a British cabinetmaker (1751–1806), with a circular revolving front from which it derives its name, a concealed basin when shut, and a toilet glass that worked with a spring and a catch. A bidet and water drawer could be drawn out from the sides.

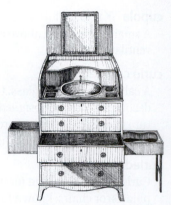

cylinder wash hand table

cyma curve (SIY mah KURV)

An S-shaped curve, one-half of which is concave and the other convex.

cyma recta (SIY mah REK tah)

A type of cyma or ogee curve in which the S-curve starts and ends in a horizontal plane with the topmost part convex and the lower concave. See also *ogee*. See *illustration in the Moldings Appendix*.

cyma reversa (SIY mah REE vur sah)

A molding in which the S-curve starts and ends in a vertical plane. See *illustration in the Moldings Appendix*.

cymatium (si MAY shee um)

The top portion or crowning member of a classical cornice, which contains a cyma curve. See *the illustration in the Moldings Appendix*.

cypress

A wood native to southern Europe and America with a dark reddish hue, very close grained, and quite popular for chests and storage pieces in the 16th and 17th centuries.

cypress chests

A cypress chest designed in the early Renaissance to hold tapestries, robes, and other items; eventually replaced by cedar because its aroma repelled moths.

Dada (DAH dah)

A nihilistic art movement of the early 20th century that sought authentic reality through the eradication of traditional culture and aesthetic forms. Famous Dada artists include Marchel Duchamps, Man Ray, and Max Ernst.

dado (DAY doh)

Based on the classical divisions of a wall, the lower part of an interior wall when set apart from the upper wall.

dado cap (DAY doh KAP)

The molding used to top a dado, commonly called a chair rail.

dado joint (DAY doh JOINT)

A common wood joining technique that involves creating a groove across the width of one piece, so it can accommodate the straight edge of another. See also *rabbet joint*.

Daedalus (De dah lis)

The Greek architect associated with the legends of the famous labyrinth of Crete, who made wings for himself and his son Icarus in order that they may escape being imprisoned within the maze.

daga (DAY gah)

Buildings made of waddle and daub in Africa.

Dagobert chair (DAY goh bayr CHAYR)

An extremely rare and famous 7th-century gilded bronze curule chair (throne) originally made for King Dagobert, a French king from the sacred Merovingian bloodline. In the 12th century, Abbot Suger added arms and a back to the chair. Napoleon used it for his coronation in 1804.

daguerreotype (de GAY roh tiyp)

Invented in France by Louis Daguerre A photographic process invented in France by Louis Daguerre in 1839 that produced faint images on a silver or silver-covered copper plate.

Dagobert chair

dais (DAY is)

A raised platform commonly used in the Great Hall of medieval castles as a place for nobles to dine.

dalbergia (dahl BUR jee-uh)

Name for a large genus of trees found primarily in tropical and subtropical locations. Dalbergia is commonly called rosewood in the Western world, but blackwood in the Far East. The beautiful heartwood of the tree is chocolate brown to purple black in color, with a very fine, usually straight grain. Used for high-end cabinetry, musical instruments, and small carved decorative elements.

dallage (DAH lahj)

French for a ground or floor surface covered with marble, stone, or tile.

damascene work (dahm ah SEEN WURK)

The originally Moorish art of inlaying precious metals such as gold, silver, or copper into a matte black steel background for which the city of Damascus is celebrated. Also called damascening, Damascus, or damasquinado.

damask (DA mesk)

A figured, jacquard-woven silk named after Damascus, Syria, that is characterized by its contracting dull woven design and shiny background. It is commonly used for draperies and upholstery.

damasquinado (DAH mah sekeen ah doh)

Spanish term for damascene work.

damassé (DAH mah say)

French term for damask.

dancette (DAN set)

A Romanesque term for a chevron or zigzag on Saxon and early Norman architecture. See also *chevron*.

dan-day chair

A type of early 19th-century Windsor chair made in Suffolk, England.

Danish Modern

See *Scandinavian Modern*.

dansu (DAN soo)
See *tansu.*

Dante chair (DAHN tay CHAYR)
An Italian Renaissance chair with legs that cross, in front and back, to form an x-shape and that continue as a support for the arm. Named for the great Italian poet, Dante Alighieri. Also called Dantesca chair.

Dantesca chair (DAHN te skuh CHAYR)
See *Dante chair.*

Dante chair

Darby and Joan settee
An 18th-century English settee designed with a double chair back. Probably named after the characters, Darby and Joan, in an 18th-century English ballad. Sometimes referred to as a Darby and Joan chair.

darnick
A 16th-century worsted wool fabric originally made at Dorneck, the Dutch name for Tournay, France. Also called Darnick or Dorneck.

daub (DAWB)
A plaster-like material, generally made with mud and straw or animal hair. It was commonly used as an infill material over wattle to form the walls of medieval timber-framed structures.

Daum (DAHM)
A French glass-making family most famous for their Art Nouveau work.

dauphine (doh FAN)
A silk fabric with a matte finish that was stylish in late 18th-century France.

davenport
A small early 19th-century English writing desk featuring a sloping

davenport

lift-top with a side drawered base. Also a 20th-century term for a large upholstered sofa. The former named for a Captain Davenport, the later for the furniture manufacturing firm of Irving, Casson & Davenport.

davenport bed
A convertible sofa bed.

davenport sofa
A convertible sofa bed.

davenport table
A narrow table that is placed behind a sofa not used along a wall.

daybed
A chaise lounge, rest bed, or other elongated seating used during the day for napping and relaxing. Commonly seen in the late 17th century and early 18th century of England and France.

daylighting
The practice of using windows and other openings to provide direct or indirect light to a space.

dead seat or dead back
An upholstered piece of furniture that does not contain springs in the seat or the back.

deal
English and Early American word for pine, especially relative to boards of the wood when used as the base for veneering.

decalcomania (de kah LOH may nee-uh)
A late 18th-century transfer technique that was a substitute for painting furniture. Popular during the early 1800s in America and commonly seen on Hitchcock chairs.

decanter
A vessel used to pour off liquids, such as wine, usually made of crystal, glass, or metal.

decanter stands
Coasters meant to hold decanters.

decastyle (De kah stiyl)
A building, also known as a portico, that has ten columns supporting it.

deception bed
An early American cabinet that hid a bed.

deck
A roofless, planked, wooden structure that extends off an existing building.

deck chair
See *Kaare Klint deck chair*. See *Kaare Klint, 1888–1954, in the Architects, Artists, and Designers Appendix*.

deckle edge
A ripped edge that looks like handmade paper.

deconstructivism or deconstruction
Architecture that made extreme examples of the Constructivist; has frequent references to popular culture, technology, common materials, and revealing structure.

décor (du KOR)
The style of the interior furnishings.

Decorated period
A late 13th- to mid 14th-century period of English Gothic architecture characterized by elaborate geometric or florid tracery, stellar vaulting, and ballflowers.

Decorated Queen Anne period
Early English style known as Georgian. Key elements were cabriole legs, rounded top rails, fiddle-shaped splats, claw-and-ball feet, and generally curved forms that were enriched in scale and heavily adorned with carvings. See also *Queen Anne Style*.

decorative drapes
Drapes that do not move. They are hung so they open in the center and are held back on the sides.

découpage (de koh PAHJ)
Art made from combining images, scraps of cloth, and other materials.

decumanus maximus (DEK uu maan us MAAK su mus)
The main street in a Roman city.

Delft (DELFT)
A highly glazed pottery from Delft, Holland, usually blue and white in color.

Della Robbia
In ceramics, richly modeled, polychromed, enameled terra-cotta or faience named after 15th-century Florentine family of sculptors and ceramists.

Della Robbia

demicelure (DE mee se lur)
A tester that does not extend to the foot of the bed.

demidome (DE mee dohm)
A half dome that is found on top of cupboards.

demi-lune (DE mee loon)
A half circle plan commonly used in furniture design.

demimetope (DE mee me tohp)
A half metope.

demi-patera (DE mee pah TAYR uh)
A half patera used on tables from the 18th century.

demi-lune table

demoiselle (dem wah ZEL)
Used to hold headdresses that were fitted to a woman's head.

demoiselle a atourner (dem wah ZEL ah' ah tur nay)
A table dressing that was also a Gothic wig stand.

demotic (de MO tik)
A simplified writing form related to Egyptian hieratic.

den

A room used as a retreat or informal study commonly seen in residential architecture.

deng (DENG)

A solid-sided Chinese stool.

deng'gua yi (DENG' GWAH YEE)

An armless Chinese chair with a curved yoke rail, used as a lamp hanger, resembling an official's hat.

denim

A heavy cotton cloth originally called serge de Nimes.

deng'gua yi

dentil

A projecting rectangular block resembling a tooth and used as a repeating ornament on crown molding and cornices. Often associated with Greek Revival and Colonial Revival architecture. See *illustration in the Motifs/Ornaments Appendix*.

dentil course

A row of dentils generally seen with a cornice. Also called a dentil band.

dentil molding

Small blocks that resemble teeth. Used as molding.

dependency

A small building commonly flanking larger American Georgian structures.

depressed arch

See *four-centered arch*.

Derbyshire chair (DUR bee sheer CHAYR)

A type of Jacobean chair.

desk

A table sometimes with drawers that was made for writing.

desk box

A small box that carries important papers and writing materials. Eventually they became larger and a part of the desk itself.

Deskey console

See *Donald Deskey console*. See *Donald Deskey, 1894–1989, in the Architects, Artists, and Designers Appendix*.

desonamentado (DE son ah men tah doh)

Spanish term for without ornament. A severely austere style of architecture and decoration developed during the 16th and 17th centuries in Spain.

desserte (DE sur tay)

A French serving table. See also *buffet* and *credence*.

desserte

De Stijl (DE STIYl)

(1917–1931) A Dutch word literally translated as "the style"; the name given to an art movement influenced by cubism; also the name for a Dutch magazine published between 1917 and 1928 and edited by Theo van Doesburg that was linked to designers, architects, and artists of the style.

deu-darn (DOO DAHRN)

A type of Welsh press cupboard.

Deutcher Werkbund (DU chur WURK bund)

A German organization (1917–1931) led by influential Bauhaus members who sought to bridge the gap between art and industry.

dhurries (DU reez)

Flat-woven carpets from India.

diaconicon (diy KOH uh kon)

A room that stored vestments, books, and other items needed for church services.

diaeta (diy AY tu)
A place to rest during the day in a Roman house.

diamond cut
Beveled edge on glass.

diamond matched veneer
A continuous molding that consists of rounded diamond shapes.

diamond ornament
A carved diamond pattern commonly used to ornament Tudor furniture.

diamond or wire chair
See *Harry Bertoia diamond or wire chair*. See *Harry Bertoia, 1915–1978, in the Architects, Artists, and Designers Appendix*.

diamond point
Straight-grained wood that has been diagonally cut and assembled to produce a diamond pattern.

diamondwork masonry
Casework with a diamond pattern that was often used in 17th-century France.

diao tian (DI Tee in)
A Chinese lacquer technique employing a carved design that is painted afterward.

diapering
A repeating pattern employing diamond shapes, commonly used during medieval times. See *illustration in the Motifs/Ornaments Appendix*.

diaphanie (DIY ah faan ee)
A common 19th-century technique overlaying glass with transparent designs in order to imitate stained glass.

diaphragm arch
A transverse wall-bearing arch that provides a firebreak by forming a partial wall dividing the ceiling of a nave.

diatreta (DIY ah tre tuh)
An ancient Roman glass vessel with an outer undercut layer that stands out from the main body. See also *cage cup*.

die
The space between the cornice and base of a pedestal.

diffuser
Stones used on an exterior wall edge with two finished sides. Also called diffusing shield.

diffusing glass
Glass with different patterns to reduce the transparency.

dime novel
Popular short stories published for young people between WWI and WWII.

dimensional stability
The ability of a material to hold its shape.

dimity (di MI ty)
The small decrease in size of a column's top made to overcome optical illusion.

dimmer
A device that controls the brightness of a light.

dinanderie (de NAAN dur ee)
An alloy of copper, tin, and lead that was a precursor to pewter.

dinette table
Small dining table often used in a kitchen.

dinette table

ding gui (DING GWEE)
A Chinese hat cupboard.

dining table
Tables made for eating meals.

Diocletian window
(DIY oh klee shun WIN doh)
A large semicircular window divided into three lights by vertical mullions. Named after the windows found at the Roman Baths of Diocletian and revived by Palladio. Also known as a thermae window.

diorite (DI Yor iyt)
A dark, speckled stone commonly used in preclassical sculpture of Egypt and Assyria.

dip dyeing
A textile dyeing process that involves dipping pieces into dye after they are woven.

dip seat
A seat also called a dropped seat or scoop seat. See *scoop seat.*

diphros (DIY frohs)
A stool without arms or back of Greek origin.

diphros okladias (DIY frohs OH klay dee-us)
Folding stool from Greece.

diprostyle (DIY proh stiyl)
A classical porch with two rows of columns.

dipteral
A four-legged Greek stool.

diptych
Two-panel screen that is hinged.

direct lighting
A lighting technique focused on distributing light directly to a surface.

Directoire Style (dee REK twahr STIYL)
A late 18th-century Neoclassical Style that served as a transitional period between Louis XVI and Empire.

Directory
The governing body of France during the Directoire Style (1795–1799).

discharge printing
A textile printing technique using bleaching agents to remove color.

diphros

dished
A term applied to the sunken areas in the top surface of card tables, used to hold money or candles.

dished corner
A hollowed out form made by turning.

disk foot
A small, flattened, ball-shaped or pad foot of the Queen Anne Style.

disk sander
A machine with a rotating disk of sand paper used to smooth rough surfaces.

disk turning
Flat, circular turning used to embellish furniture.

distant colors
Colors that recede, creating the illusion of space.

distemper
Opaque watercolor paints made of pigment, water, and an egg emulsion.

distressed
Furniture that shows scratches and holes as a result of age.

distressing
Furniture made to look old by adding imperfections often seen with age.

distyle (DI stiyl)
A building with two columns in front.

Ditzel bench for two
See *Nanna Ditzel bench for two.* See *Nanna Ditzel, 1923–2005, in Architects, Artists, and Designers Appendix.*

divan (di VAAN)
A long armless and backless sofa of the 19th century, evolved from the Turkish tazar.

divani de portego (DE vahn ee DE POR te goh)
A settee in Italian.

divider
Furniture used to separate an area of a room.

diwan (DE wahn)
An Islamic raised platform with cushions for sitting.

do (DOO)
A Japanese Shinto shrine hall.

dobby weave
A fabric woven with a small geometric pattern.

document drawer
A small vertical drawer often found on the interior of a desk or secretaire.

documentaries
Wallpapers or fabrics with authentic period designs.

dodecastyle (doh DEK ah stiyl)
A building with 12 columns in front.

doe's foot
See *cloven foot, hoof foot,* and *pied de bi.*

doe's foot leg
A long S-shaped leg of the Louis XV period.

dog ear
Projecting rectangular molding commonly used on door heads and paneling in Early Georgian interiors.

dog grate
A fire grate that is moveable.

dog-legged staircase
A set of stairs where the upper flight is directly above the lower.

dog's tooth
An Early Gothic ornamental motif that consists of four leaves radiating up from a central point and resembling a canine tooth.

dog-tooth bond
A masonry pattern using bricks laid with corners projecting from the face.

dole cupboard
A food cupboard commonly used in churches during the Middle Ages.

dolmen
A large prehistoric rock structure composed of two upright stones and a horizontal cap stone.

dole cupboard

dolphin
A marine mammal that is a motif in Stone and Bronze Age carving Also seen in 18th-century French and English Regency furniture.

dolphin hinge
A type English furniture hardware named for its dolphin-like shape, commonly used on secretaires.

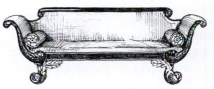

dolphin sofa

dolphin sofa
A French Empire sofa with an arm that extends to form a foot in a dolphin-like shape.

doma (Do mah)
A Japanese room with compact dirt floors meant for work and cooking.

dome
A roof made of arches that come from a center point. Various types of domes include double, elliptical, geodesic, hemispherical, imperial, melon, onion, radial, saucer, semicircular, semidome, and turkish.

dome bed
A bed that is covered by a dome or arch.

dome light
An opening in a dome.

domed top
Half round tops of cabinets during the Queen Anne period.

domestic
Products that are used in the same country they are made in.

domino
A term used early on to denote wallpaper. See also *domino wallpaper*.

domino wallpaper
Popular 16th-century wallpaper imitating marble and produced by the Dominotiers in France.

dominotiers (DAH min oh teerz)
Sixteenth-century makers of domino papers in France.

domos (DOH mohs)
The Mycenaean hearth room.

domus (DOH mus)
A town house in Rome. Usually reserved for the upper class. Also the name of a popular Italian architecture magazine.

domus de statio (DOH mus DE STAH shee oh)
An Italian residence that commonly included a workshop on the ground floor.

Donald Deskey console
Early 20th-century console by American designer Donald Deskey, one of the leading proponents of the Streamlined Modern Style, which emphasized curving forms and long horizontal lines as seen in the console's wooden body and base with boldly curved flat aluminum support See *Donald Deskey, 1894–1989, in the Architects, Artists, and Designers Appendix.*

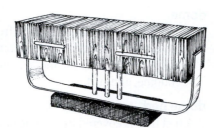

Donald Deskey console

donjon (DON jahn)
The tall, inner tower that was used as a stronghold in medieval castles. See also *keep*.

doratura (DOR ah tur uh)
Italian gilding.

doreur (Dor ur)
French for a person who applies gilt finish to wood or metal.

Doric Order
The oldest and most simplistic of the three Greek orders of architecture, characterized by a fluted column shaft, a capital formed by an echinus and abacus, and triglyphs and metopes within the frieze. See *illustration in the Architectural Orders Appendix.*

dormer window
A window that projects past the surface of the roof.

dormeuse (DOH my uus)
A chaise lounge resembling an upholstered deck chair.

dorure (DO rur)
French term for gilding, gold leaf, or gilt.

dos-à-dos (DOHS-AH-DOHS)
A chair designed with two seats facing in opposite directions. Literally translates from French as "back to back."

dosser (DOS ur)
A medieval term for fabric hanging between a wall and a piece of furniture such as a throne or bench.

dosseret (dor sur AY)
A tapered block positioned on top of a column capital during the Byzantine era. Also called an impost block.

dossier (DAW see-ay)
French for the backrest or splat of a chair.

dossier plat (DAW see-ay PLAAT)
French for a flat-backed chair.

dotted swiss

A cotton fabric that has tiny and regularly spaced dots.

double bed

A bed that is 53″ wide and 75″ long.

double bonnet

An American term for a double segmental arch used as a pediment on tallboys, secretaires, and cabinetry. Termed as "domed" or "hooded" in England. See also *hood* and *hooded top*. See *illustration in the Pediments Appendix*.

double C scroll leg

Distinctive legs with a double C-shape, commonly found on pedestal-based pie crust tables designed by Thomas Chippendale. See *illustration in the Legs Appendix*.

double chair

See *courting chair*.

double chest

Two chests stacked on one another.

double shoulder miter joint

In woodworking, a conventional-looking miter joint with a supporting shoulder or lap joint on the inside of each piece being connected. See *illustration in the Joints Appendix*.

double stretcher Flemish bond

In masonry, two stretchers that alternate with a single header. Centered over the next course of stretchers is a header.

double-acting hinge

A hinge that allows a door to open 180 degrees.

double-decker bed

Two beds stacked on top of each other.

double-hung sash

A window divided into two sliding sections.

doubled column

A double shafted column that shares a single capital.

doublet (DUB let)

A pair of patterns, one usually in reverse of the other.

Douglas fir

A curly grained wood that is often used for plywood.

dougong (dow GONG)

The Chinese system of wooden brackets that hold up the roof.

douppioni (DOO pee-oh nee)

Silk that is obtained from two silk worms that have spun a single cocoon. Also called duppion.

dovetail

A tail-shaped projection that interlocks with another piece to create a joint. See *illustration in the Joints Appendix*.

dowel

A peg that is used to hold two pieces of wood together.

dowelled joint

In woodworking, a joint secured by one or more dowels. See *illustration in the Joints Appendix*.

dower chest

A chest reserved for the custom of supplying items for a bride. Also called a hope chest.

down

Soft feathers from young birds or the insulating layer of older fowl used as upholstery filling.

down light

A light source that points downward, often recessed in a ceiling.

draft

A technical line drawing of a proposed project.

dragee (DRAH jay)

Large Tudor wing-back chair, which later became upholstered.

dragon's claw foot

An 18th-century English furniture foot representing a scaly dragon's claw which often held a ball. The motif likely stems from the Orient, symbolizing the power and intelligence of the dragon holding the pearl of wisdom.

dragon's head

A carved motif on Oriental furniture. Also found on Tudor and Jacobean chests as a symbol for Wales.

drake foot

An 18th-century English furniture foot with three prominently ribbed toes that resembles a duck's foot.

drape

A term that describes how a fabric hangs.

draperies

Pieces of fabric used to cover, dress, or hang beside a door or window.

draps de raz (DRAHPZ de rahz)

Spanish term for tapestry.

draught chair (DRAWFT chayr)

A late 18th-century chair with characteristic wings or ears designed to protect the user from drafts. See also *wing chair*.

draw curtain

A curtain that can be pulled across a rod by manual or mechanical means.

draw leaf table

See *draw table*.

draw runner

A supporting piece for the drop lid or fall front of a desk. Also called a draw slip.

draw slip

Another name for draw runner. See also *draw runner*.

draw table

A table that can be extended by the two detachable leaves that rest under the primary top when not in use. Also called a draw leaf table or draw-top table.

draw table

draw-top table

See *draw table*.

drawing book chair back

A chair back extensively copied by American cabinetmakers from Thomas Sheraton's book published in 1791 called *The Cabinet-maker and Upholsterer's Drawing Book*.

drawing

Art representing three-dimensional objects on a two-dimensional surface with pencil, pen, or crayon as opposed to paint.

drawing room

A comfortable room in which people would sit and relax after dinner. Abbreviated from withdrawing room.

drawing table

A table originally from the 18th century with an adjustable top designed for artists and designers.

drawn work

An openwork fabric pattern created by pulling warp and weft threads out or to the side.

dress

To smooth the surface of stone or wood.

dressed sizes

The actual size of lumber, smaller than the nominal dimensions.

dresser

A chest of drawers used for the storage of clothing; usually has a mirror over it.

dressing box

A box designed to hold toiletries.

dressing mirror

A small mirror on a stand, often incorporating drawers within the base.

dressing room

A small room that has a closet and mirror arrangement.

dressing table

A table designed to be used while dressing or applying makeup, generally containing storage for toiletries and often an attached mirror. See also *dresser*.

dressoir (DRE swar)

French for dresser. Originally a 16th-century cabinet with a closed cupboard designed to hold dishes. See also *dresser*.

dressoir de salle à manger (DRE swar DE SAL AH' MAHN jay)

A late Gothic sideboard with open shelves.

drier

A chemical that can be added to paint to produce quicker drying time.

drill

A heavy twill fabric that resembles denim.

drinking table

See *horseshoe table* and *hunt table*.

drip mold

A molding that projects over the top frame of a door and down the sides. See also *hoodmold*.

dressing box

dressing table

dressoir

drip stone

See *drip mold* or *hoodmold*.

dromos (DROH mus)

A processional passage leading to an ancient building. Also called a Greek race course.

drop

A decorative pendant that hangs beneath a vertical support, often pineapple or acorn-shaped in form.

drop front

A desk front designed to fall or drop forward for use.

drop handle

The hardware pull of a drawer or door that hangs on the surface like a pendant.

drop-in seat

An upholstered seat that can be removed from the chair frame for easy reupholstery and repair. See also *drop seat*.

drop-leaf

The hinged leaf or flap of a table.

drop-leaf table

A table with hinged leaves or flaps designed to enlarge a tabletop when needed.

drop-leaf table

drop lid

The hinged top or front of a desk that serves as a writing surface. When closed, the drop lid conceals a desk's inner compartment of drawers and pigeon holes.

drop ornament

A pendant ornament that extends down below the underframe of a piece of furniture; commonly used during the late 17th and early 18th centuries. See also *drop pendant*.

drop pendant
Also called a drop ornament. See also *drop ornament.*

dropped ceiling
A secondary ceiling suspended below the main or structural ceiling designed to hide mechanical and electrical elements of a building or create a more intimate and efficient environment.

dropped seat
Also called a dip seat or scoop seat. See *scoop seat.*

drugget (DRU get)
A cheap floor cloth designed to protect a more expensive floor covering beneath it.

drum
In furniture, a cylindrical extension below a foot. In architecture, a cylindrical block used to form a column or a cylindrical wall bearing a dome or cupola.

drum table
A drum-shaped table, often containing drawers within the table's apron and a leather top, generally mounted on a tripod base.

drum table

drum tower
An ancient Chinese clock tower that used water clocks and drums to announce times during the day and bells at night.

drunkard's chair
A popular Queen Anne period chair with a seat wide enough for one person to sprawl and two people to sit very closely. Also known as a lover's chair. See also *chair and a half.*

dry sink
A 19th-century kitchen cabinet designed to hold a pitcher and wash basin.

drypoint engraving
An etching made by scratching a design into a metal plate with a hard steel pencil. See also *intaglio engraving.*

drywall
A common name for gypsum board, a material used for interior walls. See also *gypsum board.*

dual bed
See *Hollywood bed.*

dual-purpose unit
A multi-use item like a convertible couch.

duchesse (DOO ches)
See *chaise longue.*

duchesse bed (DOO ches BED)
A bed without tall posts with a canopy that attaches to a wall.

duchesse brisée (DOO ches bree ZAY)
A French chaise lounge with a detached foot stool.

duchesse en bateau (DOO ches AHn BAA toh)
A one- to three-piece French duchesse with a short rounded back.

duchesse lace (DOO ches LAYS)
See *Valenciennes lace.*

duck
A cotton fabric similar to canvas.

duchesse bed

dry sink

duck foot

Sometimes used incorrectly for a Flemish and English furniture with a webbed foot. See also *drake foot*.

dumbwaiter

A three-tired and footed table from the 18th century used to serve food. See also *rafraichissoir* and *servante*.

dumbwaiter

dummy board figures

A decorative board cut into silhouettes of various human and animal figures, popular during the 17th and 18th centuries.

dun

A barrel-shaped Chinese stool with openings along the sides.

Duncan Phyfe armchair

Federal Style armchair designed by late 18th- and early 19th-century American cabinetmaker Duncan Phyfe. Many of Phyfe's chairs exhibit graceful, refined lines with either splayed, curule, straight, or tapered legs. Chair backs commonly displayed an X-shaped crossbar, a single crosspiece, a lyre-shaped splat, or a scroll-shaped splat. See *Duncan Phyfe, 1768–1854, in the Architects, Artists, and Designers Appendix.*

Duncan Phyfe armchair

Duncan Phyfe card table

A variety of card tables were designed by late 18th- and early 19th-century American cabinetmaker Duncan Phyfe in the Neoclassic Style. They are typified by beautifully figured veneers, splayed legs, and brass toecaps in the shape of animal paws. All open to reveal a felt insert used for playing cards. See also *card table*. See *Duncan Phyfe, 1768–1854, in the Architects, Artists, and Designers Appendix.*

Duncan Phyfe card table

Duncan Phyfe cornucopia leg sofa

Greek Revival sofas were a popular design of the late 18th- and early 19th-century American cabinetmaker Duncan Phyfe. They were characteristically composed of exposed wood trim of mahogany or cherry, gently rounded sleigh arms, and a straight back with low relief carvings of neoclassical motifs, such as swags along the top rail. Many legs took the form of a cornucopia in shape, and feet were generally capped by brass toecaps resembling paw feet. See *Duncan Phyfe, 1768–1854, in the Architects, Artists, and Designers Appendix.*

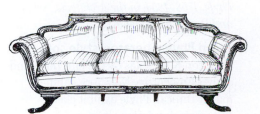

Duncan Phyfe cornucopia leg sofa

abcdefghijklmnopqrstuvwxyz

Duncan Phyfe lyre-back chair

A variety of Empire chairs were designed by late 18th- and early 19th-century American cabinetmaker Duncan Phyfe. His most popular design featured finely carved lyre backs with strings of brass or bone. The chairs also featured a gracefully rolled back, saber legs, and paw feet See also *lyre-back chair*. See *Duncan Phyfe, 1768–1854, in the Architects, Artists, and Designers Appendix*.

Duncan Phyfe sewing table

A variety of sewing tables were designed by late 18th- and early 19th-century American cabinetmaker Duncan Phyfe. These neoclassically styled pieces were designed to hold various needlework supplies. Most had a hinged top under which sat one or two drawers, all often supported by a pedestal base with three splayed legs terminated by brass paw feet. See *Duncan Phyfe, 1768–1854, in the Architects, Artists, and Designers Appendix*.

Duncan Phyfe Sheraton-style sofa

Sheraton-Style sofas by the late 18th- and early 19th-century New York cabinetmaker Duncan Phyfe exhibit classically restraint defined by a rectilinear silhouette, eight straight legs, and straight top rail containing low relief carvings of swags and other neoclassic motifs. See *Duncan Phyfe, 1768–1854, in the Architects, Artists, and Designers Appendix*.

Duncan Phyfe lyre-back chair

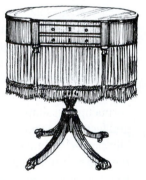

Duncan Phyfe sewing table

Duncan Phyfe Sheraton-style sofa

Duncan Phyfe table

A round table with a birdcage base supported by splayed, reeded legs and capped by brass toecaps in the shape of animal paws by late 18th- and early 19th-century New York cabinetmaker Duncan Phyfe. See *Duncan Phyfe, 1768–1854, in the Architects, Artists, and Designers Appendix*.

Duncan Phyfe table

Duncan Phyfe tall case clock

A neoclassical tall wooden clock designed by late 18th- and early 19th-century American cabinetmaker Duncan Phyfe. The case features an arch-topped bonnet with a glazed door flanked by reeded columns, a waist with an arched-topped door with carved fan motif, and a square-paneled base supported by bracket feet. See also *grandfather clock*. See *Duncan Phyfe, 1768–1854, in the Architects, Artists, and Designers Appendix*.

dust board

A thin strip of wood separating the drawers of a chest, used to keep dust out. Also called dust bottom.

dust ruffle

A piece of fabric designed to extend from a mattress to the floor in order to keep dust out.

Dutch cross bond

In masonry, a pattern that has stretchers, then a single header.

Dutch cupboard

A massive, unpretentious Dutch cupboard with simplified Baroque Style commonly seen in the American homes of 17th-century Dutch immigrants. The cupboards were generally painted and incorporated crude carvings and turned elements with simple cabriolet legs that terminated in a spoon, club, or pad foot. See also *kas*.

Duncan Phyfe tall case clock

Dutch door

A door that has independent upper and lower sections.

Dutch dresser

A large cupboard or buffet with an upper unit composed of open shelves for displaying plates. See also *Welsh dresser*.

Dutch foot

A popular 17th- or 18th-century furniture foot with a pad or spoon shape.

Dutch gable

A gable designed with sides containing one or more curves that rises above the wall to form a parapet. Also called a Flemish gable.

Dutch leg

A turned leg that has round forms spaced with oval dishes, often terminating with a flat oval foot.

Dutch settle

A wooden settle with a back that is often hinged so that it can be lowered to serve as a table.

duvet (doo VAY)

French for a comforter traditionally filled with down and designed with a removable cover. Present-day forms may be filled with other materials, such as silk or synthetic fibers.

duvet cover (doo VAY KU vur)

The removable cover for a duvet.

dwarf wall

A partition that is level with the floor but does not reach the ceiling.

dwelling tower

A multistoried medieval building constructed of stone below and wood above for defense purposes, also containing a battlement.

dyeing

The process of coloring yarn and fabric with different pigments.

Dymaxion (diy MAAK see-on)

A brand name created by designer architect inventor Richard Buckminster Fuller for industrial designs which give maximum performance at maximum economy. See *Richard Buckminster Fuller, 1895–1983, in the Architects, Artists, and Designers Appendix.*

dynasty

A series of rulers generally connected by family.

abcdefghijklmnopqrstuvwxyz

E

eagle

A popular motif first used by the Persians, Assyrians, Egyptians and continuing into modern times. Greek mythology portrayed the eagle as the companion of Zeus. It depicted the military standard during the Roman, French Empire, and American Federal Styles, and was a symbol of St. John the Evangelist in ecclesiastical art. It was also notable during the Renaissance and as a double-headed motif during the Byzantine era.

Eames Birch LCW (EEMZ BURCH LCW)

See *Charles Eames LCW chair. See Charles Eames, 1907–1978, in the Architects, Artists, and Designers Appendix.*

Eames DAR dining arm chair (EEMZ DAR DYN ing AARM CHAYR)

See *Charles Eames DAR dining arm chair. See Charles Eames, 1907–1978, in the Architects, Artists, and Designers Appendix.*

Eames lounge chair (EEMZ LOWNJ CHAYR)

See *Charles Eames lounge chair. See Charles Eames, 1907–1978, in the Architects, Artists, and Designers Appendix.*

Eames Time Life stools (EEMZ TIYM-LIYF STOOLZ)

See *Charles Eames Time Life stools. See Charles Eames, 1907–1978, in the Architects, Artists, and Designers Appendix.*

ear

The extension of a chair's crest rail past the vertical back supports, especially prominent with the Chippendale Style; or the decorative overlaps of upright pieces of surround molding on doors or windows.

Early American

The 17th to early 18th-century (c. 1608–1720) American style of architecture, furniture, and art. All furniture is constructed of native woods, and early forms are very crude because colonists were focused on survival. Later, although provincial in nature, it is reminiscent of the Jacobean, Carolean, and William and Mary Styles of their homeland.

Early English Style or period

Name given to the earliest English Gothic architecture from c. 1170–1240. Also known as the "Lancet," "First Pointed," and "Early Plantagenet" period. It is characterized by tall lancet windows, projected buttresses, pinnacles, and steep-pitched roofs.

earpiece

In 18th-century English and French furniture designs, a scroll or volute extending from the knee of a cabriole leg and terminating at the underframing; or when a lintel extends past its sides, the overlapping extension is known as an earpiece.

earthenware

Pottery made of coarse clay that is not impervious to liquids upon firing unless glazed.

Eastlake desk

See *Charles Locke Eastlake desk. See Charles Locke Eastlake, 1836–1906, in the Architects, Artists, and Designers Appendix.*

easy chair

Generally based on the bergère or wing chair, a comfortable chair designed for rest and relaxation.

Easy Edges rocking chair

See *Frank O. Gehry easy edges rocking chair. See Frank O. Gehry, 1928– , in the Architects, Artists, and Designers Appendix.*

eaves (EEVZ)

The overhang of a roof at the top of the wall.

ébéniste (AY ben eest)

A term developed in the early French Renaissance (15th and 16th centuries) to signify a cabinetmaker who worked with ebony, a popular veneer wood of the time. Later in the 18th century, a term synonymous with a skilled craftsman of marquetry and veneer.

ebonized

Wood that has been stained black to resemble ebony.

ebony

A hard, dense, brown-black colored wood popular for furniture and for veneer and inlay work during the Louis XIV and Empire periods of France. This black or gabon ebony comes from Africa. The ebony popular in 19th-century Victorian furniture is reddish-brown in color with black stipes and is called Macassar ebony after the town that exported it. See also *coromandel wood.*

ebony, Gaboon (E be nee GA boon)
A brown-black colored wood also called black ebony. See also *ebony*.

ebony, Macassar (E be nee mak ah SAR)
A reddish-brown colored wood with black stripes; also called coromandel. See also *ebony*.

echinus (ee KIY nuhs)
Located beneath the abacus and above the column shaft, the rounded, oval-shaped molding of a Doric capital.

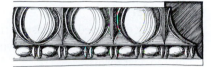
echinus

eclectic (e KLEK tik)
Evocative of multiple sources or styles.

eclecticism (e KLEK ti sizm)
A term used to describe a style combining previous styles, art forms, or motifs. Quite popular during the Victorian era.

École Des Beaux Arts (AY kohl DAY BOHZ ART)
Name of the leading 19th-century French art institute that had great influence on tastes and styles of the period.

écran (Ekrahn)
French for screen.

écran à cheval (E krahn AH she VAHL)
French for a fire screen composed of a frame with sliding panel.

écran à coulisse (E krahn AH KOO lees)
French for a cheval or fire screen.

écran à éclisse (E krahn AH Ekless)
French for pole screen. See also *pole screen*.

edging (E jing)
The term used to describe the narrow decorative band found on the rim of porcelain or other objects. It is called banding with respect to furniture and translates to filage in French.

Edo (EE doh)
Old Japanese word for Tokyo.

Edwardian period
English period covering the reign of King Edward VII from 1901 to 1910 characterized by architectural revivals of the late 17th and early 18th centuries and furniture that mixed classic lines with curvilinear details.

Eero Aarnio cognac chair
Mid 20th-century chair (1962) with a fiberglass bowl-shaped seat mounted on a steel swivel pedestal base designed by Finnish designer Eero Aarnio. Originally manufactured by Stendig. Also called the Cognac Cup chair. See *Eero Aarnio, 1932– , in the Architects, Artists, and Designers Appendix*.

Eero Aarnio globe or ball chair
Iconic chair designed by Finnish designer Eero Aarnio in 1966. The chair is crafted out of fiberglass in a simple geometric ball form mounted on a steel pedestal base. The chair's scooped-out seating area creates a personal cocoon from the outside world. See *Eero Aarnio, 1932– , in the Architects, Artists, and Designers Appendix*.

Edwardian display cabinet

Eero Aarnio cognac chair

Eero Aarnio globe or ball chair

abcdefghijklmnopqrstuvwxyz

Eero Aarnio gyro chair

A lozenged-shaped chair named after a small sweet treat, created by Finnish designer Eero Aarnio in 1967. The chair's fiberglass construction enables indoor and outdoor use, yet comfortably supports the human body with a contoured depression as a seat. Also known as the pastil chair. See *Eero Aarnio, 1932–, in the Architects, Artists, and Designers Appendix.*

Eero Aarnio Gyro chair

Eero Saarinen tulip pedestal chair

Mid 20th-century chair (1956) designed by Eero Saarinen and manufactured by Knoll. It mimics the reductively simple lines of a tulip flower. A smooth, clean modern chair of molded fiberglass with a cast aluminum base. See *Eero Saarinen, 1910–1961, in the Architects, Artists, and Designers Appendix.*

Eero Saarinen Tulip Pedestal chair

Eero Saarinen tulip table

A simple yet elegantly proportioned round pedestal table designed by Eero Saarinen in the 1940s. The table was originally designed with a cast iron base and a variety of tops, including white marble. Today, the base is generally constructed of fiberglass. See *Eero Saarinen, 1910–1961, in the Architects, Artists, and Designers Appendix.*

Eero Saarinen tulip table

Eero Saarinen womb chair

An enveloping lap-like form created from a foam-wrapped, reinforced fiberglass shell set on slender, chrome-plated steel legs. The chair was created by Finnish designer Eero Saarinen and manufactured by Knoll in 1948 and is an example of the Scandinavian organic modern style. See *Eero Saarinen, 1910–1961, in the Architects, Artists, and Designers Appendix.*

Eero Saarinen Womb chair

egg and dart

A molding developed in Classical times composed of alternating egg or ovoid and pointed dart forms.

Egg chair

See *Arne Jacobsen egg chair.* See *Arne Jacobsen, 1902-1971, in the Architects, Artists, and Designers Appendix.*

egg crate

A metal or plastic grid used to diffuse light from a fluorescent fixture. Named as such because of its resemblance to a cardboard egg separator.

eggshell finish

A paint finish with a low, soft, dewy luster resembling an eggshell and considered semiflat.

églomisé   (e GLOH mee zay)

Painting or gilding on the reverse side of glass that often incorporates gold leaf.

égouttoir   (e goo TWAR)

French term for a provincial piece of furniture containing open rack shelves for drying and storing dishes.

egret

Same as aigrette. See also *aigrette.*

Egypt

A preclassical civilization often called the land of the Pharaohs after its mighty rulers. Many motifs and decorations from this time, such as the sphinx, obelisk, x-frame, lion's paw, lotus column, etc., are still used today.

Egyptian finish

A turquoise, glasslike ceramic finish created in ancient Egypt.

eiderdown (IY dur down)

The soft fluffy inner feathers obtained from large sea ducks, used as a high-end filling for cushions, pillows, and comforters.

eight-legged table

A type of 18th-century English gate-leg table, usually made of mahogany. See also *gate-leg table*.

Eileen Gray bibendum chair

An Iconic chair of the late 1910s composed of two semicircular, padded leather tubes on a frame of chrome-plated steel tubing by furniture designer and architect Eileen Gray. See *Eileen Gray, 1878–1976, in the Architects, Artists, and Designers Appendix*.

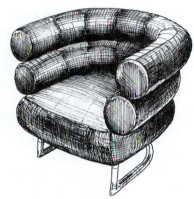

Eileen Gray bibendum chair

elbow chair

A chair designed with arms on which users can rest their elbows.

Elda chair

See *Joe Columbo Elda chair*.

electroplating

A electrical process for coating base metals with a thin, more valuable metal.

electrum

A natural alloy of gold and silver that contains a larger percentage of gold.

elevation

A flat, two-dimensional drawing of an interior or exterior wall, or cabinet face. This type of drawing does not foreshorten views as seen by the eye and is usually drawn to scale.

Elgin Marbles (EL jin MAR bulz)

A name given to the pediment sculptures of the Parthenon, on behalf of Lord Elgin, who had them removed to London's British Museum.

Elizabethan

Name given to the English Renaissance Style during the reign of Elizabeth I, 1558–1603.

Elizabethan bed

Typical Elizabethan Style bed with massive form and heavy cornice supported by four melon bulb laden posts. Other characteristics include profuse carving, columns, acanthus leaves, and arcaded arches. See also *acanthus leaf, cup and cover, melon bulb*, and *Elizabethan*.

Elizabethan bed

Elizabethan Gothic flower carving

Popular carved flower motif found in running borders on furniture of the Elizabethan era.

Elizabethan Gothic flower carving

Elizabethan shell carving

Common Elizabethan running border motif with carved scallop shell design made popular by travel to foreign seas.

Elizabethan shell carving

ell

See *three-quarter width*.

elliptical arch

An arch in the shape of half an ellipse.

elm

A strong, tough hardwood with a light, brownish red color with dark brown rings.

émaux de niellure (E moh de NIY ur)

French term for an enameling process in which lines are cut into metal and filled with enamel. Name stems from niello, a black compound commonly used to fill engraved designs.

emblem

A decorative symbol used in heraldry to denote a person or family, e.g., Napoleon's bee and Francis 1st's salamander. The emblems commonly appeared in carvings, embroideries, and painted panels.

emblema, pl. emblemata

A Roman mosaic design sold intact, within a tray, so that it could be carried and installed by less-skilled artisans.

embossed

A raised design created by stamping, hammering, or molding onto a surface. See also *repoussé*.

embossing

A textile design process that creates designs by passing fabric, such as velvet, through hot engraved rollers that press the design onto the surface. Also used with wood and other materials.

embroidery

An art developed in 16th-century Italy that decorates a fabric with raised designs of thread or yarn. Originally completed by hand, most embroidery today is machine produced.

Emile Gallé butterfly bed

Art Nouveau bed created in 1904 by French designer Emile Gallé with a headboard and footboard sculpted in the form of a butterfly with spread wings. See *Emile Gallé, 1846–1904, in the Architects, Artists, and Designers Appendix*.

Emile Gallé butterfly bed

Emile Gallé dragonfly table

Carved rectangular table with four legs in the shape of enormous dragonflies. The table was created by French Art Nouveau designer Emile Gallé in 1900. See *Emile Gallé, 1846–1904, in the Architects, Artists, and Designers Appendix*.

Emile Gallé dragonfly table

Emile-Jacques Ruhlmann cabinet

Cabinet of Macassar ebony with interlacing circle motif of inlaid ivory, designed by French Art Deco designer Emile-Jacques Ruhlman. See *Emile-Jacques Ruhlmann, 1879–1933, in the Architects, Artists, and Designers Appendix*.

empaistic (em PAY stik)

This process, developed before Boulle work, involves covering structural elements or sculpture with sheet metal that had been hammered in decorative patterns.

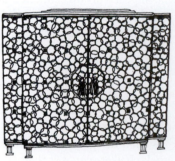

Emile-Jacques Ruhlmann cabinet

Empire

French Late Neoclassical style associated with the reign of Napoleon Bonaparte from 1804 to 1815. Also known as the Napoleonic period, it is characterized by its classical and Egyptian motifs. Charles Percier and Pierre Francios-Léonard Fontaine, the great practitioners of the style, created furniture and interiors during the period that glorified the emperor and his reign. The style was mimicked in middle-class Germany and Austria with a pared-down style called Biedermeier.

Empire bed

A typical 19th-century French bed with low sides and curved ends that was usually displayed with a long side set against the wall.

Empire chair

A typical 19th-century French bergère with tapered legs, barrel back, and neoclassic ormolu mounts.

Empire drape

A popular French 19th-century drapery treatment in which the fabric is caught at the top at points of equal distance, thereby creating rigid verticals with free-falling valleys forming in between.

Empire chair

empreintes veloutées (em pree ENT ve loo TAY)

The French term for flocked wallpapers and prints. See *flocked wallpaper*.

en cas or en case (AHN CAHS/ EN CAS)

A small French Louis XV style table generally found with a marble top with drawer and cupboard below. Similar to a table de chevet.

en charrette (AHN shah RET)

A 19th-century French term for last-minute work, derived from the practice of artists working on their paintings as they were carted for assessment at the École des Beaux Arts. Literally translated as "on the cart."

en ressaut (AHN re SOH)

The French term for an object connected to a wall or projecting from it.

en suite (AHN SWEET)

French for a matching set, i.e., part of a suite.

en tableau (AHN TA bloh)

A late 18th-century upholstery technique where the straight lines of a sofa or chair were defined with passamentarie such as gimp, braid, or cord.

en taille d'épargne (AHN TIY de PARN)

A French term for Champlevé enamel.

enamel

A colored glaze used as decoration for metal or ceramics that becomes hard and permanent after firing.

encarpus (en KAR pus)

A fruit or flower festoon used extensively during the Italian Renaissance, Louis XV, and Louis XVI periods on flat surfaces.

encaustic painting (en KAW stik PAYN ting)

A technique of painting that uses pigments mixed with hot wax.

encaustic tile (en KAW stik TIYL)

A ceramic tile inlaid with clay of a different color before firing. It was first popular during medieval times, then again in the 1830s in England, and the 1870s in America.

enclosing wall

An exterior, non-load-bearing wall within frame construction that does not have to be constructed between columns or piers like a curtain wall, yet is fastened to columns, piers, or floors.

encoignure (en KWAN yur)

The French term for a corner cupboard. See also *whatnot*.

encoignure

encorado (en koh RAH doh)

A Spanish chest lined or wrapped in leather.

encrier (en KREE ay)

In French, an inkwell.

end table

A small table used at the end of a sofa or settee, or at the side of a chair.

endive or endive marquetry (AHN deev MAR ke tree)

A sinuous marquetry design of the Queen Anne style akin to the leaves of the endive plant and similar to seaweed marquetry.

ends

Name given to the yarns found lengthwise in cloth.

enfilade (en fee LAHD)

Introduced during the reign of Louis XIV, a French term for the alignment of interior doors along a shared axis, thus creating a vista.

engaged column

A column attached to a wall by its rounded shaft. See also *half column*.

English bond

A brick pattern laid in alternating rows of headers and stretchers.

English cross bond

A brick pattern similar to English bond with alternating rows of headers and stretchers, where stretchers break joints consistently in successive courses.

English walnut

See *walnut, black*.

engraving

The process of incising a design into a hard material such as copper, steel, or wood with a sharp instrument. The resulting plate can then be inked to make impressions. Examples include woodcut, linocut, drypoint, mezzotint, aquatint, and intaglio.

engraving room

See *print room*.

enneastyle (EN i stiyl)

A building façade that contains nine columns across the front.

enrichment

A design that is repetitively painted or carved into moldings to enhance them. Examples include guilloche, egg and dart, honeysuckle, etc.

enfilade

engaged column

enroulements découpés (en rool mahn DAY koo pay)

See *strapwork*.

ensayalada (en say ah LAH dah)

A Spanish chest known for its fabric cover that is trimmed with braid.

ensemble (en SAHM bul)

The term for complimentary sets of furniture popular during the Baroque period.

entablature

In Classical architecture, the part of a building resting on columns, comprised of an architrave, frieze, and cornice.

entablature

entasis

The Greek refinement of augmenting a column shaft with an outward curve to counter the optical illusion that it appears to curve inward.

entrelac (EN tre lahk)

A French carved interlacing motif that resembles guilloche; seen during the Louis XVI period.

entresol (EN tre sohl)

French term for mezzanine.

envelope table

A late 18th-century table designed with four hinged envelope flaps that, when opened, enlarge the tabletop surface.

epergne (e PERN)

An ornamental stand with a central trumpet-like vase or branching arms that hold containers, commonly used as a table centerpiece.

entasis

envelope table

epistyle

Also known as an architrave. See also *architrave*.

epoxy

A very strong adhesive or sealant widely used to reinforce plastics. The liquid form needs a catalyst to activate it.

equipal (E keep ahl)

A popular Mexican patio chair with a cylindrical base made of cedar splits and a circular seat.

equipal

ergonomic design

A design based on the needs of humans in relation to the objects in their environment.

ergonomics

The science of studying humans with regard to health, safety, and welfare in their environments.

escabeau (esk ah BOH)

See *escabelle*.

escabelle (esk ah BEL)

An early French Renaissance stool supported on a trestle base.

escallop (e SKAL up)

See *scallop shell*.

escritoire (e SKREE twar)

French term for a small writing desk or table, or a secretaire.

escutcheons (e SKU chun)

A decorative plate for a keyhole or a shield with a heraldic device.

escritoire

espadaña (es PAH dahn yah)

A parapet at the gable end of a building that has a curved profile and arched openings for bells.

espagnolette (e SPAHN yo let)

A popular terminal ornament in 16th and 17th-century French furniture that employs a female bust as part of the support.

espalier (es PAHL yay)

Latticework used to tie fruit tree branches so that the trees assume decorative patterns.

espejos (es PAY hos)

A Spanish term for small pieces of mirror applied to a surface to reflect light.

estagnie (es TAH nyee)

A French provincial open hanging shelf, sometimes incorporating a drawer on the underside, designed to hold pewter utensils.

ester

A chemical used in the production of contemporary textiles.

estagnie

estipite (es TI pee tay)

A Spanish term for a pilaster with stacked sections that taper to the base, commonly used in the Spanish Baroque or Churriguersque styles.

estofado (es toh FAH doh)

A decorative technique that involves gold leafing an object, overpainting it, then scratching through the paint to expose a design in gold.

estrade (es TRAD)

Originally a term defining an alcove for a bed or sofa. It is also the French version of a Spanish estrado or drawing room.

estipite

estrado (e STRAHD oh)

A 17th-century term used for a raised platform or dais at one end of the main living space. Also refers to the main room of Spanish house.

étagère

Originally a French term used to describe an elegant hanging or standing display piece with open shelves. Also known as a whatnot.

etched glass

Glass that has been sandblasted to impart a milky, semi-opaque look. See also *frosted glass*.

etchings, etching

A form of intaglio engraving that uses a copper plate that has been engraved with a needle and etched with acid. The etched plate is then inked to make impressions. The 17th century was a noteworthy era for the art form. See also *intaglio engraving*.

Etruscan (e TRUS kan)

A term pertaining to a civilization in Italy before the Romans. Also infrequently used as another name for the Tuscan order.

étui (e TWEE)

French word for a box or container.

eucalyptus (yoo KAH lip tus)

A brown to pinkish-grey wood with strong distinguishing stripes used for modern decorative items and shipbuilding. See also *oriental wood* or *oriental walnut*.

even wash

Soft, even planes of light created from track, can, or eyeball spotlights.

éventail (e vahn TAY)

French word for fan.

évidence (e vee DAHNS)

A 16th-century term used for a dressoir or buffet in France.

étagère

evolute

A classical uninterrupted wave or Vitruvian scroll motif commonly used during the 18th century on bands, cornices, friezes, etc.

exedra, pl. exedrae (ek SEE drah)

In ancient Roman or Pompeian dwellings, a public room or semicircular recess for seating.

exonarthex (ek soh NAR theks)

An exterior portico, situated off the narthex or entrance vestibule, that spans the width of a building.

export wares

A term used to describe primarily Chinese and Japanese goods specifically made for sale abroad in the European and American markets.

Expressionism

An early 20th-century art movement characterized by emotional experience rather than physical reality.

extension table

A table containing a top that separates in the middle and extends outward in both directions to allow space for additional leaves to be added.

extrados (EKS tru dahs)

The outside curve of an arch. See also *intrados*.

extension table

eye

Term for the middle of an ionic volute.

eyebrow dormer

A dormer with a curiously shaped roof resembling an eyebrow, first appearing on medieval cottages, then popularized in the Shingle style.

eyebrow dormer

façade (FAH sahd)

French for frontage or face. In architecture, referring to one side or face of a building, generally the front.

façade d'honneur (FAH sahd DON ur)

French for the front façade of a building. See also *façade*.

facciata (FAH see ah tah)

Italian for the front face of a building.

face

In textiles, the side of a fabric designed to be used. In architecture, the front of a building. See also *façade*.

face brick

Brick used for exterior facing over cheaper base materials, designed with special consideration given to color and texture.

face fibers

The fibers that are most exposed to a carpet or rug's surface, thereby determining appearance and quality.

faced wall

A wall with a substructure and face of different materials that have been tied together.

facet (FAA Sit)

A flat surface on a gemstone or crystal.

facettes (FAA set)

French for the flat, vertical projections found between a column's shaft fluting.

fachwerk (FAHK verk)

German for half-timbering. See also *half-timber*.

facia (FAY sheeah)

See *fascia*.

facing

Finish material such as stone, brick, stucco, or wood used to cover or face a structure.

façonné (FAH sohn ay)

French for fancy weave. A fabric with a figured weave, usually made of silk or rayon.

faïence (FAY ehns)

French for a type of pottery originating from Faenza, Italy. An opaque, tin-glazed earthenware similar to majolica. See also *majolica*.

faille (FIYL)

A soft, finely ribbed fabric, often produced from silk, rayon, or cotton. Commonly used for trim, upholstery, and window treatments.

faldistorium

faldistorium (FOHL dist or ee um)

Latin for a faldstool. See also *faldstool*.

faldstool

A late 16th-century portable folding x-frame stool with armrests, used by a bishop when not sitting on the throne of his cathedral. Also used by the kings of England during coronation. From the old high German falden or falten, which means to fold, and stoul, a stool.

fall front

The hinged front of a desk that drops down to form a writing surface, yet when closed covers the inner compartment of drawers, doors, and pigeonholes. See also *cylinder front, drop front,* and *drop lid*.

falling table

See *gate-leg table*.

famille noire, verte, jaune, rose, etc. (FAH meel niWAHR, VAYRT, JOHN, ROHZ)

French for black family, green family, yellow family, and rose family. Names used to categorize Chinese porcelain with respect to the color palette.

abcdefghijklmnopqrstuvwxyz

fan motif

A semicircular motif resembling a fan, commonly seen in late 18th-century English and American furniture.

fan vault or vaulting

A type of vaulting resembling a fan in shape, with ribs that follow the same curvature and spacing, popular in Gothic architecture.

fanback chair

A chair with a back resembling a fan, originating in the designs of 18th-century France.

fancy chair

A simple, sturdy American chair of the early 18th century, derived from Sheraton's Klismos-based designs, characterized by hand-stenciled decorations and a rush or caned seat. Also called a Hitchcock chair, after Lambert Hitchcock, the most well-known maker of the chairs. See also *Hitchcock chair*.

fancy chair

fancy furniture

Small-scaled decorative American furniture, popular during the Federal period, ornamented with paint and stenciled designs. Although primarily associated with chairs, other items such as settees, nightstands, and cabinets were produced. See also *fancy chair*.

fanlight

A semicircular, sometimes semi-elliptical, window placed over a door, with panes of glass separated by radiating mullions.

farthingale chair   (FARth in gayl CHAYR)

A common English Renaissance side chair with a rectangular form, an upholstered seat and back, and four legs joined by low set stretchers. Aptly named for the chair's ability to accommodate the hooped farthingale skirts worn by fashionable ladies of the time.

farthingale chair

fasces   (FAAs ees)

A classical ornament composed of a bundle of rods bound around an axe with the blade projecting, commonly carried before ancient Roman magistrates as a symbol of authority.

fascia   (FAY shuh)

A flat band used as molding, commonly known as the projecting crown molding of a cornice. Also spelled facia.

fashion

A trend or fad, something in vogue or style.

fauces   (FAW seez)

The narrow passage from the atrium of a Roman house to the street.

faudesteuil   (foh DES toi)

Old form of the term faldstool. See also *faldstool* and *pliant*.

faun

A mythological creature with the body of a man and the horns, ears, tail, and sometimes legs of a goat. Commonly used as a decorative element during the French and Italian Renaissance, and again in the late 18th-century work by the Adam brothers.

fauteuil   (foh TOI)

A popular French armchair, first seen during the Louis XIV period, with open arms and an upholstered seat and back. See also *caquetoire*.

fasces

fauteuil a chassis   (foh TOI AH SHAAs eez)

A chair created during the Louis XIV period and constructed with a simple upholstered wooden frame inside the main elaborately carved frame. The inner frame could easily be removed for upholstering.

fauteuil

fauteuil à la reine (fo TOI AH LAH REN)

Literally translated from French as Queen's armchair. A variation of the fauteuil, with a high square back meant to be placed against a wall.

fauteuil de bureau (fo TOI DUH BYU roh)

French for a desk chair. Common in the Regence and Louis XV periods.

fauteuil en cabriolet (fo TOI AHN CAB ree-oh lay)

A small, portable French chair designed with a concave curve to the back to more closely fit the human form.

fauteuil en gondole (fo TOI AHN GAHN dol)

French for an armchair designed with the sweeping curved lines of a gondola. See also *gondola chair*.

fauve (FOHV)

Literally translated from French as wild beast. An art movement of the early 20th century characterized by bold colors, flat patterns, and wild distortions of form, typified by the work of Henri Matisse, Albert Marquet, André Derain, Maurice de Vlaminck, and Georges Rouault.

faux (FOH)

French for imitation. See also *faux finish*.

faux finish

Decorative painting technique to make one material resemble another; such as faux marble or faux bois (faux wood). Also used to mimic surface patinas such old plaster, etc.

faux rose (FOH ROHZ)

A wood with a pinkish brown color and distinctive striped figure. Also called Madagascar rosewood.

faux satine (FOH SAA teen)

A wood that looks similar to satinwood, acquired from the crotch of cypress trees found mainly in the southeast United States. The oily, soft wood has an amber to golden brown color and is commonly used for veneer work and for paneling.

favas (FAH vuz)

A design reminiscent of a honeycomb, used in decoration during the Louis XVI period.

favrile glass (FAH vreel GLAAS)

An art glass patented by Louis Comfort Tiffany in 1880 known for its beautiful iridescent color.

feather banding

A decorative band of inlay used on furniture with the grain laid diagonally to the main surface. See also *herringbone*.

feathered edge

A beveled or chamfered board edge that is thinner than the general board's thickness.

feathering

Gothic tracery created by the layout of cusps and foils. See also *foliation*.

Federal period

The late 18th- to early 19th-century American neoclassical period. Characterized by columns, pediments, and shallow arched fan lights over doors. The style was greatly influenced by the Hepplewhite, Sheraton, Adams, and Regency styles of England and associated with names in America such as Thomas Jefferson, Benjamin Latrobe, and Duncan Phyfe.

Federal secretaire

felt

A fabric made by matting or interlocking fibers of wool, mohair, and other furs through heat and pressure. Synthetic and vegetable fibers can also be added to the mix.

felt base rug

A durable, inexpensive, rug of the early 20th century, formed by coating an asphalted felt base printed with oil-based paint.

fender

A hearth accessory comprised of a low, metal, fence-like guard. When used in front of a fireplace, it stops logs or coals from falling out, thereby protecting floors and rugs.

fenestration (FEN e stray shun)

The arrangement and proportioning of openings, particularly windows and doors, within an architectural structure.

fenêtre à battants (fen EE tree ah be TAWN)

French for a pair of windows that extend to the floor and open like doors. See also *French window*.

feng shui (FUNG SHWAY)

A Chinese system of spatial orientation and arrangement based on the natural flow of energy (qi) taken into consideration when designing buildings and furniture. Literally translated as wind (feng) and water (shui).

fenster rose

German term for a rose window.

Feraghan rug (FAY Ruh ahn RUG)

A rug from the Feraghan district of Tehran with a dense pattern of stylized flowers.

ferrocement

A composite material of cement, sand, water, and wire mesh, used to create thin slabs utilized in construction.

ferroconcrete

Concrete reinforced with metal, usually steel or iron, to increase tensile strength.

ferronerie velvet (fay run AYR yay VEL vut)

French for ironwork velvet. An antique Venetian velvet designed with a pattern mimicking wrought iron.

ferrule (FER ul)

A metal cap used to cover the bottom of a wooden furniture leg for protection as well as reinforcement. Stems from the Latin word viriola, a small bracelet.

ferrule

festoon

A carved, molded, or painted ornamental garland of flowers, fruit, or foliage, often bound by ribbons, commonly seen in the Baroque and Neoclassic periods. Also a soft, curved window treatment introduced in the 18th century. See also *catenary, swag,* and *fruit festoon*.

festoon

fête galante (FET GALawnt)

French for gallant party. Scenes featuring elegantly attired people involved in lavish outdoor entertainment such as garden parties, picnics, or outdoor games, often seen in 18th-century murals, tapestries, and paintings.

fiadores (fee AH doh rees)

The curved wrought iron stretchers connecting diagonally opposite legs of Spanish furniture.

fiber rug

Common name for a reversible rug composed of a paper fiber called kraft. Also made of sisal fibers.

fiberboard

A construction material made by compressing fibers of wood into rigid, strong, 4' x 8' sheets used for partitions, ceilings, and the substructure of lower-quality furniture. Available under many trademark names such as Masonite, Homosote, Beaverboard, etc.

fiberglass

Glass in filament form used to make yarns, textiles, insulation, and other materials. When resin is added, it creates a reinforced plastic material used for molded seating and other furniture components.

fiddle-braced back
See *braced back*.

fiddleback
A violin-shaped splat commonly found on Queen Anne chairs of the American Colonial period. Also, a figured wood with ripples running at right angles to the grain, frequently found in maple and mahogany.

fiddle-string back
Name occasionally used for the back of a Windsor chair composed of multiple turned spindles that bear likeness to the strings of a fiddle. See also *arrow-back chair, comb back, Philadelphia chair*, and *stick-back*.

field bed
A small, portable, bed, with central arched canopy, designed for field use by military officers since the late 16th century. Also, an 18th-century Chippendale design with smaller bed posts and tester.

fielded panel
A panel set flush with the surrounding woodwork and outlined by a wide bevel.

figure
Designs, patterns, or distinctive markings found on the longitudinal surface of wood, resulting from its color, luster, texture, and grain.

filage (fee LAHJ)
French for edging.

fil d'argent (FEE DAR jawn)
French term for silver thread.

fil de bois (FEE DUH BWAH)
Veneer applied to furniture in a full, uninterrupted sheet, i.e., with no matching.

fil de chypre (FEE DUH SHEE Pruh)
French term for Cyprus thread.

fil d'or (FEE DOR)
French term for gold thread. In actuality, a gold-coated silver thread, often employed in tapestry works from the Middle Ages through the 18th century.

filament
A fine or thin spun thread or fiber that when plied together forms yarn.

filet (fi LAY)
A lace produced by embroidery on a knotted net ground. Also known as lacis, filet brodé, or poinct conté.

filigree (Fil u gree)
A delicate, lacelike pattern of openwork, usually created from fine wires of gold or silver.

filler
In textiles, another name for weft, the threads or yarn that extend from one selvage edge to another, across the width of a fabric. In woodworking, a material used to fill pores, grain, and irregularities before applying a final finish. See also *filling, pick*, and *weft*.

fillet (fi LAY)
A flat, narrow band molding often used to separate other moldings and between column fluting. See also *channel* and *fluting*. See *illustration in the Moldings Appendix*.

filling
In textiles, the thread or yarn that is shuttled between the warp and fills the area between knots or tufts in carpets and rugs.

fin de siècle (FAAN DUH see-E-kluh)
A French term for end of the century, especially associated with the end of the 19th and 20th centuries, particularly with the Art Nouveau Style.

finger joint
A woodworking joint composed of hinged interlocking parts or fingers. Often used on the leaves of drop-leaf tables. Also known as a comb joint. See also *knuckle joint*.

finial (FIN ee-ul)
A carved or turned ornament used to terminate a post or pediment and to define element intersections. Often in the form of an acorn, foliage, knob, mushroom, or pineapple.

finish

In woodworking, a treatment applied to protect the wood's surface, make it more durable, and increase desired aesthetics, with respect to color and sheen. In fabrics, a treatment completed to enhance the look, performance, or feel (a.k.a. hand) of a fabric. Finishes include napping, glazing, waterproofing, shearing, scouring, wrinkle resistance, etc.

Finn Juhl pelican chair

A 1940s Danish Modern chair by architect and designer Finn Juhl with teak legs and an organic curved form that embraces the user. See *Finn Juhl, 1912–1989, in the Architects, Artists, and Designers Appendix.*

Finn Juhl pelican chair

fir

A soft, close-grained wood known for its high elasticity and excellent dimensional stability, commonly used for framing lumber, plywood, and interior trim. See also *Douglas fir.*

fireback

A metal liner or plate, historically made of cast iron, positioned on the back wall of a fireplace to catch heat and reflect it back into the room, also to protect the masonry from the cumulative effects of numerous fires.

fire division wall

See *fire wall.*

fire irons

Fireplace accessories designed for tending a fire, generally a set composed of a poker, tongs, and shovel.

fire screen

A decorative screen used in front of a fire to protect the home from sparks and/or the inhabitants from intense heat.

fire wall

A full height (foundation to roof) wall constructed to compartmentalize a building, often into one or more floors, thereby restricting the spread of fire. Also known as a occupancy separation wall, fire division wall, or fire partition.

fire-retardant wired glass

A glass with encased wire mesh used to keep the glass intact under the high temperatures produced by fire, thereby protecting building occupants from the harmful effects of smoke and flame.

fireclay

A clay able to withstand high temperatures, used for making firebricks.

firedogs

Another name for andirons. See also *andirons.*

firehouse Windsor chair

A chair, closely resembling the Philadelphia chair, used extensively in volunteer firehouses during the Victorian era. See also *Philadelphia chair* and *captain's chair.*

firehouse Windsor chair

fireside chair

A general term, coined when it was customary to sit by the fireside, for a comfortable upholstered chair with a high rolled back and arms.

fireside figures

Popular wood and/or canvas silhouettes used as fire screens during the 16th and 17th century. Often painted to resemble royal personages, guards, pages, etc., the figures were just under life size and were also known as picture board dummies.

firing

The process of hardening clay at high temperatures in a kiln.

First Plantagenet period (FIRST plan TAA jun et PEER ee-ud)

See *Early English period.*

First Pointed period

See *Early English period*.

first style painting

A 2nd century B.C.E. style of Roman wall painting known for its faux marble, and aptly named by its position in a series of four styles. See also *Incrustation Style*.

fish tail

A carving resembling a fish tail, occasionally found on the top rail of 18th- and 19th-century American banister-back chairs.

fitments

An English term for built-in furniture, fixtures, or equipment such as bookcases, cupboards, stoves, and bathtubs.

fittings

Small parts such as metal hardware, mounts, escutcheons, etc.

five-colored wear

A Ming dynasty porcelain enriched with five colors, innovative for its time.

flag

A widely grown water plant with long sword-shaped leaves that can be twisted and woven to form rush seats.

flagstone

A hard stratified stone that can be easily split to form large, flat paving stones.

flaked

A wood figure commonly found in quartersawn oak, characterized by horizontal highlights that travel across the grain.

flambeau (FLAAM boh)

A flame or torch, often used as a decorative device in urns and finials of the 17th through early 19th centuries of England and France. Also, a large ornamental candlestick with several branches.

flamboyant (flaam BOI unt)

Literally translated from French as flaming. A late Gothic style of French architecture characterized by tracery with waving, flame-like curves. See also *tracery*.

flame carving

A swirling, flame-like effect often seen on 18th- and early 19th-century finials and springing from 17th- and 18th-century decorative urns.

flame stitch

A needlework pattern or fabric patterned with a repeating series of jagged, flame-like lines. See also *bargello*.

flâneuse (FLAN uuz)

A long garden deck chair, used for lounging, commonly found with a caned seat, back, and footrest.

flannel

A twilled or plain woven wool or cotton/wool blend fabric with a soft, slightly napped face.

flap strapping

See *strapwork*.

flap table

See *drop-leaf table*.

flare

An outward spreading element, as in an arm, leg, seat, or back of a piece of furniture.

flashed glass

Glass encased with a thin layer of molten glass of another color. This invention advanced the art of architectural stained glass, which must be 1/8" in depth. Solid-colored glass of this depth would only let a little light through and would appear quite dark in color. The invention of flashed glass opened the door for numerous bright, beautiful colors to be used. Another advantage is that the outer layer of flashed glass can be engraved or abraded to reveal the clear glass below.

flat arch

A flat horizontal arch with mutually supporting voussoirs. Also called a jack arch or straight arch.

flat-cut veneer

The most common and least expensive veneer, cut across a half log, producing a cathedral grain. Often used for wall panels and furniture. Also called plain-sliced veneer or crown cut veneer.

flat glass

Glass manufactured in flat sheets. Commonly used for windows, doors, wall, and windshields. Also known as plate glass or broad glass. See also *sheet glass*.

flatted

Furniture that has been painted, such as the pieces prevalent in the Louis XV and Louis XVI periods.

flax

A plant cultivated for its seed and bast fiber. The seed is the source of linseed oil, a product found in many wood finishing products and linoleum. The fiber has been used in the manufacture of linen since Egyptian times.

flèche

From the French word for arrow. A small, slender spire found on the ridges of Gothic cathedrals and churches. Also called a spirelet.

Flemish

Associated with Flanders, a medieval principality in the southwest region of the Low Countries, now Belgium, Holland, and part of northern France.

Flemish bond

In masonry, a brick pattern using alternating headers (ends) and stretchers (lengths) in a course. In the second course, the headers are centered over the stretchers below, creating a cross pattern.

Flemish chair

A late 17th-century English chair with a high back containing an upholstered or caned central panel, sometimes replaced with laths or balusters and topped by an elaborately carved crest. The chair is supported by boldly curved front legs, scrolled feet, and a curvy X-frame stretcher system.

Flemish cross bond

In masonry, a brick pattern similar to Flemish bond with courses of Flemish bond alternating between courses of stretchers.

Flemish ear

A furniture foot of the late French Renaissance and Baroque periods commonly seen in Louis XIV furniture, resembling the Flemish scrolled foot with an inverted S or C. See also *Flemish foot* and *Flemish scroll*.

Flemish foot

A 17th-century scrolled furniture foot, commonly seen on S- and C-shaped legs in Flanders, England, and France.

Flemish scroll

An S- or C-shaped form, generally associated with Flemish and Dutch furniture, but also used in English Restoration and William and Mary pieces.

Flemish scroll

Flemish spiral bond

In masonry, a brick pattern using courses of Flemish bond arranged with headers breaking joint over each other, forming diagonal bands. See also *bond* and *Flemish bond*.

fleur-de-lis (FLER duh lee)

A conventionalized iris symbolizing royalty, especially the French Bourbon kings of the late 16th to 18th centuries. Composed of three stylized iris petals, the popular motif was commonly used in heraldry and as a decorative motif. Also seen as fleur-de-lys.

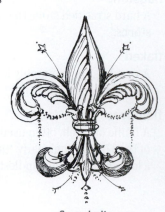

fleur-de-lis

fleurette (FLER et)

French term for small flower. A flower ornament used in art and design.

fleuretted treillage (FLER et ed TRAY aj)

French for a trellis scattered or sprinkled with flowers. A popular ornamental motif during the French and German Rococo and Louis XV periods.

fleuron (FLER on)

A flower-shaped ornament applied to the center of each side of the abacus of a Corinthian capital.

fleury cross (FLER ee CROS)

A cross, typically Greek, with fleur-de-lis ornamenting the ends of each arm.

fliers

One step in a straight flight of stairs.

flight

A string of steps connecting one floor of a building to another.

flip-top table

A table with hinges mortised between two leaves that allow one leaf to fold on top of another. Forms are generally rectangular or demi-lune in shape. See also *card table* and *mechanical card table*.

flitch

A thin, rectangular sheet of veneer cut from a log, generally stored in the sequence in which they were sliced to provide easy pattern matching.

floating construction

A method of construction for solid wood furniture that uses slotted screw holes to allow for expansion and contraction of the wood without damage.

fleury cross

flip-top table

floating furniture

Furniture that is not lined against a wall, but floated in the middle of the room. Also legless furniture that is suspended from a wall, appearing to have no base.

flock

Very short or ground fibers used to form a velvet-like surface on fabric, paper, etc. See also *flocking* or *flock printing*.

flock paper

A textured wallpaper with a velvet-like surface created by flocking, generally in a raised fabric pattern. Developed in the 17th century as velvet paper. See also *flocking* or *flock printing*.

flocking or flock printing

The practice of securing flock to an adhesive-coated surface, often seen in beautiful patterns created by strategically applying glue. Originally developed during the Middle Ages and applied to fabric, leather, paper, and other surfaces.

flokati (floh KAH tee)

Traditional Greek rugs, handwoven from wool into a thick, plush shag. Also known as flokates.

floor cloth

A popular floor covering of the 18th and early 19th centuries made of decoratively painted canvas, used to protect more expensive flooring materials. Called a wachstuch-tapete in Germany and often an oilcloth in America.

Florentine arch

A round arch that springs directly from a capital, column, or pier, whose outer arch (extrados) and inner arch (intrados) are not concentric. Commonly seen in a series or arcade.

Florentine stitch

See *flame stitch*.

Florentine table

A table with carved slab legs crowned by an octagonal top, associated with Florence, Italy.

abcdefghijklmnopqrstuvwxyz

florianware

An early 20th-century style of pottery, with strong Art Nouveau influences, manufactured by Moorcroft, a British pottery manufacturer. The design was characterized by heavy slip decoration, translucent glaze, and bright vivid colors.

floriated

Ornamented with leaf and floral forms. Commonly seen in tracery, capitals, and other elements of the Gothic period.

flower stand

A stand designed to hold flowers. Commonly seen in the 18th-century work of the Adam brothers and Chippendale. Also called a plant stand. See also *jardinière*.

flue

A duct designed to carry smoke, gases, or steam up and out of a building from a fireplace or furnace.

fluid plan

A building or plan with large, open areas containing few or no interior walls dividing the space.

flush

Elements arranged to form a single continuous plane, i.e., a flat, unbroken surface.

flush bead

A bead molding set so that the top is level with an adjacent surface.

flute

A shallow concave channel.

fluting, fluted

A series of shallow, parallel, and concave channels found on the shaft of columns and pilasters, particularly in the architectural styles of Ionic, Corinthian, and Composite. Also commonly used to ornament furniture legs and friezes. Occasionally seen in a spiral formation.

fly bracket

A bracket designed to support the flap or drop leaf of a table, often including a shaped decorative end. Examples include Pembroke tables, library tables, butterfly tables, etc.

fly rail

A hinged wooden bracket designed to support a table's drop leaf.

flying buttress

A finger-like arch that extends from a wall to a buttress, designed to counteract the thrust of a roof or vault, typically found on the exterior of Gothic cathedrals.

flying buttress

flying façade (FLIY ing FAH sahd)

See *roof comb*.

foils

The small arcs found between cusps in Gothic tracery. See also *trefoil, quatrefoil, cinquefoil,* and *multifoil.*

fold over

A table seen in 18th-century France and England, particularly in the work of Sheraton, with a folding top leaf that converts it into a desk.

folding doors

Hinged doors, generally seen in pairs and operating off a track, capable of being folded back onto each other.

folding furniture

Furniture that folds or collapses to form a more compact unit capable of easily being moved. Commonly used by the Egyptians, Greeks, and Romans through the Renaissance, French Empire, English Hepplewhite and Sheraton, up to modern day times.

folding stool

A stool that collapses or folds to form a compact and portable unit. See also *folding furniture*.

folding table

Historically, the name of a multi-legged table of the early English Renaissance, a precursor of the gate-leg table. In modern times, a table with a hinged double top that opens to expand the table-top surface or a table with legs that fold to store under the tabletop. See also *gate-leg table* and *card tables*.

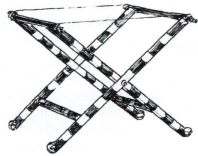

folding stool

foliage (FOHI ee-ij)

Plants, leaves, flowers, and branches used as ornamentation.

foliaged scroll (FOHI ee ijd SKROHL)

An ornamental motif using foliage in scrolling forms. Also called scrolling foliage or leaf spiral. See *illustration in the Motifs/Ornaments Appendix*.

foliated arch (FOHI ee-ay ted ARCH)

An arch created by a series of foils or lobes, common in the late Romanesque Style, but derived from Islamic architecture.

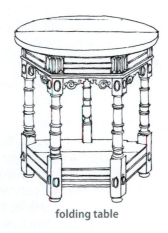

folding table

foliation (FOHI ee-ay shun)

Embellished with foliage. Also, an architectural opening ornamented with foils, such as Gothic tracery. See also *feathering*.

folio slide

A retractable element used to support folios and large books for viewing.

folly

A structure designed predominately for ornamentation, such as a Roman ruin, Chinese temple, etc., common in 18th-century French and English gardens.

fondeur (fohn DUR)

French term for a metal caster or smelter who creates mounts, embellishment, hardware, or accessories. See also *ciseleur*.

Fontainebleau (Fohn TEN bloo)

A royal French Renaissance château originating in the early 16th century during the reign of François I, but added to by many French monarchs, such as Henri II and Henri IV, in various periods and styles.

foot

The terminal part of a furniture leg. See *illustrations in the Feet Appendix*.

footboard

A supporting board creating the foot of a bed and connecting to the side rails. See also *headboard*.

footman

See *trivet*.

footrail

A low stretcher between the legs of a chair or table used as a support for the feet.

footstool

Originally a small step for a high throne.

foreshortening

In perspectives, a method of drawing in which certain dimensions of an object or figure are diminished in order to portray spatial relations correctly.

forged

Metal shaped through heat and hammering.

form

A long, backless bench or seat designed to hold two or more people, commonly seen during the Medieval and Jacobean periods.

formal

In design, generally associated with symmetrical balance, a traditional arrangement or layout of objects.

forty-winks chair

Another name, although antiquated, for a wing chair. See also *wing chair*.

forum

A marketplace forming the center of judicial, business, and public affairs in an ancient Roman city.

foulard (fooL ARD)

A lightweight silk or cotton fabric, in a twill or plain weave, containing a small printed design.

fountain

An ornamental structure, commonly constructed of marble, stone, bronze, concrete, etc., that pumps a jet, stream, or spurt of water up into the air, which then often cascades back down into a catch basin.

four square

A 20th-century American two story, simple box-shaped house with a four-over-four plan, low hipped roof, and large central dormer. Occasionally called a prairie box due to features shared with prairie style architecture.

four-centered arch

A Tudor arch commonly curved from four centers.

four-poster bed

A bed with four tall posts, one in each corner, originally designed to support an elaborate canopy or draperies, which often fully enclosed the bed. See also *ananas bed*.

four-way center and butt match

A veneer technique using four consecutive flitch sheets on a panel with a vertical and horizontal center line. Two pairs of consecutive flitches are book matched, one along the top of the vertical line and one on

the bottom. Then the butt or short ends of the pairs are also matched along the center horizontal line. Similar to diamond match veneer.

fourth style painting

The fourth of four periods distinguished in wall murals of ancient Rome, seen around c. 50 C.E. The style is characterized as a Baroque reaction to the Ornate Style. Although it exhibits less ornamentation, the style is known for its large-scale narrative painting and panoramic vistas, but it still retains the architectural detailing seen in the first and second styles. See also *Intricate Style*.

fox edge

A burlap-covered padding used on the edges of upholstered furniture to build up the edge rail and provide a smoother appearance. Also called edge roll paper.

foyer (FOI yur)

The entrance hall of a home or lobby of a commercial building.

frailero (FRAY le hroh)

A 17th-century Spanish Renaissance arm or side chair with a simple rectangular shape, plain legs, and a seat and back of leather stretched between the rails and uprights. Spanish for friar, so called because of its austere form.

frailero chair

fraktur painting (fraak TOOR PAYN ting)

Ornately embellished 18th- and 19th-century documents of birth, baptism, marriage, or death created by Pennsylvania artists of German descent in a formal script called fractur and illuminated with colorful birds, flowers, and other motifs. Alternately spelled as fractur.

frame

The elemental structure that lends shape or strength to a building or piece of furniture or that surrounds an object, such as a door, window, or piece of art. See also *carcass*.

François I

Early Renaissance King of France (1515–1547), known for his patronage of the arts, including architecture, which at the time combined Gothic elements with the splendor of the Italian Renaissance Style. His most well-known reconstruction projects are the Chateau de Blois, Chateau de Chambord, the royal Chateau of Fontainebleau, and the Louvre.

François I style

A French neoclassical style synonymous with the reign of King François I during the first half of the 16th century.

Frank L. Wright barrel-back chair

A barrel-backed chair of natural cherry designed by Frank Lloyd Wright in 1904. The chair also includes a flared backrest, square spindles, and a circular upholstered seat. Wright was so fond of the chair that he used it in his Spring Green, Wisconsin home, Taliesin. A variation of the chair called the "Wingspread" was created in 1937 for the Herbert F. Johnson House. See *Frank Lloyd Wright, 1867–1959, in the Architects, Artists, and Designers Appendix.*

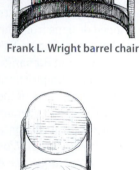

Frank L. Wright barrel chair

Frank L. Wright Johnson Wax chair

A painted tubular steel chair with wooden paddle-like arms and a tilting back rest designed by American architect Frank Lloyd Wright in 1939 for the Johnson Wax Headquarters. See *Frank Lloyd Wright, 1867–1959, in the Architects, Artists, and Designers Appendix.*

Frank L. Wright Johnson Wax chair

Frank L. Wright peacock chair

An oak-framed chair with hexagonal back and yellow oilcloth upholstery designed by American architect Frank Lloyd Wright in 1921 for the Imperial Hotel in Tokyo. The strong geometric shapes of hexagons, squares, and triangles found in the chair where pulled from the hotel's architectural details. See *Frank Lloyd Wright, 1867–1959, in the Architects, Artists, and Designers Appendix.*

Frank L. Wright peacock chair

Frank L. Wright swivel chair

Metal swivel chair designed by American architect Frank Lloyd Wright in 1904 for the Larkin Administration Building in Buffalo, New York. The perforated grid of the seat back was designed to mimic the open grid plan of the building. The chair is constructed of cast iron and bent steel with leather upholstery. See *Frank Lloyd Wright, 1867–1959, in the Architects, Artists, and Designers Appendix.*

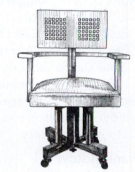

Frank L. Wright swivel chair

Frank O. Gehry easy edges rocking chair

A corrugated cardboard rocking chair designed for the Easy Edges furniture line by Canadian American architect, Frank Gehry in 1972. See *Frank O. Gehry, 1929–, in the Architects, Artists, and Designers Appendix.*

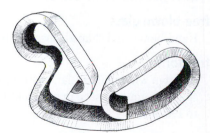

Frank O. Gehry easy edges rocking chair

abcdefghijklmnopqrstuvwxyz

131

Frank O. Gehry powerplay chair

A ribbon-like chair created from laminated strips of maple that are bent, woven, and curved, designed by Canadian American architect, Frank Gehry in 1990. The chair is one of a collection of pieces created for Knoll and named after ice hockey terms. See *Frank O. Gehry, 1929 –, in the Architects, Artists, and Designers Appendix.*

Frank O. Gehry powerplay chair

Frank O. Gehry wiggle chair

A 1970s corrugated cardboard side chair designed for the Easy Edges furniture line by Canadian American architect Frank Gehry. The designer is known for using unusual materials for his architecture and furniture. See *Frank O. Gehry, 1929 –, in the Architects, Artists, and Designers Appendix.*

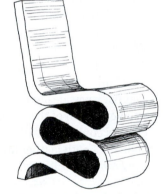
Frank O. Gehry wiggle chair

Franklin stove

A metal-lined fireplace created in 1741 by Benjamin Franklin, designed with an inverted siphon and hollow rear baffle that worked to distribute more heat and less smoke into a room. Also known as a Pennsylvania fireplace or circulating stove.

free-blown glass

Hand-blown and shaped glass created without the use of molds.

free form

A design with an irregular, abstract, and generally asymmetrical shape, commonly seen in mid-century modern designs of the 1940s to 1960s.

freestanding column

A column without support of the structure around it; standing by itself.

freestanding pole

A metal or wooden pole with an attached adjustable sleeve connection allowing height variations, often used as a temporary weight-bearing structure, to support pole lights and traveling displays, etc.

French bed

Older term used for a sleigh bed. See also *sleigh bed.*

French bracket foot

See *French foot.*

French chair

Generic 18th-century term for an English upholstered chair typified by the Rococo bergère.

French directoire   (FRENCH dee rek TWAR)

An austere, simplified neoclassic style of late 18th-century (1795–1799) France, concurrent with the post-revolution French Directory. The period transitioned designs from the Greek-based style of Louis XVI to the Egyptian and Roman-based style of the Empire period. Chief establishers of the style were Charles Percier and Pierre François Léonard Fontaine. See *Charles Percier, 1764–1838,* and *Pierre François Léonard Fontaine, 1762–1853,* in the Architects, Artists, and Designers Appendix.

French directoire commode

French Early Renaissance

An end of 15th- to mid 16th-century transitional French period encompassing the reigns of Charles VIII, Louis XII, and François I and mixing gothic forms with new Italian Renaissance ornamentation. Also called the François I period.

French Empire

See *Empire period*.

French foot

A slender bracket foot that resembles a stunted saber leg, popular on 18th-century English and American case pieces in the Hepplewhite, Sheraton, and Federal styles. Also called a French bracket foot.

French heading

A drapery or curtain heading containing pleats that alternate with open flat areas thereby creating neat orderly folds as the curtain falls. Also called French pleated or pinch pleated.

French Late Renaissance

An end of 16th- to mid 17th-century French period encompassing the reigns of Henri IV and Louis XIII with the aid of Cardinal Richelieu, noted for its profuse, massive, heavy ornamentation. Also called the Louis XIII period.

French leg

A popular 17th- and 18th-century scrolled furniture leg, often embellished with carvings and other ornamentation.

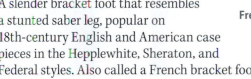

French Early Renaissance bed

French Late Renaissance music cabinet

French Middle Renaissance

A mid to late 16th-century French period encompassing the reigns Henri II, François II, Charles IX, and Henry III and the patronage of Henri II's wife, Catherine de Medici, in which design more closely resembles Italian prototypes and walnut becomes the wood of choice in furniture making. Also called the Henri II period.

French polish

A high-gloss wood finish produced by applying multiple thin layers of shellac dissolved in alcohol with a rubbing pad.

French provincial (FRENCH pru VIN chul)

A simple style generally associated with furniture from the French provinces or countryside, based on Louis XV characteristics, often using less formal woods such as fruitwood.

French Régence period (FRENCH REE jun see PEER ee-ud)

A transitional French period of the early 18th century (1700–1730), named after a time when France was under the leadership of a French regent, the Duc d'Orleans, who served for the five-year-old heir to the throne, Louis XV. The period encompasses the time between the reigns of Louis XIV and Louis XV and is characterized by slight curves, ribbon ornament, the use of walnut, mahogany, and rosewood, as well as the appearance of the bombé chest. Also called French Regency period.

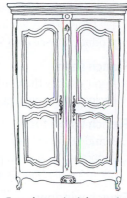

French provincial armoire

French Régence period console

French Restoration period

An early 19th-century period (1814–1830) marked by the abdication of Napoleon I and the return of the Bourbon monarchs to the French throne. The period encompasses the reigns of Louis XVIII, Charles X, Louis-Philippe, and Napoleon III. Designs of the time were eclectic, but marked by declines in taste and machine production. See also *Second Empire or Late Empire period*.

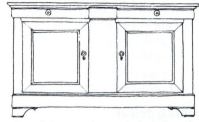
French Restoration period cupboard

French seam

A top-quality finish used in tailoring and upholstery work that encloses the raw edges of fabric by a seam on both sides.

French whorl foot

A mid 18th-century furniture foot with an upward scroll often supported by a shoe, popular in the Régence and Louis XV periods. See also *knurl foot* or *scroll foot*.

French window

A casement window that extends down to the floor, generally seen in pairs that allow access to a balcony, porch, terrace, or garden.

fresco

Italian term for fresh. A method of painting on wet plaster that integrates the pigment, making it harder and more durable when dry. First seen in 14th-century Italy, but perfected during the Italian Renaissance of the 16th century.

fresco paper

Wallpaper that mimics the subtle effects, layers, colors, textures, patterns, and designs of actual frescos.

fresquera (fres KAY Rah)

A Spanish hanging food cupboard, designed especially for storing meats, characterized by latticework or spindle fronted doors that provide ventilation.

fret

A form of Greek ornament, generally used in borders and bands, composed of intersecting lines at right angles. Also called Chinese Key Design, Greek key, or meander. See also *Greek fret*. See *illustration of Greek fret in the Motifs/Ornaments Appendix*.

fretwork

Open or relief carved woodwork in geometric patterns composed of intersecting lines at right angles. Commonly seen on aprons, arms, legs, and stretchers of Rococo or Chinese-inspired furniture, particularly the 18th-century work of Thomas Chippendale.

fretwork mirror

See *silhouette mirror*.

friar's chair

See *frailero*.

Friesian carving

See *Frisian carving*.

Friesland (FREES laand)

A northern province of the Netherlands famous for its 17th-century Baroque Style furniture.

frieze (FREEZ)

In architecture, the middle part of a classical entablature, located between the architrave and the cornice. In interiors, a decorated band found beneath the crown molding of walls. In furniture, another name for a table apron. See also *apron*.

friezé (FREEZ ay)

A heavy woolen, mohair, or cotton fabric with uncut loops, originally made in Friesland. Also a textile manufacturing technique used to make wool carpeting with a heavy twist that produces better resiliency. Also known as frisé in French. See also *frisé*.

frieze drawer

A drawer located within the apron of a table. Or, an upper drawer that extends out over the main body of a cabinet, chest, or cupboard; commonly seen in Empire and Biedermeier furniture of the early 19th century.

frieze rail

A grooved horizontal molding, attached near the top of a wall, designed for hanging pictures. In furniture, the horizontal rail found below a table's top. In doors, the center rail located below the frieze panel. See also *picture molding or rail*.

frigger

Small objects, designed at a glassmaker's whim, out of leftover pieces of glass. Also called friggars or whimsy glass.

fringe

Trim used to edge, finish, or ornament drapery treatments and upholstery, composed of twisted threads, loops, or tassels that hang beneath a band. See also *bullion*.

frisé (free ZAY)

French for curled. See also *friezé*.

Frisian carving (FRIZH un CAHRV ing)

A type of light chiseled carving, often in simple geometric patterns, seen on furniture made by the Pennsylvania Germans, who emigrated from Friesland. Common during the American Colonial period. Also called Friesian carving.

frit

A fused mixture of glass materials used in enamelwork and ceramic glazes.

Fritware

A type of pottery able to be fired at low temperatures because of the glassy frit added to the clay, dated to the late first millennium from the Near East. Also known as Islamic stone-paste.

front

The forward part of a piece of furniture, found in various forms such as flat rectangular. See also *bombé, serpentine, bowed, block front, breakfront,* or *demilune*.

frosted glass

Clear glass that has been sandblasted, acid etched, or silk screened to produce a frosted, translucent surface that obstructs clear view.

frosting

A chemical process used on glass bulbs or lamps that makes the surface uneven and hence translucent, thereby reducing glare.

fruchtgehange (fruukt GU hayngu)

German for fruit garlands.

fruit festoon

A draped garland of fruit, foliage, and flowers, often bound by ribbons, popular in ancient Rome and the Renaissance. See also *festoon*.

fruitwood

The wood of a fruit tree such as cherry, apple, or pear, commonly used in 18th-century provincial furniture.

fruitwood finish

A light tan or honey-colored finish, commonly applied to softwoods to mimic fruitwood.

fulcrum

In furniture, the curved headboard of a Roman couch, used for reclining during banquets, decorated with figural attachments of bronze, ivory, or bone in the form of animal heads, busts, or satyrs.

full-lead crystal

Glass containing at least 24 percent lead.

fulcrum

135

fully tempered glass

A type of glass that is three to five times more resistant to breaking than annealed glass, hence its use as a safety glass. It is produced by heating glass almost to the point of softening, then quickly cooling it with air or liquid.

fumed oak

A popular 19th- and 20th-century furniture finish using ammonia to create a dark, rich color on oak, famous through the work of Gustav Stickley.

fumeuse (foo MOOZ)

An 18th-century French smoking chair designed with a broad crest rail for storing pipes and tobacco and a seat that is straddled by the user. Similar to a voyeuse. See also *cockfight chair* and *ponteuse*.

functional furniture

Utilitarian furniture that places function over aesthetic form.

Functionalism

An early 20th-century design movement, heralded by architect Adolph Loos and the Bauhaus school, grounded in the idea that "form follows function."

fur

A hair-on pelt or skin from animals, commonly used as a rug or upholstery material.

furring

A method of insulating the interior of masonry walls by anchoring strips of lumber or metal to the wall to provide space for insulation.

fustic (FUS tik)

A fine-grained wood with a golden yellow color and good weathering characteristics, historically used for making fabric dyes and in 17th- and 18th-century marquetry and parquetry. Indigenous to the West Indies and Central and South America. Also called Argentine Osage Orange.

fusuma (foos oo MAH)

Rectangular sliding panels used in Japan as doors and to redefine spaces, historically painted with scenes from nature. Generally covered in plain or printed thick rice paper today.

futon (foo TAHN)

A bed or bed covering comprised of a thick, rolled comforter.

Futurism

An early 20th-century Italian art movement associated with contemporary concepts such as technology, modes of transportation, and the industrial city. Although limited primarily to Italy, the movement did have influence over other movements such as Art Deco, etc.

fusuma-e (FOO soo mah EE)

Paintings on Japanese sliding panels. Also known as fusuma.

gable
The triangular end of a building formed by a pitched roof.

gable roof
A roof composed of two sloping sides, forming a gable at each end.

gaboon (ga BOON)
A wood from Central Africa's Gaboon region with a soft, straight grain and golden to pinkish-brown color, typically used for plywood, interior work, and furniture in Europe.

gadroon
A short, oval or egg-shaped form applied around the edges or rim of furniture, silver, or glass and commonly seen on the bulbous legs and supports of Elizabethan and Jacobean furniture. The term is derived from the French word gadron. Also called lobed decoration or thumb molding. See also *lip molding*. See *illustration in the Motifs/Ornaments Appendix*.

gaine
A post or pedestal that tapers downward and is generally crowned with a head or bust, terminating with human or animal feet.

galerie (GAHl er ee)
A French term for a covered porch on a house.

Gallé butterfly bed
See *Emile Gallé butterfly bed*. See *Émile Gallé, 1846–1904, in the Architects, Artists, and Designers Appendix*.

Gallé dragonfly table
See *Emile Gallé dragonfly table*. See *Émile Gallé, 1846–1904, in the Architects, Artists, and Designers Appendix*.

gallery
In furniture, a small decorative railing attached to the top of 18th-century sideboards and rimming tabletops. In architecture, a covered outdoor balcony, porch, or veranda; also an early corridor that predated the hall, generally found on the second story of a home during the Elizabethan period.

gallery grave
A prehistoric grave with divided chamber.

galloon or galon (ge LOON/ ga LON)
A narrow, closely woven braid utilized to trim upholstery and draperies, often finishing off rough edges.

galvanized iron
Iron that has been coated with zinc to make it rust resistant.

gambrel roof
A roof with two pitches on both sides of the ridge, characteristic of Dutch Colonial Revival architecture.

gambrel roof

game table
A table created for playing board games or cards. Also called a card table. See also *card table* and *flip-top table*.

garde du vin (GARD DOO VAHN)
A late 18th-century term used by Hepplewhite for a cellarette, a wine cooler. See also *cellarette* and *sarcophagus*.

garde-manger (GARD-MAHN jay)
French term for a food cupboard.

garden apartment
A multifamily residence, situated within a landscaped setting of a suburban residential locale.

garden seat
See *garden stool*.

garden stool
A Chinese stool resembling a small barrel, primarily produced in porcelain for an outdoor area, originally carved from stone. Also called a garden seat.

garden stool

garderobe (GAR de rohb)

In furniture another name for a wardrobe or armoire. In architecture, a private room within a suite utilized for dressing and storing garments. See also *armoire*.

gargoyle (GAR goi-ul)

A grotesque carved human or animal figure often used as a rain spout in Gothic architecture.

garland

A wreath of flowers, leaves, or fruit used as a carved or painted decoration.

garniture (GAR nee chur)

A French term for motifs designed for embellishment. Also defines a set of decorative objects.

garniture de cheminée (GAR nee chur DE SHE mee nay)

A set of decorative objects designed to be used on a mantle, generally consisting of a central clock with flanking candlesticks or a set of vases or urns.

garreting

The practice of placing small pebbles or stones into a wet mortar joint.

garrett

Originally, an old French term for a place of refuge or lookout. Today, it defines a room or unfinished area within an attic space.

garrison

A common feature of Colonial houses, where a second story extends past the first. Also a term denoting a permanent military post.

gatch

An Oriental term for molded plaster ornaments, such as anaglypta or Robert Adam's carton-pierre.

gargoyle

gate-leg table

A 19th-century term for a 17th-century English table with drop leaves supported by hinged, gate-like legs.

gauffrage (GOH frahj)

A decorative embossing technique commonly used on leather.

gauze

A thin, transparent fabric woven in a leno or plain weave, commonly used as curtains.

gazebo (gah ZEE boh)

A turret-roofed garden shelter with open sides, often constructed of lattice.

gejin (ge JIN)

An area within the outer area of a Japanese temple utilized by the uninitiated.

genie

A folkloric entity with supernatural powers that becomes a human when summoned, utilized as a decorative motif.

genius

In Roman society, the protective spirit of males. See also *juno*.

genkan (GEN kahn)

The foyer of a traditional Japanese home.

genre (JAHN re)

French term for art depicting scenes common in everyday life; also a reference to an artistic style or subject matter.

gate-leg table

gazebo

gentleman and lady chairs

During the Victorian era, a pair of matching chairs developed for a gentleman and lady.

geodesic dome (JEE oh de sik DOHM)

A dome constructed of similar, interlocking, straight structural elements, otherwise known as geodesics.

geodesic dome

geometric design

Designs created from the repeated use of geometric shapes such as circles, triangles, and squares.

George Hepplewhite heart-shaped chair back

A mid 18th-century Hepplewhite chair back composed of interlaced hearts; one of the two most characteristic shapes used. See *George Hepplewhite, d. 1786, in the Architects, Artists, and Designers Appendix*.

George Hepplewhite heart-shaped chair

George Hepplewhite oval-back armchair

A mid 18th-century English chair with an oval-shaped back popularized by George Hepplewhite, often incorporating a splat of Prince of Wales feathers and/or swags. See *George Hepplewhite, d. 1786, in the Architects, Artists, and Designers Appendix*.

George Hepplewhite oval-back armchair

George Hepplewhite shield-back side chair

A mid 18th-century English chair with a shield-shaped back popularized by George Hepplewhite, often incorporating a splat of Prince of Wales feathers and/or swags. See *George Hepplewhite, d. 1786, in the Architects, Artists, and Designers Appendix*.

George Hepplewhite shield-back side chair

George Nelson coconut chair

A chair designed by noted American industrial designer George Nelson and first introduced by Herman Miller in 1955, composed of a fiberglass-reinforced plastic shell on a chromed tubular steel base with soft contours resembling a chunk of coconut. See *George Nelson, 1908–1986, in the Architects, Artists, and Designers Appendix*.

George Nelson coconut chair

George Nelson marshmallow sofa

A sofa with multiple disk-shaped cushions atop a steel frame designed by American industrial designer George Nelson and Irving Harper of George Nelson Associates in 1957 and manufactured by Herman Miller. See *George Nelson, 1908–1986, in the Architects, Artists, and Designers Appendix*.

George Nelson sling sofa

A 1960s mid-century modern sofa designed by George Nelson and manufactured by Herman Miller with a chromed steel frame with rubber slings supporting leather cushions. See *George Nelson, 1908–1986, in the Architects, Artists, and Designers Appendix*.

George Nelson marshmallow sofa

George Nelson sling sofa

abcdefg**g**hijklmnopqrstuvwxyz

139

Georgian period

The golden era of English design, synonymous with the reigns of King George I, II, and III in England from 1714 to 1811. Notable designers of the period are Chippendale, Sheraton, Hepplewhite, and the Adam brothers.

ger (GAR)

See *yurt*.

German silver

A corrosion-resistant, malleable alloy composed of copper, zinc, and nickel that is silvery white in color. Also called nickel silver.

Gerrit Rietveld red-blue chair

Planar plywood chair with cantilevered seat originally designed by Gerrit Rietveld in 1917 in a natural wood color. The chair was painted in primary colors of red, blue, and yellow in 1923. It represents one of the first expressions of the De Stijl style. See also *De Stijl*. See *Gerrit Thomson Rietveld, 1888–1964, in the Architects, Artists, and Designers Appendix*.

Gerrit Rietveld red-blue chair

Gesamtkunstwerk (GEZ ahmt kuns twahk)

A nonhierarchical philosophy supporting unity and collaboration of the arts in Germany.

gesso (JE soh)

A 17th-century plaster of paris composition used as a base coat for decorative painting and for creating bas-reliefs. See also *anaglypta*, *carton-pierre*, and *composition*.

getabako (GE tah bah koh)

A cupboard designed to hold shoes at the entrance of a Japanese home.

Ghiordes knot (GEE ordez NAHT)

A symmetrical, hand-tied knot used in Oriental rugs that is constructed by wrapping two warp threads with yarn in such a way that the ends emerge between them.

ghorfa (CHOR fah)

A North African barrel-vaulted storage unit with rooms opening off a central court yard. The structure is often built partially below ground to take advantage of the earth's ability to regulate temperature.

giant order

A style using columns that are more than one story in height.

gilding

A technique for applying thin sheets of gold over a surface.

gilt or gilded furniture

Furniture finished by the technique of gilding. Commonly seen in the late French Renaissance, Louis XIV, and Louis XV periods, as well as in England during the early Queen Anne period.

gimp

Braided trim used to cover an upholstery tacked edge or as a decorative trim on draperies, bedspreads, and other textile items. Also spelled guimpe or guimp.

gingerbread

The lacy decorative woodwork often applied to Victorian houses.

gingham

A lightweight, yarn-dyed cotton fabric, generally woven in characteristic checks or stripes.

girandole (JEER en dohl)

A multibranched wall sconce common in the late 17th and 18th centuries. Used in the 19th century to describe a circular convex mirror, often designed with an attached candle sconce. In the mid 19th century, the term also represented a Bohemian glass candlestick, encircled with prisms. See also *luster* and *bull's eye mirror*.

girder

A large structural beam used to support the vertical load of a building.

Glasgow School

A noted art school in Glasgow, Scotland, with building and interior designed by Charles Rennie Mackintosh. His earlier ties to the school, as a student with the other members of the famous "Glasgow Four," led to the development of his approach to modern applied art. See *Charles Rennie Mackintosh, 1868–1928, in the Architects, Artists, and Designers Appendix.*

glass

A mixture of primarily silica, formed by fusing materials at high temperatures.

glass block

A translucent hollow block made from two pieces of glass sealed with air space in-between, commonly used to form non-load-bearing walls that transmit light.

glass cameos

Glass ornaments covered with a layer of different colored glass imitating relief carved onyx cameos.

glass curtain

A window covering made of a sheer, translucent material.

Glastonbury chair (GLAS tun bar ee CHAYR)

A 19th-century term for a late 16th-century folding chair, originally designed for churches before pews became popular. The wooden chair features an x-frame with carved arms that extend from the chair's crest rail to the seat front.

glazed door

A glass-paned door used on case pieces to facilitate the display of items found inside.

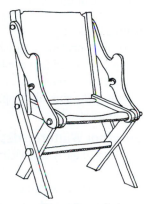

Glastonbury chair

glazing

In decorative painting, a technique that involves applying a transparent color wash or glaze over a base coat of paint. With respect to textiles, the practice of treating fabric with starch, glue, paraffin, or shellac, followed by heat, to create a smooth, highly polished finish.

globe or ball chair

See *Eero Aarnio globe or ball chair.* See *Eero Aarnio, 1932-, in the Architects, Artists, and Designers Appendix.*

glory

A ring of light depicted in sculptures as gilded rays radiating from behind a figure's head.

gloss paint

A paint with a high luster finish.

glyph (GLIF)

A groove within the frieze in classical Greek architecture.

Gobelins (GOH be linz)

A 16th-century tapestry factory located in Paris and run by the Gobelin brothers. It was purchased in 1662 by Louis XIV, who appointed Charles Le Brun as director and chief designer.

Goddard chest

A four-drawer block-front chest with the central vertical section recessed from the flacking sections, usually capped by shell carvings and originally designed by John Goddard. See *John Goddard, 1724–1785, in the Architects, Artists, and Designers Appendix.*

Goddard chest

Göggingen (GAH king en)

An 18th-century German ceramics factory, active from 1748 to 1754, that produced faience in the Bavarian town of Göggingen.

gold lacquer

A varnish often used to mimic a gilded surface.

gold leaf

A very thin sheet of gold utilized for gilding.

gold size

The adhesive used to cover a surface to prepare for gold leaf.

Golden Rectangle

A rectangle with a ratio of length to width that equals the Golden Ratio of 1:1.618. See also *Golden Section*.

Golden Section

A classical proportion based on a rectangle, divided in such a way that the ratio of the whole to the larger part is the same as the ratio of the larger part to the smaller part. It is the foundation for multiple proportioning systems, such as Le Corbusier's Modulor.

gondola chair (GAHN de lah CHAYR)

A mid to late 18th-century chair, popular during the French Empire, with a deep concave back and curved stiles that sweep forward to the seat rail.

gooseneck

A pediment popular in 18th-century England and America curved like the neck of a goose, i.e., with a double curve. The term is also used with furniture of the Victorian period that exhibits the telltale curve. With respect to a pediment, it is also called a broken arch or swan neck. See also *swan neck pediment*.

gooseneck lamp

A lamp designed with a flexible metal shaft that allows redirection of the light beam.

Gothic arch

A pointed arch commonly seen from the 12th to 16th centuries during the Gothic period.

Gothic Style

The dominant style of the Middle Ages from the 12th to the 16th centuries. It is commonly associated with ecclesiastical art and architecture, especially elaborate cathedrals. Design features include the pointed arch, rib vaults, clustered columns, flying buttresses, trefoils, and gargoyles. The name of the style is derived from the Goths, the Germanic tribes that caused the collapse of the Roman Empire.

Gothic Style chair

gothique troubadour (GAH theek TROO bah dor)

Name for the Gothic Revival style in 19th-century France.

gouache (GWAHSH)

An opaque watercolor paint, as well as a technique for producing studies for oil paintings. The Italian term for gouache is *tempera*.

gouge carving

A type of carving created by using a scoop-shaped tool that gouged the surface of the wood.

gout stool

An 18th-century English padded stool designed for people suffering from gout, sometimes incorporating a ratchet adjustable top. Also called a gouty stool.

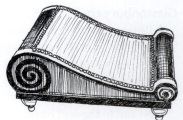

gout stool

Governor Winthrop desk

A typical early American (c. 1750) slant-front desk with three to four graduated drawers, named after the first governor of Massachusetts, John Winthrop.

go-with
A fabric that compliments the principle fabric of a design.

grain
The arrangement of fibers in wood; the direction parallel to the selvage in fabric.

grained furniture
Late 19th-century furniture that was inexpensive, dark in color, and painted with a grain to mimic oak.

graining
A decorative paint technique that simulates the grain of wood, often those that are rare or expensive.

Grand Confort
See *Le Corbusier Grand Confort.* See *Le Corbusier, (born Charles-Édouard Jeanneret) 1887–1965, in the Architects, Artists, and Designers Appendix.*

grand miroir à la psyché
A French Empire pier mirror suspended between two pillars and resting on a footed base. Also called a psyche. See also *pier glass.*

Grand Rapids, Michigan
A city known for manufacturing well-priced, mass-produced furniture for over a century.

grandfather chair
A 19th-century term for a wing chair, popular in early 18th-century England during the Queen Anne period. See also *wing chair.*

grandfather clock
A pendulum clock enclosed in a tall, narrow, wooden case that usually stood over six feet high. See also *long clock* or *tall case clock.*

graneros (GRAH na rohs)
A Spanish chest used for storing grain.

granite
A very hard igneous rock of quartz, feldspar, and mica with a visible crystalline texture, used in the building and interior materials industry.

great hall
A large, two-storied room considered to be the most important room of 16th- and 17th-century medieval castles or manor houses, used primarily for dining and entertaining.

great hall

Greek cross
A cross with two horizontal and two vertical arms of equal length.

Greek fret
See *Greek key.* See *illustration in the Motifs/Ornaments Appendix.*

Greek key
A fret design created by the repetition of interlocking squared hook-shaped forms. Also called Greek fret or Greek meander. See *illustration of Greek fret in the Motifs/Ornaments Appendix.*

Greek meander (GREEK mee AAN dur)
See *Greek key.* See *illustration of Greek fret in the Motifs/Ornaments Appendix.*

greenware
Clay objects that have not been fired.

greige (GRAYZH)
A greyish-beige hue that is considered to be a neutral color.

greige goods (GRAYZH GUUDZ)
Woven fabrics in their natural state before any dye or treatment has occurred.

grés (GRE)
French for stoneware.

griffin
A mythological animal with the head and wings of an eagle and the body of a lion. See *illustration in the Motifs/Ornaments Appendix.*

grille

A wood or metal lattice used in place of glass on doors. Employed extensively by Hepplewhite and Adam.

grisaille (gree SAY)

Decorative painting in monochromatic grays designed to produce a three-dimensional effect like trompe l'oeil. See also *chiaroscuro* and *clare-obscure.*

groin

The curved, sharp edge created where two barrel vaults intersect.

groin rib

A projecting band following the line of a groin on a vaulted surface. See also *rib.*

groin vault

A compound vault created by the intersection of two barrel vaults at right angles.

groote kamer (GROOT KAY mer)

The "best room" used for entertaining in a Dutch home.

groove and rabbet joint

See *barefaced tongue joint.*

grosgrain (GROH grayn)

A close-ribbed silk used for draperies and ribbon, produced by inserting heavier weft filler threads.

grospoint

A cross-stitch produced on a double net with embroidery threads generally made of wool. The process produces a fabric with a coarse tapestry effect that is often used as upholstery on office task chairs.

grotesque (groh TESK)

Fanciful classical ornament, characterized by a hybrid human-animal or human-plant form, that was rediscovered in grottos during the Renaissance. See *illustration in the Motifs/Ornaments Appendix.*

grotto (GRAH toh)

A natural or human-made cave or recess.

ground

Material that serves as a substrate.

ground color

The color of a fabric's background.

grout

A thin mortar used to fill the spaces between tiles or stone, also used to join or attach them. Produced with a sanded or unsanded finish.

guadamicil (GWAH dah mee see)

The Spanish term for the decorated leather first produced in Guadamacileria, Spain, in the 16th century. The technique was originally introduced into Europe from Morocco in the 11th century. See also *arras* and *wachstuchtapet.*

guanmaovi (GWAHN mo hvee)

A Chinese armchair containing a crest rail with an upward curve at the center, named for its resemblance to an official's cap. Also called an official's hat chair.

Guelph window (GWELF WIN doh)

A common Italian Renaissance window containing two perpendicular wood members forming an exterior cross that is sometimes decorated with a boss. Named after a prominent Renaissance family.

guéridon (GAR ee don)

A small ornamental stand originally designed in the mid 17th century, during the reign of Louis XIV, to hold a candelabra. By the end of the 18th century, the term was also used for a small circular table with splayed legs. The name was derived from the young male Africans serving Louis XIV's court as pages, commonly called guéridons. Hence, a base for the stand sometimes represented the carved figures of these elaborately uniformed young African servants.

guéridon à crémailliére (GAR ee don AH KREM ee yar)

A small round table or stand of the Louis XVI period of adjustable height. The French word crémailliére, means toothed, representing the toothed support that allowed for height adjustments.

guerite (GAR it)

French term for a high-backed, hooded chair popular during the 18th century in France. Also called a porter's chair.

guild

A medieval organization of craftsmen and merchants established for the purpose of providing apprenticeship and controlling crafts and its members.

guilloche (gee LOHSH)

A classical border ornament composed of interlacing curved bands. See *illustration in the Motifs/Ornaments Appendix.*

Guimard corner cabinet

See *Hector Guimard corner cabinet. See Hector Guimard, 1867–1942, in the Architects, Artists, and Designers Appendix.*

Guimard desk

See *Hector Guimard desk. See Hector Guimard, 1867–1942, in the Architects, Artists, and Designers Appendix.*

guimpe (GAMP)

See *gimp.*

guinea holes or pockets

An 18th-century term for the dished areas designed to hold money or chips in gaming tables.

gul

A repeated octagonal motif representing a stylized flower or tribal symbol, originally used in Turkoman rugs.

gumwood

A fine-grained, reddish-brown wood whose heartwood is commonly used for cabinetwork and general interior trim. See also *red gum.*

Gunston Hall

An American Georgian home built in 1755 for George Mason, author of the United States Bill of Rights, known for its dining room, with magnificent woodwork, designed by William Buckland. See *William Buckland, 1734–1774, in the Architects, Artists, and Designers Appendix.*

gusset

A triangular insert placed in a seam between two pieces of fabric to allow expansion or to reinforce construction.

Gustav Stickley reclining armchair

An early 1900s reclining armchair designed by American Arts and Crafts furniture designer Gustav Stickley. A sturdy, simple, spindled chair constructed of fumed white oak with broad open arms and a repositionable back. See *Gustav Stickley, 1858–1942, in the Architects, Artists, and Designers Appendix.*

Gustav Stickley reclining armchair

guttae (GOO tiy)

Small conelike ornaments used under the mutules in a Doric entablature. The singular form is gutta.

gynaeceum (JIN aysee-um)

The segment of a Greek house for women.

gypsum

A mineral made of hydrous calcium sulfate that is used to create plaster of paris.

gypsum board

A building material sold in a 4' × 8' panels, available in various thicknesses and composed of gypsum traditionally encased in a tough, heavy paper. The panel is used to cover framing members of interior walls and can be painted or wallpapered after it has been primed with a sealer. A new paperless board has been designed to prohibit mold. Also called wallboard or plasterboard. See also *building board.*

gyro chair

See *Eero Aarnio gyro chair. See Eero Aarnio, 1932-, in the Architects, Artist, and Designers Appendix.*

gyronny (JIY roh nee)

A pattern composed of triangles in alternating colors or textures.

H

H hinge

A metal-shaped hinge with vertical, long flat leaves that are held together by a center horizontal bar, so when opened, the hinge resembles the letter "H." See also *HL hinge*.

H stretcher

A stretcher connecting the front to back legs on each side and a cross stretcher connecting the two side stretchers to form the shape of the letter "H."

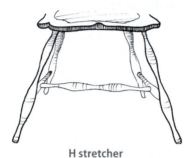

H stretcher

hacienda (HAH see-en dah)

A Spanish term for a large estate or plantation.

hackberry (HAK ber ee)

A native North American deciduous tree or shrub that is often mistaken for its cousin, the American elm, bearing edible berries and a soft yellowish color that stains and finishes well, usually used for shade and firewood.

Hackensack cupboard (HAK en sak cu burd)

A two-piece cupboard of Dutch origin with an upper portion enclosed with a pair of glazed doors and a lower portion consisting of a combination of panel doors and drawers.

hacket

Triangular forms often in the form of an S-scroll used to fill the space when the cresting extends beyond the stiles on the back of wainscot chairs.

Hadley chest

An early American chest from the Hadley area of New England that stands on four legs with one to three drawers; only about 32" to 46" high

hacket

and decorated with shallow, crude incised carvings, usually of a stylized tulip or a Tudor rose. See also *Connecticut chest* or *Wethersfield chest*.

Hadley chest

Hagia Sophia (HAH gee-ah SOH fee-ah)

A cathedral in Constantinople, a masterpiece of Byzantine architecture, built in 532-37 C.E., with its spacious nave covered by a lofty central dome carried on pendentives; later became a mosque and now a museum.

haircloth

A cloth made of cotton, worsted, or linen warp and horse hair filler; very durable and popular in England and America in the mid 19th century for upholstery.

Hagia Sophia

hairy paw

See *illustration in the Feet Appendix*.

half column

A column projecting from a wall by only half, or approximately half. See also *engaged column*.

half-headed bed

A bed with corner posts at all four ends but no canopy.

half lap joint or half joint

One of the simplest joinery methods for connecting two pieces of wood or metal fittings by cutting half the depth of the material away so the two pieces fit together flush; used to make frames and bracket supports for either inside or outside. See also *joint*. See *illustration in the Joints Appendix*.

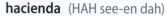

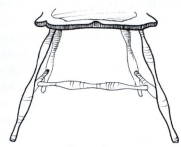

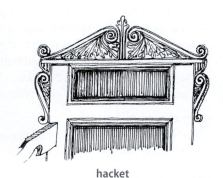

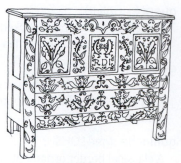
Hadley chest

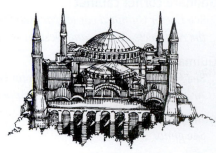
Hagia Sophia

half-tester bed

A term for a bed with the canopy over just the head half of the bed; a full tester has a canopy that covers the entire bed. See also *angel bed*.

half-timber

A type of exposed wood framing with an infill of plaster, brick, stone, or masonry, often filled with a daub of clay, sticks, and mud.

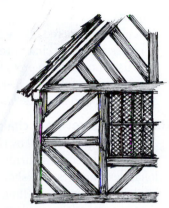

half-timber

half turning

Turned piece cut in half lengthwise used as an ornament, applied to a flat surface on a case piece or the back of a chair. See also *split spindle*.

hall and parlor house

An early colonial house with a front door leading into a vestibule called a porch and leading either to one of two rooms; on one side a room called the hall where the center of activity occurred and on the other side a room called a parlor where the best furniture was located along with the bed for the parents. Same as center-hall plan.

hall chair

Formal ornamental chairs with decorative backs originating in the 18th century, found in halls and corridors of Palladian mansions. See also *light chair* and *side chair*.

hall church

Church with nave and aisles but no clerestory and with an interior of approximately uniform height throughout, often under a single immense roof with tall windows, no transept, and the chancel defined only by furniture.

hall clock

Usually referred to as a grandfather clock; can be any tall clock. See also *grandfather clock* and *long clock*.

hall tree

A coat or hat rack made of wood or metal as a floor-standing unit; often placed in the front hall.

hallenkirche   (HAL en kursh eh)

See *hall church*.

hallmark

Designated mark on silverwork or goldwork as an official approval of quality; also called plate mark.

halved joint

A woodworking joint in which two wood members of equal thickness are joined by removing material from each at the point of intersection so that they overlap and fit together to form a flush surface. Also called checking and half-checking. See also *half lap joint*.

hamman   (HA men)

Public bath house in Islamic towns.

hammer beam or hammer beam truss

Description of a roof truss during the early English Renaissance where one of a pair of horizontal members attached to the foot of a principal rafter. The roof is framed so as not to have a tie beam at the top.

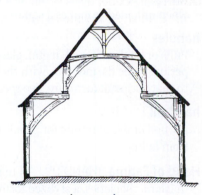

hammer beam

Han Dynasty   (HAHN DIY nas tee)

Second imperial dynasty of China, 206 B.C.E.–220 C.E., followed by the Qin Dynasty and preceded the Three Kingdoms of China; considered by the Chinese to be one of the greatest periods in the entire history of China.

hand

The feel or tactile property of a fabric. See also *finish*.

abcdefghijklmnopqrstuvwxyz

hand-blown glass

Glass formed or shaped by using a hand-held blowpipe.

hand prints

A process of hand screening wallpapers, murals, accessories, fabrics, etc., instead of using a machine.

Handicraft, Guild of

An association of craftsmen started in London, England, in 1888 by C. R. Ashbee as an experiment in medieval craftsman ideas and traditions, producing some fine metalwork of the Arts and Crafts period. See *C. R. Ashbee, 1863–1942, in the Architects, Artists, and Designers Appendix.*

handkerchief table

A triangular folding table, introduced in America in the 17th century, designed to fit into the corner of a room with a triangular single leaf; when unfolded, it makes a square.

handles

Pulls or knobs of wood, metal, glass, ivory, etc., adapted over all periods to be harmonious with the design; constitutes an index to that period of furniture. See *specific types of handles* or *pulls.*

handrail

A wood or metal railing for people to grip for support or protection from falling.

Hand of Fatima (HAND UV FAH te mah)

In Islamic societies, a stylized form of a hand with three fingers raised and sometimes with two thumbs arranged symmetrically; worn on charms, jewelry, cars, and other places to ward off the evil eye. In the Jewish lore, it is known as the Hand of Miriam; also known as "Khamsa" from Hebrew and Arabic, meaning "five."

hanging shelves

A shelf suspended from a wall, popular but very crude in the late 17th through the 18th centuries in France and England, used to meet the desire to show china collections, books, and plates; in the 19th century, hanging whatnots or knickknack shelves became the vogue.

hangings

A richly embroidered textile hung on a bed to create a place to chat or receive guests. Also used on a wall to provide comfort in harsh castle interiors. See also *arras, guadamicil,* and *wachstuchtapete.*

Hans Wegner cowhorn chair

A chair designed in 1952 by Hans J. Wegner, a successful Denmark furniture designer, for Johannes Hansen's workshop, characterized by elegant joining, a swelling and tapering of the top rail, and its excellent, but playful abstract and organic design. See *Hans J. Wegner, 1914–2007, in the Architects, Artists, and Designers Appendix.*

Hans Wegner cowhorn chair

Hans Wegner ox chair

A bull-shaped chair designed in 1960 by Hans J. Wegner, a Danish furniture designer, for strength and comfort with its heavily padded high-density foam form and cover of top-quality Italian leather. See *Hans J. Wegner, 1914–2007, in the Architects, Artists, and Designers Appendix.*

Hans Wegner ox chair

Hans Wegner peacock chair

A chair designed by Hans J. Wegner, a Danish furniture designer, in 1947 and manufactured by Johannes Hansen; the nickname "peacock" came from the distinctive back silhouette that looks like a peacock made of solid ash with teak armrests; a postmodern look based on the idea of a traditional English Windsor chair. See *Hans J. Wegner, 1914–2007, in the Architects, Artists, and Designers Appendix.*

Hans Wegner peacock chair

Hans Wegner round chair or "The Chair"

The round chair, designed by Hans J. Wegner in 1949 and often referred to as "The Chair," has been called "the most beautiful chair in the world," characterized by a simplified semicircle solid wood design and leather upholstered seat resting on four tapered legs. See *Hans J. Wegner, 1914–2007, in the Architects, Artists, and Designers Appendix.*

Hans Wegner round chair

Hans Wegner valet chair

A multipurpose chair designed by Hans J. Wegner in 1953 with a solid teak seat and brass fittings, designed with a rail to hold trousers or store other pieces of a man's suit; some items can even be stored underneath the seat. See *Hans J. Wegner, 1914–2007, in the Architects, Artists, and Designers Appendix.*

Hans Wegner valet chair

Hans Wegner Y chair or wishbone chair

A classic modern chair designed in 1949 by Hans J. Wegner, a cabinetmaker, and produced by Carl Hansen & Son in 1950; hailed as one of the Danish modernist's "most identifiable designs" with its solid wood frame, Y-shaped back (or its wishbone look), curved hind legs, and semicircular top rail. See *Hans J. Wegner, 1914–2007, in the Architects, Artists, and Designers Appendix.*

hard paste or hard-paste porcelain

A term used by the Chinese to identify hard-bodied or true porcelain. See also *porcelain.*

Hardoy chair (HAR doy CHAYR)

A popular portable recreational chair characterized by a folding frame and a cloth sling hung from a metal frame. It was designed by the Austral Group in Buenos Aires, Argentina in 1938 and is also referred

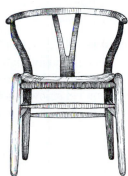

Hans Wegner Y chair

to as the BFK chair, named for the three partners of the group, Antonio Bonet, Juan Kurchan and Jorge Ferrari-Hardoy. Also known as the Hardoy butterfly chair. See also *sling chair.*

hardware

A term for general parts of cabinet trim, such as drawer pulls, handles, knobs, hinges, etc.; also a term for computer components. See also *specific type of hardware.*

hardwood

A conventional term for lumber from broad-leaf trees, such as oak, walnut, maple, and birch; used for furniture and interior trim. See also *softwood.*

haremlik (HAR em lik)

Women's quarters of the home or palace in the Middle East or in Muslim architecture. Same as haremand harim.

harewood

Common English name is sycamore; in America it is curly maple, dyed a silvery gray with oxide of iron, used for cabinetwork, decorative veneering, and inlays.

hari-bako (HAH ree-BAH koh)

Japanese sewing box with multiple trays to hold sewing objects.

haricot (AH ree koht)

French name for Louis XV kidney bean motif and the same for the C motif of the Louis XIV style; also a favored shape for the tops of small marquetry tables during Louis XV's time. See also *kidney desk, kidney table, rognon,* and *table à rognon.*

harlequin table (HAR le kin TAY bul)

An 18th-century writing or dressing table in which the center part rises automatically when drop leaves are raised, revealing a central set of compartments for toilet articles and/or writing materials.

harlequin table

harmonium (har MOH nee-um)
All pedal-pumped free-reed keyboard instruments, whether they have a pressure or suction bellow, are referred to as "harmonium."

harp
A triangular stringed musical instrument, which stands on a heavy base with pedals to influence the tone; also referred to as a Clarsach in ancient Ireland and Scotland; a Celtic harp in Wales and Brittany; a Blues harp; and a Jew's harp.

harpsichord (HAHRP si KORD)
A keyboard instrument resembling a grand piano whose strings are plucked by quills or jacks, existing by the mid 15 century, but becoming popular in the 17th and 18th centuries, and being replaced by the pianoforte in the late 18th century.

harrateen
A coarse cloth made of wool in the 18th century.

Harry Bertoia diamond or wire chair
A 1950s chair designed for the Knoll Group by Harry Bertoia, an Italian-born designer, artist, and sculptor, who experimented with bending metal rods to produce an innovative piece of art in the diamond chair. See *Harry Bertoia, 1915–1978, in the Architects, Artists, and Designers Appendix.*

Harry Bertoia diamond chair

Harvard chair
A three-cornered wooden chair with a triangular seat, similar to the Gothic three-cornered chair made of wood turnings; used since the 18th century by the president of Harvard University when conferring degrees.

harvest table
A simple American long, narrow, drop-leaf table designed to seat many people during the harvest time; associated with the 18th and 19th centuries.

hashira (HAH shee rah)
A generic term for a type of post, column, or pier that supports the roof of Japanese timber architecture.

hasp
A metal fastener for a chest or a door with a hinged, slotted part that fits over a staple and is secured by a pin or padlock; highly decorated during the Gothic period, particularly on Spanish Gothic chests.

hassock (HA sek)
A low thickly stuffed footstool on which to kneel or rest one's feet.

Hathor column (HA thor KAH lum)
A column popular in Egypt, found in their temples during the Middle Kingdom, surmounted by a capital representing the cow-headed goddess Hathor.

hatrack
A means of hanging hats, ranging from a frame, stand, wall rack with hooks or pegs to a freestanding structure. See also *costumer* and *umbrella stand.*

hausmalerei (HOWS mah lur iy)
German or Bohemian white pottery made in the home by Hausmaler (term for freelance home painter or decorator), very homemade and amateurish, started in the 17th century but quite common by the 18th century.

haut boy (HOHT BOI)
See *highboy.*

haut relief (HOHT-REE leef)
French term for high relief meaning that sculptural figures project at least half of their circumference from the background as opposed to bas-relief or low relief. Alto-relievo is the term used in Italian for high relief. See also *alto-relief* and *high relief.*

hawksbeak

A molding on the upper edge of an exterior surface with a convex curve above and a concave curve beneath it; also a decorative molding at the top of the wall, such as a crown molding, or at the top of certain pieces of furniture, such as a highboy.

headboard

A vertical panel or board forming the head of a bed. See also *footboard.*

header

The short side of the brick when laid sideways to the face of a wall.

header bond

Bricks arranged by rows of headers, only being displaced by a half a brick on each row. See also *header.*

heart and crown chair

Baluster-backed chair with a rush seat, painted black with cutouts of hearts and crowns on the cresting, developed in Connecticut in the 1730s by a country artisan's interpretation of fancy Boston or Philadelphia chairs.

heart and crown chair

hearth

The floor, usually of brick, tile, or stone (fire-resistant material), around a fireplace or extending outward into the room in front of the fireplace.

Hector Guimard corner cabinet

A late 19th-century corner cabinet designed by one of the most influential architects, Hector Guimard of Lyons, who incorporated materials into a curvilinear and plastic style, working the wood to look like soft twisted satin, yet embodying the very essence of the French Art Nouveau movement into the cabinet design. See *Hector Guimard, 1867–1942, in the Architects, Artists, and Designers Appendix.*

Hector Guimard corner cabinet

Hector Guimard desk

An olive wood desk with ash panels designed by one of the leading French Art Nouveau architects, Hector Guimard, in the late 19th century or early 20th century; the desk is considered to be a "work of art" using nature as a source of inspiration. See *Hector Guimard, 1867–1942, in the Architects, Artists, and Designers Appendix.*

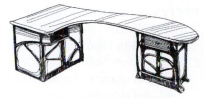

Hector Guimard desk

helix (HEE liks)

Something spiral in form, such as an ornamental volute on a Corinthian or Ionic capital or a spiral staircase moving in a circular motion.

Hellenistic period (he lu NIS tik PEER ee ud)

Pertaining to the era of Greek art, architecture, and culture from the death of Alexander the Great in 323 B.C.E. to the annexation of the classical Greek heartland by Rome in 146 B.C.E.; considered to be a time when Greek influence and power was at its zenith in Europe and Asia.

hemlock

A wood from a coniferous tree found across Canada and the United States that resembles the white pine.

hemp

A strong coarse fiber used for fabrics, ropes, and sacks, derived from the mulberry family, which grows in many temperate zone countries.

henge

A prehistoric monument, sometimes in a circular form, but not always, created of stones, wood, or earth.

Henri II (Deux) style (HEN ree THEE SE kend STIYL)

A French name for the second phase of the three principal styles of the French Renaissance, named after Henri II (1547–1559), when refined and restrained classic Italian motifs replace Gothic elements in architecture and decoration.

abcdefghijklmnopqrstuvwxyz

Henry van de Velde armchair

An Art Nouveau chair designed in 1904/05 by Henry van de Velde for Alfred von Nostitz-Wallwitz's dining room, characterized by its highly polished mahogany with dark leather upholstery; a very large chair designed for spacious dining rooms or cozy corners. See *Henry van de Velde, 1863–1957, in the Architects, Artists, and Designers Appendix.*

Henry van de Velde armchair

Hepplewhite heart-shaped chair back

See *George Hepplewhite heart-shaped chair back.* See *George Hepplewhite, d. 1786, in the Architects, Artists, and Designers Appendix.*

Hepplewhite Style (HEP ul wiyt STIYL)

A style of English furniture of the late 18th century, characterized by square tapering legs; light, graceful lines; and subtle decoration achieved by inlays, veneers, and delicate carvings, with chair backs in shield or heart shapes and with popular motifs, such as bellflowers, wheat sheaves, and paterae. See also *George Hepplewhite shield-back side chair.* See *George Hepplewhite, d. 1786, in the Architects, Artists, and Designers Appendix.*

heptastyle (hep tah STIYL)

A porticus with seven columns, at one end or at each end.

heraldic symbols

In the Middle Ages personal insignia on seals and shields, emblazoned with symbols that identified individuals or families; a feudal system that carries the arms and heraldic marks of a noble owner. See *illustration in the Motifs/Ornaments Appendix.*

herati (hayr AH tee)

A Persian rug design consisting of a rosette surrounded by four leaves or fish, usually found inside a lozenge shape.

Herculaneum (her kyoo LAN ee-um)

A popular ancient resort town located in southern Italy on the bay of Naples during the Roman Empire, which was destroyed by the eruption of Mount Vesuvius in 79 C.E. The excavation of this city in 1738 revived interest in the classical styles, particularly during the time of the French Louis XVI style and the English Adam Style. See also *Pompeii.*

hereke or herek rug (HAYR ek)

Recognized as one of the finest hand-knotted carpets in the world with designs inspired by both traditional Turkish carpets and the elaborate curvilinear designs of Persia and Egypt; made of silk, a combination of wool and cotton, and often gold or silver threads.

herma, pl. hermes (HUR mah)

A square stone pillar that tapered downward with a bust or head of Hermes or some other divinity, used by the Romans as milestones or outdoor decoration. See also *term.*

herma

herringbone

A pattern of rows of short, slanted parallel lines in which the grain of each runs diagonally to that of the previous producing a herringbone effect, used in parquet flooring, weaving or cloth designs, embroidery, and masonry. See also *feather banding.*

herringbone

hetre (Ee tru)

A French term for beechwood used by French artisans during the 18th century for furniture.

hex sign

A round sign with stylized six-pointed stars, rosettes, wheels, or other geometric motifs, thought to be magical, painted on Pennsylvania Dutch barns as a symbol of good luck or to ward off evil, but today largely for decoration.

hexagonal court cupboard

A court cupboard with a hexagon-shaped profile popular in late 16th-century England and France. See also *court cupboard*.

hexastyle (heks ah STIYL)

A building or temple with six columns across the front.

hibachi (hi BAH chee)

A Japanese designed small portable charcoal-burning brazier with a grill used chiefly for cooking.

hexagonal court cupboard

hickory

A heavy, strong, tough wood of the walnut family, indigenous to America and used for cabinetmaking, not for decorative purposes.

hideaway bed

A bed that can be folded away vertically against the wall or into a closet for concealment, designed by William L. Murphy as an means of having more room in a small apartment. See also *Murphy bed* and *trundle bed*.

hieracosphinx (hiy RAH koh sfinks)

An ancient Egyptian sphinx with the head of a hawk. See also *achech*.

hieracosphinx

hieratic (hiy RA tik)

Cursive form of ancient Egyptian writing, simpler than hieroglyphic, and reserved for religious writings.

hieroglyph or hieroglyphics (HIY roh glihf)

A system of writing by ancient Egyptians using pictures or symbols to represent words or thoughts; some found on walls tell pictorial stories.

hieroglyph

high altar

Central primary altar in the church, which is raised so that it can be seen by all the faithful in the sanctuary.

high chair

A long-legged chair with a footrest and a tray for a baby or a young child to sit in while eating.

high daddy

An 18th-century American highboy without drawers in the supporting frame.

High Gothic

A style of architecture and art developed in 13th-century Europe, particularly in France where cathedrals increased in height and were embellished by large stained glass windows.

high relief

Sculptural relief in which forms extend out from the background at least fifty percent, or half of the depth. See also *haut relief.*

high style

A trendsetting style of fashion or design used by exclusive clientele; usually more elaborate than previous provincial styles.

highboy

A tall chest of drawers appearing in the 17th century developed in England with William and Mary and Queen Anne influences and in Colonial America in the 18th century, usually in two sections, with larger drawers above and smaller ones below, supported on four legs fifteen inches or more in height; derived from the French term hautbois, meaning high wood. See also *chest-on-chest* and *tall boy.*

highboy

abcdefghijklmnopqrstuvwxyz

high-post bedstead

A bed holding a tentlike canopy; another name for the bed is tester.

high-riser

A single bed used as a couch designed with a mattress and frame beneath it; when pulled out, the unit underneath can be raised up to the level of the upper mattress and locked into place to form a double bed.

high-tech

Twentieth-century style of architecture featuring and emphasizing elements of advanced technology, structure, and materials; also known as Late Modernism or Structural Expressionism.

hijki   (HIYJ kee)

Bracket arm used by the Japanese for support.

hinge

A folding device that permits doors, lids, or other swinging parts to open, close, or swing on a pivotal center. See also *specific hinge* or *pull*.

hip

A reference to the knee of a chair or table leg. See also *knee*.

hipped carved decoration

Decoration on the knee of a furniture leg that extends onto the seat rail.

hipped roof or hip roof

A roof with sloping ends as well as sloping sides.

hippodrome   (hi poh DROHM)

An open-air arena surrounded by tiers of seats in an oval for horse and chariot races in ancient Greece; corresponds to the Roman circus.

high-post bedstead

hipped roof

hirashi   (hi RAH shee)

Support columns or posts for a Japanese hall.

Hispano Mauresque or Hispano-Moresque architecture   (hi SPAN oh-MOR esk)

Term used to designate the Spanish style of architecture or decoration with Moorish influences from the 8th to 15th centuries; a fine example is the Alhambra (1338–1390); also referred to as Hispano-Moresque architecture.

historiated   (his TOR ee-a ted)

Initial letters decorated with animals, flowers, or other designs, which are representational or symbolic; popular in medieval manuscripts.

historicism   (hi STOR i si zum)

A theory that stresses the importance of history as a basic criterion of value or the practice of using historic styles in the design of contemporary works.

Hitchcock chair

An American chair, 1820–1850, made by Lambert Hitchcock of Connecticut, composed of a light, sturdy, cane or rush-seat with a stenciled frame, derived from the Sheraton "fancy" chair. See *Lambert Hitchcock, 1795–1852, in the Architects, Artists, and Designers Appendix*.

Hitchcock chair

HL hinge

A common provincial hinge used for passage doors, room doors, and closet doors during the 17th, 18th, and 19th centuries with a design resembling an H due to the pivotal joint between the I and L creating the image of the H. See also *H hinge*.

Hobby Horse, The

A quarterly magazine published in 1882 by Arthur Heygate Mackmurdo (British architect and friend of William Morris) for the Century Guild; the magazine was one of the most iconic official mouthpieces of the Arts and Crafts movement. See *Arthur Heygate Mackmurdo, 1851–1942, in the Architects, Artists, and Designers Appendix*.

hock leg

A cabriole leg with the curve broken on the inner side just below the knee; often the sides of the knee will be decorated with carved spirals called ears. See also *cabriole leg*. See *illustration in the Legs Appendix*.

hodo (HOH doh)

The treasure room in a Buddhist temple or monastery where rare objects of worship such as statutes of divinities, relics, and precious items are stored.

Hogarth chair (HAH garth CHAYR)

Name for an 18th-century English chair of the Queen Anne style with heavily decorated knees and modified cabriole legs, a hoop back, and pierced splat.

hogyo (HOG yoh)

A type of Japanese sloped roof used mainly on pavilions or Buddhist structures with a square, hexagonal, or octagonal plan.

holly, white

The whitest of all wood, very hard, grayish-white with small flecked grain; used in modern work for large surfaces.

Hollywood bed

A bed with a headboard only that is attached to the frame or wall; varies in size from twin to king. See also *dual bed*.

hom (HOHM)

Pattern representing the Assyrian "tree of life." See also *"tree of life" pattern* and *palampores*.

hondo (HAHN doh)

Japanese main hall located in a Buddhist temple.

honeysuckle

A conventionalized fanlike Greek ornament; a common name for the Greek anthemion. See *illustration in the Motifs/Ornaments Appendix*.

hood

Shaped cabinet top; usually a bonnet or arch top on a clock case or highboy. See also *hooded top* and *bonnet top*.

hooded chimney piece

A projecting metal or masonry cover above a fireplace opening that forms the upper part of the fireplace and keeps the smoke going into the flue.

hooded top

Early 18th-century English cabinets with rounded tops, especially found during the Queen Anne period; also referred to as domed, curved, or semicircular tops.

hooded chimney piece

hoodmold

A projecting molding, originally designed to carry away water, located over the interior or exterior of a door or window. See also *drip stone* or *drip mold*.

hoof foot

A type of foot representing a goat hoof on a cabriole leg and seen on very ancient furniture; first found in Egypt, then on English furniture of the late 17th century throughout the 18th century. See also *cloven foot, doe's foot*, and *pied de biche*. See *illustration in the Feet Appendix*.

hoopback chair

A term used to describe a chair back when the uprights and top rail merge to form a continuous curve, denoting the bow-back classification of the Windsor chair.

hoopback chair

hooped stretcher

See *arched stretcher* and *rising stretcher*.

hope chest

A chest that is a traditional form of furniture kept by a young woman for storing clothing and household goods, such as silver and linens, in anticipation of her marriage. See also *cassone* and *cedar chest*.

horror vacui (HOR ur Vak yoo-iy)
Term describes the fear of empty spaces; in art it describes the filling of empty space with a design or image of some sort.

horse
A rear strut designed to support a hinged flap by engaging the ratchet; it could be an invented V or a shaped piece. See also *rachet*.

horse dressing glass
See cheval glass.

horse screen
A fire screen with two bracketed feet. Also known as a cheval screen. See also *cheval screen*.

horse screen

horsehair
A furniture covering, popular in the late 18th and 19th centuries, woven from the hair of a horse's mane or tail and wrapped with cotton or linen; used as an upholstery material.

horseshoe arch
A rounded or pointed arch, often found in Moorish and/or Spanish architecture, whose curve is greater than a semicircle.

horseshoe back
A term for the outward sweep at the bottom of a chair where it joins the seat; a good example can be found on Windsor chairs.

horseshoe-shaped seat
The contour of a seat in the shape of a horseshoe, i.e., the upholstered seat of a Queen Anne chair that is fitted within the seat rails.

horseshoe table
An 18th-century table shaped like a horseshoe. See also *drinking table* and *hunt table*.

hortulus (HOR tu lus)
A small, enclosed garden in a Roman house.

hortus (HOR tus)
A Latin term meaning "a pleasure garden in a Roman villa."

hosho (HOH shoh)
A Japanese term for the finial on the pagoda roof.

hotel (HOH tel)
A French term for a luxurious townhouse or private residence of a French aristocrat.

houndstooth
A type of broken check or four-pointed star design on fabric or wallpaper; also called four-and-four check.

hourglass base
An early 18th-century base made up of two curved elements, one set on top of the other to form a rounded X shape; used by Adam, Sheraton, Hepplewhite, and Chippendale on stools and chairs.

housse (OOS)
A French word for slipcover or dust cover.

howdah or houdah (HOW dah)
The carriage used to ride an elephant; usually highly decorated.

Hsia Dynasty
The ancient, semi-legendary first dynasty of China; now thought to have actually existed according to traditional dates from c. 2204 to c. 1766 B.C.E. or before.

hu chuang (HOO CHANG)
Chinese chair in the form of a foldable stool, introduced into China, possibly from central Asia, toward the late Eastern Han period.

hua zhuo (WHAH ZHOO)
Chinese term for a square-topped table used as a surface for writing or painting.

huche (EHSH)
French term for hutch. See also *hutch*.

huchier-menuisiers

French term for a cabinetmaker; a person making fine cabinets by the panel method of construction.

Hudson River School (1825–1870)

A mid 19th-century American school of romantic landscape painters, influenced by European Romanticism, whose aesthetic vision depicted the grandeur of the Hudson River Valley, the Catskill Mountains, and Niagara Falls.

humpback sofa

A Georgian sofa with a central raised, rounded back.

humpback sofa

hunt table

An English semicircular table, popular from the late 18th century through the 19th century, with an open middle, often having drop leaves at the end or other expansions; see also *drinking table, horseshoe table*, and *wine table*.

hunting chair

An 18th-century Sheraton chair designed with a frame that slides out in front upon which to rest the feet.

hurricane lamp

A 17th- and 18th-century lamp with a tall, glass cylinder shade to protect the flame, often used in pairs and similar to the 19th-century girandole or lustre.

husk ornament

A chainlike arrangement used on 18th-century furniture and architectural woodwork, representing the outer coat or outer covering of seed; derived from the ancient Greek ear of wheat. See also *bellflower ornament* and *catkins*. See *illustration in the Motifs/Ornaments Appendix*.

hutch or huche (HUTCH)

A term derived from the French word huche meaning a chest or cupboard, from the Gothic period; designed for storage, with the open upper shelves used for dishes. See also *ménagère*.

hydria (HIY dree-ah)

A Greek water jar with a rounded body, a small neck, and three handles used for pouring or carrying water.

hypaethral (hiy PEE thrul)

An ancient temple wholly or partly open to the sky.

hypocaust (HIY pu kawst)

An underfloor heating system in the hollow space beneath the floors of an ancient Roman building providing a type of radiant heat into the room from the masonry floor; later flues were used to carry the heat from a remote furnace.

hypostyle hall (hi pe STIYL HAHL)

An Egyptian building or hall constructed by rows of columns to support a roof or ceiling.

hypotrachelion (hi poh tra KEE lee-um)

The lower part of the capital of an architectural column or a groove encircling a column between the capital and the main shaft.

icon or **ikon** (IY kahn)
A Greek term for a portrait of a sacred image of saints, Christ, and the Virgin Mary that started in the 6th-century Byzantine church.

Iconoclastic period (iy KAHN oh klas tik PEEr ee-ud)
Floral and geometric patterns in rich colors and textures typically found in Byzantine and Eastern churches; this style replaced sculptural representations of humans and animals, which were prohibited by Emperor Leo III who feared that the statues fostered paganism and idolatry.

iconograph (iy KAHN oh graf)
A pictorial illustration formed by a word or words.

iconostasis (iy KAHN oh stay sis)
A decorated screen with icons separating the sanctuary from the rest of the church found in Byzantine or Eastern Orthodox churches.

icthus (Ik thus)
The Greek word for fish and the early Christian symbol that combined the initials of the Greek words of "Jesus Christ, Son of God, Savior."

IDEC
An acronym for Interior Design Educators Council.

IIDA
An acronym for International Interior Design Association.

illumination (I loo mu NAY shun)
A type of decoration, such as scrolls; decorated borders with gold and silver, foliage, etc., used in the medieval times on manuscripts, especially religious manuscripts produced in Italy and the Eastern Roman Empire during the period 400 to 600 C.E.

illusionism (I LOO zhu ni zm)
Pictorial methods using images to deceive the eye, often referred to as trompe l'oéil. See also *trompe l'oéil*.

ima (Ee mah)
A term for a Japanese living area with wood floors where shoes must be removed before entering.

imagine d'epinal (ee MAH jeen de pee NAHL)
A simple print made using a block of wood.

Imari ware (i MAR ee WAYR)
A gilded and enameled porcelain with elaborate patterns in strong reds, golds, and blues; the first porcelain made in Japan, produced around the early 17th century.

imbrication (im bri KAY shun)
A decorated molding or ornament resembling overlapping fish scales used on tile roofs, columns, walls, etc., adapted from antique Roman during the Italian Renaissance. See also *scaling*.

imbrication

imbuya (im BWEE yah)
Brazilian wood with interesting variation of color from olive to deep, rich, red-brown, often used for veneer on high-quality furniture. It has a medium density with a figured and variegated grain.

imitation
An act of replicating another's work; a contrast to innovation. Method of instruction in ancient Roman and Renaissance humanist curricula.

impluvium (im PLOO vee-um)
A basin or pool in the ancient Roman house used to collect water from the roof by means of the compluvium. See also *compluvium*.

impluvium

impost block

A plain or decorated masonry block (also called a dosseret) mounted between the capital of a column and the entablature or arch that receives and distributes the weight of an arch.

impost capital

The crowning member of a column, pilaster, or pier, often tapered, that provides structural support and transition for the thrust of vaults or arches; similar to an impost block.

Impressionism

A style of painting that originated in France during the 1870s and 1880s that aimed to achieve naturalism by using unmixed primary colors and short strokes of paint to simulate reflected light. Claude Monet and Alfred Sisley were two of the major impressionists. Also, refers to a literary style that used details and mental associations to evoke sensory impressions, and a style of music that used vague harmony to evoke a mood, place, or natural phenomena.

in antis

in antis (IN An tis)

An architectural term describing a condition created when columns are located between antae.

in situ (IN Si too)

A Latin term for work done by a craftsman directly on the job instead of being performed in a workshop for later application or installation.

incised carving

Low-relief carving in which the ornament is cut below the surface but is flush with the surrounding wood. See also *intaglio*.

incised lacquer

A Chinese pattern technique used during the Sung period (960–1279 C.E.) by applying several coats of lacquer, then a design was incised into the lacquer surface with a fine chisel to form decoration, especially used on screens and furniture.

Incrustation Style (200-60 B.C.E.) (in krus TAY shun STIYL)

First style of Pompeii paintings with the emphasis on stucco relief to imitate texture and to simulate a material, using predominantly red and yellow as colors. See *first style painting and Pompeii*.

India papers

Chinese papers dating from the 17th century, characterized by flower designs and exotic birds with a jewel-like delicacy; they were imported to Europe by great trading companies, Dutch East India and English East India Company, hence, the name of India papers; also referred to as Japan paper.

India print

A plain-weave printed cotton fabric made in India or Persia with brilliantly clear colors and designs on a white or natural background.

Indian head

A cotton fabric that is smooth and lightweight, and has a permanent finish that has low shrinkage and is guaranteed color fast.

Indian red

A terra cotta color used on American provincial pine furniture in the 18th century.

Indian rugs

Handmade India rugs with Persian design influence of flora or "tree of life."

indienne fabrics (IN dee-en FA briks)

In textiles, the French imitation of a lightweight, India-printed or painted cotton fabric imported from India into France during the late 17th and 18th centuries. See also *toiles d'indy*.

indiscret (in dis KRAY)

A French upholstered settee, comprised of three armchairs linked in a spiral arrangement from a central point, popular during the Second Empire.

inginocchiatoio (in jee NAH kee-ah toi-oh)

A term used by the Italians for prie-dieu. See also *prie-dieu*.

inglenook (in gul NUK)
A recessed opening, usually with seating, formed next to the fireplace creating a space that is small, sheltered, and cozy. It came into being in the mid to late 16th century.

ingrain
Machine-made reversible carpet with a flat-woven wool or wool and cotton carpet made with on a Jacquard loom.

inlay
A decorative design formed by embedding pieces of material, such as woods, metals, ivory, precious stones, tortoise shell, etc., into another part of a surface ornamentation to create a flat surface. See also *Boulle work, certosina, intarsia or tarsia*, and *marquetry*.

inscrolling foot
A variation of the scroll foot where it curves inward and back on itself. Another name is knurl foot. See also *knurl foot*.

insula (in soo LAH)
An ancient Roman apartment building with shared walls that filled a block; occupants were of lower to middle class.

intaglio (in TAI ee-oh)
Countersunk decoration as opposed to carving in relief. See also *crayon engraving, intaglio engraving*, and *stipple*.

intaglio engraving (in TAAL yoh en GRAYV ing)
A printmaking process where lines or textures are incised into a smooth plate, normally copper or zinc, then ink is spread across the plate and wiped smooth, leaving ink within the lines or texture. The ink within these lines print onto the paper when assisted by an etching press or roller. See also *aquatint, crayon engraving, drypoint engraving, etching, intaglio*, and *mezzotint print*.

intarsia or tarsia (in TAR see-ah)
A decorative inlay technique used during the Italian Renaissance where small pieces of wood or other materials, such as ivory, shell,

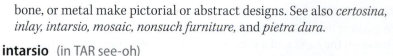

inglenook

bone, or metal make pictorial or abstract designs. See also *certosina, inlay, intarsio, mosaic, nonsuch furniture*, and *pietra dura*.

intarsio (in TAR see-oh)
An Italian type of wood inlay used to ornament a surface by setting wood or materials of different colors into a cut-out space to execute a decorative design. See also *intarsia*.

intercolumniation (in ter kah lum ni-ay shun)
The space between the columns at the bottom of the shaft.

interlaced chair backs
In the late 18th century the French and English (Chippendale and Hepplewhite styles) used a ribbon back or interlaced strap, formed by two long C-scrolls knotted to appear like tied ribbons. See also *ribbon-back chair*.

International Style
A modern architectural style developed in the 20th century characterized by flat roofs and large glass areas, usually without ornament.

interpenetrating moldings
A decoration in the late Gothic architecture where moldings intersect each other and seem to pass through solid uprights, transoms, or other members.

interrupted arch
A segmental pediment with the center omitted to accommodate a decoration or ornament, usually found on cabinets or chests of the 18th century; same as broken pediment. See also *arch*.

interrupted pediment
See *broken pediment*.

interstice (in ter STIYS)
A small or narrow space that intervenes between vertical parts in a building.

intrados (in TRAY dos)
The interior curve or face of an arch or vault. See also *extrados*.

Intricate Style (c.50 C.E.)   (in tri KAT STIYL)

Fourth style of Roman painting at Pompeii with architectural representations, but no attempt to copy architecture; more reminiscent of stage building of the Roman theater. See *fourth style painting and Pompeii*.

inverted cup leg

Popular in the William and Mary period in England; the shaping of the uppermost part of the leg resembles an inverted cup. See *illustration in the Legs Appendix*.

Ionic Order

The second of the three orders of architecture; originated by the Ionian Greeks, characterized by a column capital with large volutes of spiral form. See also *zoophorus*. See *illustration in the Architectural Orders Appendix*.

ireme   (eer EEM u)

African wood that varies from golden orange to light brown with a pale yellow sapwood and darker brown heartwood used for interior and exterior joinery, furniture making, cabinetry, and carving. See also *iroka*.

irimoya-zukuri   (ee REE moh yah zoo KOO ree)

A hipped-and-gable-style roof used in the kondo or lecture hall of Buddhist temples, with the gabled part covering the moya (core of building) while the hipped covers the aisles.

Irish Chippendale

In the mid 18th century in Ireland, furniture based on Chippendale drawings that was not as refined and light as the original Chippendale. Usually it had lion masks and paw feet.

iroko   (eer OH koh)

A hardwood from tropical Africa initially yellow that darkens to a rich brown and used for many purposes such as flooring and furniture; often referred to as African teak or ireme, and also called kambala. See also *ireme*.

ironstone

In the 19th century, a type of stoneware introduced by Staffordshire potters of England to imitate porcelain that could be mass produced. It was dense, hard, and durable with several names used to describe the same product. See also *China, creamware, Queen's ware,* and *Staffordshire*.

ironware

Household utensils and other products made of iron.

ironwood

An extremely hard wood with one species found in North America in the eastern part of the United States and Canada; often called musclewood due to its large trunk and limbs.

Isabellina   (iz ah be LEE nah)

A Spanish style named for Queen Isabella and the first style of the Plateresco style; flourished in the late 14th century to early 15th century, characterized by a mixture of Moorish and Gothic architectural elements. See also *Manuelino* and *Plateresco*.

Isamu Noguchi Akari lamps   (ee SAH moo noh GOO chee ah KAH ree LAMPS)

Lamps designed by Isamu Noguchi in the mid 1950s based on Japanese traditional designs of folding rice paper in varied shapes and sizes with modern concepts. See *Isamu Noguchi, 1904–1988, in the Architects, Artists, and Designers Appendix*.

Isamu Noguchi Akari lamp

Isamu Noguchi rocking stool

A 1954 rocking stool designed by Isamu Noguchi evoking the hourglass shape of African stools. Featuring a seat and foot made of wood and chrome-plated steel rods, it utilizes ergonomic effects as it rocks gently in all directions and is protected by a contour edge and plastic support. See *Isamu Noguchi, 1904–1988, in the Architects, Artists, and Designers Appendix*.

Isamu Noguchi rocking stool

abcdefghijklmnopqrstuvwxyz

Isfahan or Esfahan rugs (Is fahn RUGZ)

One of the most sought after rugs in the world markets, woven in the Iranian city of Isfahan or often spelled Esfahan (city famous for Persian rugs) having ivory backgrounds with blue, rose, and indigo motifs with symmetrical designs. Also referred to as Esfahan rugs.

isho-dansu (EE shoh DAHN soo)

Japanese clothing chests with multiple drawers used to store clothing, often with iron carrying handles and ornate decoration.

isinglass (iy zun glaas)

Transparent sheets of mica used instead of glass in windows for stoves and kerosene heaters because mica was less likely to shatter than glass; also used as "isinglass curtains" in horse-drawn carriages.

island

An unattached unit that stands away from the walls and permits access from all sides.

island bed

A bed that sits in the middle of the room and can be viewed from all sides. Sometimes a screen or some form of shelving may be placed behind the head of the bed. See also *platform bed*.

Italian Neoclassic Style

Inspired by the rediscoveries of Pompeii and Herculaneum in the late 18th century and a reaction against the Baroque and Rococo styles with a desire to return to style of Louis XVI of France, but with unique usage of exaggerated Italian flairs.

Italian Provincial Style

Italian furniture of the 18th and 19th centuries designated as a rural style with straight lines and simple decoration, usually of fruitwood or mahogany. See also *Palladian*.

Italian Renaissance

The opening phase of the architecture of the Renaissance, a word meaning "rebirth." A period between early 15th and 17th centuries in Europe starting in Florence with Brunelleschi as one of the innovators and spreading to other European cities, it featured a conscious revival of the elements of ancient Greek and Roman culture. Emphasis was placed on symmetry, proportion, geometry, and classical antiquity. See also *Renaissance*.

Italian Renaissance

Italianate architecture

A distinct style of the 19th-century phase of Classical architecture based on 16th-century Italian Renaissance, started in England in the early 19th century by John Nash and becoming very popular in the United States in the mid to late 19th century, promoted by Alexander Jackson Davis.

ivory

Elephant tusks used for decorative inlay features on furniture; often imitated with plastic material.

ivy

A leaf design symbolizing both pagan and Christian traditions. It dates back to the Romans where it was the ancient symbol of Bacchus, god of wine and revelry.

iwan (AY vahn)

A part of a common place or Islamic dwelling with an open-fronted semi-domed room faced with glazed tiles and located on the south side of the courtyard.

Iznik ware (IZ nik WAYR)

A highly decorated pottery that reached its zenith in the late 17th century and is recognized as one of the most admired, collected, and emulated of the Islamic world.

jabot (JA boh)

A fabric or small panel with folded deep pleats at the top and cut at an angle that cascades down each side of the window.

jacaranda (ja kah RAN dah)

A Brazilian rosewood belonging to the genus Jacaranda, one of Brazil's finest woods. The trees or shrubs usually have blue or blue-violet flowers and fernlike leaves. See also *rosewood, Brazilian.*

jackknife sofa bed

A sofa bed that opens into a bed by lifting the seat part up from the front and the back folds down flat to form the bed; a "jackknife" method of opening a bed. See also *sofa bed.*

Jacobean moldings (Ja koh bee-an MOHLD ings)

Applied moldings in geometric patterns creating a paneled effect on furniture, particularly the chest drawers, used during the Jacobean period 1603–1649.

Jacobean Style (Ja koh bee an STIYL)

The English architectural and decorative style from 1603 to 1649, extending over the reigns of James I and Charles I. The Tudor design was merged with the early Renaissance style in England.

jabot

Jacobean Style

Jacquard loom (ja KARD LOOM)

A loom, invented in the 19th century and named after its French inventor, that produced intricate and elaborate patterns, such as damask, brocades, and tapestries. See *Joseph-Marie Jacquard, 1752–1834, in the Architects, Artists, and Designers Appendix.*

Jacquemart and Bernard (ZHAK mar AND bur NARD)

French wallpaper manufacturers (1791–1840) and successors to Réveillon.

jade

A term applied to two distinct species, one rare variety is jade (a sodium aluminum silicate), and the other is nephrite (a calcium magnesium silicate). Jade used for fine carvings and jewelry has flourished in China since 2000 B.C.E.

jale, jalee, or jali (jah LEE)

Pierced slabs of marble primarily used as a screen or lattice in Indian architecture, as found on the Taj Mahal.

jale

jalousie or louvre window (JAAL wuu zee OR LOOV ru WIN doh)

A window with a series of thin, narrow strips of glass that open outward to shield the interior from rain, yet provide ventilation and privacy. See also *awning windows.*

jamb

The vertical member of a door or window frame to which the window sash or door attaches.

Japanese lacquer

A resinous varnish from a Japanese tree used to create a highly polished wood surface, generally black in color with gold and silver motifs.

japanning

A type of finish used in the 18th century in England and Europe that imitated Japanese lacquer, usually with a background of black but other colored backgrounds could be used. See also *pontypool* and *vernis Martin*. See *Martin brothers in the Architects, Artists, and Designers Appendix*.

japonisme (Ja pah neez mah)

A late 19th-century and early 20th-century style that developed in England and American based on Japanese inspired design.

jardinière (ZHAR din yayr)

French term for a large stand, pot, urn, or jar intended to hold plants or flowers, generally highly decorative. It also has other meanings relating to the culinary world and to a type of garden beetle. See also *flower stand*.

jasper

Usually a dark red, but also yellow, dark green, or brown opaque quartz used as a gemstone.

jasperware

The name for a type of hard biscuit ware (pottery) introduced in England in the 18th century by Wedgwood.

Jenny Lind bed

A bed with spool turnings designed between 1850 and 1852 and named for Jenny Lind, a Swedish opera singer known as the "Swedish Nightingale," who visited America during that time and slept in a bed with turned spindles. See also *spool furniture*.

Jenny Lind bed

jardinière

jetty (JE tee)

An upper story overhang that projects beyond the wall below.

jewel box

A receptacle or small chest made especially for storage and transportation of jewelry. See also *coffer*.

jetty

jewel work

A term used to describe applied ornaments such as split spindles, turnings, and bosses on 17th-century and Colonial American cabinets, cupboards, etc.

jeweled strapwork

A decorative design of low relief interlacing scrollwork, crosshatching, braiding, or shield, commonly used on wood, metal, or plaster. See also *strapwork*.

ji (JEE)

A term used for a Chinese armrest.

ji tai shi an (JEE TAY SHEE AHN)

A tall, narrow Chinese altar table, used for religious functions, designed with turned up ends and sometimes simple carvings on the apron and braces.

ji tai shi an

jià zi chuáng (JEE ah zhi CHOO ang)

Chinese word for a four-poster bed.

jichimu (JEE chee moo)

A Chinese term for a wood used during the Tang dynasty that translates into "chicken-wing wood"; because of its strongly grained pattern with lines of purple and yellow, it resembles bird feathers when cut tangentially.

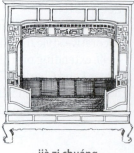

jià zi chuáng

jigsaw

An early power tool used to create cutouts or fretwork to enhance buildings in the mid to late 19th century, especially on late Victorian structures labeled "gingerbread" or "steamboat Gothic," the most ornate forms of that period. See also *scrollwork* and *Steamboat Gothic*.

jigsaw mirror

Nineteenth-century framed mirrors popular in America and England, cut with a power-operated tool called the jigsaw.

jigsaw mirror

Joe Colombo elda chair

An armchair designed in 1963 by Joe Colombo, an Italian designer; it is one of his most significant works and is considered a classic of the 20th century. The shell is made of fiberglass (the first to be made of fiberglass of this size) and the interior upholstery is fabric or leather; on exhibit in New York at the "Modern Art Museum" and in Paris at the "Louvre." See *Joe Colombo, 1930–1971, in the Architects, Artists, and Designers Appendix*.

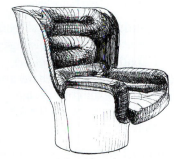

Joe Colombo elda chair

Joe Colombo tube chair

Italian designer and architect, Joe Colombo, radically reinvented furniture forms in the components of his "tube" chair, which can be arranged in several combinations to fit the user; made up entirely of synthetic materials, it reflects the interest of the 1960s in using human-made materials in residential environments. See *Joe Colombo, 1930–1971, in the Architects, Artists, and Designers Appendix*.

Joe Colombo tube chair

Joe DiMaggio baseball glove chair

A classic modern leather lounge chair shaped like an oversized baseball glove, created in 1971 and inspired by the New York Yankees baseball legend Joe DiMaggio, who was married to Marilyn Monroe. Also known as Joe chair.

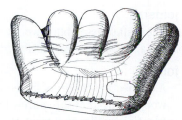

Joe DiMaggio baseball glove chair

jodan (joh DAHN)

A Japanese Shoin-style room with a raised area or platform.

joggled lintel

A lintel composed of a series of masonry joggle joints, in which one fits into another by a notch or projection in one piece, fitted to a projection or notch in a second piece to prevent one piece from slipping.

jogyo-do (JOG yoh DOH)

One of two twin halls in Japan (jogyo-do and hokke-odo) linked by a corridor under one roof; only Mt. Hiei and Rinnoji Temple use this temple design. jogyo-do, built in the Japanese style, was used for "gyozanmai training."

John Henry Belter chair

A mid 19th-century rosewood laminated chair with a low seat, undulating back, and carved pierced work decorated in the Rococo Revival Style by cabinetmaker and designer John Belter, a German immigrant to the United States in 1833. See *John Henry Belter, 1804–1863, in the Architects, Artists, and Designers Appendix*.

John Henry Belter chair

Johnson Wax chair

See *Frank L. Wright Johnson Wax chair. See Frank Lloyd Wright, 1867–1959, in the Architects, Artists, and Designers Appendix*.

joiner

A person skilled in constructing articles by joining pieces of wood, especially a cabinetmaker. See also *joinery*.

joinery

The craft of assembling woodworking by joining together pieces of wood. See also *dovetail, mortise and tenon joint*, and *tongue and groove joint*.

joint

A connection or way of fastening two pieces of wood; some joints are purely for support and function, while others can be both functional and decorative. See also *specific joints*.

joint stool

A 17th- and 18th-century English stool made of turnings joined together with mortise and tenon joints.

joint stool

joist

A horizontal construction member of wood, steel, or concrete that runs from wall to wall, wall to beam, or beam to beam to support a floor, ceiling, or roof.

Josef Hoffmann cabaret fledermaus

(kaa bu RAY fle DUR mows)

A beech wood chair designed by Josef Hoffmann in 1908 for the Cabaret Fledermaus in Vienna, with the characteristic bold, geometric style and fine lines of Charles Rennie Mackintosh, Scottish architect and furniture designer. It is often described as a "total work of art" by Vienna critics. See *Josef Hoffmann, 1870–1956, in the Architects, Artists, and Designers Appendix*.

Josef Hoffmann cabaret fledermaus

Josef Hoffmann sitzmaschine, model No. 670 (zitz MAH shee nu)

Described as a "machine for sitting," the 1905 chair was originally designed by Josef Hoffmann for the Purkersdorf Sanatorium in Vienna; it represents one of his earliest experiments in unifying a building and its furnishings. See *Josef Hoffmann, 1870–1956, in the Architects, Artists, and Designers Appendix*.

Josef Hoffmann sitzmaschine, model No. 670

jouy (JOH ee)

See *toile du juoy*.

juansha (JWAHN shah)

In Chinese architecture, the convex-shaped wood blocks at the ends of brackets.

judge's chair

A chair with an upholstered high back that is curved to support the head and shoulders and with upholstered arms curved at the same level as the bottom of the chair back. Legs are wood and square with a stretcher connecting the two front and two back legs.

Jugendstil (YOO gent shteel)

Name derived from Die Jugend ("Youth") at the end of the 19th century in Germany and Austria, exhibiting design contemporary with the Art Nouveau in France.

Jugendstil

juno, pl. junones (JOO noh)

In Roman religion, the chief goddess and wife of Jupiter, connected with all aspects of women's lives, particularly marriage, and the female guardian spirit. See also *genius*.

jute

A sturdy, cheap, durable plant fiber that is woven and used as carpet backing to add strength and stiffness; also used for making mats.

K

Kaare Klint (KOR KLINT) **deck chair**
A teak deck chair designed by Danish designer Kaare Klint in 1933, characterized by its wicker seat, ergonomic design, and superior craftsmanship. See *Kaare Klint, 1888–1954, in the Architects, Artists, and Designers Appendix.*

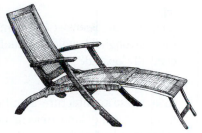
Kaare Klint deck chair

kachelofen (kah ke LOH fen)
A German ceramic-tile stove.

kaidan-dansu (KAY dahn DAHN soo)
A Japanese step chest that usually opens only on one side and is used for storage and stairs to climb to the second floor. When the tax collector comes, however, the step chest is moved so that the upper level can be hidden.

kairō (KAY roh)
Covered walkways in Buddhist temples and nobles' residence linking pavilions or rooms.

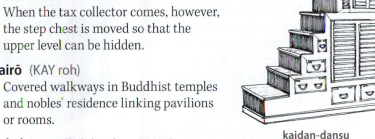
kaidan-dansu

kakebuton (kah kay boo TAHN)
Traditional Japanese comforter that is a part of a futon set, also includes the shikibuton (futon) and the makura (pillow).

kakemono (kah kay MOH noh)
Chinese or Japanese unframed painting equipped with bamboo rods at both top and bottom, mounted on brocade and hung on the wall. See also *makimono.*

kakesuzuri (kah ku SOO zoo ree)
A small chest, one of three fana-dansu "ship chests" from the Edo period into the Meiji era, with a single swinging door and multiple internal drawers.

kakiemon (kah KEE e-im ahn)
The first enameled porcelain produced in Japan at the factories of Arita, Saga Prefecture, Japan, from the mid 17th century.

kambala (kahm BAH lah)
See *iroko.*

k'ang (KANG)
Chinese term for a platform for sitting or sleeping.

k'ang-hsi porcelain (KANG see POR se lin)
Magnificent Chinese porcelain created during the K'ang-hsi period of the Ching dynasty (1661–1722), usually blue and white.

kan'g table (KANG TAYbul)
A Chinese long, low table, typically rectangular with short cabriole legs, placed on a kang, a raised three-walled platform used for sleeping or relaxing; dates back to 3rd century B.C.E. See also *zhuo table.*

kan'g table

kantharos kan (THAH rohs)
A Greek pottery drinking cup characterized by high swung handles that extend above the lip of the pot; from the period of the red-figure and black-figure styles.

kaolin (KAY oh lin)
A white clay, also called china clay, used in making porcelain. See also *china clay.*

kapok (KAY pok)
A fine, fibrous material obtained from the seeds of a tropical tree called kapok; used for stuffing cushions, mattresses, soft toys, and for insulation.

Karabagh or Karabakh rugs (KA re bah RUGZ)
Handmade floor coverings from the Karabakh district, north of the Iranian border, with different designs and color schemes in bold color combinations, very similar to those of Persian rugs.

Karuselli chair (Ka roo sel ee CHAYR)
See *Yrjo Kukkapuro Karuselli chair*. See *Yrjo Kukkapuro, 1933–, in the Architects, Artists, and Designers Appendix*.

kas, kast (KAHS, KAHST)
A tall, upright Dutch wardrobe with ball feet and two doors and an overhanging cornice found in Dutch-American colonies, usually painted with primitive ornaments. See also *armoire, garderobe*, and *wardrobe*.

kas

kasbah (KAZ bah)
An Islamic city often built on top of a hill as a means of defense to protect the local leader when the city was under attack.

katagami (kah tah GAH mee)
A Japanese term for a method of fabric dyeing that uses a resist paste through a hand-cut stencil.

katana-dansu (kah TAN ah DAHN soo)
A Japanese chest designed for storing Samurai swords.

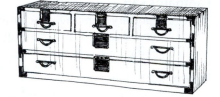

katana-dansu

katsuogi (KAT soo-oh gee)
Decorative logs placed at a right angle to the ridgeline of Japanese and Shinto religious or imperial buildings; usually featured today on Shinto buildings to distinguish them from other religious structures, such as Buddhist temples in Japan.

keel molding
Molding created by using the keel arch, which resembles the keel of a boat.

keep
A castle's tall defensive tower and the inner stronghold, which is usually centrally located.

ken
In Japanese architecture, a unit of measurement of land areas in an effort to calculate taxes.

keep

Kent Style
A term used to describe a movement of architecture associated with the characteristics of William Kent, whose architecture was inspired by the great Italian architect Andrea Palladio, and whose early Georgian interiors and furniture had Baroque features of symmetry, regularity, and correctness of detail. See *William Kent, 1685–1748, in the Architects, Artists, and Designers Appendix*.

kerf (KURF)
A groove or slit made by a saw; it also can refer to the width of the cut made by the sawn notch.

Kent Style

kettle base
A piece of furniture with a bombé-shaped base that has a swelling or bulging front and sides, prevalent in the 18th century in America and England. See also *bombé*.

kettle front
See *swell front*.

kettle base

kettle stand

An 18th-century small table, very popular in America and England, used to hold a tea kettle. Sometimes incorporating a sliding tray within the apron to hold a tea cup while pouring water.

key cornered

A decorative ornamentation with a broken corner filled with a paterae or rosette, used in England by Adam during the late 18th century and also used in France during the Louis XVI, Directoire, and Empire periods.

key hole cover

Decorative piece of hardware that covers the key hole of a door.

key pattern

A Greek geometric border design of interlocking right angles and vertical lines in a continuous pattern with motifs often inserted between the meandering elements; sometimes, but not often, the continuous pattern will be intermittently broken. See also *Greek fret*. See *illustration of Greek fret in the Motifs/ Ornaments Appendix.*

keystone

The wedge-shaped or topmost central stone of an arch. See also *arch, intrados,* and *voussoir.*

keystone

khekher (KE kur)

An ancient Egyptian design for a decorative frieze using papyrus stalks bundled together with floral parts at the top.

Khilim rugs (KI lum RUGZ)

In Oriental countries, a rug used as a floor covering or as a curtain hung to separate the dwelling area of the tent from the area for cattle; in Turkey, a rug with a smooth surface, alike on both sides, used on the floor or wall. Very popular in the United States as a wall hanging or coverlet on the sofa. See also *kilim.*

kibotos, pl. kibotoi (ki boh TOHS)

A wooden chest or box with a flat or angled lid used by the ancient Greeks.

kidan (kee DAHN)

Japanese term for a base platform or a variously shaped slab of rock often present under the base.

Kidderminster carpets (ki dur MIN stur CAR pets)

Light, medium, and heavy-tufted wall-to-wall carpets, rugs, and runners designed and manufactured at Kidderminster factory in the United Kingdom.

kidney desk

A kidney-shaped desk with an inset leather top, used in 18th-century England, especially by Sheraton; also found in France. See also *haricot, rognon,* and *table à rognon.*

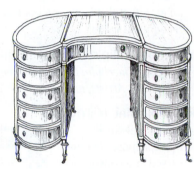

kidney desk

kilim or kelim (KI lum)

A flat-woven tapestry rug from the Middle East with decorative geometric designs in rich, brilliant colors. Same as *khelim.* See also *Khilim rugs.*

kiln dried (KILN DRIYD)

Wood that has been control-dried or seasonsed in a kiln to reduce the moisture content to a predetermined amount. See also *seasoned lumber.*

kingwood

A fine-textured, violet-streaked wood from a Sumatran and Brazilian tree used in cabinet-making, especially in France during Louis XV and XVI periods and in England during the Queen Anne and Late Georgian periods. It is also referred to as bois de violette.

kilim

kiosk (kee OSK)

A term coined from the French word kiosque meaning a small shelter or pavilion, set up in a public place and used for many purposes.

kirizuma-zukuri (ki ree ZOO mah zoo KUR ee)

One of the traditional architectural roof styles, the gable, used on Japanese buildings.

kitch (KITCH)

A German term describing an inferior, low-quality, worthless copy of an extant style of art; or a poor taste imitation of artwork that has a recognized value.

Kjaerholm tulip chair (kee YAY Rhohm TOO lip CHAYR)

See *Poul Kjaerholm tulip chair*. See *Poul Kjaerholm, 1929–1980, in the Architects, Artists, and Designers Appendix*.

kline, pl. klini (KLIYN)

An ancient Greek multipurpose sofa that served as a couch, bed, or reclining surface while dining.

kline

klinium (kli nee-UM)

A certain type of couch used in the Roman dining room (triclinium) at meals. It was also referred to as the lectus tricliniaris. See also *lectus*.

klinium

klismos, pl. klismoi (kliz MOHS)

An ancient Greek chair characterized by the saber legs splayed at both front and back and with a concave curved back. Later the Romans designed the cathedra chair, which is similar in form and shape to the Greek klismo. See also *cathedra*.

klismos

kkloosterkozyn (kloo stur KOH zen)

A Dutch word for a casement window with a fixed window located above it.

kneading table

A French country utilitarian table used for kneading dough.

knee

The upper bulging or convex curve of the cabriole leg, which is often decorated with a shell, acanthus leaf, mask, etc. See also *hip*. See *illustration of cabriole leg in the Legs Appendix*.

kneehole desk

A desk with a central opening below the writing surface for the sitter's knees, while the spaces on either side of the opening are filled with drawers or cabinets that continue to the floor. See also *pedestal desk*.

kneehole desk

kneehole panel

See *modesty panel*.

knife box or knife case

Decorative boxes, usually in pairs, first appearing in England during the 18th century, placed on the buffet or sideboard and filled with vertical slots for table silver. See also *prong box*.

knife urns

A 1760s English urn placed on top of pedestals flanking a dining room sideboard used to hold tableware or hot/cold water; replaced by knife boxes.

knob turning or knob-turned

Seventeenth-century turnings containing a series of balls or knobs, used for furniture legs and stretchers.

knockdown or K.D. furniture

Unassembled furniture shipped in a kit with all its parts so it can be easily constructed by the buyer. Same as knocked down or knock-down furniture.

Knole sofa

The Knole sofa, a classy work of art made in the 17th century and housed at Knole, England, at the Sackville-Wests. It has a cushioned headrest hinged to the arms and held by ratchets.

knife box

Knole sofa

knop

An archaic term for knob, bulb, or protuberance, used to open doors, drawers, etc., or used as handles on the lids of tureens; also found on the stem of drinking glasses.

knot

A heraldic motif of interlaced cords or ropes stitched on a surcoat; also it could be where a knot or oval interrupts the grain of wood.

knot garden

A garden of formal design in a square frame with a variety of aromatic plants and culinary herbs; first established in England during the reign of Queen Elizabeth I.

knotted column

A late Byzantine or Romanesque column where two or more columns are laced or knotted together.

knotty pine

A pine wood used especially for furniture and paneling; known for its large number of knots.

knubstol (NUB stohl)

An early 18th-century Scandinavian peasant chair made from a hollowed tree trunk because the weight made it a safer chair.

knuckle

The outer edge of the arms of chairs resembling the knuckles of a human hand; often found on Chippendale or Windsor styles.

knuckle joint

A hinged joint used to support the drop leaf of a table, allowing the table leg to swing 180 degrees.

knurl foot (NURL FUUT)

A furniture foot formed by an inward-turning scroll continuing down the leg and outward; used in Europe during the late 17th century to the mid 18th century. See also *inscrolling foot, paintbrush foot, scroll foot,* and *whorl*. See *illustration in the Feet Appendix.*

koa (KOH ah)

A reddish wood, similar in strength and weight to black walnut; the wood comes from the largest endemic tree in Hawaii; often used for musical instruments, other art objects, and some furniture.

kodo (KOH doh)

A Japanese lecture hall within a Buddhist monastery.

abcdefghijklmnopqrstuvwxyz

koilon (KOI lun)
Seating area of an ancient Greek theater, which had three major parts: the orchestra, the scene, and the main theater or koilon.

kokera-buki (koh KE rah-BOO kee)
Traditional Japanese roof made with a layer of thin cypress shingles.

kokoshniki (koh KOH shnik)
A semicircular or keel-like exterior decoration used in traditional Russian architecture in the 16th century, which gained great popularity in the 17th century, where it was placed on walls, over window frames, or in rows above vaults.

kondo (KAHN doh)
A Japanese term for the chief room in a Buddhist temple where the images of Buddha exist.

korai (KOR ay)
An ancient Greek sculptural representation of the Archaic period depicting a standing young woman dressed in a long Greek robe. See also *kouros* for the young male sculpture equivalent.

korai

korina (ko ree NAH)
A wood native to tropical western Africa with the trademark name for limba, either "white limba" or dark stripes "black limba," used for making furniture and musical instruments due to its workability, color, and finish. See also *afara* and *limba*.

Korya period (KOR yah PEE ree-ud)
A great period in Korean history, along with Yi, that constituted the "golden age," beginning in the 10th century and ending in 1392.

kotatsu (koh TAT soo)
A Japanese low, wooden table covered by a comforter so another table can sit on top, while underneath is a heating device built into the table.

kotatsu

kouros, pl. kouroi (KOR ohs)
A life-sized Greek sculpture of a standing nude young man, especially produced between the 7th century and 5th century B.C.E. The statue was typically made of marble, but also rendered in ivory, terracotta, wood, and/or bronze. See also *korai*.

kraal (KRAHL)
An African rural village consisting of huts with an open space surrounded by a stockade. It also can mean an enclosure for livestock.

krater (KRAY tur)
An ancient Greek and Roman vessel made out of metal or clay with a wide neck, large body, two handles, and a base used for mixing wine and water.

kuche (KOO chah)
A Pennsylvania-German term for a kitchen.

kufic (koo FIHK)
An angular form of the Arabic alphabet, particularly used for inscriptions or for making fine copies of the Koran.

kumimono (koo mee MOH noh)
Brackets used in Japanese architecture to support wide overhanging eaves.

kuri (KOO ree)
Japanese for chestnut, the wood choice among wood craftsmen and furniture designers for its striking natural grain, light weight, strength, and durability.

kuruma-dansu (koo roo MAH DAHN soo)
A Japanese moveable chest of drawers for valuables and merchandise; an essential possession, often a part of a daughter's dowry.

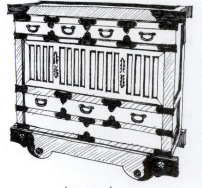
kuruma-dansu

kusuri-dansu (koo soo ree DAHN soo)

A Japanese traditional apothecary chest with numerous small drawers used to store herbs, tree bark, or powders, which could be made into prescriptions by a pharmacist.

kusuri-dansu

kuwa (koo WAH)

Japanese word for mulberry.

kylikeia (ki li KEE yah)

A large classical Greek cupboard, like a pantry with shelves hidden behind doors, usually placed near the kitchen.

kylin (KI lin)

A mythical beast often used in Chinese art and decoration.

kylin

kylix (ki LIKS)

A flat, two-handled ancient Greek drinking cup set on a slender center foot.

kylix

kyodai (kee YOH diy)

An ancient Japanese dressing table with mirrors or a miniature table with tiny drawers.

kyosoku (kee YOH soh koo)

Japanese term for a wooden upholstered armrest used for comfort while sitting at the traditional low table.

kyodai

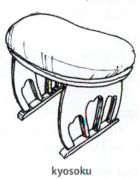

kyosoku

L

labrys (la BUR eez)

A Minoan term for a double axe often used as a motif within the civilization.

laburnum (lu BUR num)

A European hardwood, yellowish in color, used in the late 17th and early 18th centuries as a veneer. It was especially popular for Oysterwork.

labyrinth (LA bu rinth)

Latin word for an intricate maze commonly used as a structure or as a design motif.

lacca povera (LAH ka POH vay rah)

Italian for découpage.

lace

A openwork fabric constructed by an arrangement of threads to form a decorative pattern. See also *fillet lace, Nottingham lace, reticella,* and *Valenciennes lace.*

lacewood

An decorative wood from Australia that displays a lacy figure and is pink to light brown in color.

laconicum (la KOHN ee kum)

In a Roman bath, a room with hot, dry air that was typically circular in form, allowing the air to flow to every part of the room.

lacquer (LA kur)

A hard, dense furniture finish originating from China and made from the sap of *Toxicodendron vernicifluum,* commonly known as the Chinese lacquer tree. The finish was first exposed to the Western world during the Renaissance.

lacquer work (LA kur WURK)

Decorative articles of flat or relief design, generally of wood, that are coated with lacquer. Popular in Europe during the mid 17th to late 18th centuries.

lacunaria (la KOO nar ee-ah)

See *caissons* and *coffered panels.*

ladder-back chair

A chair with a back containing horizontal slats between two posts that resembles a ladder. See also *Chippendale ladder-back chair.*

ladies desk

A small, delicately legged desk originating in France and England in the late 17th century.

ladrillos (la DREE ohs)

Spanish for fired brick.

lady-chapel

Highly valued and decorated chapel within a cathedral that is dedicated to the Virgin Mary.

lag

An excretion of resinous material from the insect Coccas lacca, which is treated to create shellac.

lagynos (LAH jee NOHS)

A Greek wine jug with a broad bottom, narrow neck, and loop handle.

Lamassu (Lam i shoo)

Proper name for the sculpture of a bull with a human head, wings, and five legs. Only two legs can be viewed from the front, but four from the side.

lambelle (LAM bel)

A light, damask fabric with a texture created by coarser weft threads woven with fine, usually mercerized, warp threads.

lambrequin (LAM bri kin)

A hard window treatment that is fixed at the top of a window, similar to a cornice, but that generally extends partially down the sides. The unit is usually covered in fabric, but can be reproduced in carved wood or metal.

ladder-back chair

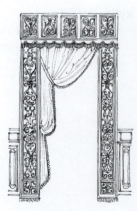

ladies desk

lambrequin

lambris d'appul (LAHM bree duh PUUL)
French for waist-high paneling.

lambris de hauteur (LAHM bree DUH HOH tur)
French for cornice or picture-rail-high paneling.

laminate
A product made by the process of lamination, such as plywood or plastic laminate.

lamination
The process of binding three or more layers of materials, such as wood or sheets of plastic, to form a permanent material. See also *laminate*.

lamp
A device used to produce light. Most present day sources are electrified and use a light bulb or tube; until the19th century, oil followed by gas was employed.

lampadaire (LAHMP u dayr)
In classical times, a pedestal specifically designed to hold a lamp or candlestick.

lampas (LAHM pus)
A patterned textile formed by using two warps and two or more wefts and employing a plain or twill weave for the pattern and a plain or satin weave for the ground.

lampshade
A cover for a light bulb, designed to shield the viewer from glare, to diffuse light, and/or to direct the stream of light. Usually constructed with a wire frame covered in fabric, paper, or opaque board. May also be constructed of glass, metal, or other materials.

lanai (la NIY)
A term used in Hawaii for an outdoor patio or terrace.

Lancashire spindle-back chair (LAN ku sheer SPIN dul-BAK CHAYR)
A turned English country chair with a rush seat, distinguished by one or two rows of spindles within the chair's back, a shell-like ornament in the center of the top rail, and a front stretcher with a knoblike centerpiece.

lancet arch
A narrow, sharply pointed arch.

lancet window
A tall, narrow window with a sharply pointed, arched top typical of the English Gothic Style.

landing
A level area found at the beginning, end, and sometimes middle of a flight of stairs.

lantern
A structure with glazed or open sides used on top of a roof to provide light or ventilation. The term is also used for a metal or wood protective case with panes of transparent material at the sides used for light emission, often cupola-shaped with open windows.

lap joint
A form of joinery made by overlapping one edge over another.

lap siding
See *clapboard*.

lapis lazuli (LAP us La zu lee)
A rich azure blue semiprecious stone.

laqué (LAH kay)
French term for lacquered.

lararium (LAH rayr ee um)
A room within a Roman home reserved for worship of household gods.

L'Art Moderne (LART MOH dayrn)
Name of a Belgian weekly periodical published from 1884 to 1893 that espoused "Art is the eternally spontaneous and free action of man on his environment, for the purpose of transforming it and making it conform to a new idea." See also *Art Nouveau*.

Late Empire period
See *Second Empire*.

lath (LATH)
Thin strips of wood nailed to studs, joists, or rafters to provide support or backing to plaster or stucco.

latilla (la TEEL ah)
A Spanish term for small poles laid across vigas to support a roof's finish material.

Latin cross
A cross with three short equal arms and one extended lower arm.

latten (Lat in)
German term for thin plates or laths used for engraved panels and cast statues during the Gothic era.

lattice
Thin pieces of wood or other material diagonally interwoven to form a repeating diamond shape pattern.

Latin cross

lattice window
A leaded window with panes in a diamond or lozenge shape.

latticework
A chair back design by Sheraton that encompasses a lattice design. Also the lattice framework of gazebos, pavilions, porches, and trellises, particularly popular during the Victorian and Aesthetic Style periods.

lattimo (la TEE moh)
Glass with an opaque milky color.

lauan (LOO-on)
A reddish-brown wood also known as Philippine mahogany because of its close resemblance to the wood.

laurel
A long-standing symbol of glory, this ornamental motif resembling bay leaves has been utilized on architecture and furniture since classical Greece and Rome. It can also be found in the styles of Louis XVI, English 18th century, and early 19th-century European.

laurel wood
An East Indian hardwood with a brown or gray color, characterized by its coarse, wavy grain, used predominately for fine cabinetry.

lavabo (lah VAH boh)
An 18th-century French term for a wash bowl or basin that contains one or two spigots and hangs on a wall beneath a fountain. Often used as a decorative planter today.

lawn
Originally a fine sheer linen fabric of plain weave. Currently also woven from cotton.

Lawson lounge
An overstuffed chair with square seat and rolled arms positioned mid-height between the seat and back. This style is also translated to sofas and loveseats.

Lawson lounge

layette (LAY et)
In furniture, a small chest designed to hold gloves and other lady's accessories.

laylight
A flush glass or translucent ceiling panel used to transmit natural or artificial light into a space.

lazy Susan
An American term for a revolving tabletop or tray, usually placed at the center of a dining table, used for passing condiments or food.

Le Corbusier adjustable lounge chair

Adjustable chaise lounge designed by Swiss-born architect and designer Le Corbusier in 1935 from chromed-plated tubular steel and leather. Also called the LC-4 Adjustable Chaise Lounge. See *Le Corbusier, born Charles-Édouard Jeanneret, 1887–1965, in the Architects, Artists, and Designers Appendix.*

Le Corbusier adjustable lounge chair

Le Corbusier basculant chair

A chrome-plated tubular steel frame chair with a back, seat, and armrests of leather slings stretched between the frame, designed by Swiss-born architect Le Corbusier in 1929. The chair was called the basculant because of it's pivoting back. Also called the LC1 chair. See *Le Corbusier, born Charles-Édouard Jeanneret, 1887–1965, in the Architects, Artists, and Designers Appendix.*

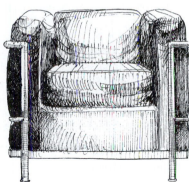

Le Corbusier basculant chair

Le Corbusier grand confort

A chair by Swiss-born architect Le Corbusier in 1929 designed with a tubular steel frame and cushions that mimic the geometric massing favored in his architecture. See *Le Corbusier, born Charles-Édouard Jeanneret, 1887–1965, in the Architects, Artists, and Designers Appendix.*

Le Corbusier grand confort

Le Corbusier Villa Savoye

Residence in Poissy, France, designed by Swiss born architect Le Corbusier in 1929 out of simple geometric massing.

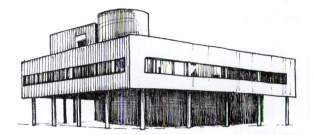

Le Corbusier Villa Savoye

An early example of the International Style of concrete and plaster over masonry; noted for its use of pilotis and lower level glass, which appears to make the building hover above the ground. See *Le Corbusier, born Charles-Édouard Jeanneret, 1887–1965, in the Architects, Artists, and Designers Appendix.*

le médaillon (LUH mee DAL yohn)

A Louis XVI oval-backed chair with square, tapered legs and arms that fastened directly above the front legs. Also called a cameo back or oval back.

lead glass

Glass containing a high amount of lead oxide, which gives it extraordinary brilliance and clarity.

leaded glazing

Small pieces of glass soldered together with lead strips. Various colors, patterns, and textures can be used. Colored or stained glass was commonly used in religious and educational institutions. Small diamond shapes were commonly used during the Tudor period.

leaf

Removable or hinged section of a tabletop, used to extend the surface area. Or, a very thin sheet or plate of any substance.

leaf scroll foot

A variation of the scroll foot containing foliage. See *scroll foot in the Feet Appendix.*

abcdefghijklmnopqrstuvwxyz

leaf work

Small collections of carved leaves common on legs, splats, and cabinets of late 18th-century English furniture.

leather

The hide of an animal that has been tanned, commonly used on furniture, books, and accessories.

leatherette

An artificial leather, carved to simulate leather graining, composed of nitrocellulose and used as upholstery, writing surfaces for desks, and wall coverings. Comes in a variety of colors, textures, and weights. See also *Naugahyde*.

leaves

Plural for *leaf.*

lectern

A desk or stand with a sloping top used to support books that are generally large, such as bibles and dictionaries.

lectica (lek TEE kah)

A portable Roman funeral bed used by women or by ill or wounded individuals.

lectus

A Roman bed or reclining sofa designed for sleeping and dining.

lectus adversus (LEK tus AD ver sus)

A Roman wedding bed, named for its placement across from the atrium.

lectus cubicular (LEK tus koo BIK yoo lar)

A Roman sleeping sofa typically requiring a footstool for entry because of its height, unlike the lectus triclinaris.

lectus triclinaris (LEK tus triy KLIN ar is)

A three-person sofa designed for the dining room or triclinium of a Roman house, generally arranged in threes around a central table.

lectern

ledge

A flat, horizontal surface projecting from a wall such as a mantle.

LEED

An acronym for Leadership in Energy and Environmental Design, a point-based building rating system with regard to green design.

leg

A support used on tables, chairs, couches, and other pieces of furniture. See *illustrations of common legs in the Legs Appendix.*

lekythos (Lek ee thohs)

A tall, slender-necked, single-handled Greek vase used for pouring oil.

leno weave (LE noh WEEV)

An open, netlike weave created by crossing pairs of warp yarns.

leonine base (LEE oh niyn BAYS)

A furniture support system carved with the legs and paws of a lion.

lekythos

lepel bortie (Le pel BOR tee-ay)

A traditional Dutch wooden spoon board made to hold twelve spoons.

lesenes (LAY say nez)

A narrow strip of stone used to form a panel that is devoid of base or capital.

lettiera (le tee AYR ah)

An Italian Renaissance bed designed to rest on a platform of chests that were used for storage and seating.

letto (LE toh)

The Italian term for bed.

letto con baldacchino (LE toh KON bal DA kee noh)

Italian tester bed.

Iewan (Iuu WAHN)

A room with a side open to an inner courtyard found within Oriental houses.

library

A room generally fitted with bookcases, a desk or writing table, and a comfortable chair.

library case

A late 18th-century English term used for a bookcase by Hepplewhite.

library chair

A chair with a built-in lectern and candleholder designed for reading within a library. Also, a convertible chair, first seen in the late 18th century, whose hinged seat flips over to form a small stepped unit used to access the higher shelves of library bookcases.

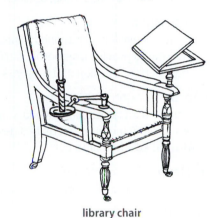

library chair

library press bedstead

A popular 18th-century convertible piece of furniture such as a cupboard, bureau, or bookcase that housed a bed folded inside. Commonly seen during the Sheraton and Hepplewhite periods in sitting rooms that doubled as a bedroom.

library steps

Various devices, popular during the mid to late 18th century, used to access the higher shelves of library bookcases.

library table

Large table with drawers designed for use as a study or writing surface within a library.

Lido sofa

See *Memphis Lido sofa.*

lierne (lee-AYRN)

A short rib found in Gothic architecture that connects one principle rib to another, but does not spring from a capital.

light chair

A lightweight, portable side chair. See also *hall chair* and *side chair.*

lighting louvers

A plastic, metal, or glass device used to filter light and/or soften glare from a light fixture.

Lignereux (lee NAYR oh)

Noted French Empire cabinetmaker of the early 19th century. See *Martin-Éloi Lignereux, 1750–1809, in the Architects, Artists, and Designers Appendix.*

lignum vitae (LIG num VIY tee)

A very hard, heavy, greenish-brown wood first used in the 16th century for its medicinal value, hence its name meaning wood of life. Also used for 17th-century Dutch and Flemish furniture, especially linen chests and cupboards.

limba (LIM buh)

French for korina wood. See also *afara.*

lime

A calcium oxide product obtained by pulverizing limestone with high heat; used for building and agriculture.

lime mortar

Mortar made from sand, water, and lime used to set bricks and stone masonry.

limed oak

A finish used to give oak a frosted look, created by rubbing a whitish filler or paint into the grain.

lime-soda glass

A common glass produced from sand and large amounts of lime.

limestone

Common sedimentary rock, usually gray or beige in color, used as a building material.

limewood

A light, close-grained wood that is white in color, excellent for carving and favored by the late 17th-century wood carver, Grinling Gibbons.

Limoges (lim OHJ)

Porcelain made in Limoges, France, since the 18th century.

Lincoln rocker

A Victorian Rococo Revival rocker with a tufted back named after the uphol-stered rocking chair on which President Abraham Lincoln was sitting in the Washington Theater box when he was assassinated.

Lincoln rocker

linden

A fine, light, white-grained wood of the linden family, such as limewood and basswood. Excellent for carving. Commonly used by 17th-century master wood carver, Grinling Gibbons.

linen press

A cupboard or chest designed to hold linens; named after an earlier board and screw device used to press sheets and table linens.

linenfold (lin in FOHLD)

Ornamental carving, common in the Gothic and Tudor periods, that resembles folded linen or a scroll of linen.

linen press

lingerie chest (lon ju RAY CHEST)

A tall, narrow chest of drawers used for storing undergarments.

lining

In furniture, a fine line of veneer, such as stringing. In window treatments and upholstery, a backing used for fine face fabrics to add additional weight and body. May also be used to protect fabrics from the sun, provide insulation, or block out light.

lining paper

An inexpensive paper applied beneath a wall-covering to provide a smoother surface, which offers better adhesion and prevents cracking.

lingerie chest

linocut (LIY noh kut)

A modern adaptation of a woodcut print technique that uses linoleum as a carving medium to create a design that can be used for printing. Also called a linoleum cut.

linoleum (li NOH lee-um)

A resilient flooring material made from linseed oil, resin, and powdered cork.

linseed oil

A drying oil from flaxseed, commonly used in house paints, furniture finishes, and linoleum.

lintel

A horizontal, structural building member used to span an opening such as a door or window. Usually made of wood or stone.

lion motif

A decorative motif used in various forms in furniture, interiors, art, and architecture since ancient times. It is commonly associated with strength, courage, and royalty.

Lion period

An English period from about 1720 to 1735 when carved lions were the most popular motif. The beast took the form of masks on the knees of cabriolet legs, heads as terminators on the arms of settees and chairs, and paws served as feet.

lions paw foot

A furry-pawed furniture foot representing that of a lion, first appearing in classical times. It is also common in French, English, and Italian designs of the Renaissance and of the French Empire and Early Georgian periods. See *illustration in the Feet Appendix.*

lip molding

A small convex molding used around drawers in casework of the Queen Anne and Early Chippendale periods.

lips sofa

See *Salvador Dali Mae West lips sofa.* See *Salvador Dali, 1904–1989, in the Architects, Artists, and Designers Appendix.*

lisière (liz YAYR)

French for selvage. See also *selvage.*

listel or list (LIS tel OR LIST)

A narrow band of molding.

lit

French for bed.

lit à colonnes (LEE AH KOHL un)

French four poster bed with a full canopy.

lit à couronne (LEE AH KOR un)

A French bed, common during the Empire period that was crowned with a round or oval canopy and draped with fabric that extended to the bed's corners.

lit à la duchess (LEE AH LAH doo CHES)

A French bed with a full canopy or tester that attached to the wall.

lit à la Francaise (LEE AH LAH frahn SEZ)

A French Empire canopy bed of the late 18th century that has a headboard and footboard of equal height. It is arranged in a room with one long side against a wall and display draperies that hang to the bed's short sides.

lit à la polonaise (LEE AH LAH pah lah NAYZ)

A French four poster bed with four iron rods that extend upward to form a central dome-shaped canopy that is draped in fabric.

lit à la turque (LEE AH LAH TURK)

A French bed with sides and a back that resembles a sofa or settee.

lit à travers (LEE AH tra VAYR)

French term for sofa bed.

lit canapé (LEE KAN ah pay)

French term for sofa bed.

lit clos (LEE KLOH)

A built-in bed with wooden panels enclosing the sleeping area, commonly found in 17th- through 19th-century French country estates. Also called a cupboard bed.

lit à la turque

lit d'ange (LEE DAHNJ)

A bed of 18th-century France, with a small canopy attached to the wall above the bed. In England it is called an angle bed.

lit de repos (LEE DUH RAY poh)

French term for a daybed.

lit en bateau (LEE ON bah TOH)

A French 19th-century boat-shaped bed.

lit en housse (LEE ON OHS)

A bed of the French Renaissance with curtains that can be raised and lowered.

lithograph

A method of printing using a grease pencil or crayon to draw a design on stone.

lits jumeaux (LEE ju MOH)

French term for twin beds.

liu xian zhou (loo shee EN joh)

A six-Chinese-immortals table commonly located in front of a tang hua an.

abcdefghijklmnopqrstuvwxyz

livery cupboard

A 17th-century English food cupboard with doors containing grilles of spindles or tracery for ventilation.

load-bearing wall

Exterior and interior walls that bear part of the structural weight of a building.

lobby chest

An early 18th-century small chest of drawers, about three feet in height, with four rows of drawers and at times a pullout writing surface beneath the top.

lobe

A Gothic term for a foil used in tracery.

lobing

See *gadroon.*

lock rail

The horizontal rail found at the center of a door, generally where the lock or door knob is fixed.

locker

The small central cupboard found in the interior of a writing desk or secretaire.

loggia (LOH jee ah)

A porch or gallery with an open colonnade on one or more sides.

lohan chair (LO han CHAYR)

A Chinese chair distinguished by a crest rail that curves around to form the arms of the chair and whose seat height often leads to using the front stretcher as a footrest.

Lombard Style

The Northern Italian edition of the Romanesque Style.

long clock

An 18th-century tall floor clock; also called a grandfather clock, hall clock, or tall case clock.

livery cupboard

long gallery

In Elizabethan homes, a long narrow space located above the entry, spanning the entire width of the building, and commonly used for socializing, entertaining, and exercising.

loo table

A Victorian pedestal table, with a circular or oval top, designed for playing the card game loo.

looking glass

See *mirror.*

loop back

A chair with an oval back. Also an American term for an armless Windsor bow-back chair.

loop pile

A tufted carpet or rug in which yarn loops are uncut.

loose seat

A chair seat with an independent upholstered frame that fits within the chair seat. See also *slip seat* or *drop-in seat.*

loper (LOH pur)

Sliding arms designed to support the fall or drop front of a desk.

lotiform column (LOH ti form KOL um)

An Egyptian column with a lotus flower capital including outer calyxes.

lotus

A type of water lily used as a decorative motif in ancient times in the Orient and Egypt.

lotus bud

Stylized water lily often used as ornamentation and as a capital in ancient Egypt or Greece. See *illustration in the Motifs/Ornaments Appendix.*

Louis XIII Style

See *French Late Renaissance.*

lotus bud capital

Louis XIV Style

The French Baroque Style period, from 1643 to 1715, also known as the Golden Age of the French Renaissance. Under the reign of Louis XIV, the Sun King, the style exhibited splendor and magnificence through massive furniture with S-shaped or pedestal legs, rich heavy gilt ornamentation, and bold jewel-toned colors. A predominately masculine style with rectangular shapes softened by compass curves.

Louis XV Style

The French style period, from 1723 to 1774, also known as the French Rococo period. Louis XV was king and the style was characterized by asymmetry, increasing ornateness, florid forms, the cabriolet leg, and pastel colors.

Louis XVI Style

The French style period, from 1774 to 1793, also known as the French Neoclassic period. Louis XVI was in reign and the style exhibited a return to naturalism, simplicity, and reason in the forms of classical Greece and Rome. Straight lines, symmetry, and the quadrangular tapered leg proliferated.

Louis Majorelle orchidée desk

Art Nouveau desk designed and manufactured by French decorator and designer Louis Majorelle in 1903, a designer known for transforming the Rococo Style with organic forms such as the orchid. Attached art glass lamps are by Daum. See *Louis Majorelle, 1859–1926, in the Architects, Artists, and Designers Appendix.*

Louis Majorelle orchidée desk

Louis-Philippe period

The period in France relative to the reign of Louis-Philippe from 1830 to 1848. The eclectic style looked back to the Rococo Style of Louis XV, but never captured its grace and quality in craftsmanship.

Louis Quatorze (LOO ee KAT orz)

Style name referring to Louis XIV.

Louis Quinze (LOO ee KANZ)

Style name referring to Louis XV.

Louis Seize (LOO ee SEZ)

Style name referring to Louis XVI.

lounge

A popular late 19th-century sofa, that resembled a daybed, with one arm higher than the other which enabled it to serve as a headrest. Also the name given to a large sitting room within a public building.

lounge chair

A fully upholstered armchair developed in the mid-19th century that was designed for lounging.

lounge chair

See *Le Corbusier adjustable lounge chair.* See *Le Corbusier, born Charles-Édouard Jeanneret, 1887–1965, in the Architects, Artists, and Designers Appendix.*

louver (LOO vur)

An opening fitted with one or more fixed or moveable angled slats that allow for air circulation, but keep rain or sun from entering.

louvered door (LOO vurd DOR)

A door with the center fitted with fixed or moveable horizontal slats.

Louvre (LOO vruh)

One of the world's largest art museums located in Paris, France. The largely French Baroque building was originally designed as a royal fortress in the 12th century under Philip II, and was later transformed into a palace for François I and then Louis XIV.

love seat

A small upholstered sofa designed for two people, first popular in the Louis XIV period of France and Queen Anne period of England.

lover's chair

See *drunkard's chair.*

low-back chair

Small side chairs, such as the farthingale chair, that succeeded stools and benches in middle-class homes of mid 17th-century England.

lowboy

A low chest or table popular in the 18th century that usually has three side-by-side drawers and long legs. It originally served as a ladies dressing table, but currently is seen as a serving table.

lowboy

low relief

Relief carving that has low projection from the background.

lozenge

A diamond-shaped motif commonly used throughout history in decoration of architecture, furniture, ceramics, silver, and textiles. See *illustration in the Motifs/Ornaments Appendix.*

lucarne (loo KARN)

French term for a small dormer window set in a roof or spire. Commonly seen during the Gothic and Romanesque periods.

lüftmalerei (luuft MAL u ZIY)

Literally translated as "air painting." A type of trompe l'oeil used on houses in Bavaria.

lug

A projection used on building materials to improve hold or support.

luminaire (loo mi NAYR)

A light fixture.

lunette (LOO net)

Semicircular motif, resembling a crescent or half-moon. See *illustration in the Motifs/Ornaments Appendix.*

luohan chuang (LOO hahn chung)

A Chinese bed, with low rails on three sides, used for sleeping, sitting, or reclining. Also called a monk's bed.

lustre (LUS tur)

A decorative table light containing crystal drops or pendants.

lustre à cristeaux (LUS trah AH krees TOH)

A chandelier.

lusterware

Pottery that has a thin iridescent metallic glaze applied to the surface.

luthern (LOO thurn)

A window of various shapes, placed above the cornice and lined up with the front of a classical building.

lu-tou (LOO toh)

A Chinese border or capital covering a notch in a building beam.

lyre (LIY ur)

A common Neoclassical motif representing an ancient Greek harplike instrument.

lyre-back chair (LIY ur-BAK CHAYR)

A chair with a carved lyre in the back, commonly seen in 18th-century Neoclassic English design such as the work of Adam, Hepplewhite, Sheraton, and Duncan Phyfe.

lyre-back chair

M

macaroon or macaron (MA kah roon / MA kah ron)

A carved decorative rosette commonly seen on Louis XVI furniture, consisting of an eight-petaled flower with a central bud and resembling a cookie, hence its name. Also seen as macaron. See also *patera*.

Macassar (MAH ka sur)

A Dutch West Indies seaport known for exporting a Macassar ebony. Also known as Makasar, calamander wood, and variegated ebony. See also *antimacassar* and *tidy*.

Macassar ebony (MAH ka sur E be nee)

An exotic species of wood with a beautiful striped pattern of blacks and chocolates used in furniture and cabinetwork, named after the Dutch West Indies seaport from which it is exported. Also known as calamander wood and variegated ebony.

macellum (MAH sell em)

An ancient Roman structure designed as an indoor market primarily for fruits and vegetables, generally located near the forum and basilica.

machicolation (me chi koh LAY shun)

A projecting defense structure of medieval castles, generally supported by corbels and designed with openings through which stones, boiling oil, etc., can be dropped to fend off attackers.

Mackintosh argyle chair

See *Charles Rennie Mackintosh argyle chair*. See *Charles Rennie Mackintosh, 1868–1928*, in the Architects, Artists, and Designers Appendix.

Mackintosh Hill House chair

See *Charles Rennie Mackintosh Hill House chair*. See *Charles Rennie Mackintosh, 1868–1928*, in the Architects, Artists, and Designers Appendix.

Mackmurdo ebonized carved chair

See *Arthur Mackmurdo ebonized carved chair*. See *Charles Rennie Mackintosh, 1868–1928*, in the Architects, Artists, and Designers Appendix.

macramé (MA kre may)

A technique for knotting yarns, twine, or other cords into open, lace-like patterns for use as wall hangings, decorative trim, hanging pot holders, etc.

Madame Jumel chair (me DAM JOO mel CHAYR)

Early 19th-century American chair whose top rail sweeps forward to meet the front legs. The chair's splat is commonly vase or lyre in shape. Similar to the English Regency spoon-back chair. See also *spoon-back chair*.

madio (MAH dee-oh)

A sideboard of the Italian Renaissance.

madou (MAH doo)

See *maidou* and *padouk*.

madrasa (mah DRA sah)

A school of higher learning for Islamic religious and cultural studies. Also known as a madrasah.

madio

Magasin au Bon Marché (MA gah zin OH BON MAR chay)

Renowned as the first department store of the modern glass and iron era. Built in 1876 by designer Louis Auguste Boileau and engineer Alexandre Gustve Eiffel, the store was full of glass sky lights, iron bridges and stairs, ornamental iron columns, and continuous ground floor display windows.

magnolia

A dense hardwood native to the southern United States, noted for its straight grain and close uniform texture that resembles yellow poplar. Principally used in the production of furniture, blinds, doors, sashes, and cabinetwork

Mahal (MAH hahl)

Indian for an eminent structure or palace. Alternatively, an area of Central Persia that is known for carpets of the same name. Also known as Malhal.

mahogany

A hardwood from South America and the West Indies, known for its beautiful reddish color, handsome straight grain, wonderful ability to take a high polish, and beautiful figures such as striped, mottled, fiddlebacked, or swirled. Commonly used in making British and American furniture since the 18th century. See also *acajou, Age of Mahogany*, and *primavera*.

185

mahogany, Honduras
A species of mahogany found in Central and South America, mainly Honduras and El Salvador, with a color that varies from pale pinkish-brown to reddish-brown and medium red, often with a rich mottle or straight grain with crossfire.

mahogany, Spanish
Considered the best of the mahogany species, with a medium to dark reddish-brown color. Originally indigenous to Cuba, trees were also planted by Spanish missionaries in Indonesia and Oceania hundreds of years ago, hence the name. Also known as Cuban mahogany and Santo Domingan mahogany.

mahogany, white
See *primavera*.

maidou or madou (MAY doo or MAH doo)
An exotic, rare wood of the East Indies and Indo-China with a light yellow to red color and long grain or fine burled figure similar to amboyna. Valued for furniture and cabinetwork.

maiolica (MIY oh lee kah)
Originally an Italian Renaissance lusterware, separated from the tin-glazed, white body wares known as bianchi. Later, all tin glazed earthenware, including those with luster, were labeled maiolica. See also *majolica*.

Maître Ébéniste (MET re E ben eest)
French for master cabinetmaker. A title bestowed by French kings. See also *Ébéniste*.

majolica (mah JAH li kah)
A tin-glazed pottery that mimicked Italian maiolica, popular in 19th-century England, France, the European continent, and America. Majolica was introduced to the public at the Great Exhibition of London in 1851. Famous manufacturers and potters include Minton, Wedgwood, Copeland, Bernard Pallisy, and Choisy-le-Roi. See also *maiolica*.

Majorca chair (MAH yor kah CHAYR)
See *caderira de sola*.

Majorelle orchidée desk
See *Louis Majorelle orchidée desk*. See *Louis Majorelle, 1859–1925, in the Architects, Artists, and Designers Appendix*.

maki-e (MAH kee-ee)
Literally translated as sprinkled picture. A type of Japanese lacquerware, developed as early as the 8th century, decoratively dusted with gold or silver powder. Most popular during the Edo period of the 17th through mid 19th centuries.

makimono (MAH kee moh noh)
A Japanese scrolled ink brush painting or calligraphy, designed for portability, ease of storage, and to be viewed horizontally. See also *kakemono*.

makore or makori (MAH kor or MAH kor ee)
An African cherry hardwood that closely resembles American cherry, with a fine texture that sometimes contains a mottled figure and a pink to pinkish-brown color. Commonly used for furniture, cabinetwork, turning, and as a veneer. Also known as baku, douka, and ukola.

maksura (MAHK soo rah)
The sanctuary or pray chamber of the caliph and his entourage in an Islamic mosque, generally screened by an intricately perforated enclosure.

makura (MAH koo rah)
A Japanese buckwheat hull stuffed pillow.

malachite (MA le kiyt)
A semiprecious stone known for its beautiful green color, popular since Egyptian times and in the Byzantine era, and also the favorite gemstone of Louis XIV. Often called Peacock Stone in Italy.

Maltese cross (MAHL teez KRAWS)
A cross formed by four V-shaped arms of equal length, ending in eight points. A 16th-century symbol for the Knights of Malta, an order of Christian warriors. Also known as an Amalfi cross.

Mamluk rugs (MA me look RUGZ)
Cut pile rugs originally created during the mid 13th through early 16th centuries by the Mamluk of Egypt and Syria, known for their superb quality and intricate designs of arabesque and geometric forms.

manara (MAH na rah)

An early term for minaret, a tower originally used on Islamic mosques used to call muslims to prayer. See also *minaret*.

manchette (mahn CHET)

French for a small upholstered arm cushion, commonly seen on the wooden frames of chairs, sofas, and settees. See also *arm pad*.

Manchu Dynasty (MAN choo DIY nes tee)

See *Ch'ing Dynasty*.

mandala (MAN dah lah)

The sanskrit word for circle. Also, a symbol of the same form representing the universe, with spiritual and ritual importance in the Hindu and Buddhist religions.

mandapa (MAN dah pah)

A covered porch-like structure leading to the temple of a Hindu temple complex, utilized for religious dancing and music.

mandorla (MAN dor lah)

Italian for almond. In design, an almond-shaped figure or halo used in Christian iconography, derived from an ancient symbol representing the convergence of heaven and earth. See also *aureole* or *vesica piscis*.

Mannerism or Mannerist School

An Italian style of art and architecture of the 16th century, characterized by unconventional, exaggerated, and distorted elements and bright, harsh colors that stirred emotions. Two of the most prominent artists of the style were El Greco and Tintoretto.

mansard roof

A roof containing two slopes on all four sides, with the lower slope being steeper in pitch than the upper slope.

mansard roof

mansonia (man SOH nee AH)

A wood indigenous to tropical West Africa with a yellowish or grayish-brown color, straight grain, and fine texture very similar to walnut. Commonly used for furniture, cabinetwork, turning, and as a decorative veneer. Also known as aprono, bete, koul, and ofun.

manta de techo (MAN tah DAY TEK oh)

Literally translated as ceiling blanket. A cloth attached below a ceiling to keep dust from entering a room.

mantel

A shelf projecting above a fireplace opening, originating from a medieval hood used to catch rising smoke. Also known as a mantelshelf.

mantelpiece

The decorative frame of brick, stone, or wood around a fireplace opening. See also *chimneypiece*.

mantelshelf

See *mantel*.

Manuelino (MAN yoo-e lee noh)

A Portuguese style of architecture, a variation of the final Gothic Style. See also *Plateresco*.

maple

A close-grained hardwood, similar to birch, with a light cream to light brown color. Indigenous to England, Central Europe, and America, maple was commonly employed in marquetry and as a veneer in 17th- and 18th-century English furniture and in American provincial furniture. Currently used for furniture, cabinetwork, molding, paneling, and flooring, some species offer highly decorative figures such as flame, quilted, bird's eye, and burled for veneer.

maqsurea (MAHK soo rah)

Literally a closed-off space. In architecture, a wooden screen or grill located near the mihrab of an Islamic mosque, originally intended to offer protection to a worshipping ruler.

maquette (MAH ket)
French term for a scaled model. A small study model or sketch created in preparation of a larger painting, sculpture, or space.

marble
A relatively hard metamorphic stone prized throughout history for its use in sculpting, furniture design, and as a building material. Made of recrystallized carbonate material and available in a variety of colors, patterns, and decorative effects. Today it is commonly used for flooring, tabletops, bar tops, and fireplace surrounds or hearths.

marbling
A faux finish designed to imitate the veining and texture of marble.

Marcel Breuer cesca chair
Chair with an industrial age aesthetic of chromed tubular steel, user-friendly caning, and wood, designed by Marcel Breuer in 1928 during the Bauhaus era and manufactured by Knoll. See *Marcel Breuer, 1902–1981, in the Architects, Artists, and Designers Appendix*.

Marcel Breuer cesca chair

Marcel Breuer wassily chair
A chair composed of a chrome-plated tubular steel frame with seats and arm rests of leather slings stretched between the frame; designed by Marcel Breuer in 1925, first manufactured by Thonet in the 1920s, and later manufactured by Knoll. The chair was designed while Breuer was head of the Bauhaus cabinet-making workshop and was also known as the Model B3 chair. See *Marcel Breuer, 1902–1981, in the Architects, Artists, and Designers Appendix*.

Marcel Breuer wassily chair

marlborough foot
See *block foot*. See *illustration in the Feet Appendix*.

marlborough leg
A straight, sometimes fluted leg usually terminating with a block foot. Popular on mid 18th-century English and American furniture, especially the work of Thomas Chippendale. See *illustration in the Legs Appendix*.

marmo
Italian term for marble.

marouflage (MAR oh flahj)
A method developed over 3,000 years ago to attach a mural-sized painted canvas to a wall, ceiling, or other large surface.

marquee (MAR kee)
An alternate term for marquise. See also *marquise*.

marquetry (MAR ke tree)
Decorative veneer work, popular during the Renaissance and in 18th-century England and France, created by inlaying different colored woods and/or other materials such as brass, tortoiseshell, ivory, bone, and mother-of-pearl into furniture, walls, or other surfaces.

marquetry

marquise (mar KEEZ)
A canopy projecting out from a wall over a building's entrance, often crafted of metal and glass. Also known as a marquee.

marquise chair (mar KEEZ CHAYR)
A late 17th-century French chair designed with a very broad seat that accommodated the wide skirts and panniers of the time.

marquisette (mar kee ZET)
A sheer gauze-like fabric of cotton, silk, wool, rayon, or other synthetic fiber woven in a leno weave, commonly used as a glass curtain material.

marriage chest

A 15th-century Italian Renaissance chest, also called a *cassone*, designed to hold a bride's dowry or offered as a wedding present, generally decorated with elaborate carvings and paintings. See also *cassone*.

marshmallow sofa

See *George Nelson marshmallow sofa*. See *George Nelson, 1908–1986, in the Architects, Artists, and Designers Appendix*.

Mart Stam model 533 chair

Cantilevered tubular steel framed chair designed by Dutch architect and Bauhaus teacher, Mart Stam, in 1926. The revolutionary streamlined design produced a rocking effect and eliminated the need for elaborate upholstery. See *Mart Stam, 1899–1986, in the Architects, Artists, and Designers Appendix*.

Mart Stam model 533 chair

Martha Washington chair

An 18th-century armchair with a high upholstered back and seat, shaped crest, and receding arm posts topped by incurvate arms. Generally supported by fluted marlborough legs.

Martha Washington chair

Martha Washington sewing table

A late 18th- or early 19th-century oval-shaped table with semicircular end pockets flanking turned or reeded legs. A hinged top allowed access to a fitted center tray and the two end pockets. The pocket ends were generally covered in a pleated fabric or reeded to mimic tambour.

martyrium, pl. martyria

(MAR tee ree-um / MAR tee ree-ah)
In medieval times, a tomb or edifice designed to honor a Christian martyr.

Martha Washington sewing table

maru (MA roo)

The primary defense of a Japanese castle, known in English as a bailey. Also called a kuruwa.

mascaron (MAS kah ron)

A deformed face or mask ornament with a frightening grin, originally designed to keep evil spirits away. The decoration was commonly painted or carved onto Gothic, Renaissance, and Baroque Style architecture and furniture. See also *grotesques*.

mascherone (MAS ku roh nee)

Italian for mask, particularly a gotesque one. See also *mascaron* and *grotesques*.

mascaron

mashrabiyyah (MASH rah bee yah)

A latticework or spoolwork grille used over windows of Islamic structures. Also known as mesherabijeh in Spain.

masjid (mas JID)

Arabic for mosque.

mask

See *masques*.

Masonite

A trademark name for a rigid composition board made from wood fiber, commonly used as siding material. Invented in 1924 by William H. Mason.

masonry

The laying of stone, brick, tile, or other materials set by mortar.

masques (MASKS)

An ornamental representation of a human face, often in an exaggerated or grotesque form, commonly seen in classic architecture and design and the Renaissance. See also *mascarons*.

masques

mass production

A product of the Industrial Revolution to mechanically produce identical versions of a design in mass quantities for the market.

masswerk (MAS wurk)

German term for tracery.

mastaba (MAH stah bah)

A rectangular Egyptian tomb with outward sloping sides and a flat roof. Also, a built-in wall bench, usually of stone, commonly found within Islamic structures.

mastaba

mastic

A resin from the mastic tree used in the production of varnish. Also, an adhesive used for setting vinyl tiles, mirrors, and glass.

masu (MAH soo)

A square wooden box used to measure the day's rice for one person during Japan's feudal period.

masu

match board or matched board

A tongue and grooved board, commonly used for paneling, with a chamfered or beaded edge that makes a joint feature when placed beside another match board.

matelassé (MET lahs)

French for padded or cushioned. A fabric with an embossed quilt-like pattern constructed on a Jacquard or dobby loom.

mate's chair

An armless captain's chair. See also *captain's chair*.

Mathsson miranda chair

See *Bruno Mathsson miranda chair*. See *Bruno Mathsson, 1907–1988, in the Architects, Artists, and Designers Appendix*.

matte

A dull, lusterless finish.

matted

A 17th-century English woodcarving technique, commonly used on oak, where the background is repeatedly dented with a punch to create contrast to the carved decoration.

mattress

A fabric-cased sleeping unit generally filled with a combination of cotton, feathers, foam, and sometimes springs, customarily placed over a box spring or slats. See also *box spring*.

Mauresque (MOR esk)

A variant of Moresque. See also *Moresque*.

mausoleum (mah soh LEE um)

A commemorative structure designed as a burial tomb.

meander (MEE an dur)

A geometric band or border motif of Greek origin composed of lattice-like interlocking lines. See also *Chinese key* or *fret*.

mechanical card table

An early 19th-century pedestal-based card table invented by American furniture designer Duncan Phyfe, designed with automatic supports that move into position when the table's hinged top leaf is flipped open.

mechanical desk

A bureau plat style desk with an adjustable writing surface housed in the center drawer and hinged covers on the flanking side drawers. The desk's top is generally rimmed with a brass gallery or wooden lip that keeps items from sliding or rolling off the surface.

médaillier (me DIY-yay)

A small, 18th-century French cabinet designed for the display of medals or decorations.

médaillier

médaillon (ME dal yen)

See *le médaillon*.

medallion

A circular or oval-framed panel containing an ornament or figure in low relief within the center.

medallion

Medieval period (MEE dee vul PEE ree-ud)

A period relating to the Middle Ages, containing the Romanesque, Byzantine, and Gothic Styles.

Mediterranean Style

A 20th-century style based on the bold colors and carvings, curved lines, deep moldings, iron detailing, grillwork, rough plaster, arched openings, and wall niches found in Mediterranean countries such as Italy, Greece, and especially Spain.

medium

The material or substance used by an artist to create a work of art, such as marble, wood, paint, paper, etc. In painting, a liquid substance used for mixing pigments.

megalith

A very large, undressed stone monument or building block employed during prehistoric times.

megaron

A large central hall with a rectangular plan fronted by a columned porch found in Mycenaean palaces.

Meissen (MIY sen)

An 18th-century porcelain manufacturer known for its fine white hard-paste porcelain, considered to be the first European equivalent to the Chinese porcelains.

melon bulb

A heavy, elaborately carved, bulbous turning resembling a melon in shape, commonly used as a support on Elizabethan and Jacobean furniture. See also *cup and cover turning*. See *the illustration in the Legs Appendix*.

melon bulb table

A 16th-century English Tudor table with large bulbous turned legs. See also *melon bulb*.

melon turning

See *melon bulb* and *cup and cover turning*.

Memphis lido sofa

A multicolored cushion sofa on a black and white laminate base designed by Michele De Lucci in 1982 for the Italian design firm, Memphis.

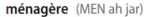

Memphis lido sofa

ménagère (MEN ah jar)

French for a low dresser with open shelves used to store pottery. See also *hutch* and *vaisselier*.

Mendlesham chair

A small armchair of the early 19th century designed by Daniel Day of Mendlesham, England. Considered a variation of the Windsor chair because of its similar undercarriage, but with a splat and balled spindled back that is more similar to Sheraton designs.

menhir (MEN eer)

A large upright stone, generally with an uneven square shape and tapered top, of prehistoric origin.

Mendlesham chair

abcdefghijklmnopqrstuvwxyz

mensa, pl. mensae
Latin for table, a general term used during ancient Roman times.

mensa delphica (MEN sah DEL fee kah)
An ornamental table from ancient Greece and Rome with three legs and a round tabletop.

mensa tripes (MEN sah TRIYPS)
A Roman table supported by three legs.

mensa vasaria (MEN sah vah SAR ee-ah)
A table of ancient Greece and Rome designed to hold the jugs, cans, and other utensils (vasa) used for domestic purposes.

mensa viuaria (MEN sah vlu ar ee-ah)
A table used to receive wine for drinking.

menuisier (me noo zee-AY)
A French woodjoiner or carpenter of furniture carcasses.

meri-boteh (me REE-BOH tee)
A pinecone motif commonly used in Persian rugs. See also *boteh*.

méridienne (mer i DEE-en)
A short sofa with one arm higher than the other, introduced during the French Empire period and repopularized during the American Rococo Revival Style.

merlon
The solid projections of a crenelated wall, designed to be used as a shield during battles.

mensa delphica

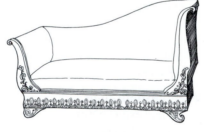

méridienne

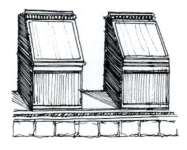

merlon

merino
The fine, soft cashmere-like wool of Spanish merino sheep.

merisier (MER ee zee-ay)
French wild cherry wood.

Merovingian (MER e vin jee-an)
Referring to the art and architecture of the 5th through 8th century Merovingian Dynasty in Gaul, present-day France and Germany.

mesa
Spanish and Portuguese for table.

mesherabijeh (ME ser ah bee hay)
Spanish term for mashrabiyyah. See also *mashrabiyyah*.

Mesoamerican
A term encapsulating the North American and Central American regions of the Americas.

Mesolithic
The midpoint of the stone age from the 7th to the 8th century B.C.E.

Mesopotamia
An area of very early civilization in Western Asia on the fertile plains of the Lower Tigris and Lower Euphrates rivers; commonly known as the "Cradle of Civilization." See also *Assyrian*.

mesquita (me SKEE tah)
Spanish for mosque.

Mestiço (mes TEE koh)
Spanish for a person of mixed European and Native American ancestry.

metal mounts
See *mounts*.

metates (me TAH teez)
An oblong mortar used for grinding and perhaps as a seat or an alter for sacrifices.

metates

metoche (me TOHSH)
The area between two dentils or between two triglyphs.

metope (MEH teh pay)
The flat recessed slabs between triglyphs of a classical Doric frieze, commonly decorated with sculpted reliefwork.

meubles (MEB le)
French for furniture. Also known as mobilier.

meubles à hauteur d'appui (MEB le AH OH tur DAH pee)
French for a cupboard, bookcase, or low secretaire that could serve as a comfortable place to lean. Literally translates as furniture of high support.

meubles à transformations (MEB le AH TRANS for mah shun)
French for mechanical furniture. Commonly seen in the Louis XV and 18th-century Sheraton designs.

Mexican tiles
Thick, porous, handmade tiles, generally made of terra-cotta and dried in sunlight before firing in an oven. Also known as saltillo tile.

mezzanine
An intermediate story or floor that projects as a balcony. Also, an intermediate floor with a low ceiling located between two main floors.

mezzo-rilievo (MEZ-REE yay voh)
Italian for medium relief carvings.

mezzotint
A mid 17th-century form of intaglio printmaking that employs a copper or steel plate that is roughened to produce a design that can then be inked for making prints. See also *intaglio engraving.*

Michael Thonet bentwood rocker
An early 1900s lounge chair rocker designed by Michael

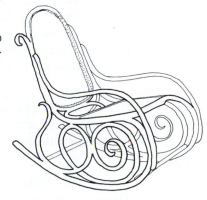

Michael Thonet bentwood rocker

Thonet using a unique late 19th-century steam-bending process to create a bentwood frame on which a caned seat is applied. See *Michael Thonet, 1796–1871, in the Architects, Artists, and Designers Appendix.*

Michael Thonet Le Corbusier chair
A bentwood armchair with a caned seat created by Michael Thonet in the early 1900s from a unique steam-bending process. The name stems from the wide use of the chair by Le Corbusier. See *Michael Thonet, 1796–1871, in the Architects, Artists, and Designers Appendix.*

mi-clos
See *clos.*

micro mosaic
A Renaissance form of mosaic using very small pieces of glass or enamel, often only slightly wider than a human hair. The technique reached its height of popularity in the mid 19th century.

Middle Ages
See *Gothic period.*

Middle Pointed period
See *Decorated period.*

Mies van der Rohe Barcelona chair
Chrome-plated steel-framed chair with tufted seat and back cushion designed by German architect Ludwig Mies van der Rohe in 1929 for the German Pavilion of the Barcelona exposition and manufactured by Knoll. See *Ludwig Mies van der Rohe, 1886–1969, in the Architects, Artists, and Designers Appendix.*

Michael Thonet Le Corbusier chair

Mies van der Rohe Barcelona chair

Mies van der Rohe MR chair

A cantilever armchair with a chrome-plated tubular steel frame and upholstered seat and back designed by German architect Ludwig Mies van der Rohe in 1929 and manufactured by Knoll. See *Ludwig Mies van der Rohe, 1886–1969, in the Architects, Artists, and Designers Appendix.*

**Mies van der Rohe
MR chair**

Mies van der Rohe Tugendhat chair

An armless chair with a cantilever chrome-plated steel frame and tufted seat and back cushions designed by German architect Ludwig Mies van der Rohe in 1930 for the Grete and Fritz Tugendhat residence in Czechoslovakia. Manufactured by Knoll. See *Ludwig Mies van der Rohe, 1886–1969, in the Architects, Artists, and Designers Appendix.*

**Mies van der Rohe
Tugendhat chair**

mignatures (MIG nah churz)

A small sprig pattern repeat used on textiles since the late 18th century.

mignonnettes (min ye NETS)

A small, orderly pattern, seen since the 19th century, that fills the background space between larger elements in a design.

mihrab (MEE reb)

A niche found in the qibla or wall closest to Mecca of an Islamic mosque. Also, a niche-shaped design in a prayer rug.

milk or pie safes

A 19th-century American cupboard designed for storing milk, pies, and other foods that did not need immediate refrigeration. Common to Pennsylvania and the Midwest, the cupboard doors were framed tin panels punched in decorative patterns that allowed for air circulation and hence delayed spoilage.

millefleurs (meel FLER)

Literally translated from French as a thousand flowers, millefleurs are particularly associated with a late 15th- and early 16th-century Gothic tapestry pattern that depicted numerous small leaves, plants, and flowers.

minaret

A tall, slender tower or turret associated with Islamic mosques and used for calling the faithful to prayer.

minbar

The pulpit of an Islamic mosque used by the imam (prayer leader) to deliver sermons; located to the right of the mihrab. Also spelled mimbar.

Ming Dynasty

The dynasty that provided native rule to China from 1368 to 1644, between the Mongul and Manchu eras. Architecturally famous for building the Forbidden City, the era was also culturally important for its contributions to cloisonné, enamelware, bronzework, lacquerwork, furniture, painting, and pottery; particularly the red unglazed stoneware later known in the West as Bocarro.

Ming Dynasty chair

miniature

Any small painting, sculpture, or other art object, first tied to 7th-century illuminated manuscripts, but particularly noted during Elizabethan England when miniature portraits on vellum, ivory, or metal became fashionable and served as photographs do today.

minimalism

An 1950s art and design trend associated with extreme sparseness and simplicity, often associated with the work of Mies van der Rohe and the De Stijl artists. See also *De Stijl*.

minka

Literally translated from Japanese as a "house of the people," a private residence of the non-ruling class in the 18th century.

minster

Originally a 7th-century English term for an endowed settlement of clergy. Since the 11th century, a title of dignity for a large or important church with Anglo-Saxon roots.

minstrel gallery

A small balcony found above the main entrance of a castle's great hall, used to hold performing musicians (minstrels) during feasts.

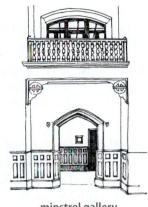

minstrel gallery

Minton

Famous English porcelain and pottery factory founded by Thomas Minton in 1796, particularly known for high-quality porcelains, Parian, pâte-sur-pâte, and majolica.

mirador (MEER ah dor)

Spanish for a window, balcony, or small tower that offers a good view.

miroir (MEER war)

French for mirror or looking glass.

mirror

A polished surface that reflects images. The earliest known mirrors stem from Egypt and were of polished silver. During the Gothic era other metals were used. The first silvered glass mirrors were created in Venice during the early 14th century. Also known as a looking glass.

miserere (mi zu RAYR ee)

See *misericord*.

misericord (me ZUR e kord)

A small projection found on the underside of hinged choir stall seats, used for support when standing and the seat is raised. Also called a miserere.

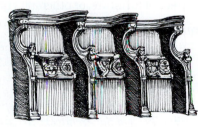

misericord

Mission chair

An inexpensive adaptation of the Spanish frailero, created in the early 20th century. See also *Mission Style*.

Mission Style

A late 19th- to early 20th-century furniture style characterized by heavy forms, simple lines, oak wood, leather upholstery, often trimmed with oversized nail heads. Based on furniture created by priests and Indians for missions of the Southwest United States. See also *Gustav Stickley reclining armchair*. See *Gustave Stickley, 1858–1942, in the Architects, Artists, and Designers Appendix*.

misu (mi SOO)

See *sudare*.

miter joint

A woodworking joint created by cutting two pieces of wood at an angle before joining. Also spelled as mitre. See *illustration in the Joints Appendix*.

mitesaki (MI te sah kee)

The third in a system of three brackets that support the eaves of Japanese buildings such as a temples or shrines.

mixing table

A small sideboard or cabinet designed with one partitioned end for storing bottles.

mizuya- tansu (MI zoo yah-dahn soo)

A Japanese kitchen chest designed in two sections, full of various sized drawers, designed for storing food, tea articles, utensils, and other kitchen supplies. Also spelled as mizuya-dansu.

mobile

A suspended form of kinetic sculpture originally created from wire and sheet metal by American artist Alexander Calder during the second quarter of the 20th century.

mobilier (MOH bil yay)

French for furniture. Also known as meubles.

Mocarbe (MOH kar bee)
Spanish for muqarna. See also *muqarna*.

mock-up
A study model, usually built to scale.

model
A scaled, three-dimensional representation of a design such as a room, a building, or a piece of furniture.

modern
Designs of the present or near present; 20th-century modern furniture follows new technological developments, is functional, and is composed of clean, generally straight lines. If curves are seen, they are refined. See also *oriental modern, Scandinavian modern, Shaker modern*.

Modern Baroque
An early 21st-century design trend mixing Baroque patterns, ornament, furniture, and lighting with modern elements.

Moderne
A streamlined style of the mid 1920s related to Art Deco. Influenced by advancing technologies such as aviation and ballistics, designs were composed of aerodynamic forms, clean lines, rounded corners, bands, and stepped skyscraper forms. Also called Streamline Moderne. See also *Art Deco*.

Modernism
A 20th-century movement that embraced a break from the past, rejecting useless ornamentation, historic styles, and tradition for functionalism and simplification of form.

Modernisme
A Catalan movement best described as Spain's equivalent of Art Nouveau and Jugenstil. The style's best-known architectural exponent was Antonio Gaudi. See *Antonio Gaudi, 1852–1926, in the Architects, Artists, and Designers Appendix*.

modesty panel
A thin sheet of wood, metal, or plastic that shields a seated person's upper legs from view on a desk, table, or other piece of furniture.

An adaptation of 18th- and 19th-century modesty boards used in churches, Quaker meeting houses, and stairways. Also called a kneehole panel.

modiglione (MOH dig lee oh nee)
Italian term for a corbel or bracket or modillion. See also *modillion*.

modillion (moh DIL yen)
One bracket or corbel of a series that supports a Corinthian or Composite cornice. See also *modiglione*.

modillion

modular furniture
An early 20th-century furniture design concept where units are designed of components with set sizes that create flexible and expandable options for layout.

modular home
Home built with self-contained, prefabricated modules or sections that are constructed in a factory, delivered to the building site, and assembled by a crane. See also *prefabricated houses* and *module*.

modular seating
Seating designed with various prefabricated units that may fit together in multiple ways to fulfill space requirements. See also *module*.

module
A standard that regulates the size or proportion of a structure, interior, piece of furniture, or other item of design.

modulor (MAHJ u lur)
An anthropomorphic system of proportioning created by the French architect Le Corbusier.

Mogensen model No. 1789
See *Børge Mogensen model 1789 spoke-back sofa*. See *Børge Mogensen, 1914–1972, in the Architects, Artists, and Designers Appendix*.

mohair

Yarn or cloth made from the fleece of Angora goats, widely used for upholstery since the 18th century because of its strength, resilience, and durability. Commonly mixed with cotton and linen today.

moiré (mwah RAY)

A ribbed silk, cotton, or wool that has been subjected to heat and pressure to give it a watermarked or wavy grained effect.

mokoshi (MOH koh shee)

A decorative pent (skirt) roof used on Buddhist temples and pagodas in Japan. Also known as a yuta.

molded base

A base constructed of molding generally seen on case goods.

molding or moulding

A shaped strip used to finish or decorate features in architecture and furniture, generally constructed of wood, stone, or plaster. See *illustrations in the Molding Appendix*.

monastery

See *abbey*.

monastery chair

A multi-legged, armless x-framed chair that folded and was commonly used in monasteries during the 16th century.

money motif

A series of overlapping coin-like discs often used as a border design.

monial (MAH nee-ul)

See *mullion*.

monk's chair

A chair whose back pivots to form a table. See also *frailero* and *table chair*.

monk's cloth

A coarse woven, heavy cotton fabric in a plain or basket weave. Historically used as a textile border, monk's cloth is presently utilized for hangings and upholstery in informal rooms. Also called friar's cloth.

monk's table

A settle whose back pivots to form an elongated table. See also *table chair*.

monochromatic

A color scheme produced from tints or shades of a single hue. Also known as monochrome. See also *grisaille*.

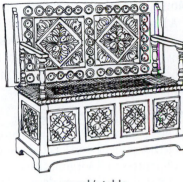

monk's table

monolith

A massive single erect stone that functions as a monument, column, or obelisk.

monolithic

Composed from one piece of stone, without any joints or seams.

monopodium (mah noh POH dee-um)

In furniture, a support featuring the head and chest of a lion attached to one paw, commonly used during the French Empire and English Regency periods.

monoprostyle (MAH noh proh stiyul)

A porch designed with one row of columns.

monopteral (MAH nohp te rul)

A circular edifice, especially a round temple, with a single row of columns on the outside. Also called a cyclostyle.

monopodium

monostyle

A design with a single column.

monoxylous (MAH nok se les)

Formed from a single piece of material.

montage (MAHN tahj)

A composition composed by the juxtaposition of several pictures. See also *collage*.

Montgolfier chair (mahnt GAHL fee-ur CHAYR)
A late 18th-century chair with a wooden back shaped like a hot air balloon. Designed in honor of the successful balloon flight of the Montgolfier brothers in 1783; the accession made France the first country to take to the air.

Monticello (MON te sell oh)
Late 18th-century Colonial Georgian home of Thomas Jefferson located just outside of Charlottesville, Virginia. An avid student of architecture, Jefferson designed the home with flanking octagonal projections and a central dome based on the work of Andrea Palladio. He also included many impressive inventions of his own within the design.

Montgolfier chair

moon gate
A circular opening used as a passageway in Chinese gardens.

Moorish arch (MOR ish ARCH)
Also known as a horseshoe arch. See also *horseshoe arch.*

moquette (moh KET)
A thick pile fabric, predominantly woven from wool and linen, utilized for upholstery and carpets. Produced during the 16th through 18th centuries in France and England. It was also known as Brussels carpet.

mordant
A chemical substance used to set fabric dyes.

moreen
See *morine.*

Moresque (MOR esk)
Moorish style in art, architecture, and other designs. Commonly seen in Spain and Portugal during the Middle Ages.

morine
A 17th- and 18th-century upholstery material generally composed of wool warp yarns and linen, cotton, or wool weft yarns. Later called moreen.

morning room
In English architecture, a sitting room used for morning activities such as correspondence, etc.

Moroccan tapestries
A decorated leather wall hanging or tapestry. See also *guadamicil.*

Morocco leather
A goatskin leather, originally from Morocco, used as a luxury binding material during the 16th century. To process, the hide is dyed red on the grain side and hand tanned to pull up the grain and create a beautiful bird's-eye-like pattern.

Morris chair
An early reclining chair marketed by Morris & Company, William Morris's firm, during the mid 19th century in the Arts & Crafts Style. The straight-lined chair featured a pegged and hinged reclining back, wooden arms and frame, and loose cushions in the seat and back. See *William Morris, 1834–1896, in the Architects, Artists, and Designers Appendix.*

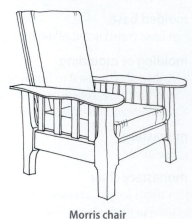

Morris chair

mortar
In masonry, a material composed of lime, sand, and water, used to bind and bed masonry and brickwork.

mortise
In woodworking, a pocket or hole cut into a piece of wood in order to receive a tenon. See also *joinery, mortise and tenon joint,* and *tenon.*

mortise and tenon joint
A woodworking joint composed of a projection or tenon on one piece that is inserted into a mortise or hole cut into another. See *illustration in the Joints Appendix.*

Mortlake Tapestry Works
Principle manufacturer of tapestries and textiles during the Restoration period (17th century) in England. Founded by Sir Francis Crane in 1619, through the help of Charles I.

mosaic
Small pieces (tesserae) of glass, stone, marble, or tile set in mortar to form a pattern or design. Although dating back to ancient Greek times, mosaics were a highly popular form of decorating walls, ceilings, and floors of Early Christian and Byzantine churches. See also *intarsia* and *pietra dura*.

moshee (MAH shee)
Another term for decorative borders in the 18th century.

mosque (MAHSK)
In Islamic architecture, a structure designed for public prayer and worship.

moss
A chenille-like edge used on braiding that decorates or finishes upholstery and drapery treatments.

mother of pearl
The iridescent lining of pearl oysters and various other shells, commonly used for inlay.

motif or motive
A distinct decorative feature or pattern.

motte
The raised earthen mound on which a castle sits.

mottle
A short, irregular wavy grain produced in wood.

mount
Another name for furniture hardware. See also *hardware*.

mouse-tooth brickwork
A zigzag pattern of bricks set where a sloping course intersects a horizontal course. Known as muisetanden in Dutch.

moya (MOI-ah)
The central room or core of a Japanese structure.

Moyen Âge (MOI-en AHJ)
French term for Middle Ages.

Mozarabic (MOH zar a bik)
Islamic designs infused with Christian elements created in Moorish Spain from the 9th to the 11th centuries.

MR chair
See *Mies van der Rohe MR chair*. See *Ludwig Mies van der Rohe, 1886–1969, in the Architects, Artists, and Designers Appendix*.

Mudéjar (moo THAY har)
A 12th- through 16th-century style of architecture and design found in Spain, after Moorish control was expelled, superimposing Moorish details over medieval, Gothic, and Renaissance styles. See also *Plateresco*.

muffin stand
muffin standA small tiered table used at a proper tea to hold plates of food during the 18th and 19th centuries in England and America.

Mughal architecture (MOO gul AHR ki tek cher)
A distinct fusion of Islamic, Persian, and Indian architecture developed by the Mughals in what is now known as India, Pakistan, and Bangladesh during the 16th and 17th centuries. The most well-known example of the style is the Taj Mahal.

muffin stand

muhaqqaq (MOO hah kahk)
A 13th-century form of Arabic calligraphy developed by lengthening the horizontals of Thuluth script. The style was abandoned in the 16th century.

muisetanden (MWEEZ than den)
Dutch for mouse-toothed brickwork.

mulatto (ME lah toh)
An 18th-century term used to denote a person of African and Caucasian descent. Derived from the Spanish term mulato meaning hybrid.

mule chest

A low chest of drawers mounted on a low frame with an upper storage compartment accessed by a hinged top and one or two drawers beneath it. Also called a blanket chest.

mule chest

mullion

A vertical member separating windows or glass panels.

mulqaf (MUL kaf)

Arabic for wind catcher. In architecture, a shaft with lateral openings on the roof, used to catch breezes and ventilate ancient Egyptian structures.

multifoil

A design composed of more than five lobes.

multifoil arch

An arch composed of more than five lobes, commonly seen in the Moorish architecture of Spain. Sometimes described as a scalloped arch.

mummy cloth

A heavy, plain-woven fabric, created from unbleached linen or cotton, utilized as a base for embroidery work.

Munsell color system

A color system developed by Albert F. Munsell in the early 20th century that classified colors based on the attributes of hue, value, and intensity.

muntin

The central vertical member dividing the panels of a door. In windows, the narrow wood members used to divide individual panes of glass. Also called glazing bars, muntin bars, or sash bars.

muqarnas (meh GAYR nehs)

A system of small corbels used as decorative devices in traditional Islamic architecture, often beneath vaults or arches.

mural

A large wall painting that is either painted directly or printed and applied to a wall. See also *fresco*.

Murano glass

A specially treated glass developed in a variety of beautiful colors on the Italian island of Murano, just off the shores of Venice. Known since the 13th century for its prized glassmakers.

Murphy bed

A trademark name, which developed into a generic term, for a bed that is hinged on one end, allowing it to be flipped up and stored in a wall recess, closet, or cabinet. Also called a cabinet bed, wall bed, or hideaway.

Murphy bed

murrhine glass (MUR een GLAS)

A type of glass designed to imitate the murrhine (stone) vases and cups of ancient Rome.

mushrebeeyeh (MUSH re bee yeh)

Arabic for an oriel window or balcony enclosed with decorative lattice screens. Also known as a shanasheel or rushan.

mushroom turning

A turning with a domed top and trumpet-shaped stem resembling a mushroom cap, commonly found on Sheraton and American Empire furniture.

mushroom turning

muslin

A plain, loosely woven cotton, bleached or unbleached, commonly used as a subsurface material for upholstery, and for sheeting, patterns, curtains, and clothing. It was introduced to Europe from the Middle East in the 17th century.

musalla (MOO sah lah)

A prayer hall found within an Islamic mosque.

müster (MUS ter)

German for an abbey church.

muted

Colors that are soft, restrained, and subdued.

mutule (MOO tool)

In architecture, a projecting block found on the underside of the horizontal geison (soffit) of a Doric cornice. Commonly decorated with rows of guttae and aligned with the metopes and triglyphs of a frieze.

muxarabi (MUK sa rah bee)

Traditional wooden grilles, geometric in design, used on the windows of Spanish and Portuguese architecture for ventilation and filtering of light.

myrtle burl

A highly figured yellow wood with a dark brown heart that forms within the tree's stump. Indigenous to the Pacific Coast of the United States and commonly used for cabinetwork, inlay, and veneer.

N

Napoleon's initial used as a key decorative motif during the early 19th century of the French Empire Style. The monogram was carved, inlaid, painted, woven, and embroidered onto a multitude of goods.

nacre (NA kor)

French for mother of pearl. See also *mother of pearl*.

naijin (NAY jin)

A sacred area within a Japanese temple hall in which only those initiated are permitted.

nail claw

Term for a tool used to remove nails.

nailheads

Plain or decorated nails or brads used to attach leather and other upholstery fabrics to a frame or panel. They are typically made of brass, copper, and other metals and originated from Spain and Italy during the Gothic era.

Nakora (na KOR ah)

A trademark name for a Japanese hardwood that is exceedingly light in its blond color and exhibits a definite pattern when rotary cut.

nanguan mao yi (non GWUN MOW HEE)

A Chinese official's chair characterized by arms that curve downward to form the front arm supports. The back of the arms also curves to meet the chair's uprights.

nanmu (na MOO)

An aromatic Chinese wood that exhibits a rich deep brown color with age. Primarily used for building and decoration, it is also known as Persian cedar.

nanguan mao yi

Nanna Ditzel bench for two

A two-seater bench composed of plywood with a silk screened striped print created by Nanna Ditzel in 1989 and manufactured by Frederica Furniture. See *Nanna Ditzel, 1923–2005, in the Architects, Artists, and Designers Appendix*.

Nanna Ditzel bench for two

naos (NOWS)

The most sacred location within classical Greek and Roman temples that housed the cult statue. The term later becomes synonymous with nave. See also *cella*.

nap

A fuzzy surface found on fabrics composed of short raised fibers.

narrawood

A Philippine hardwood exceptional for use in furniture construction and veneer that varies from light golden to brown, or light to dark red in color. Because of its ripples and mottled effect, it may look similar to mahogany and satinwood.

narthex

The arcaded porch of a church that leads to the nave.

nattes

A textile surface enhancement that resembles a plaited, basket-weave pattern.

naturalism

In art, a realistic representation of natural objects.

narthex

Naugahyde

United States Rubber Company's trademark name for a vinyl fabric used for upholstery and wallcoverings.

Naugaweave

A trademark name for a breathable vinyl created by the United States Rubber Company.

Navajo rugs

Traditional handwoven American Navajo Indian rugs, distinguished by bold geometric patterns of black, gray, and white accented with red.

nave

The central section of a Latin cross church, generally terminated by an apse and flanked by aisles. See also *apse* and *transept*.

nave

near colors

Colors that tend to advance and make a room seem visually smaller. Prominently seen with darker shades and brighter hues.

nebule ornament

A form of Norman ornament employing continuous wavy lines to enrich moldings.

nécessaire (NE se sayr)

French for a small writing or toilet accessory case.

necessary stool

See *close stool*.

neck

The horizontal band, often ornamented with relief work, found near the top of a column shaft in the Roman and Doric architectural orders.

necking

See *collar*.

needlepoint

Cross-stitch embroidery completed with wool on net, heavy canvas, or coarse linen. See also *petit point*.

Neoclassicism

A movement originating in Rome and France in the mid 18th century exhibiting a revival of classical ornament as a reaction to the Rococo excess. The styles of Louis XVI in France and Adam in England were part of this new style.

Néo-Grec Style

A name specific to the new Greek style of the Louis XVI period that was spurred by the discoveries at Herculaneum and Pompeii.

Néo-Greek period

A term that is seldom used for the period of American art and architecture exhibited in the early to mid 19th century that favored classical Greek ornament.

nesting tables

A graduated series of small tables, designed to slide one inside another. See also *quartetto tables*.

net

A general term for an open-weave fabric.

neutral color

Colors with no identifiable hue, nearly achromatic, such as beige, gray, white, or black.

New Colonial or Modern Colonial period

An early 20th-century style of furniture. The classic features from both the colonial era and the later Federal and American Empire Styles were retained, but the ormolu and brass mounts were omitted. The S-shaped scroll, scroll foot, lion's paw foot and classic columns were often in evidence.

newel post
The heavy main post found at the termination of the handrail on a staircase.

nib
See *lug*.

niche (NEECH)
A recessed space found within a wall, generally used to hold a statue or other decorative item.

niche-pilaster (NICH-PI les ter)
An architectural element characteristic of the Spanish Baroque and Spanish Colonial Styles featuring a pilaster whose shaft contains a niche holding a figure or other decorative element.

nicho (nee CHOH)
Spanish word for niche. See also *niche*.

nicking
A notched or gauging process used to ornament 17th-century English furniture.

niello
A method of embellishing metal objects in which engraved lines are filled with a black material.

night clos (NIYT KLOH)
See *close chair*.

night stool
See *close chair*.

night table
A small table used at a bedside to hold a lamp, clock, etc. Also called a night stand.

nijiri-guchi (ni JEER ee-goo CHEE)
Japanese term for a low entry to a tea house.

niche

nimbus
A halo or ring commonly seen behind the head of Christ, the Madonna, or a saint in medieval art.

ninon (NEE nahn)
A smooth, shear rayon used for glass curtains, at times called triple voile.

noeud (NOHD)
Knot found at the crossing of an x-shaped stretcher during the Baroque and Rococo periods.

no-fines
A concrete mixture of cement and coarse aggregate.

nogging
Contemporarily noted as the practice of inserting a horizontal member between two vertical studs during construction of a partition wall. In medieval times, the term defined the application of brick, instead of wattle and daub, between timbers of a timber-framed house.

noil (NOYL)
A short fiber added to wool, cotton, or silk in the making of high-quality yarns.

nomen-dansu (NOH mun DAHN soo)
A small Japanese chest containing square drawers utilized to store masks used in traditional Japanese dramas.

nominal dimensions
The dimensions associated with sawn lumber before it has been dried and planed.

non-load-bearing wall
A wall or partition that does not support any weight other than its own. Also called a non-bearing wall.

nonsuch furniture

English furniture of the 16th and 17th century decorated with trompe l'oeil, especially views of Henry VIII's Nonsuch Palace.

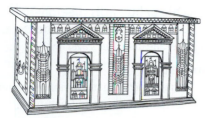

nonsuch furniture

norens (NOR enz)

A Japanese term for split privacy curtains.

Norman

A term used to denote Romanesque architecture in England after the country was conquered by the Normans in 1066. See also *Romanesque Style*.

Normandy

A province of France known for its quaint, country-style furniture in the 18th century.

nosing

The curved forward edge projection of a stair tread.

Nøstetangen (NOH stu than gen)

Norwegian glass factory in production from 1741 to 1779 patronized by Christian VI.

notching

See *nicking*.

nottingham lace

A machine-made lace named after the town that first produced it, Nottingham, England.

Nove (NOH vay)

An area of Italy, near Venice, known for ceramics since the 18th century.

nub yarn

See *slub yarn*.

nulling

A wood-carving technique of the English Jacobean period of the 17th century, characterized by heavy knots.

numdah (num DAH)

A wool felted rug made in the Kashmir region of India that is characterized by vines and blossoms embroidered on the surface in brightly colored yarns.

nursing chair

An English word for a chauffeuse. See also *chauffeuse*.

O

oak

A generic term used to describe the tough, hard, durable wood used extensively to make furniture, cabinets, and flooring. It was also commonly carved. The term may refer to species of English or American oaks. There are two classes of American oaks: the red oak, which is red in color, and the white oak, which is whitish in color.

oak, pollard

Commonly known as English oak. It possesses a rich, medium to deep brown color, spotted with black.

oak, quartered

Term referring to an oak tree trunk cut through the center into four equal parts, resulting in a plank or veneer with a characteristic straight grain.

obelisk (AH be lisk)

A tall, tapering, four-sided pillar terminating with a pyramid-shaped cap. Original examples date to preclassical Egypt.

objects of vertu (AHB jikts OF VUR too)

A term used in the antiques trade to distinguish an object of high quality, especially small decorative objects containing precious metals and stones.

objet d'art (ohb JAY DAR)

French term referring to any small art object.

obscure glass

A translucent glass that slightly masks or obscures views through it.

obverse

The main or front surface of an object such as coin, medal, etc.

occasional chair

A generic term for a small odd chair of any period or style called into service as the occasion demands.

occasional table

A small, general-purpose table of any period or style that can be used to fill a variety of roles such as end table, sofa table, coffee table, lamp table, etc.

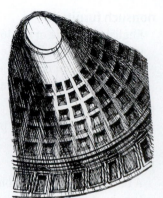

obelisk

occhio di bue (OH chee-oh DUH BOY)

Literally translated from Italian as bull's eye. See also *bull's eye*.

octastyle

A building style or element characteristically including eight columns.

oculus

A circular opening found in the top of a dome or a round window.

odalisque (OH du lisk)

A popular motif of the Louis XV period featuring a female slave or concubine of a harem.

oculus

odanoma (ah DAH nu mah)

Japanese term for a room elevated on a platform.

odeion (OH dee-ay-un)

Greek term for an odeum. See also *odeum*.

odeum

A small roofed ancient Roman theater designed for poetry readings, plays, and musical concerts.

oecus (OH kus)

A large room within an ancient Roman house designed for entertaining guests.

oecus Corinthius (OH kus KOR in thee-us)

A roof opening defined and supported by a colonnade in a Greek or Roman house.

oecus tetrastylos (OH kus TE tru stiy lohs)

A roof opening defined and supported by four columns, one at each corner, in a Greek or Roman house.

oeil-de-boeuf (OH DUH BUF)

Literally translated from French as bull's eye. See also *bull's eye*.

oeil-de-perdrix (OH DUH PAYR dree)

Translated from French as partridge's eye, an ornamentation used on porcelain comprised of small circles enclosed by smaller ones.

office landscape

Contemporary term used to describe an office designed with workstations positioned to enhance communication and efficiency between employees. This new idea redesigned the office workplace from an environment predominated by private offices.

offset

A change in face, projecting to create a small ledge or lip.

ofuro (oh FUR oh)

A room designed in a Japanese house for bathing.

ogee (OH jee)

A molding exhibiting an S-shaped profile in section. Also identified as ogive. See also *keel molding*. See *illustration in the Moldings Appendix*.

ogee arch (OH jee ARCH)

An arch containing S-shaped curves on either side that converge to form a point, commonly found in Islamic architecture. Also identified as an ogive or keel arch.

ogee bracket foot (OH jee BRA kut)

A foot commonly used in furniture that contains a reverse S-shape or cyma recta on the outside face of a bracket. See *illustration in the Feet Appendix*.

ogee arch

ogival arch (OH jee vul ARCH)

See also *ogee arch*.

oil cloth

A fabric treated with oil or paint to provide a waterproof and easy-to-clean surface used for clothing, coverings for tables and shelves, and often as a floor mat in modest Early American homes.

oil finish

A protective wood finish of linseed or tung oil that imparts a low sheen similar to satin, commonly used on woods such as teak.

oil golf

A manner of gilding using linseed oil as a medium.

oil painting

The art of painting using oil paints, which contain pigments ground in oil.

oiled silk

A fine silk fabric that has been treated with linseed oil to waterproof it.

oinochoe (OY nuk oh)

An ancient Greek vase used for pouring wine. See also *aryballos* and *lagynos*.

olive wood

A wood that is light yellow in color with greenish yellow figures, used primarily in small pieces or as an inlay, similar to English ash.

oinochoe

ombre (AHM bray)

A graduated pattern from one hue, generally resulting in a striped effect, from the French word for shadowed.

on the glaze

In ceramics, the term defining the technique of applying color over the glaze of biscuit pottery, as seen in majolica.

one-point perspective

Developed during the Italian Renaissance, a mathematical approach used to illustrate three-dimensional objects or space on a flat surface.

abcdefghijklmnopqrstuvwxyz

onion dome
A dome with a bulbous form shaped like an onion commonly seen in Russian, Indian, and Islamic architecture.

onion foot
An Early Renaissance turned foot shaped like an onion.

onlay
A form of decoration similar to sheathing or veneer using materials laid on top of a surface instead of into it.

onyx (AHN iks)
A semiprecious chalcedony, exhibiting parallel bands of color and slight translucence.

opalescent (oh pu LE sent)
Displaying a glistening rainbow of colors in light reflection.

open back
A chair back with a decorative open frame or one that has no upholstery between back supports.

open pediment
A pediment that is open along the base. See also *broken pediment*. See *illustration in the Pediments Appendix*.

open planning
A space planning concept incorporating large, flexible, open areas that minimize permanent walls or partitions and feature systems furniture.

open string staircase
A staircase whose stringer has been notched so that the treads stick out at the side of the stair on one or both sides. Also called a cut string staircase or saw tooth staircase.

onion dome

open string staircase

open well stair
A series of steps that rise up the walls of a vertical shaft, leaving the center open.

opisthodomos
(OH pis toh du mohs)
A room located behind the naos of a Greek temple that was usually utilized as a storage space for valuables.

optical balance
A visual perception of balance even when a composition does not have identical halves. See also *asymmetrical balance.*

opus Alexandrinum (OH pus AL ik san dri num)
A type of mosaic used on the floors in churches of the Byzantine and Romanesque eras.

opus sectile (OH pus SEK tiyl)
A geometrically patterned mosaic consisting of large pieces of stone utilized by the Romans.

opus spicatum (OH pus SPIK ah tum)
A Roman technique of facing a wall with stones set diagonally into a herringbone pattern.

opus tesselatum (OH pus TES ul ah tum)
Mosaic pavement containing tesserae set into various patterns or pictures.

opus vermiculatum (OH pus VUR mik yoo lay tum)
Roman mosaics using long, diamond, or irregularly shaped stones.

orangery or orangerie (OR in jur ee OR ORNJ u ree)
A greenhouse for cultivating oranges.

orchestra
The circular space in front of a stage reserved for the chorus and dancers within an ancient Greek theater.

orchidée desk

See *Louis Majorelle Orchidée desk.* See *Louis Majorelle, 1859–1926, in the Architects, Artists, and Designers Appendix.*

order

In architecture, one of the classical treatments of a column, base, and entablature. There are five orders of architecture: Doric, Ionic, Corinthian, Tuscan, and Composite. See *illustrations in the Architectural Orders Appendix.*

organic architecture

A term developed by noted architect Frank Lloyd Wright defining architecture created as an organic whole, harmonizing with the natural landscape, each part interacting with another.

oriel window (OR ee-ul WIN doh)

A large bay window supported by corbels or brackets.

oriental

Referring to items from the Far East, particularly China and Japan.

oriental modern

Popularized in the mid 20th century, a style combining the basic lines of Chinese and Japanese design with uncluttered modern ideas.

oriental rugs

General term for handmade rugs from Eastern countries such as Iran, Afghanistan, Tibet, India, and China.

oriental walnut

See *oriental wood.*

oriental wood

A wood with brown to pink gray color and bold, distinctive striped figure found in Australia.

oriel window

orientation

The relationship of an object such as a building, wall, or piece of furniture to a compass setting.

ormolu (OR me loo)

Gilded bronze ornaments applied to furniture, used as mounts for fine porcelain, or as stand-alone objects, made popular during the Louis XIV period.

ornament

A decorative trim, or enhancement used to embellish. See *illustrations in the Ornament and Motifs/Ornaments Appendix.*

ornamentation

The process of embellishing.

Ornate Style (20 B.C.E.–50 C.E.)

See *third style painting* and *Pompeii.*

Orrefors (or u FORZ)

A Swedish glass factory established in 1898, known for high-quality crystal.

orthogonal

A drawing constructed of lines parallel or perpendicular to each other.

os de mouton (OH DUH MOO ton)

French term for mutton bone. A carved motif utilized for legs and arms during the French Louis XIII period.

oshiire (OH shir uh)

Japanese term for a closet used to store futons when not in use.

Osiride pillar (OH su ree duh PIL ar)

A pillar containing a sculpture of the Egyptian god Osiris with characteristically crossed arms.

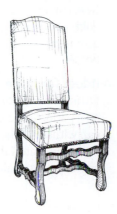

os de mouton base

209

ostium (AHS tee-um)

With respect to a Roman home, the passage leading from the entrance to the atrium.

Ostvald color system

A color system named after its German developer, Wilhelm Ostvald, which uses hue, value, and saturation to identify colors.

ottoman

On upholstered seat without back and arms, designed to be used with an easy chair; a large footstool.

ottomane

French term for a Louis XV Style upholstered canapé with curved enclosing sides that are an extension of the back.

Oushak (oo SHAHK)

An Oriental rug characterized by earth tones such as beige, gold, and orange and containing geometric designs within a wide border.

outdoor furniture

Furniture manufactured for use on a patio, terrace, or porch that can withstand the elements. Common materials include woods such as teak, cypress, and redwood, as well as glass, aluminum, fiberglass, and PVC.

ottoman

ottomane

outrounded corners

Corners of furniture that have been produced with semicircular curves.

outshot house

An American colonial house characterized by the addition of rooms at the back that produce an L-shaped plan.

oval back

A common Hepplewhite chair back with oval shape, similar to French Louis XVI Style chairs. See also *cameo back*.

overdoor

An architectural treatment over front entrance doors.

oversailing front

A front elevation that extends horizontally from the façade.

overstuffed

An upholstered piece that has been substantially filled.

ovolo (OH vu loh)

A classical term given to molding with the convex profile of a quarter circle. Also called quarter round. See *illustration in the Moldings Appendix*.

ox chair

See *Hans Wegner ox chair*. See *Hans Wegner, 1914–2007, in the Architects, Artists, and Designers Appendix*.

oyster veneer

A richly figured veneer comprised of distinctive concentric ovals, created by transversely cutting through small tree branches or trucks. Commonly used during the English William and Mary Style.

pad foot

A foot used to terminate a cabriole leg, characterized by a flat circular bottom with little or no carved ornamentation; similar to a club foot without the disk at the base. See *illustration in the Feet Appendix*.

padauk (pu DOWK)

Richly colored wood, imported from Anadaman Islands and Burma, very durable with a firm texture similar to rosewood, varying from pinkish to a reddish color, used for decorative cabinetwork. Sometimes sold under the name madou or Andaman redwood. See also *vermilion*.

pagoda (pah GOH dah)

A Buddhist sacred tower or temple found in China and India, rising several series of stories, each diminishing in area and height and usually circular, square, or octagonal in form with multiple-tiered roofs.

pagoda

paillon (pah YAWN)

French term for spangles or thin rolls of gold, silver, or colored foils cut in geometrical shapes and fired between two layers of translucent enamel, developed in France in the 18th century.

pailou (PAY loo)

A decorative Chinese gateway made of wood, brick, or stone with one, three, or five openings and a decorative roof, often carrying an inscription in the middle beam; also known as paifang.

Paimio chair (PAY mee oh CHAYR)

See *Alvar Aalto Paimio chair*. See *Alvar Aalto, 1898–1976, in the Architects, Artists, and Designers Appendix*.

paintbrush foot

See *knurled foot* or *whorl foot*. See *illustration in the Feet Appendix*.

painted furniture

Furniture painted with any opaque colored finish to hide the natural grain, also painted for protection and decoration.

paisley (PAYZlee)

Distinctive pattern made in Paisley, Scotland, to imitate the shawls imported from India.

paktong (PAK tong)

Chinese term used for "white copper," which is an alloy of copper, zinc, and nickel with a color resembling silver but slightly tinged with yellow; imported from China in the 18th century for use in the manufacture of candlesticks, fire irons, chimney grates, etc. Same as white copper.

palaistra, pl. palaistrai (piy LIY strah)

A gymnasium or wrestling sports school in ancient Greece or Rome.

palampores (PAH lem por)

East Indian printed cottons painted with foliage or flowers and/or the "tree of life" motif.

palanquin (pa lun KEEN)

A large, box-shaped litter or conveyance for a single person and carried by four to six men by means of poles projected fore and aft on both sides. See also *sedan chair*.

palazzo, pl. palazzi (pa LAT zoh)

An Italian three-storied urban palace, which featured a rusticated stone exterior to express power and affluence during the Italian Renaissance.

paldao (pahl DAY oh)

A wood rich with golden color that can be spalted, giving it a bluish-gray steak, adding a beautiful color.

palestra (pa LEE-es trah)

An ancient Greek or Roman public facility devoted to the training of athletes.

palette (PAAL it)

A surface, board, or tablet where an artist lays out pigments; also in computer graphics, it is the set of colors available for use on a project.

palisade (pa lu SAYD)

A fence of side-by-side posts constructed especially for a defense barrier or fortifications.

palisander (pa LEE son day)

French word for rosewood, particularly the hard dark purplish-red wood, imported into Europe from East India in the late 18th century and early 19th century and used as decorative element on French furniture. See also *rosewood, Honduras.*

Palladian motif (pa LAY dee-un MOH teef)

A row of open arches modeled after ancient Classical Roman architecture and used by Palladio to cover the Gothic façade on the 15th-century Basilica Vicenza, which centuries later inspired what became known as the Palladian window.

Palladian Style (pa LAY dee-un STIYL)

An architectural style inspired by the works and designs of the buildings and published works of the Italian architect Andrea Palladio during the 16th century and later revived in the 18th century. See *Andrea Palladio, 1508–1580, in the Architects, Artists, and Designers Appendix.*

Palladian window

(pa LAY dee-en WIN doh)

A three-part window, with a larger arched central section and two side windows with flat cornices. See also *Venetian window.*

Palladian window

palm

A decorative motif widely used by early civilizations, appearing in Egypt, Greek, and early Christian church art.

palm vaulting

See *fan vaulting.*

palmate column (PAHL mayt KOL um)

A column capital in ancient Egypt resembling the leaves of a palm tree that appear to be tied with bands to the shaft.

palmated (PAHL may tud)

A decorative motif of the palm leaf, shaped like an open hand, having lobes radiating from a common point.

palmette (PAHL met)

An ancient Egyptian stylized palm leaf, used as a decorative motif, fanlike in arrangement, similar to the anthemion. See *illustration in the Modlings Appendix.*

pampre (PAHM pruh)

A French word for a decorative ornament composed of grape and vine leaves, often found draped around spiral columns.

panache (pu NASH)

A French term for a feather plume, often used at the corners of an 18th-century canopy bed.

panchetto (pahn KE toh)

A small Italian Renaissance chair supported by three splayed legs and a fanlike carving on the back; similar to sgabello. See also *sgabello.*

palmate column

panache

panchetto

panel

A sunken or flush panel framed by horizontal and vertical members, known as rails and stiles. See also *bolection molding* and *sunk panel*.

panel, bolection

A raised panel that is above or in front of the frame.

panel wall

A panel used in the skeleton construction of walls, which is non-load-bearing and built between columns or piers serving only to separate spaces, supported at each story by the building frame.

panel-back chair

A chair used by the head of the family during the Tudor and Jacobean periods, cumbrous and high-seated, made of oak with heavy legs, stretchers, and a quite high wainscoted back. Also referred to as wainscot chair. See also *wainscot chair*.

panetière (pahn e tee AYR)

A small, decorated French provincial bread box or cupboard, usually hung on the wall and often found in Provence and Normandy.

panier (pon YAY)

A French word for a large container or basket used for provisions; often carried on a person's shoulders or on the back of an animal.

panneau (pon OH)

French term for panel, sign, or signpost.

panorama (pan oh RAH mah)

A continuous series of pictures of a landscape with an unbroken view of the entire surroundings, or unrolling a picture a part at a time before the audience, which occurred in the mid 19th century through traveling shows touring the country.

panetière

pantile (PAN tiyl)

A curved or S-shaped roofing tile commonly found on Mediterranean houses, and on English, Scottish, and Dutch buildings.

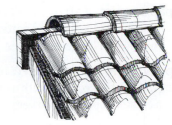

pantile

Panton chair (PAAN tun CHAYR)

See *Verner Panton chair*. See *Verner Panton, 1926–1998*, in the Architects, Artists, and Designers Appendix.

panurge (pon YURJ)

French term for a Louis XVI bed; also for a harness.

papelera (PAH pah lay rah)

A small, elaborate Spanish cabinet similar to vargueno, except it did not have a drop front or permanent base; used to hold writing materials. See also *varqueno*.

papelera

paper scroll

A term defining the scroll sometimes carved on the top rails of chairs and quite popular toward the mid 18th century; referred to under several names, such as spiral whorl, spiral scroll, spiral volute, conical volute, and helicoidal volute.

papier-mâché (PAH pee-ay-MAH shay)

A French word for a material made from paper pulp that could be molded into shapes and then baked; introduced in the 17th and 18th centuries into Europe and becoming quite popular in the 19th century in both Europe and America for table tops, boxes, trays, etc., often decorated with Eastern designs.

papier-mâché

papier peint (PAH pee-ay PAHN)

French word for printed patterned wallpaper used in the late 17th century.

papyriform column (pu PIY roh form KOL um)

An Egyptian column with a capital decorated with a cluster of papyrus flowers.

papyrus bed (pu PIY rus BED)

An ancient Egyptian wooden rectangular bed with a mat of woven papyrus.

papyrus bud (pu PIY rus BUD)

Closed papyrus often used on ancient Egyptian column, which was extremely popular during the 19th and 20th dynasties.

papyrus flower (pu PIY rus FLOW ur)

An aquatic plant abundant in ancient Egypt processed into a form of paper used as writing material and popular as a design for Egyptian columns, usually with a base representing the lotus.

parapet (PAYR u pet)

A low protective wall at the edge of a roof, terrace, balcony, or structure to protect the edge of a platform, roof, or bridge.

parcel gilding

Selective gilding or partial gilding applied to parts of a design, practiced in the late 17th and early 18th centuries in England and particularly during the Decorated Queen Anne period.

papyrus bud

papyrus flower

parapet

parcheman (par SHIM ahn)

An ornate carving appearing to be folded fabric as it bulges outward at intervals.

parchemin (PAHR shu mohn)

An early 16th-century linenfold panel, often referred to as parchemin; a Gothic motif, but used with Renaissance details. See also *linenfold*.

parchemin

parchment

A creamy or yellowish material prepared from the dried and treated skin of a sheep or goat on which to write or paint; also used to define a document or a strong, tough, high-quality paper.

parchment panel

Another term referring to linenfold paneling. See also *linenfold*.

pargework pargetry (PARJ wurk / PARJ u tree)

A decorated plastered design applied to walls and ceilings, especially during the Elizabethan and Jacobean periods.

pargework

parian ware (PAYR ee-un WAYR)

A fired, but unglazed bisque porcelain introduced around 1840 in England and used mainly for biscuit figures.

Paris Exposition des Arts Decoratifs et Industriels (PAR ee EKS poh zi see-ohn DAYZ AR de kor AH teef AY AHN doo stree-el)

International exhibition in Paris in 1925 that had a major focus on design and the decorative arts, which was also where the term Art Deco originated with the underlying aim to reestablish France as the forefront of design in fashion, decorative arts, and luxury goods.

parliament chair

A side chair with a high back and shaped splat, cabriole legs, and club feet made in the 18th-century Queen Anne Style in the British colony of Bermuda.

Parliament clock

See *Act of Parliament clock*.

parlor lamp

A Victorian table lamp with a ball shade, consisting of two bulbous globes one on top of the other, generally a removable fount, with matching painted or embossed decoration on both the top and the base.

parlor stand

A Victorian square or rectangular lamp table supported by four splayed legs.

parlor suite

Victorian furniture for the parlor or living area, usually consisting of armchairs, side chairs, a sofa or settee, sometimes a rocker, and occasional table to match.

parlour

From the French word parloir, a private room for reception and entertainment; currently in England, it is the drawing room or comfortable sitting room.

parlour or parlor chair

Carved mahogany Victorian armchairs with padded armrest and an upholstered back and seat.

parlour lamp

Same as *parlor lamp*.

parquet (PAR kay)

Strips of wood inlaid on a floor, usually laid in a geometric pattern, sometimes using different colors of wood. See also *block flooring* and *marquetry*.

parlour chair

parquetry or parquetrie (PAR ku tree)

Same as parquet.

Parson's table

Square or rectangular table of molded plastic with flush surface and straight block legs; named from the Parson's School of Design, where the design originated in the 1950s.

Parson's table

parterres (PAR tayr)

A French term for a formal garden, often symmetrical, with paths between the beds of flowers and decorative plantings.

Parthenon

(PAR thu non)
Chief temple sacred to Athena, built on the Acropolis in Greece in the 5th century, considered a supreme example of the Doric architectural order.

Parthenon

parti (PAR tee)

French word for the basic concept or scheme of an architectural design.

partners desk

An antique desk from the 18th century consisting of two pedestal desks with drawers on both faces of the pedestal, making it possible for two users to work while facing each other; also characterized by paneled end pieces and often a tooled leather top.

partners desk

abcdefghijklmnopqrstuvwxyz

partridge wood (PAR trij WUUD)

Brazilian hard, straight-grained wood with brown and dark red streaks resembling partridge feathers; used in the 17th century as an inlay wood.

passementerie (PAHS mohn tree)

French word for an ornamental trimming or edging of cord, gimp, beading, braid, or metallic thread; from the word passement.

pastas (pah STUS)

A classical Greek house with a free space in the court area extending unimpeded to the exterior walls.

pastiglia (pah STEE lyah)

A technique used during the Italian Renaissance on furniture using gesso to form a raised design that could be painted or gilded. See also *anaglypta, carton-pierre,* and *composition ornament.*

Pastil chair (PAA steel CHAYR)

See *Eero Aarnio Pastil chair.* See *Eero Aarnio, 1932– , in the Architects, Artists, and Designers Appendix.*

patera, pl. paterae (PAH ter ah/PAH ter ay)

Round or oval ornamental disk enriched with a rosette, used during the 18th-century classical revivals on chair splats, furniture crests and mirrors, decorative friezes, and many other items. See also *macaroon* or *macaron.* See *illustration in the Motifs/Ornaments Appendix.*

pâte-sur-pâte (PAT-SEER-PAT)

A French term used in reference to ceramics, in which a low relief design is developed by building successive layers of slip, creating a unique and very attractive design.

patina (pu TEE nuh)

A rich surface color produced on wood, metal, or other materials by oxidization. See also *bronze.*

patio

A Spanish building with an inner courtyard open to the sky. See also *atrium.*

pattern

A decoration or design for wallpaper, china, textile fabrics, or flooring; also an orderly arrangement of motifs.

pavilion (pu VIL yun)

A large building or a tent used for exhibition, sports, or public entertainment; usually has a lot of space and light.

paw and ball

A variation of the claw and ball foot introduced as a replacement in the mid 18th century. See also *ball and claw foot.*

paw foot

A carved stylized furniture foot representing an animal's paw, often that of a lion, bear, or dog, popular in the late 17th- to early 18th-century French and English furniture; can be seen on anything from tables to chests, even on antique bathtubs today. See *illustration in the Feet Appendix.*

paysages or paysages-décors (PAY zahj OR PAY zahj day KOR)

A French word meaning country landscapes for wall murals that were applied in the early 19th century and formed continuous scenes around the room from the chair rail to the cornice; a similar art of painted scenes in England were called perspectives.

Peacock (Wright chair)

See *Frank L. Wright Peacock chair.* See *Frank L. Wright, 1867–1959, in the Architects, Artists, and Designers Appendix.*

Peacock (Wegner chair)

See *Hans Wegner Peacock chair.* See *Hans Wegner, 1914–2007, in the Architects, Artists, and Designers Appendix.*

peacock chair (Victorian wicker)

An armchair with a very high, rounded fanback, usually of rattan or wicker.

pear-drop handle

A brass pendant shaped like a pear and used as drawer pull; typical of 17th-century English work; also a support for an arch in 18th-century architecture.

pear-drop ornament

An ornament usually decorating the upper part of a plain frieze, also found in some of the work of Hepplewhite and Sheraton, characterized as a series of Gothic arches in relief with drops appearing at the lower points suggesting capitals.

pearling

Repetitive form of beads resembling pearls used as a decorative molding or used to embellish furniture in straight lines, swaged, or arced.

pearwood, African

An interlocking finely grained wood that is beautiful with a clear finish; used for furniture and smaller accessories. It was often used by country cabinetmakers for furniture pieces during the 16th and 17th centuries.

peche mortel (PESH MOR tel)

A mid 18th-century two-part chaise longue in which one part was made into an oversized easy chair, while the other part was made into an upholstered stool with the feet joined in the middle; forerunner of the modern easy chair with footstool. See also *chaise longue* and *duchesse*.

peche mortel

pedestal

A central supporting base or block for a table top or a statue vase; also in the order of architecture, it is the lowest portion of a classic order.

pedestal desk

A simple rectangular free-standing desk, used as a writing or library table, with a flat top resting on two pedestals or small cabinets of stacked drawers; sometimes there is a central large

pedestal

drawer and a modesty panel in the front to hide the legs and knees of the user, appearing in England in the mid 18th century. See also *kneehole desk*.

pedestal table

A round, square, or oval table supported by a single member base; also known as a tripod table.

pediment

A triangular gable in classical Greek and Roman architecture, crowned with a projecting cornice and used over a portico. Later in the 18th century this feature was adopted by Renaissance architects for furniture and interior features, with adaptation of the triangular form into segmental (rounded), broken scroll, swan's neck (double curve), and other types. See *illustrations in the Pediments Appendix*.

peg

A small wooden dowel, usually cylindrical and pointed or tapered, used to fasten things, such as joining furniture, panels, or floors, or to plug a hole; usually implies that the peg is exposed.

pegged lap joint

Wood joint in which two pieces are overlapped and held together using dowels for reinforcement. See also *joint*.

Pelican chair

See *Finn Juhl Pelican chair*. See *Finn Juhl, 1912–1989, in the Architects, Artists, and Designers Appendix*.

pelike (pel i kee)

A Greek storage jar with two handles and a wider rounded lower portion, giving the vessel a more stable but heavier appearance; same use as an amphora.

pellet ornament (PEL it Or nu munt)

Gothic or Norman ornament resembling disks or flattened balls.

pelmet (PEL met)

A narrow, flat addition at the top of a window, designed to conceal the curtain rail and complement the side curtains; same as a valance. See also *lambrequin*.

abcdefghijklmnopqrstuvwxyz

pelta (PEL tah)

A small shield, crescent-shaped, of Thracian design.

Pembroke table

A late 18th-century table with drop leaves supported by brackets with a drawer in the apron and tapering legs usually on castors; named after the Countess of Pembroke who ordered a table of this type.

Pembroke table

penasco door (pen AH scoh DOR)

A Spanish-style door with decorative panels, handcrafted by Southwest Spanish craftsmen.

pencil and pearl

A synonym for bead and reel molding.

pendant

A term to describe a hanging ornament or drop. See also *boss* and *cul-de-lampe*.

pendentive (pen DEN tiv)

The triangular concave form that transmits the weight of a circular dome over a square to the four corner supports; originating in Byzantine architecture.

pendule à gaine (PAHN dyool AH GEN)

A French term for a grandfather clock or tall clock.

peniures-vivantes (pe nee YOOR ays vee VAHN tays)

Three-dimensional sculptural forms framed in architectural detail and enhanced by light of natural and artificial means; used extensively in Italy and Spain.

pendentive

penne d'oiseau (PEN duz OH)

French word interpreted to mean "bird's feather"; in reference to wooden furniture, an ornamental carving.

Pennsylvania Dutch

Plain sturdy furniture left unfinished or brightly painted featuring traditional German and Swiss folk motifs, such as tulips, tree of life, hearts, birds, leaves, or geometric designs; made in southeastern Pennsylvania where the German and Swiss Mennonites settled at the end of the 17th century.

Pennsylvania stove

See *Franklin stove.*

pent roof

A small shed-type roof above the first floor of a structure, separating stories and covering all four sides of the building to protect doors, windows, and lower walls; also called a shed roof.

pentastyle (pen TA stiyl)

In classical architecture a temple or portico having five columns across the front.

penthouse

During medieval times, a term meaning an attic structure formed by a lean-to roof; in present day, the term is used to describe an apartment on the uppermost story of a large building, typically set back from the main building wall to allow for an outside terrace or garden.

pentice (pen TEE chay)

An unsupported extension of a building's roof used over an entrance to protect the area beneath; often found in Pennsylvania Dutch buildings.

pepper pot tower

A circular stone tower with a conical roof.

pergamene capital (payr gu MEEN ay KAP i tal)

An ancient Greek capital with palm fronds.

pergola (PAYR goh lah)

An Italian covered walkway in a garden, usually designed with a double row of spaced posts or columns supported by joints that form a frame for climbing plants.

peribolus (per EE bul us)

An ancient Greek term for a wall or colonnade surrounding a Greek temple and its sacred space, or to separate the sacred space from the other areas.

perimeter stretcher

A perimeter stretcher at floor level or slightly above connecting the legs on a piece of furniture, usually a chair or table.

peripteral (pe RIP ter ul)

A temple or structure with a single row of columns on all sides; almost all ancient Greek temples were peripteral, regardless of the architectural order.

peripteros (pe RIP ter us)

An ancient Greek portico, a kiosk, or a chapel; usually it is rectangular in plan and framed on all sides by a colonnade. An example of a peripteros is the Parthenon in Athens (447–435 B.C.E.).

peristyle (PER i stiyl)

A columned porch or open colonnade surrounding a court that may have an internal garden.

pergola

perimeter stretcher

peristyle

peristyle plan (PER i stiyl PLAN)

Same as peristyle.

peristylium (PAYR u stiyl ee-um)

An ancient Roman building or court enclosed by columns. See also *peristyle*.

periwig chair (PAYR u wig CHAYR)

A high, caned-back chair of the late 17th century with elaborate carved cresting, designed with or without arms.

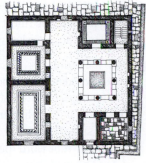

peristyle plan

Perpendicular Style

Final phase of English Gothic period (1350–1550), characterized by rich visual effects, predominant vertical lines in its tracery, windows enlarged to great proportions, and slender vertical lines on the interiors; oldest surviving example is the choir of Gloucester Cathedral (begun ca. 1335); style also known as the Rectilinear or Late Pointed Style.

perroquet (payr OO kay)

A French chair with legs crossed in the shape of an X.

Persian knot (Senneh)

The Persian knot is one of two knots used to make hand-knotted oriental rugs, also known by the name Senneh, and is an asymmetrical knot; the other knot, known as the Turkish knot, is a symmetrical knot. See also *Senneh knot.*

Persian rugs

Carpets and oriental rugs from Persia (currently produced in Iran) with the highest reputation, unequalled in technique, design, and soft, rich color; they are characterized by traditional and stylized symbolic imagery according to the province where they are made.

petit commode (PET ee Ku mohd)

A small French table with two or three drawers, usually one under the other.

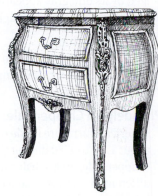

petit commode

petit point (PET ee PWAHN)

Needlepoint of the finest stitch, using a smaller needle, often used for upholstery, accessories, wall hangings, etc. See also *needlepoint*.

petrin (PET run)

French wooden coffer chest with four legs elevated off the floor and a lid that lifts up or off; used to store flour or for holding dough. The root word "petrin" means kneaded or molded.

petrin

petticoat mirror

A low mirror set over a console or table, typically hard to see since it is so close to the floor; commonly found in formal halls and used by ladies to see if their petticoats were showing. See also *console mirror*.

petuntse (peh TUN seh)

Chinese white porcelain made by the combination of two integral ingredients, white kaolin (china clay) and pai-tun-tze (china stone) or "petuntse" as it is called in England.

pewter

An alloy of tin with lead, copper, and various other metals, characterized by its dull gray appearance; used for domestic utensils, tankards, bowls, and ornaments; originally it substituted for silver.

Philadelphia chair

An American version of the Windsor-style chair, manufactured by Gilbert and Robert Gaw, important Philadelphia manufacturers. See also *Windsor chair*.

Philadelphia Chippendale

American furniture made of mahogany in the Chippendale style from about 1750 to 1780 during the colonial period and named after Thomas Chippendale, an English cabinetmaker. American Chippendale was different in style, very conservative compared to the English designs, but closely related to the early Queen Anne Style, yet it overlapped other styles as taste changed in America.

Philippine mahogany

See *lauan*.

phoenix (FEE niks)

A mythical bird common in ancient Egypt and in Classical antiquity that is a fire spirit with colorful plumage, tail of gold and scarlet; also a Chinese motif symbolic of the Empress.

Phyfe armchair (FIFE)

See *Duncan Phyfe armchair*. See *Duncan Phyfe, 1768–1854*, in the *Architects, Artists, and Designers Appendix*.

Phyfe card table (FIFE)

See *Duncan Phyfe card table*. See *Duncan Phyfe, 1768–1854*, in the *Architects, Artists, and Designers Appendix*.

Phyfe console (FIFE)

See *Duncan Phyfe console*. See *Duncan Phyfe, 1768–1854*, in the *Architects, Artists, and Designers Appendix*.

Phyfe cornucopia leg sofa (FIFE)

See *Duncan Phyfe cornucopia leg sofa*. See *Duncan Phyfe, 1768–1854*, in the *Architects, Artists, and Designers Appendix*.

Phyfe lyre-back chair (FIFE)

See *Duncan Phyfe lyre-back chair*. See *Duncan Phyfe, 1768–1854*, in the *Architects, Artists, and Designers Appendix*.

Phyfe sewing table (FIFE)

See *Duncan Phyfe sewing table*. See *Duncan Phyfe, 1768–1854*, in the *Architects, Artists, and Designers Appendix*.

Phyfe Sheraton-type sofa (FIFE)

See *Duncan Phyfe Sheraton-type sofa*. See *Duncan Phyfe, 1768–1854*, in the *Architects, Artists, and Designers Appendix*.

Phyfe table

See *Duncan Phyfe table*. See *Duncan Phyfe, 1768–1845*, in the *Architects, Artists, and Designers Appendix*.

Phyfe tall case clock (FIFE)

See *Duncan Phyfe tall case clock*. See *Duncan Phyfe, 1768–1854*, in the *Architects, Artists, and Designers Appendix*.

piano nobile (PEE anoh NOH bee lay)

Italian term for the main floor, which is the second floor of the building, usually containing the main apartments; also Italian for "noble floor." See also *bel étage*.

piano stool

A special type of chair or stool adjustable in height dating back to the 19th century for use when playing the piano. See also *stool*.

piano nobile

pianoforte (pee AAN u for tay)

An Italian term for piano invented by Cristofer in the 18th century.

piazza (pee AHT suh)

An Italian term for a open square in a city, surrounded by buildings that form an enclosure; often used as a public marketplace.

pick

A filling yarn inserted through a shed by the carrier device, a shuttle, as it moves across the loom. This single crossing of the shuttle from one side of the loom to the other is known as the pick.

pickled finish

A method of treating wood by rubbing white or off-white paint into previously stained or finished wood; often used to make the wood look old.

picture molding or rail

A simple grooved horizontal strip of wood running around the perimeter of the room below the frieze or close to the ceiling line from which pictures can be hung. Same as frieze rail or frisé.

picture rugs

Modern rugs handwoven by Scandinavian artisans, characterized by abstract designs; used as wall-mounted decorations or area rugs.

pie safe

A wooden cupboard with decorative pierced tin doors for ventilating pies after baking; introduced by Pennsylvania Germans in the 19th century. See also *milk safe*.

piece-sur-piece (PEES-SUR-PEES)

A French-Canadian log house where horizontal timbers are stacked vertically and held in place by grooved vertical corner posts.

piecrust table

An 18th-century English or American small round tripod table with a curved, scalloped edge resembling a pie crust; usually made of mahogany.

pied-de-biche (pee AY deh-BEESH)

French term for a carved hoof or cloven hoof-shaped foot used on early cabriolet legs of the 18th century. See also *doe's foot, cloven foot, or hoof foot*. See *illustration in the Feet Appendix*.

pier

A type of support for a superstructure; very heavy, vertical masonry attaching to the wall where a heavy load is imposed.

pier glass

A tall, narrow wall mirror designed to stand on the floor against a wall surface; later it was hung on the wall or pier often between windows or over a chimney piece or console table; also called a cheval glass. See also *cheval glass*.

pier table

A table designed to be placed against a pier or wall, usually between windows with a pier glass or mirror; many were made in pairs during the 18th century.

pier table

abcdefghijklmnopqrstuvwxyz

piercing or pierced tracery or pierced carving

Carved designs that penetrate through a surface for ornamentation, as in crestings, aprons, chair backs, and other places where open design work is needed; similar to fretwork. See also *ajoure* and *fretwork*.

piercing

pierrotage (pee ay roh TAHJ)

A filling of stones and clay in the space between the hewn logs.

pieta (pee AY tah)

An Italian term for a painting or sculpture depicting the Virgin Mary holding the dead body of Jesus; more often found in sculpture.

pietra dura, pl. pietre dure (pee AY trah DOO rah)

A mosaic or inlay using pieces of marble and semiprecious stones, cut to fit to create a picture or pattern; especially used to embellish Renaissance cabinets and table tops. See also *intarsia, mosaic,* or *tarsia.*

pietre intarsiate (PEE e tray in TAHR see ah tay)

See *pietra dura.*

pigeonholes

Small compartments built in desks and cabinets to hold papers, letters, and other items.

pilaster

A representation of one of the architectural orders, yet rectangular and flattened against a surface to appear as a visual support; usually projects a third of its width.

pilaster located on side of door

pilastrade (pi LAHS tur)

A row of continuous pilasters in a series.

pillar

An architectural column or shaft; a vertical, free-standing structural member made of stone, brick, or other materials, used as a building support or as an isolated commemorative shaft.

pillar and claw table

A fashionable breakfast table of the late 18th century through the Victorian period, often referred to as a tripod table, which has a single column-like pedestal support with three carved lion or bear paw feet, giving the table more stability.

pillar and scroll style

A furniture style widely popularized in America during the 19th century through a 1840 publication by John Hall called "The Cabinet Maker's Assistant," which characterized the design being dominated by single and double scrolls and the belief that the elliptical curve was the single most beautiful ingredient to design; often used by clockmakers of the period.

pillow capital

A Romanesque cubic capital resembling a cushion, rounded at the corners, and decorated in bas-relief sculpture.

pillow capital

pillowback chair

An American "fancy" chair made in the late 18th and early 19th centuries with the distinctive characteristics of Hitchcock work, particularly the pillow or central block with carved decorations resembling a cushion or pillow, the usual rush seat, decorated rails with stencil designs, and turned front legs.

pilotis or piloti (pi LAH tee)

A concept introduced by Le Corbusier using piers or columns to support a structure by elevating it above ground level, thus providing free space beneath the building.

pinacotheca, pl. pinacothecae (pin ah KOTH i kah)

A place in ancient Rome for the display of the artwork of private collectors; currently in Italy it applies to public galleries.

pinched trailing

See *quillwork*.

pincushion chair

See *compass seat*.

pine

The wood of any pine tree, highly valued in carpentry to make such items as furniture, window frames, paneling, and flooring because it is abundant with an interesting grain and very easy to use.

pine, pickled

A method of finishing wood that produces a beautiful look with a whitish patina by using off-white semitransparent stain applied to open pored wood, such as pine.

pine, southern yellow

A hard pine native to Northern America, very strong and much heavier than white pine, characterized by its durability and beautiful light natural color that can be shaped into paneling, molding, flooring, and other uses; even used by the colonists at Williamsburg in their houses.

pine, white

A soft wood that is light in weight but very strong, characterized by its pale, yellow appearance that is quite uninteresting and smooth with few markings; hence, it is often used for structural purposes because it holds its shape well, showing no warping, welling, splitting, or shrinking.

pineapple

A stylized and very popular motif, adopted in America during the 19th century as a symbol of hospitality, prosperity, and friendship; used on furniture as terminals on chairs and bedposts, buildings, textiles, china, and so forth.

ping (PING)

An early Chinese folding screen, originating as early as the 4th century B.C.E., with widespread use in the 7th century in the Tang Dynasty of China; also called ping feng.

pinnacle (PIN ah kul)

Small pyramidal or cone-shaped turret used in Gothic architecture to crown the roof or cap a tower; also used as a finial at the top of a piece of furniture.

pipkin (PIP kin)

An English term for an 18th-century metal coal container used at fireside.

piqua (PIK way)

An African exotic wood with a uniform pinkish-brown color often used for veneer. See also *bosse*.

pishtag (PISH tahk)

A high arch set within a rectangular frame, most common in Anatolian and Iranian architecture, also in India; sometimes decorated with glazed tilework, geometric designs, calligraphy, and vegetal designs.

pithos, pl. pithoi (PITH ohs)

A large storage jar of a characteristic shape uncovered in ancient Greece and in Crete.

placage (PLAH kaj)

French word for a thin covering of fine wood, commonly referred to as veneer.

placita (plah SIT ah)

A Spanish word for an enclosed courtyard surrounded by a high wall with a massive gate for entrance; usually found on Spanish Colonial ranches in the Americas.

plain butt joint

A joint used in woodwork, which is one of the simplest and most frequently used, consisting of one piece of material held against another piece and fastened by glue, nails, or screws. It is used specifically in cheap box construction and also house framing and bridge construction. See *illustration in the Joints Appendix.*

plank flooring

Solid wood flooring made of planks that are three inches and wider, installed in random lengths.

plantation shutters

A window shutter made from a variety of materials with wide louver sizes.

planted molding

A molding that is fastened to the work by nailing rather than cut into solid material. See also *applied molding* and *stuck molding.*

plaque (PLAK)

A term for a plate or piece of metal, glass, or pottery with a picture, design in relief, or some other surface enrichment, used to hang on the wall for decorative purposes; it also defines a wall tablet to commemorate an event or identify a place. See also *cartouche.*

plate tracery

A form of tracery found in early Gothic architecture that uses a series of ornamental patterns cut through thick areas of stone, making the window look as if it had been filled in with stone and small openings that appear to have been cut through the glass; hence the stone dominates the window, not the glass.

plate warmer

An 18th-century metal unit designed to hold plates and equipped with a heater; also in the 18th century a plate made of pewter would have a port for hot water, which would warm the plate.

plateau

A flat 19th-century stand with low feet, used to raise a centerpiece above the table's surface, sometimes even extending the full length of the table; very decorative and made of silver, brass, glass, or wood.

Plateresco or Plateresque (PLA tu res koh / PLA tu resk)

Spanish term identifying the period of art in Spain during the first half of the 16th century, characterized by the imitation of the fine detail suggesting the work of a silversmith (platero); also related to Baroque in style. See also *Mudéjar.*

platform bed

A bed with a mattress raised off the floor by a solid wood or plastic platform with the space beneath used for storage or living space. See also *island bed.*

platform bed

platform rocker

A rocking chair in which the chair rocks on a stationary base rather than on the floor; hence, the movable section can be kept at a comfortable angle without oscillating.

Platner Model 1725A chair

See *Warren Platner Model 1725A chair.* See *Warren Platner, 1919–2006, in the Architects, Artists, and Designers Appendix.*

platform rocker

plaza (PLAH sah)

A marketplace or large open public square in a town or city or a paved area between buildings. Currently it refers to a widened area approaching a tollbooth or a shopping complex.

pliant (PLEE ohn)

A French word for easily bent or flexible; also a folding stool with legs crossed in the shape of an X. See also *faudesteuil.*

plinth (PLINTH)

Lowest part of the column in the shape of a square or rectangular block; also the base under a statue, pilaster, or door frame. In furniture, it is the square, continuous base resting on the floor.

plinth

pliqué à jour enameling (PLEE kay AH JOR)

A French term for a vitreous enamel technique from the 14th century where enamel was applied in cells, similar to a form of cloisonné, but with no backing, creating a translucent or transparent effect.

pluteus, pl. plutei (PLOO tays)

A short screen between columns, especially one surrounding the choir of the church.

podium, pl. podus (POH dee um)

A pedestal supporting columns or continuous base for a building. See also *stylobate*.

pointed arch

An arch used in Gothic architecture, quite strong, with a pointed apex.

pole screen

A fire or draft screen mounted on a wood or metal upright pole and supported on a tripod base with a sliding panel of painted wood or framed needlepoint; evolved during the late 17th century and popular for the next 100 years. See also *banner screen* and *écran à éclisse*.

pole table

See *pote table*.

polis, pl. poleis (POH lis)

A city-state in Greece.

Polish bed

See *dome bed*.

polychromy or polychrome (POI u krohm)

A multicolored ornament or pattern; something of several colors.

pomegranate (PO mu gran et)

A decorative motif used in classical times as a symbol of fertility, based on the pomegranate fruit, which has a hard rind and an apple shape.

pomegranate

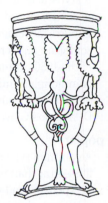

Pompeiian Style

pommes, pl. pomme (POM)

Apple-shaped finials, used by Daniel Marot (1661–1752), a French architect and furniture designer, on the corners of tester bed posts. See *Daniel Marot, 1661–1752, in the Architects, Artists, and Designers Appendix.*

Pompeii (POM pay)

An ancient Roman city southeast of Naples, founded in the 6th or early 5th century B.C.E., and becoming quite prosperous as a port and resort with villas, theaters, temples, and baths; destroyed and completely buried during the eruption of Mount Vesuvius in 79 C.E.; rediscovered in 1748.

Pompeiian Style (POM pay un STIYL)

A Neoclassical Style, inspired by the rediscovery of Herculaneum in I738 C.E. and of Pompeii in 1748 C.E., particularly influential in interior design and furnishing during the mid 18th century.

Ponies

See *Eero Aarnio Pony chairs*. See *Eero Aarnio, 1932– , in the Architects, Artists, and Designers Appendix.*

ponteuse (PON tus)

An 18th-century gaming chair used around a game table, with the player straddling the chair; also has a wide back rail sometimes upholstered or containing compartments for game chips, cards, etc. See also *fumeuse*.

pontil (PON til)

An iron rod, also called a punty, used in glassmaking during the hand-blown process to carry hot materials; when detached a circular "pontil mark" is left on the bottom of the glass.

pontypool (PAHN tu pool)

A name for a process of japanning on metal with the use of oil varnish and heat, originated by Thomas Allgood of Pontypool, England, in the late 17th century.

pole screen

Pop Art

A modern art movement from the 1950s to the 1970s, using imagery, styles, and themes of advertising, mass media, and modern popular culture.

Pop Art furniture

A stylistic trend in furniture that emerged in the 1950s and 1960s inspired by the Pop Art movement in painting and sculpture and a reaction against the taste of the 1950s; often used gaudy colors, commonplace motifs, and vulgar imagery of popular consumerist culture, such as Joe DiMaggio's Glove chair.

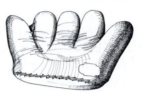

**Pop Art furniture
(Joe DiMaggio Glove chair)**

poplar

A common type of wood often classified as a hardwood by species, but it is softer than pine. It is creamy white with brown or gray streaks, inexpensive and very workable; sometimes it is referred to as yellow poplar or whitewood, but other varieties are European black poplar, cottonwood, and some types of aspen. It is used in furniture making, boat building, and other woodworking projects. See also *whitewood.*

poppy head

Ornaments or finials, sometimes human heads, carved animals, foliage knots, and even fleurs-de-lis cutouts, decorating the end of a Gothic bench.

porcelain (POR se lin)

True porcelain or hard-paste porcelain, originating in China over 1,000 years ago, with a white translucent body made of kaolin, quartz, and feldspar; fired at high temperatures. See also *china, hard paste,* and *kaolin.*

porcelaine noir (POR su len n WAHR)

A refined Chinese porcelain with an overglaze black enamel as a ground color.

porch

A covered entrance or platform to a building, usually having a separate roof that forms a covered approach to a vestibule or doorway. See also *portico.*

porphyry (POR fu ree)

A type of rock with large feldspar crystals embedded in dark red or purplish groundmass; architectural or ornamental usage.

porta (POR tah)

A monumental gate, doorway, or entrance to a Roman city or fortress or any grand entrance.

portable server

A small table on wheels outfitted with all utility connections and other removable items, such as trays, shelves, etc., so it can be used as a portable bar or as a small mobile kitchen.

portal

A word synonymous with a gate, entrance, or doorway, especially an entrance to a large and important structure. See also *porta.*

portcullis (port KU lus)

A heavy wood or iron gate in the form of grating suspended by chains and lowered into place at the entrance to a castle, fort, or fortified town.

porte-cochère (PORT koh SHAYR)

A covered passageway that is large enough to admit a carriage or automobile and also to provide shelter for passengers leaving the carriage to enter the building, usually attached to the structure; often found in French Renaissance architecture.

porte-cochère

porter chair

A chair that sat in the entry hall for use by the porter, who greeted visitors as protection for the owner; the sides on the chair kept off the draughts, and the small shelf, which would flap down when not in use, was to hold a lantern.

portico (por ti KOH)

A covered entry porch that is supported by columns forming the entrance or center to a façade.

portico

porticus (por ti KUS)

See *portico*.

portiere (POR tee-ayr)

A French term for a curtain or drapery hung over a doorway as a means of preventing drafts, providing privacy, serving as decoration, or separating a room from an alcove.

Portland vase

An antique Roman cameo vase, dating back to 1st century B.C.E., made of violet-blue glass and designed with a continuous opaque white depicting several figures (humans and gods). Joseph Wedgwood reproduced the cameo glass vase; it has become a hallmark of the Wedgwood company.

portrait chair

Chair usually with a porcelain picture of an individual on its back.

Portuguese bulb (POR chu geez BULB)

A stretcher with prominent bulbs of Portuguese origin, used in the early years of William and Mary for furniture supports. Knobs or bulbs were used in place of squares into which the stretcher was socketed with one or two more bulbs on the stretcher itself.

post

A vertical support for a beam in the framework of a building.

post and lintel

A basic form of construction that employs vertical elements, such as posts, to support a horizontal member called a beam or lintel. See also *trabeated*.

postern (POH stern)

An entrance, back door, or gate other than the main one. See also *façade d'honneur*.

posticum (POH sti kum)

The rear vestibule or back part of the portico in a classical Roman temple; also called epinaos or opisthodomua.

Postmodernism or postmodern design

Design and architectural style of the late 1970s and 1980s that rejected the plain, unadorned forms of modernism and restored color and ornament by using historical inspiration; architect Robert Venturi, one of the architects associated with Postmodernism, stated that "less is a bore." See *Robert Venturi, 1925– , in the Architects, Artists, and Designers Appendix*.

pot board

Closest shelf to the floor of dresser.

pot cupboard

Small cabinets, especially popular during the Victorian and Edwardian England periods, used to store chamber pots, extremely compact and small, some equipped with drawers. See also *bedside cupboard*.

pot cupboard

pote table (POHT TAY bul)

A single pedestal table resembing the lower portion of a fluted column with exposed shelves on one face or a tambour door; also called a pole table.

pouch table (POWCH TAY bul)

A small, elegant lady's work table with fitted drawers and compartments for reels and bobbins, and a place for fancy needlework, which was widely produced in the late 18th and early 19th centuries, and described by Sheraton in "The Cabinet Dictionary" published in 1803 as a "Table with a Bag." See also *bag table* and *table* à *ouvrage*.

227

abcdefghijklmno**p**qrstuvwxyz

poudreuse (PUH drooz)

A small 18th-century toilet table or powder table with mirrored lid used by ladies; the table was an innovation of Louis XV. See also *table de dame, tricoteuse,* and *work table.*

pouf or pouffe (POOF)

Large, low, backless, upholstered cushion-like seat, usually round and sometimes with visible wooden legs, resembling a foot stool; appearing in France in 1845 and very popular in Europe and America during the 19th century.

pouf

Poul Kjaerholm tulip chair (POHL KAYR holm TOO lip CHAYR)

A 1961 Danish classic, satin-brushed stainless steel base side chair covered in leather, available in different colors; designed by Poul Kjaerholm, often referred to as the Tulip chair. See *Poul Kjaerholm, 1929–1980, in the Architects, Artists, and Designers Appendix.*

powder room

A closet-sized room of the early 18th century where those wearing wigs had them repowdered; today, the term refers to a lavatory for women or for guests in a private home. See also *poudreuse.*

powder table

French term for a small dressing table with folding mirror and side leaves from the 18th century. See also *poudreuse.*

Poul Kjaerholm tulip chair

powder table

Powerplay chair

See *Frank O. Gehry Powerplay chair.* See *Frank O. Gehry, 1929–, in the Architects, Artists, and Designers Appendix.*

poyntell (POIN tel)

A paving or flooring pattern made of small, square tiles or lozenge-shaped blocks laid diagonally.

pozzetto (POHT ze toh)

An Italian upholstered sofa or divan.

Prague chair (PRAHG CHAYR)

A furnishing classic made of bent birchwood and seats made of cane.

Prairie Style

A style used to describe Frank Lloyd Wright's Midwestern American architecture movement that employed the principles of organic architecture.

prayer hall

A large hall devoid of furniture, decorated with Qu'ranic texts on the walls and with no images of humans or animals, as these are forbidden in Islam.

prayer rug

A small rug, carpet, or mat designed for Muslims to kneel on during devotion. See also *Turkish rugs.*

Preclassic

Also known as the Formative period, a division of the pre-Columbian Mesoamerican civilization (2000 BCE-200 CE), in which large-scale ceremonial architecture, writing, cities, and states can be traced, along with key elements, such as dominance of corn, building of pyramids, complex calendar, many gods, human sacrifice, etc.

predella (pree DEL ah)

Italian term for a platform used for beds in the Italian Baroque or for a small painted panel at the base of an altarpiece especially one containing a series of panels, used mainly in Italy from the 13th to the 16th centuries.

prefabricated houses

Homes that have been partially or fully constructed in a factory off-site; also known as a manufactured home. See also *modular home*.

première partie (prem YAYR pahr TEE)

A type of Boulle in which the piece of work is brass-in-tortoiseshell marquetry. See also *Boulle work* and *contra-partie*.

Pre-Raphaelite brotherhood (PREE-RAF ay u liyt BRU thur huud)

A movement started in the second half of the 19th century with a group of artists inspired by John Ruskin, who revolted against the mechanization and eclecticism of the arts and crafts of the Victorian era, which led to the Arts and Crafts movement.

presbytery (PREZ be ter ee/PRES be tree)

An area of significant importance within a church reserved for the officiating clergy; also can be the name for a ruling body in the Presbyterian church.

press bed

A folding bed hinged at the top and enclosed in a press or closet.

press cupboard

A mid 16th-century English and mid 17th-century American cupboard, characterized by the lower two or three tiers usually enclosed; an upper section was often arranged in three small compartments; and when removed, the bulbous supports were replaced by pendants.

press cupboard

pressed glass

Shaped glass made by an inexpensive method of pouring molten glass into a mold under pressure or using a plunger to press inside the mold to create objects, such as flat dishes, bowls, saucers, and plates. The earliest glass cast into molds was by the Egyptians in 5 B.C.E., but glassmakers did not learn to shape glass by pressing until the 19th century.

pricket candlestick

A brass candlestick from the 15th century with a high bell-shaped drip pan centered on a picket with a candle held erect by a spike.

prie-dieu (PREE-DYOO)

A narrow desk-like bench with a padded kneeling piece near the floor and high back with a shelf for devotional books, for a person at prayer; originated from France, meaning pray to God.

prie-dieu

primavera (pree mah VER ah)

A close-grained, light-colored wood from Central America, also called white mahogany, used for cabinetry; the hard, yellowish-white wood is primarily used for making furniture. See also *acajou moe, Age of Mahogany,* and *mahogany, white*.

primitive art

A term used to identify paintings and drawings made by artists without formal training who have not mastered the principles of art.

Prince of Wales motif

A decorative motive of three ostrich feathers tied together; a symbol of the Prince of Wales, heir to the British throne; also a popular motif on the Hepplewhite chair back.

Prince of Wales motif

princewood

Tropical American timber tree of the genus Cordia grown for its valuable wood of a brownish-red color, veined with lighter color, and for its creamy white flowers. Same as *Spanish elm*.

print

A surface of fabric, wood, paper, etc., having artworks printed by transferring ink or a dye using blocks of wood, screens, stencils, polymer plates, and rollers.

abcdefghijklmnopqrstuvwxyz

print room

An 18th-century fashion in England when a room was decorated by pasting prints directly onto the walls in a quasi-collage form with borders, ribbons, etc., used as accent for the wall. Several rooms survive as Chippendale made use of this form of decoration.

priscilla curtains

Solid or sheer curtains with deep ruffles gathered on rods and sometimes tied back or crossed.

prodigy house (PRAH du jee HOWS)

Large, showy mansion built in the late Elizabethan or Jacobean period with features and detailing from north European Renaissance and post Gothic; such features are found in Wollaston Hall (1580–1588), Nottingham, England, with its mullioned and transomed windows.

prodomos (poh DROH moz)

An open vestibule in a Greek house or at the entrance of the cella of a Greek temple.

promotoma, pl. protomai (proh MOH toh mah)

The column capital, pilaster, or pier with Romanesque and Gothic forms, usually animal figures, on the front.

prong box (PRAHNG BAHKS)

An antique 18th- or 19th-century box used to store cutlery or silver, usually found in pairs on the sideboard.

propylon (PRAHP u lahn)

A monumental gateway in ancient Egyptian architecture that occurred between two towers, with one or a series standing before the pylon of the temples or other important buildings.

proscenium (pro SEE nee-um)

The stage of an ancient Greek or Roman theater located between the orchestra and the background; in the modern theater, the area between the curtain and the orchestra.

proscenium arch (pro SEE nee-um ARCH)

An arch or frame separating the auditorium from the stage. See also *proscenium*.

provincial (pru VIN chul)

Country furniture made in the provinces or outlying areas but after the high style of the well-known leaders; usually a simplified and unsophisticated version. See also *French Provincial*.

pseudo-peripteral (soo DOH-pe RIP ter ul)

A temple or building in which engaged columns or pilasters surround the naos but in which no freestanding columns are used on three sides; only the portico has the freestanding columns.

psyche (SEESH)

French Empire mirror, later called a cheval glass, which stood on the floor supported by a frame that could be tilted backward and forward. The word also refers to an upholstered Greek sofa with curves from the 19th century. See also *cheval mirror*.

puce (PYOOS)

An old French variant of the word flea, defining the deep red to dark grayish purple color.

pueblo (PWE bloh)

A Spanish name for the Native Americans who lived in the southwestern part of the United States; also the term for the villages occupied by the Pueblo with communal houses made of adobe and stone surfaces, characterized by flat roofs with projecting beams called vigas.

puente stand (PWEN tay STAND)

A Spanish carved table with trestle ends connected by a stretcher, designed to support the Vargueno.

puffing

Decorative pleating on the edge of a coffin panel or on an upholstered seat or the back of furniture.

pulldown front

A lid, sliding doors, or a curved cover, such as tambour, cylinder, or roll, found on a bureau, secretary, or desk to hide the writing surface or area used for storing documents. See also *tambour*.

Pullman kitchen

A type of kitchen usually recessed into a wall or concealed, equipped with kitchen fixtures, including a stove, sink, refrigerator, etc., and named after the Pullman railroad cars and its inventor George Mortimer Pullman.

pulls

Handles or hardware used on cabinets and drawers. See also *handles* or *hardware*.

pulpit

An elevated platform or stand where a member of the clergy conducts a worship service or delivers a sermon.

pulpit

pulvinaria (also called pulvinus) (PUL vi na ree-ah)

Two convex forms on either side of an Ionic capital that have on their ends two of the volutes.

pulvinated frieze (poo VIN ay tud FREEZ)

A frieze with a cornice molding that is convex in profile.

pulvinated frieze

punchwork

Any form of craftwork or artwork where the background, whether pierced, shaped, stamped, or cut, is made with a fine steel punch.

purlin (PUR lin)

Horizontal support that runs perpendicular to rafters and to which rafters are attached.

purpleheart

A straight-grained wood with a fine even texture that grows in the tropical rainforests of Central and South America; when cut its original creamy white turns to purple; used for inlay and other ornamental purposes. See also *amaranth* and *violet wood*.

putto, pl. putti (POO toh)

An Italian term for a small, chubby figure of a young boy, sometimes with wings and depicted as a cherub; often as subjects in Italian Renaissance paintings and sculptures. See also *cherub*.

putto

pylon (PIY lahn)

A Greek term for a monumental gateway shaped like a truncated pyramid flanking the entrance to an ancient Egyptian temple.

pyramid

A tomb in ancient Egypt designed in a pyramidal shape.

pyramid

pyxis (PIK sus)

An ancient Greek or Roman cylindrical-shaped box with a lid and knob in the center, used to store toilet articles or jewelry.

abcdefghijklmnopqrstuvwxyz

qamariyyah (KAH mah ree yah)
See *mashrabiyyah*.

qibla (ke BLAH)
An Arabic term referring to the direction toward which Muslims turn during their daily prayers.

Qing Dynasty (CHING DIY nes tee)
Last ruling dynasty of China, ruling from 1644 to 1912; also known as the Manchu Dynasty. See also *Ch'ing Dynasty*.

Qing-style armchair (CHING-STIY ul ARM chayr)
A Chinese armchair made with latticework or steps on the sides commonly seen during the Qing Dynasty. It was often known by the term taishiyi, which is defined differently in various regions, but during the Qing Dynasty, the armchair was distinguish from other armchairs by its name.

Qing-style armchair

quadra (KWAHD ru)
A small architectural molding, as a fillet, used to accent a relief sculpture; also the plinth block of a podium or platform.

quadrangular tapered leg (kwah DRAANG gyoo lur)
A term used to describe a furniture leg with four sides usually tapering, popular with Thomas Sheraton and the Regency periods in England. See *illustration in the Legs Appendix*.

quadrants (KWAH drents)
One of two metal sliding pieces used in the 18th and 19th centuries in England and America to support the fall front of a desk.

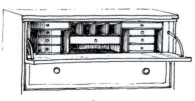

quadrants

quadrant vault (KWAH drent VAHLT)
A half-barrel vault.

quadratura (KWAH drah tur ah)
A term used during the Baroque period to describe the use of illusionistic mural painting (trompe l'oeil) on flat ceilings and wall surfaces creating a perspective view to visually extend space.

quadriga (kwah DREE gah)
A two-wheel chariot drawn by four horses harnessed side-by-side, especially used in chariot racing, Olympic games, and sacred games; also, a national symbol of victory, triumph, and fame.

quadripartite vaulting (kwah dre PAR tiyt VAHL ting)
A groin vault defined by ribs and divided into four parts by intersecting diagonals.

quadro riportato (KWAH droh REE por tah toh)
Paintings on Neoclassical ceilings without foreshortening illusionistic effects and with figures designed to be viewed at normal eye level; a reaction against Baroque quadratura.

quadruped (KWAH dre ped)
A term describing an animal with four limbs.

quadruple spiral (kwah DROO pul)
Spirals that occur in quadruple swirls in Egypt. See *illustration in the Motifs/Ornaments Appendix*.

quanyi chair (KWAHN yee CHAYR)
A Chinese term for a chair shaped with a horseshoe back, often referred to as a horseshoe chair. See also *Iohan chair*.

quarries or quarrel or quarry
A pane of square glass or lozenge-shaped paving tile.

quarry tile
A tile with a square or diamond shape that is ceramic or unglazed and used for flooring.

quarter landing
The 45-degree turn dividing straight pieces of a stairway.

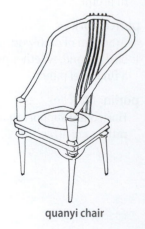

quanyi chair

quartered tables

Same as quartette tables. See also *quartetto tables*.

quartering

Boards from a log cut into four quarters through the center, and then into parallel slices to produce a decorative pattern from symmetrically arranged grain.

quartering

quarter-round

A convex molding shaped into a quarter circle. See also *shoe*. See *illustration in the Moldings/Ornaments Appendix*.

quarter-sawing or quartersawn

Method of sawing a log radially, or toward the heart of the log, at right angles producing a ribboned grain effect, which adds greater stability of size and form and a more decorative effect. Gustav Stickley of the American Arts and Crafts movement used quartersawn wood as a key feature for his furniture.

quarter-sliced veneer

Cutting the log into four quarters and then slicing from those four quarters produces a grain pattern that is more desirable.

quartetto tables (KOR te toh TAY bulz)

Four tables graduating in size to be stored one beneath the other and often referred to as nesting tables. In the Cabinet Dictionary in 1803, Sheraton used this term to refer to a nest of four tables. See also *nesting tables*.

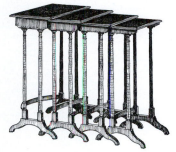

quartetto tables

quatrefoil (KA tur foi-ul)

A four-lobed Gothic ornament of a conventionalized four-leaf clover enclosed in a circle, used in tracery designs and for decorating furniture and interiors. See also *cusps*. See *illustration in the Motifs/Ornaments Appendix*.

quattrocento (KWAH troh chayn toh)

An Italian word for the 15th century or early Italian Renaissance, a time of classical architecture and very formal, austere furniture.

Quattro Libri (KWAH troh LIB ree)

An Italian treatise on architecture published in Venice in 1570 in four volumes by Andrea Palladio with illustrated engravings by the author. See *Andrea Palladio, 1508–1580, in the Architects, Artists, and Designers Appendix*.

Queen Anne Style

The style/period of furniture in the 1700s in England, during the reign of Queen Anne (1702–1714) and extending to George I and George II; it is noted for its rich, innovative design, characterized by graceful curves, such as cabriole legs and broken scroll pediments. See also *Decorated Queen Anne* and *yoke-back*.

Queen Anne Style

Queen Hetepheres chair (KWEEN he tu FER es CHAYR)

An Egyptian chair with papyrus-flower decoration in gold, belonging to Queen Hetepheres from the fourth dynasty (Old Kingdom) of Ancient Egypt, one of the most powerful women of ancient world, with an inscription on the chair recovered from her tomb stating, "Mother of the King of Upper and Lower Egypt, Flower of Horus, Guide of the Ruler, Favourite one. She whose every word is done for her, the daughter of the god's body, Hetepheres."

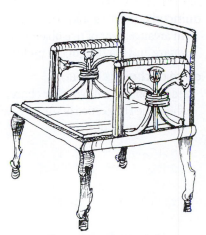

Queen Hetepheres chair

Queen's ware

An earthenware developed by Wedgwood and named in honor of Queen Charlotte in 1765, known also as creamware. It rivaled any porcelain throughout Europe in the 1760s and 1770s due to its durable standard but also its refined, brilliant glaze. See also *china*.

Quickborner team (KWIK bor nur TEEM)

A team of management consultants from Hamburg, Germany, who developed a radical office layout known as office landscape in 1955. Office landscape then became known as systems furniture.

quillwork

Decorative textiles made by Native Americans from Maine to Alaska, characterized by bands of rectangles creating geometrical patterns with overlaid porcupine quills. See also *pinched trailing*.

Quimper pottery or quimperware (KWIM pur PAH tu ree/ KWIM pur war)

Faience ware made in Quimper, France, which goes back to the Gallo-Roman times, with individualistic and authentic designs depicting life in Brittany with various flowers, birds, and peasant figures.

quincunx (KWIN kunk)

An arrangement of five objects; four symmetrically at the corners of a square and the fifth in the middle of the square.

quire or choir (KWIY-ur)

A division in a cathedral or church between the nave and sanctuary where the Holy office is sung by a choir of men and boys and referred to as a choir or quire.

quirk (KWURK)

A term for a molding with a small grove in it, sometimes referred to as a "sunken fillet." See *illustration in the Moldings Appendix*.

quirked cyma (KWURKD SIY mah)

A molding formed by the combination of a cyma with a flat vertical band added to the top and bottom; in profile it is shaped like an S. See *illustration in the Moldings Appendix*.

quirked ogee (KWURKT oh JEE)

A Greek molding with the upper portion turned back and the lower portion brought forward. See *illustration in the Moldings Appendix*.

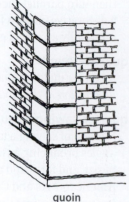

quoin

quoin (KOIN)

The term used for masonry units at the corner of a building, characterized by its decorative element, such as rustication, color, material, and size. See also *coign*.

quysshen (qui SHUN)

A 16th-century Chinese term for a comfortable cushion.

rabbet (RA bet)

A continuous rectangular slot or groove cut into one board in a way that the raised edge of another piece of board fits together to form a joint.

rabbet joint (RA bet JOINT)

A form of joinery in which a recess cut into one piece of wood receives another piece of wood. See also *dado joint*.

rachet (RAACH it)

See *ratchet*.

rack

A frame or stand on which items are hung or displayed, such as a gun rack, cup rack, trophy rack, etc.

raden (RAH den)

A type of Japanese decorative effect using lacquerwork and powdered mother of pearl; especially combined with gold or silver lacquer sprinkled with metal powder and applied to lacquer while wet. Referred to as *japanning* in the United Kingdom.

radiates

To send out rays from a center point through carving or inlay, as in a fan or shell motif.

Raeburn armchair

An English armchair with an upholstered rectangular back, short upholstered arms with an arm support that sweeps up and back, and legs that are either cabriole or straight with stretchers.

raffle leaves

An 18th-century English adaptation of an Italian design for ornamental foliage, similar to an acanthus, that has a serrated leaf edge with asymmetrical curves, often having characteristics of the C or S scroll.

rafraîchissoir (RAH fresh ees war)

An 18th-century French small serving table on casters with a drawer and shelves below and two receptacles on top that could be filled with cold water to keep wine bottles chilled. See also *dumb waiter, servante,* and *serviteur fidèle*.

rafters

A structural beam that supports the upper parts of the roof as it slopes from the eaves to the ridge of the roof.

rag rug

A braided or plaited rug of strips of rags or fabric sewn into a circle or oval to resemble provincial Early American handmade rugs. See also *braided rug*.

raies de coeur (RAI AY DE KOOR)

A molding decorated with heart-shaped leaves with alternating spearheads, used in Greek architecture. See *illustration in the Moldings Appendix*.

rail

A term used to identify the horizontal strip of a frame or panel that joins to the stiles or vertical posts and holds the sides together.

rainbow roof

A gable or pitched roof with a sloping convex surface, often referred to as whaleback.

raised ranch

Homes developed as a natural progression of the Ranch movement in the 1960s and 1970s in the United States, depicting a single story on the front but a variation on the back where the basement is above ground and both stories can be seen and used as an additional floor.

R

rake or raked

A deviation of a vertical or upright member to an angle or slant, such as the slope of a chair back or table leg that is not strictly vertical.

raku (RA koo)

A low-fired, lead-glazed Japanese pottery with a crackled glaze and colors ranging from dark brown to light red created by Raku-Chojiro (1515–1592) and in the Kyota area afterwards.

raked-back chair

ramada (RAH mah dah)

An open or semi-enclosed pavilion designed for shade with a thatched roof of twined branches, especially found in the southwestern United States. Derived from the Spanish word "ramje" meaning "arbor."

ramie or ramee (RAY mee / RAH mee)

One of the oldest textile fibers, commonly referred to as "China grass," and dating back to Egyptian mummy cloths from 5000 B.C.E. It is quite durable, very strong, resistant to bacteria, and absorbent, with a smooth, lustrous look making it quite versatile for uses in textiles, upholstery, and sacking.

ramma, rama, or ranma (RAH mah)

A transom located above sliding doors in a traditional Japanese structure, which is elaborately carved and designed to artistically fill those spaces and still allow ventilation and light into the interior.

ramp

An inclined flat surface rising from a lower-level floor to a higher level, often taking the place of steps. In furniture, a sharp curve ending in an angle at the end of the post. See also *Hogarth chair*.

ram's head

A popular classical decorative motif borrowed from the Greeks and Romans and popular in France during Louis XIV Style, then reintroduced in the 18th century in England by Robert Adam on furniture and accessories. See also *ram's horn arms*.

ram's horn arms

The outward turn of the armrest that extends beyond the arm supports.

ranch windows

See *strip windows*.

ranch-style house

American domestic architectural style, first built in the 1920s and characterized by a low, long one-story house with a low-pitched roof, sometimes with a cellar and low attic. See also *splanch* and *split-level house*.

ram's horn arms

range tables

Small tables identical in size used in the late 18th century that could be put together to form a larger table.

ratchet (RA chet)

An 18th-century mechanism consisting of a bar or wheel having inclined teeth into which a pawl drops, permitting motion in one direction only. See also *harlequin table*.

ratchet chair

An English reclining chair from the 18th century with a high moveable back attached to the armrest by means of a ratchet, making it possible to move the chair back several degrees, often referred to as a "sleeping charye." See also *sleeping chair*.

rat-claw foot

Sharp spiny claws of a rodent grasping a ball as the decoration for mid to late 18th-century English and American furniture feet.

Rateau chaise lounge (raa TOH SHEZ LOWNJ)

See *Armand Rateau chaise longue*. See *Armand-Albert Rateau, 1882–1938, in the Architects, Artists, and Designers Appendix*.

ratona (RAH toh nah)

A Spanish/Moorish term for a low circular coffee table with a brazier in the center.

rattan

A slender, long, solid, vinelike stem of a palm species found in India and southern Asia, used for caning and to weave wicker furniture.

rayonnant (RAY oh nahn)

A term denoting French Gothic architecture of the mid 13th century, which was characterized by rich and complex window tracery in the form of radiating lines.

rayonnant

reading stand or desk

An 18th-century wooden stand with an adjustable sloping top designed to hold books and resembling a lectern.

rebate joint (RAAB et JOINT)

A version of a butt joint that provides contact between components in two planes instead of one. See also *rabbet joint*. See *illustration in the Joints Appendix*.

Récamier chaise (RE kah mee-ay SHEZ)

A French 19th-century chaise used in the Directoire or Empire Styles and named after Mme. Juliette Récamier (1777–1849), characterized by one end slightly higher than the other and gracefully curved; often referred to as a Grecian sofa.

reading stand or desk

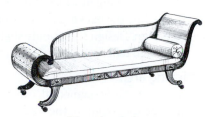

Récamier chaise

recess

An alcove in the wall that is sunken or depressed especially for holding a statute or other decorative object; referred to as a niche. See also *niche*.

recess cabinet

A cabinet set within an alcove in the wall.

réchampi (RE shahm pee)

French word for decorating a carved ornament in gold leaf or in contrasting color.

Rectilinear period

An architectural style that flourished in England (late 14th to middle 16th centuries) because of the predominant vertical lines, called Perpendicular Style. See also *Perpendicular Style*.

red-blue chair

See *Gerrit Rietveld red-blue chair*. See *Gerrit Thomas Rietveld, 1888–1964, in the Architects, Artists, and Designers Appendix*.

red-figure vase

Greek vases that developed in Athens around 530 B.C.E. to 300 B.C.E. that portrayed the figure in red unglazed on the red clay of the vase, with background in glossy black.

reeding

Parallel convex ridges next to each other; a reverse of concave parallel lines called fluting. See *illustration in the Architectural Orders Appendix*.

re-entrant angles (REE-en trent AYN gulz)

Corners of rectangular panels with angles turning inward, often decorated with a patera. Scooped or slightly rounded corners of rectangular panels are referred to as segmental corners.

cabinet door with re-entrant angles

abcdefghijklmnopq**r**stuvwxyz

refectory (re FEK tu ree)

A dining room or hall, especially in an institution or collegiate building, where meals are served.

refectory table

A long narrow dining table with stretchers and ornate carved panels at either end used in the refectory (dining hall) of monasteries during the Middle Ages.

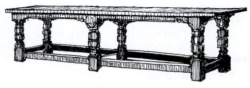

refectory table

reflecting dressing table

A mid 18th-century dressing table branded by Hepplewhite as being the most complete dressing table ever invented with its complex, mechanical devices. See also *Rudd's dressing table.*

Régence Style (RE jahns STIY ul)

Transitional French period covering the end of Louis XIV's reign, spanning from about 1715 to 1723, when France was ruled by a regent, until the accession of Louis XV, providing a combination of Louis XIV's massive straight lines and Louis XV's more gracious curves. See also *French Régence period.*

Régence Style

Regency Style (REE jen see STIY ul)

English style in architecture and design from 1811 to 1820 corresponding in dates to the regency of the future George IV, coinciding and resembling the Directoire and Empire Styles with Greek, Roman, and Egyptian motifs. See *Thomas Hope,*

Regency Style

1769–1831, and *Sir John Soane, 1753–1837, in the Architects, Artists, and Designers Appendix.*

reglet (REG lit)

A flat, narrow molding or fillet used to separate panels or other moldings; also a groove to hold or guide a window sash, etc.

regula (REG yu lu)

In a Doric entablature, a narrow, ribbonlike band that separates the tenia from the guttae; also called a guttae band.

regulator or régulateur (RE gyoo lay tur/REG yoo lah toor)

A precision pendulum clock popular in Europe in the mid 19th century.

reignier work (ren YAY WURK)

French decorative inlay similar to Boulle work. See also *reisner work.*

reisner work (RIYS nur WURK)

Ornamental technique using inlaid colored wood in 17th-century Germany, similar to reignier work and Boulle work. See also *reignier work.*

régulateur

reja or rejas (ray HAH / re HAHS)

Spanish term for a 16th-century monumental iron grille or screen, elaborately decorated; found in the great cathedrals of Spain.

relief

A type of carving in which the design is raised or embossed from the plane while the background is removed, giving more prominence to the design. Design that is only slightly raised is low relief (bas-relief), while high relief is raised much higher.

relieving arch

An arch, usually segmental, over the lintel of a window or door to alleviate the weight of the wall; also referred to as a blind arch.

reliquary (RE lek wa ree)

A container or small receptacle usually decorated with precious metals and jewels to hold sacred relics of a revered saint or personage.

Renaissance (re ne SAHNS)

A "rebirth" in Europe around 1400 to 1500, starting in Italy, in which intellectual and artistic development was based on classical sources and adapted into the architecture and decorative themes. See also *specific Renaissance Styles.*

Renaissance Revival

A term that covers many aspects of 19th-century architectural Revival Styles, drawing inspiration from a wide range of classical Italian Styles and reminiscent of Renaissance structures.

rent table

An English 18th-century circular or octagonal pedestal table with drawers in the frieze labeled with the seven days of the week and used by landlords for collecting and filing rent. Several were designed in mahogany by Sheraton.

replica

An exact copy of a piece or structure, usually historic or very old, in all details including material, details, finishes, and techniques.

repoussé (re POO say)

A process of relief decoration on a metal material in which the metal is hammered on the reverse side so the design is raised on the front. See also *embossed.*

reproduction

The act of copying old pieces of historic styles; a close imitation or duplication of its resemblance to the form and elements of the original.

reredos (rey e dohs)

A screen, usually ornamental and made of wood or stone, facing the wall or at the back of an altar; also called a retable. See also *retable.*

reserve panels

Panels with decorative elements to bring emphasis to a specific part as opposed to the overall design.

respond

A 15th-century term describing an engaged pillar or half-pier engaged to a wall and supporting an arch, usually closing an arcade or colonnade.

ressaut (re SOH)

An architectural term meaning a projection of an entablature covering a column and placed in front of a structure but returning to the building on both sides of the projection. It also can mean an entablature with a projection on a building above each column.

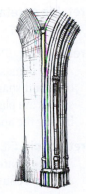

respond

rest bed

A daybed, couch, or cushioned bench used during the day for repose, appearing in France during the early Louis XIV period when the beds were excessively large and formal. See also *chaise longue.*

restoration

Using methods, such as examination, conservation, and preservation, to bring back a former place, object, or building to as close to its original appearance and condition as possible; also referred to as conservation.

Restoration chair

A typical English 17th-century Carolean chair named after Charles II, characterized by its high caned back, spiral-turned legs, and a cresting representing a crown but with emphasis placed on the heavily carved upright front stretcher and top rail. Same as Carolean.

Restoration Style

Known as the Carolean Style, meaning Charles in Latin, and a period in England in which the decorative arts became popular due to the return of the monarchy of Charles II (reigned 1660–1685) following the austere leadership of the Commonwealth. See also *Carolean Style.*

retable or retablos (REE tay bul)
See *reredos*.

reticulated (REE tik yoo layt ed)
A type of masonry in which
diamond-shaped stones or square
stones are placed diagonally,
having the appearance of a net.

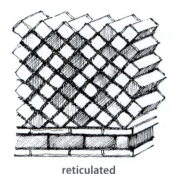
reticulated

retrochoir (RE troh kwiy-ur)
A space located behind the main
altar in a church or cathedral.

reveal
The area or depth of the masonry
frame between the wall surface and
the glass in a door or a window.

reverse serpentine
Opposite of a serpentine curve when the center is concave and
receding; also referred to as oxbow front.

revivalism
A word used to characterized the desire or inclination to restore what
belongs to an earlier time.

rez-de-chausée (RAY-de-SHOH see)
French term for the ground floor of a building that is on the same level
as the street or slightly raised above the street.

rhyton (RIY tahn)
A drinking vessel from ancient Greece shaped like an animal horn
with a hole in the bottom through which to drink.

rib
A projecting band crossing a ceiling, vault, bay, or other surface.
See also *groin rib* and *vault*.

rib arch
An arch often seen in Gothic architecture consisting of ribs placed
side by side, extending from the springings on one end to those on the
other end; some ribbed vaults have six in each bay. The use of vaulting
allowed for more windows high in the building, leading to new heights.

ribband-back chair
See *Chippendale ribband-back chair*.
See *Thomas Chippendale II, 1718–1779,
in the Architects, Artists, and Designers
Appendix*.

ribbed vault
A vault in which decorated diagonal ribs
support the web of the vault. See also
vault.

ribbed vault

Richardsonian Romanesque
A revival style associated with Henry
Hobson Richardson that became one of
the most popular styles ca. 1880–1900 in
the United States for a wide variety of building types, characterized by
revival of Roman architecture with its massive stone walls, impressive
strength, and durability. See *Henry Hobson Richardson, 1838–1886, in
the Architects, Artists, and Designers Appendix*.

ridgepole
A horizontal beam situated at the top of the roof where two sloping
sides meet; providing a means to fasten the rafters; also called a ridge
board.

rilievo stiacciato (ree LAY voh stee ah CHAH toh)
A type of sculptural relief that is shallow, low, and flattened.

rinceau, pl. rinceaux (rin SOH)
French architectural term for a running border or strip that is usually
decorated with acanthus leaves, fruit, and foliage, used on such
surfaces as a panel, frieze, or some other architectural feature. See
illustration in the Motifs/Ornaments Appendix.

ring and bobbin

Common name for a support or fancy turned and carved leg. See *illustration in the Legs Appendix.*

riser

The vertical face between two stair treads.

rising stretcher

An X-stretcher rising in a curve upward toward the intersection between the legs it braces; found on chairs and tables in Louis XIV and other allied styles. See also *arched stretcher, hooped stretcher, saltire,* and *X-shaped stretcher.*

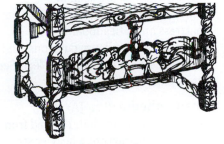

rising stretcher

riwaq (ri WAHK)

An Islamic walkway or arcade around a courtyard within a mosque, open at least on one side.

Robbia family sculptors

Eminent Italian sculptors, particularly Luca della Robbia and Andrea della Robbia, of the 15th and 16th centuries from Florence, whose names are associated with terra-cotta roundels or polychromed medallions of fruit and foliage and ceramics. See *Luca della Robbia, 1400–1482, and Andrea della Robbia, 1435–1525, in the Architects, Artists, and Designers Appendix.*

Robert Venturi Art Deco and Sheraton chairs

Two of the chairs designed by Robert Venturi, made by Knoll International in 1984, Art Deco and Sheraton design, contemporary in construction with bent plywood and plastic laminate surfaces, shaped by Venturi to suggest a historical furniture style. See *Robert Venturi, 1925–, in the Architects, Artists, and Designers Appendix.*

rocaille (roh KIY)

A French term for natural irregular stones in an artificial grotto in French gardens; the decorative shell applied to furniture ornament resembles these irregular rocks, so the term is used as a synonym for Rococo. See also *cockleshell, scallop shell or specific shell motifs,* and *Rococo.*

rock-cut church

Churches in Ethiopia hewn from living rock in the 12th and 13th centuries.

rocking stool

See *Isamu Noguchi rocking stool.* See *Isamu Noguchi, 1904–1988, in the Architects, Artists, and Designers Appendix.*

Robert Venturi Art Deco and Sheraton chairs

Rococo Style (ROH koh koh STIY ul)

A French 18th-century style of decoration and architecture originating during the reign of Louis XV, identified by asymmetry, curvilinearity, lightness, delicacy of line, and flora and fauna borrowed from nature, with the name of the style derived from rocaille and coquille (rock and shell), both prominent motifs. See also *cockleshell, coquille, scallop shell or specific sea shell,* and *rocaille.*

Rococo Style

rognon

In France the word means kidney and it is used in relation to desks or tables with a kidney shape. See also *haricot, kidney desk, kidney table,* and *table à rognon.*

rolltop desk

A writing desk with many compartments and a flexible tambour, which rolls down to cover the work space.

rolltop desk

Roman arch

A semicircular arch used in ancient Roman architecture made of wedge-shaped voussoirs or thin, tile-like brick.

Roman architecture

Architecture from the Ancient Roman republic of the Classical period dating from 44 B.C.E. to 476 C.E., which adopted the external Greek architectural style, but remained quite different from Greek buildings. As a result, a new architectural style was created including buildings such as the Roman basilica based on Greek temples, Roman baths based on Greek gymnasia, innovative freestanding amphitheaters, and the purely Roman invention, the triumphal arch.

Roman bed or couch

Ancient Roman bed, referred to as a lectus, used for sleeping, relaxing, sitting, or eating and one of the most important furniture items. It was made of wood that held a stuffed mattress and a headboard, furnished with pillows, cushions, and coverlet and highly decorated legs. See also *lectus.*

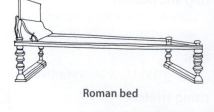

Roman bed

Roman cathedra (kaa TAY drah)

An ancient Roman chair derived from the Greek klismos but a heavier structure than the light, delicate ancient Greek chair. See also *cathedra.*

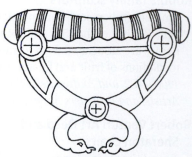

Roman cathedra

Roman curule (ko roo LAY)

An ancient Roman folding stool based on the Egyptian and Greek prototypes, made for the senior magistrates or promagistrates to sit upon; characterized as uncomfortable so the official would carry out his public function in a timely manner. The stool had curved legs forming a wide X and no back; also referred to sella curulis. See also *curule* and *sella curulis.*

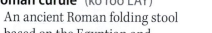

Roman curule

Roman eagle

The eagle was the potent symbol of Roman honor and of the Ancient Roman Empire; also over centuries it became a motif adopted by different countries as a symbol of power.

Roman guilloche (gweel OH kay)

See *guilloche*. See *illustration in the Motifs/Ornaments Appendix.*

Roman marble table

Various types of Roman tables from trestle to tripod were made of marble and often decorated with griffins, satyrs, and other winged animals or monsters.

Roman marble table

Roman shade

A window covering that raised and lowered with a cord system and when raised is drawn up into evenly sized folds, when lowered the shade creates a relatively smooth appearance. See also *Austrian shade* and *blind*.

Roman throne chair

An ancient Roman ceremonial chair, with the earliest found at Herculaneum, made of wood and ivory; usually depicted with a variety of complex leg turnings, paneled backs, and solid sides, following closely the Greek model. See also *throne chair*.

Roman throne chair

Romanesque arch

Similar to the ancient Roman arch, nearly always semicircular in structure and design, characterized by rough stone instead of brick and well-dressed stone of ancient Roman arches. See also *Romanesque arcade*.

Romanesque arcade

A succession of arches found on medieval churches during the Romanesque period, often used to divide the nave from the aisles or forming the front of a covered ambulatory. See also *arch* and *Romanesque arch*.

Romanesque Style

An architectural style prevalent during the early Middle Ages in Europe and in England after 1066 (called Norman), characterized by semicircular or round-headed arches, evolving into the Gothic Style with its pointed arches. See also *Norman*.

Romanticism movement

A late 18th- and early 19th-century literary and arts movement originating in Europe; characterized by individual expression including strong emotion and imagination with a heightened interest in nature.

romayne work (roh MAYN WORK)

Decorative motif of a human head carved in high relief within a roundel.

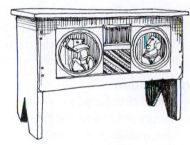

romayne work

rondavel (RAHN day vul)

An African thatched hut, single-cell, circular in form with a conical roof; also known in Southern Africa as a mokhoro.

rondel (RAHN dul)

Same as *roundel*.

rood

A crucifix symbolizing the cross used in the crucifixion of Christ.

rood screen

A large wooden crucifix supported by a rood beam or a decorative rood screen, serving as a partition between the chancel and the nave of a medieval church.

roof comb

An architectural feature located above the roof of Mesoamerican temples, which includes carved glyphs or figures that seem to indicate specific sacred meanings.

rope bed

A bed from the early to mid 19th century, mostly from the rural areas, with rope laced to the frame to hold the mattress.

243

rope molding
A decorative molding imitating the spiral twist of a rope; also called cable molding. See also *cable molding*.

rosace (roh ZAYS)
An architectural term meaning the same as a rose window. See also *rose window*.

rose
A conventionalized and stylized rose motif that comes in many forms and styles, basically adopted by England as the Tudor rose in the 15th century, where it has become a traditional floral heraldic emblem, frequently appearing as a decoration on furniture and stained glass. The rose motif as an architectural and furniture decoration can be found in many parts of the world. See also *rosette*.

rose window
A large circular window with tracery resembling a stylized rose, usually in the façade of a Gothic church or cathedral. See also *rosace*.

rosette
A circular motif formed by a series of leaves radiating from a center point with the appearance of a stylized flower. See *illustration in the Motifs/Ornaments Appendix*.

rose window

rosewood, Brazilian
A tropical wood of many varieties, the most popular from Brazil called jacarandi, with fine, reddish-brown, richly black streakings. See also *jacaranda*.

rosewood, Honduras
A rare wood with excellent acoustic properties and colors ranging from light violet to light red. It works well and finishes to a high natural polish.

roshan (ROH shahn)
A protruding window in Islamic domestic architecture that has open screens, preventing visual access but allowing air to circulate.

rostral column (RAH strel KAH lum)
An ancient Roman pillar decorated with the prow of a ship or sculptured representation of ships erected in honor of victories at sea or to serve as a naval monument.

rostrum, pl. rostrum (RAH strum)
A dais or platform, decorated with beaks of captured ships, used for speeches given in the ancient Roman Forum to give prominence to the speaker. It was also used in reference to the curved, beaklike prow of an ancient Roman warship.

rotunda or rotondo (ROH tun dah)
A circular building or room, such as the Pantheon in Rome, usually topped with a dome. See also *Pantheon*.

round chair
See *Hans Wegner round chair*. See *Hans Wegner, 1914–2007, in the Architects, Artists, and Designers Appendix*.

roundabout chair
An armchair with four legs (one in front, one in back, and two on the sides) developed in the early 18th century to save space by nestling in the corner; often referred to as a corner chair or conversation chair. See also *burgomaster chair, conversation chair, corner chair*, and *fauteuil de bureau*.

roundel (ROWN dul)
A round carved ornament that contains a representation or a motif; also a circular lead glazed window, usually stained and containing heraldic devices. Same as *rondel*.

roundel

row house
Identical or similar houses built into a continuous row and joined by common walls.

royal portal

A large entranceway to a building, such as doorways into a medieval cathedral that include sculptures of royal personage.

rubble

Irregular shapes and sizes of rock or stone set in mortar and used in the construction of walls, pavements, buildings, etc.

rudder

A wooden support, which resembles a ship's rudder, for a drop-leaf table or shelf; similar to a butterfly support.

Rudd's dressing table

An English dressing table from the mid 18th century described by Hepplewhite as being one of the most complete dressing tables ever made due to its mechanism that makes every item convenient; its name came from a popular personality. See also *reflecting dressing table.*

ruelles (ROO-el)

A French term for the space on each side of the bed where social gathering of a fashionable lady could take place. See also *levée.*

Ruhlmann's cabinet (RU menz KAb i nit)

See *Émile-Jacques Ruhlmann cabinet.* See *Émile-Jacques Ruhlmann, 1879–1933,* in the Architects, Artists, and Designers Appendix.

rule joint

A special backside joint used on drop-leaf tables from the 17th century; also found on tabletops, desks, screens, etc., where continuity of design is desired; it also provides a flat surface on the front side. See also *knuckle joint.*

runic knot (ROO nik NAHT)

Characters from the ancient Germanic alphabet which formed interlaced and twisted ornamental designs, especially during the Celtic and Scandinavian periods from the 3rd century C.E. to the end of the Middle Ages; it is believed that each character had magical significance.

runner

A term used in various ways in relation to furniture: (1) a curved member on the base of a rocking chair; (2) a horizontal member used at the floor to brace furniture legs; (3) a center or side drawer guide; (4) a curved member on the base of a rocking chair; (5) a decorative long strip of material used as a center cover for the length of the table.

runner foot

See *bar foot.*

running bond

See *stretcher bond.*

running dog

A common classical motif made up of a series of scrolls connected by a wavelike band; also called Vitruvian scroll or wave scroll. See also *Vitruvian scroll.*

rush

A twisted woven grass seat. See also *flag.*

rush seat chair

A woven chair seat made of long grass, twisted and woven, and used for provincial chairs from medieval times or earlier but more acceptable during the 17th century and throughout the 18th and 19th centuries. See also *flag.*

Russian Constructivism

A Russian avant-garde movement, active from 1913 to the 1940s, committed to abstraction, utilitarian, and technological form of modernism where art themes are quite minimal and broken down into basic elements.

rustication or rusticated (rus ti KAY shun / rus ti kayt ed)

Smooth or rough-cut masonry with deeply cut joints to give a textural appearance that makes the stones more conspicuous. See also *Romanesque.*

Rya rug (REE ah RUG)

A traditional Scandinavian rug of long-piled, heavy covers used by mariners in the early 15th century. Today the rug is lighter and more colorful and used as a decorative rug in contemporary or provincial residences.

Saarinen pedestal table

See *Eero Saarinen tulip table*. See *Eero Saarinen, 1910–1961, in the Architects, Artists, and Designers Appendix*.

Saarinen tulip pedestal chair

See Eero Saarinen tulip pedestal chair. See *Eero Saarinen, 1910–1961, in the Architects, Artsists, and Designers Appendix*.

Saarinen womb chair

See *Eero Saarinen* womb chair. See *Eero Saarinen, 1910–1961, in the Architects, Artists, and Designers Appendix*.

saber leg

A furniture leg that is splayed and tapered, resembling a cavalry saber. First seen on the Greek klismos; also commonly found on early 19th-century Sheraton chairs. See also *splayed leg*. See *illustration in the Legs Appendix*.

sabicu (SAAB I kyoo)

A wood indigenous to the West Indies, known for its rich mahogany color and durability, hence the reason it was chosen for the stairs of the Crystal Palace in London's Great Exhibition of 1851.

sabot foot (SAAB oh FUUT)

See *spade foot*.

sabots (SAAB ohz)

French term for wooden shoes. In furniture design, the metal ferrules or "shoes" covering the wooden feet of furniture.

sack back

Another name for the double-bowed back of a Windsor chair.

sacristy (SAAK ris tee)

A small room, usually adjoining a church's sanctuary, used to store vestments, altar vessels, and other like items.

saddle

A threshold or sill of a door, often made of wood or stone. See also *sill*.

saddle back

An American term for a double-bowed back Windsor chair.

saddle-check chair

A mid to late 18th-century English and American wing chair designed for use in bedrooms.

saddle seat

A solid wood seat with a raised central ridge flanked by shallow depressions, which bears resemblance to a saddle's contour. Often seen on Windsor chairs.

sakura (SAH koo rah)

A wood native to Japan; also known as ornamental cherry.

sala (SAH lah)

An open pavilion used for meetings and protection from the elements in Thailand. In Spanish, a living room or the main reception space of a home.

Salem rocker

Salem rocker

An early 19th-century New England rocking chair characterized by a scrolled seat, straight spindled back, heavy top rail, and shorter stature than the Boston rocker.

salle à manger (SAHL AH mahn JAY)

French for dining room.

salon (sah LOHN)

An refined apartment or living area within a large home or palace, often the center of cultural and political society in the late 18th and 19th centuries.

salon

saltbox house

An early 17th-century American Colonial house style with a two-story front and single-story back under a steeply pitched roof with unequal sides.

salt glaze

A ceramic glaze produced by adding salt into the kiln during firing, characterized by a glossy, pebbled, surface. First seen on stoneware of Rhineland Germany in the mid 14th century. Also used to produce a brown-glazed brick and tile popular in the early 20th century.

saltire (SAAL teer)

A heraldic device in the form of a diagonal cross or x-shape. Also called St. Andrew's Cross. In furniture, the name for an x-shaped stretcher of Italian origin. See also *arch stretcher, hooped stretcher, rising stretchers, x-shaped stretcher,* and *x-stretcher.*

Salvador Dali Mae West lips sofa

Surrealist lip-shaped sofa inspired by actress Mae West and designed in 1937 by Spanish architect Salvador Dali. The sofa is constructed on a wooden frame upholstered with red satin. See *Salvador Dali, 1904–1989, in the Architects, Artists, and Designers Appendix.*

Salvador Dali Mae West lips sofa

salver (SAAL vur)

A flat, round, handleless tray, generally made of silver and sometimes footed, used for serving food and beverages or for the presentation of a letter or card.

Salviati (SAAL vee ah tee)

A famous Venetian glass factory founded in 1859 by Dr. Antonio Salviati, Enrico Podio, and Lorenzo Radi. Also, the name of a famous Florentine banking family of the 15th century.

samara (SAAM er u)

Another name for gaboon, a hardwood from West Africa. Also called okoume. See also *gaboon.*

samite (SAAM iyt)

A heavy, twill woven silk fabric of the Middle Ages, often incorporating gold and silver threads, commonly used for clothing and upholstery.

sample

In furniture, a prototype constructed for marketing to prospective buyers. In textiles, a small piece or swatch of a fabric.

sampler

A small embroidered work, often incorporating the alphabet or verses, designed to display the skills of young girls of the 18th and 19th centuries.

san cai ti jui (SAHN TSIY TEE JWAY)

A Chinese folding chair with a footstool that extends from beneath the seat; similar to the zuiwengyi.

sanctuary

The most sacred location that houses the alter within a Christian church. Also, the place where worship services are held.

sand shaking

A 17th-century Dutch technique used to darken or shade the color of small pieces of inlay by dipping them into hot sand.

sandalwood

An aromatic wood of the East Indian and Pacific islands with a close grain and yellow color, primarily used for ornamental objects such as boxes and small chests.

sandblasting

A technique used for engraving, cutting, cleaning, or polishing glass or stone by streaming sand in compressed air onto the surface.

sandwich glass
The glassware made by the Boston and Sandwich Glass Company of Sandwich, Massachusetts, in the 19th century. Also, the decorative pressed glass, often lacey in pattern, made by a number of American companies from the 1920s onward.

sang de boeuf (SAHN DU BUUF)
Literally translated as blood of the bull. A rich, blood-red glaze first used by Chinese potters hundreds of years ago, imitated by many European pottery and porcelain manufacturers in the 19th century.

sanguine (SAANG gwin)
A reddish-brown colored mineral or chalk popular in the Renaissance era for drawings or studies.

santo (SAHN toh)
A statue of a saint, commonly found in Mexico and Spanish-speaking areas of the southwestern United States.

sapele (su PEE lee)
An African wood with a striped figure, resembling mahogany in color and texture. Commonly sought as a flooring material and for furniture making. Also known as sapeli. See also *aboudikro*.

sappanwood (SAAP pun wuud)
A wood indigenous to Southeast Asia and the East Indies that closely resembles brazilwood; used as a major trade good during the 17th century.

Sarabend rugs (SAAR u bend RUGZ)
Persian rugs made in the district of Sarawan using the tereh Mir, or small conical devices, almost exclusively in their design.

Saracenic (SAAR u sen ik)
Designs showing Arabian or Mohammedan influence, such as geometric motifs, minarets, and horseshoe arches.

sarcophagus (sahr KAHF u gus)
A stone coffin of ancient times; also the name for an 18th-century wine cooler or cellaret. See also *cellaret* and *wine cooler*.

sarcophagus

sardivan (sahr DIV en)
A central fountain found in the courtyard of a mosque, used for ritual cleansing.

sardonyx (sahr DAHN iks)
An onyx containing parallel layers of reddish-brown chalcedony.

Sarouk rugs (su ROOK RUGZ)
Persian rugs predominately woven in dark blues and reds with a lighter floral design.

sash
The moveable frame of a window.

sash bar
The strips of wood or metal that hold panes of glass within a window sash.

sash curtains
A lightweight or sheer curtain hung on a rod attached to the sash of a window.

sash door
An 18th-century term for a glazed door with rectangular panes used on a bookcase or cabinet.

sash window
A window with one or more framed glass panels or sashes that move up or down.

sashikake (sah shee KAH ke)
A Japanese shed roof that covers a building extension and is positioned below the primary roof of the main structure.

sateen

A fabric that resembles satin in weave with a lustrous face and dull back. It is usually made of cotton and commonly used as a lining for draperies.

satin

A lustrous faced silk fabric originally imported from China and called Zaytun, after the Chinese seaport. Available in a variety of types, the silk material is often blended with linen and cotton today, in order to increase the fabric's strength. See also *satin, antique; satin, charmeuse; satin, hammered; satin, ribbed;* and *satin, slipper.*

satin, antique

A rich, heavy satin fabric woven with slub warp yarns to create an uneven texture that appears handwoven, hence the name. Commonly used for upholstery.

satin, charmeuse (SAAT un, shahr MOOZ)

A lightweight satin fabric with an organzine warp and a spun silk weft. Commonly made of silk or a synthetic lookalike such as polyester.

satin, hammered

A thick, heavy satin fabric with a bumpy surface texture that looks like hammered metal.

satin, ribbed

A bengaline or faille fabric with lustrous ribs across the face.

satin, slipper

A heavyweight fabric woven from silk or synthetic fibers and backed with cotton; commonly used to make slippers in the 18th and 19th centuries.

satin finish

A low luster finish associated with paint, fabric, paper, and other materials.

satine

See *sateen.*

satine rubanne (saa TEEN, roo BAAN)

A straight-grained South African wood with a deep red-orange to reddish-brown color, known for its strength, durability, and ribbonlike markings. Commonly used for furniture, inlay, and veneer work.

satinwood

A lustrous, highly figured wood with a light yellow to golden yellow color, indigenous to Ceylon and the East Indies. Favored during the Louis XV and Louis XVI periods, satinwood was also popular with English furniture makers such as Adam, Chippendale, Hepplewhite, and Sheraton. See also *Age of Satinwood.*

Satsuma ware (saht SOO mah WAYR)

Various types of Japanese ceramics produced in the Satsuma province since the 16th century. One of the most popular types created for export in the 19th century featured a soft, ivory-colored, crackled ground decorated with minute polychrome designs highlighted by gold.

satyr mask (SAY tur MAASK)

A motif featuring a relief of a satyr head, a woodland creature from Greek mythology, popularly displayed in mid 18th-century English furniture and in Italian and French Renaissance designs.

satyr mask

sausage turning

A wood turning resembling a string of sausage links, favored during the German Renaissance and in 19th-century American furniture.

Saville chair

A late 18th-century English Arts and Crafts chair made by Morris & Co. with curvy outlined arm spindles and legs.

sausage turning

Saville chair

249

Savonarola chair (sah VOHN ah roh lah CHAYR)

An Italian Renaissance folding chair with an x-frame, multiple legs that curve upward to meet the chair's arms, and carved or inlaid decoration. Named after the martyred 15th-century Italian monk, Girolamo Savonarola.

Savonarola chair

Savonnerie (sah VUN e ree)

Prestigious French manufacturer of rugs and tapestries founded by Louis XIII in 1627. The name also applies to the high pile, handwoven rugs made within the manufactory, adorned with pastel floral and scroll patterns.

sawbuck table

A primitive 17th-century table with a simple board top and x-shaped legs.

sawbuck table

saxony

A plush, dense cut pile carpet known for its softness and comfort underfoot. Constructed from a bulky yarn that is twisted to create a more crush-resistant and matt-resistant product, although the height of the pile may still flatten under heavy traffic.

scaena frons (skiy AY nu FRAHNZ)

The elaborate architectural backdrop of a Roman theater stage.

scaffolding

A temporary framework used in the construction or repair of buildings or other large permanent structures for the support of workers and their materials.

scagliola (skiy OHL u)

From the Italian term scaglia, meaning chip. A faux marble produced from plaster or cement and marble chips. Evidence shows use of scagliola in ancient Rome. It was also popular during the Italian Baroque and continued through the19th century, particularly with the Adam brothers in England.

scale

The relative size of an object within its surroundings or of one piece of furniture to another. In architectural drafting, the proportional ratio between an actual space and a drawing of it.

scale-back chair

A Queen Anne chair with a pattern resembling fish scales carved into the splat. See also *scaling* and *imbricate*.

scaling

A surface with a finish resembling fish scales. Dating back to ancient times, but more recently seen on Victorian era homes and carved furniture of the Greek Revival Style. See also *imbrication*.

scallop shell

A semicircular, fan-shaped shell with radiating ridges popularly used as a decorative motif in the late Renaissance, Louis XIV, Louis XV, Queen Anne, and Georgian periods. See also *cockleshell* or specific shell motif and *rocaille*.

scallop shell

scalloped arch

An arch with more than five lobes that render a scalloped effect, common in Moorish architecture.

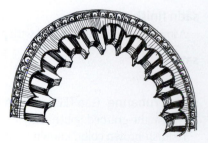

scalloped arch

scalloped-back Windsor bench

A Windsor bench with a scalloped back, an edge shaped with positive circular segments. See also *Windsor chair*.

scalloped-back Windsor bench

scalloped borders

Wallpaper borders with a horizontal edge cut in a scalloped effect, often following the outlines of the printed design. See also *cutout borders*.

scalloped edge

An edge shaped with positive and negative circular segments.

Scandinavian Modern

A style introduced in the 1930s that fused the minimalist ideas of modernism with traditional materials. Furniture of the style is primarily made of walnut and teak wood, lacks applied decoration, displays simple hardware, and is sculptural in form. Also known as Swedish or Danish Modern. See also *Alvar Aalto, 1898–1976, Arne Jacobsen, 1902–1971, Poul Kjaerholm, 1929–1980, Finn Juhl,* and *Hans Wegner, 1914–2007, in the Architects, Artists, and Designers Appendix.*

scarab

An Egyptian decorative motif modeled after the dung beetle, associated with life-giving powers and protection.

scaramouche (SKAAR u mowch)

A boastful, cowardly clown character of 17th- and 18th-century Italian commedia dell'arte, generally seen in black mask, trousers, shirt, and hat; commonly used as a decorative element in 18th-century English, French, and Italian designs. Also known as scaramouch.

scarf joint

A joint used to attach two metal or wood members end to end into a continuous form, created by chamfering or tapering ends so that they overlap each other. Commonly used when installing baseboards and other moldings. See *illustration in the Joints Appendix.*

scarves

A fabric runner created to protect and decorate the tops of dressers, sideboards, or tables.

scatter rug

A small rug commonly utilized at entries, bedsides, or sinks bases. Also known as a throw rug.

scenic

A graphic representation of a scene, vista, or event printed onto a background of paper, vinyl, or cloth and used as wallpaper, often in multiple panels.

school

A group of artists, architects, and designers with similar design ideas or focus, sometimes regionally. See also *Bauhaus* and *Hudson River School.*

scissors chair

A folding chair with transverse pairs of crossed legs for support, used since Egyptian times. See also *Dante chair, Savonarola chair,* and *x-shaped chair.*

sconce

Historically, a protective shield or lantern for a flame or light. From the Latin word abscondere, which means "to hide." Later the term adapted to an electric or candle-powered light fixture that attaches to a wall.

sconce

scoop

See *nulling*.

scoop seat

A dished or concave seat, designed since classical times to fit the human body. Popular in the Empire Style and the work of England's Thomas Sheraton. Also known as a dropped seat or dip seat.

scotia (SKOH shu)

A semicircular or elliptical concave molding commonly used at the base of classical columns. See *illustration in the Moldings Appendix*.

scraffito (skraaf FEE toh)

See *sgraffito*.

scratch carving

A wood carving technique of small incised lines, commonly used to outline designs on 16th- and 17th-century furniture.

scratch coat

The rough base coat of plaster applied to a surface and then scratched or troweled with a serrated blade to encourage adhesion of the second coat.

screen

A device employed as a protective or ornamental partition from drafts, heat, or views.

screen table

A lady's desk, designed by Thomas Sheraton in the late 18th century, with a slot behind the surface containing a retractable screen to protect the user from flying fireplace embers.

screens passage

The entrance at one end of an English great hall, shielded by screens to protect the service passage from view.

screw stair

A set of spiral steps that wind around a pole or newel post. Also called a newel stair.

scribanne (skri BAAN)

A Louis XIV period slant-front desk.

scribe

A person who copies manuscripts by hand, generally referring to a monk. In cabinetry, to mark a line by scratching or cutting.

scribe molding

Small pliable molding used to cover the seams where two surfaces such as a cabinet and wall meet.

scribing

A technique used to fit cabinets, countertops, and built-in woodwork to irregular surface contours.

scrinium (SKRIN ee um)

A round wooden box, that could be locked or sealed, used to hold scrolls in classical Rome.

scriptorium (skrip TOR ee um)

Literally translated as "a place for writing." A room within a monastery used by scribes who copied manuscripts.

scritoire (skri TWAHR)

French term for a writing table.

scroll - C-scroll

A curved design in the shape of a C, often mimicking a loosely rolled document, commonly designed with acanthus leaves, ivy, and wheat. See *illustration in the Motifs/Ornaments Appendix*.

scroll - S-scroll

A curved design in the shape of an S, often mimicking a loosely rolled document, commonly designed with acanthus leaves, ivy, and wheat. See *illustration in the Motifs/Ornaments Appendix*.

scroll bed

See *gondola bed* and *sleigh bed*.

scroll foot

A Louis XIV furniture foot in the shape of a flattened scroll, used at the end of a cabriole leg. Also popular with William and Mary and Chippendale furniture in England. See *illustration in the Feet Appendix*.

scroll molding

A popular English Gothic molding resembling a rolled document.

scroll pediment

A broken pediment with a raking cornice formed from reverse curves. See also *swan's neck pediment.*

scroll top mirror

A mirror designed with a scroll pediment and carved central ornament. The design was popularized by Thomas Chippendale in the mid 18th century and commonly made of mahogany with gilt decoration.

scrollwork

Lacey, scroll fretwork created from wood by jigsaws and popular during the American Steamboat Gothic period of the 19th century. See also *jigsaw.*

scrowled chair (SKROWLD CHAYR)

A popular 16th- to 17th-century English armchair with a high panel back, heavy top rail, and turned baluster legs supported by low stretchers. During the latter part of the period, the chair was often covered with profuse carving and topped by heavy cresting supported by the chair stiles and carved outer brackets. See also *bible chair, chancel chair, panel-back chair,* and *wainscot chair.*

scrubbed pine

Early American and French provincial pine furniture with a natural looking, light oil finish.

scrutoire (skru TWAHR)

A writing desk. See also *escritoire.*

sculpture

Art in three-dimensional form, created by an additive or subtractive technique. Carving is a subtractive form of sculpture produced from wood, stone, or marble, etc. Modeling is an additive form of sculpture produced with clay or wax.

sculptured rug

See *carved rug.*

scutcheon

See *escutcheon.*

seam

The physical connection of two material surfaces such as fabric, wallpaper, veneer, etc.

seasoned lumber

Natural or kiln-dried wood. A process that controls warping, splitting, and checking of lumber and improves durability. See also *kiln dried.*

seaweed marquetry

A popular 17th- and 18th-century marquetry pattern composed of small foliated forms that resemble seaweed. Commonly found on English William and Mary and Queen Anne period cabinetwork.

Secession movement

A succession of artistic revolutions in which artists withdrew from mainstream academy ideals and organized progressive exhibitions in Impressionist and Art Nouveau Styles. There have been three major documented secessions: Munich in 1892, Vienna in 1897, and Berlin in 1899. See also *Art Nouveau.*

Second Empire

A late 19th-century period originating in France, architecturally characterized by the use of short, steep mansard roofs and often a rectangular tower. With respect to furniture, Louis XV motifs were added to Empire Style pieces. Also called the Late Empire period or Napoleon III Style.

second style painting

The second phase of Pompeian mural painting, from 60-20 B.C.E., characterized by architectural features and trompe l'oeil compositions. Famous examples include the Villa P. Fannius Synistor at Boscoreale and the Dionysiac mystery frieze of the Villa of the Mysteries. See also *Architectural Style.*

secrétaire (sek ru TAYR)

French for secretary. See also *secretary.*

secrétaire à abattant (sek ru TAYR AH aa BAA tahnt)

An upright desk or writing cabinet with a vertical drop-front writing surface set above several drawers or a doored compartment. Also called a fall-front desk or drop-front desk. See also *abattant.*

secrétaire en dos d'âne (sek ru TAYR AHN DOH D'AAN)
A French desk that looks like two slant-top desks connected back to back, enabling users to face one another.

secretary
A writing desk with a bookcase cabinet above and a drawered or doored base. Also called a secrétaire bookcase.

section
A vertically sliced view of a structure or object that reveals internal details.

sectional furniture
Furniture manufactured in modules that are completely finished on all sides allowing for various configurations, often referring to a sofa.

sedan chair
A 17th-century enclosed chair used as a form of transportation borne on poles and carried by men. Originally designed in Sedan, France. See also *palanquin*.

sedia (SED ee ah)
A box-shaped Italian Renaissance armchair with an upholstered seat, bulky block legs, and runner feet.

sediolum (SED ee oh lum)
Latin for a four-legged bench or stool used in ancient Rome.

segmental arch
An elliptical or less than semicircular arch.

segmental corners
The curved cutout corners of a rectangular panel. Popularized in the 18th-century ceilings, walls, and doors of England's Adam brothers.

segmental front
See *bow front* and *swell front*.

sedia

segmental pediment
An elliptical or less than semicircular pediment, often used over doors and windows of the English Renaissance. See *illustration in the Pediments Appendix*.

sehna knot (zay NAH NAHT)
An asymmetrical hand-tied rug knot that creates a close, fine, velvety surface. The knot is created by yarn that encircles one warp, one end emerging between a pair and the other outside the second warp thread from below. Also called a Persian knot. See also *ghiordes knot*.

seignorial chair (say NOR ee aal CHAYR)
A Gothic or Renaissance armchair, often canopied, with a very high back, hinged seat, and solid paneled base that are elaborately carved. See also *canopy chair*.

sekkaidan (sek KIY dun)
A space within a Japanese emperor's living quarters, with dirt covering part of the floor, enabling the emperor to participate in rituals requiring contact with the earth regardless of the weather.

selamlik (si LAHM lik)
A space used for entertaining guests, male friends, and business associates within a Middle Eastern home.

self-covered seat deck
In upholstery, a term used when the primary upholstery fabric covers the area beneath the loose cushions of a piece of furniture.

sella
Latin for chair. A general term used for Roman seating, denoting specific types when followed by another term. See also *sella curulis* and *sella gestoria*.

sella curulis
An x-framed folding stool used by Roman curules, magistrates, and other politically important people. See also *curule*.

sella curulis

sella gestatoria (SAY lah ges TAH tor ee u)

A sedan chair, generally enclosed by curtains, used for town and country travel in ancient Rome. See also *sedan chair.*

semainier (su MEN yay)

A tall narrow chest of drawers with seven drawers, one for each day of the week, originating in the Louis XV period. The term is derived from the French word semaine, which translates to week. See also *chiffonier.*

semé (su MEE)

French for sown, as in seeds. In textiles, a small floral motif scattered over the field of a brocade fabric.

semicircular arch

A rounded arch formed from a single central point, creating a half circle. See also *Roman arch.*

semi-lead crystal

Lead crystal containing approximately half the amount of lead as full lead crystal, which decreases the brilliance and clarity.

semi-vitreous

A semi-porous clay body that can absorb between 3 and 7 percent water. Recommended for indoor use in low water contact situations such as tile back splashes in kitchens.

senneh (SEN nu)

See *Persian knot.*

sepia print

A print created from a reddish-brown pigment called sepia, originally made from cuttlefish.

seqt (SEKT)

Egyptian mathematical proportion system equivalent to the Golden Mean, used in the design of buildings and art.

semainier

seraglio (si RAAL yoh)

The sequestered living quarters of a harem within a Turkish palace. Also called a serail.

serdab (ser DAHB)

A small chamber within Egyptian tombs used for housing the deceased's Ka statue, which provided a place of resting for the spirit.

serigraph

A print created by silk-screening. See also *silk-screened.*

serpentine (SUR pun teen)

A compound curve with a convex center flanked by two concave curves; commonly used on 18th-century French and English furniture. When inverted the sinuous line is called a reverse serpentine.

serpentine crest (SUR pun teen KREST)

A top rail with a serpentine shape. See also *serpentine.*

serrated edge

An edge formed from zigzags or inverted Vs, similar to the toothed edge of a saw.

serra-papiers (sayr RAH PAAP yay)

See *table à grandin.*

servante (SAYR vahnt)

See *rafraîchissior* or *serviteur fidèle.*

server or serving table

A piece of dining room furniture whose top surface is designed to hold food or drinks. The piece is usually outfitted with drawers and may also contain cabinet space for storing dishes, glassware, silver, and other dining room items.

serviteur fidèle (sur VEE tur FEE del)

French for faithful servant. A French multitiered table or dumbwaiter. See also *dumbwaiter* and *rafraîchissior.*

set

In furniture, a matched suite of items designed to be used together. Also called a suite.

255

settee (set TEE)

A long upholstered seat with upholstered back and arms, designed to hold two or three people. The settee developed from the 17th-century settle.

settee

settle

A wooden bench with a solid high back and arms that developed during the Gothic era. A settle with a hinged seat allowing for base storage is called a box settle. See also *box settle* and *William Morris Settle*.

Sèvres (SEV ru)

Famous French porcelain factory, founded outside Paris in 1756 and made famous by the patronage of Louis XV's mistress, Madame de Pompadour. Also, the products of the Sèvres factory, typically elaborately decorated, often with ormolu mounts. See also *ormolu*.

sewing table

A small mid to late 18th-century work table equipped with various items used to hold sewing materials such as drawers, trays, spool racks, and a cloth bag that hung from below. Popular in France and England, particularly the work of Thomas Sheraton and George Hepplewhite. Also known as a pouch table. See also *pouch table*.

sexpartite vault (seks PAHR tiyt VAWLT)

A rib vault divided into six sections by two diagonal ribs and three transverse ribs.

Sezession

See *Secession movement*.

sgabello (skah BEL loh)

A small Italian Renaissance chair with an octagonal seat, thin fan-shaped back (plain or paneled), and trestle base, often used in hallways.

sgabello

sgraffito (grahf FEE toh)

A decorative wall and unglazed ceramic body technique produced by applying contrasting colored layers of plaster or slip and then scratching or incising a design into the surface. From the Italian word "to scratch." A particularly popular architectural treatment in Renaissance Italy.

shade

A color with black added to it. Also, a protective covering for a light source such as a lampshade or window shade. See also *lampshade* and *window shade*.

shaft

The vertical component of a column, between the capital and the base.

shag

A carpet or rug with a deep cut pile, textured loops, or a combination of the two.

shaggy paw foot

A foot resembling a hairy animal paw, commonly found on Chippendale and American Empire Style furniture. Also called a hairy paw foot. See *illustration in the Feet Appendix*.

shagreen (shu GREEN)

Originally, the rough, grainy untanned hides of horses and mules, dyed a soft green and popularly used to cover small 18th-century pieces. Today, the term is more closely associated with the pebbled shark-skin, also dyed green, fashionable in the Art Deco era.

shake

A shingle split from a log, traditionally used for roofing and siding.

Shaker furniture

Simple, clean lined, functional furniture created by the Shakers, a religious sect, throughout the late 18th and 19th centuries in America.

Shaker ladder-back chair

Shaker Modern
A simple, modern version of early 19th-century Shaker furniture, predominantly of oil finished maple, cherry, and other fruitwoods; characterized by clean lines, gentle tapers, pegged and dovetail joints.

shams
A decorative pillow cover, often matching quilts and comforters.

shantung (SHAAN tuun)
A heavy, plain-woven fabric with a slightly irregular surface constructed from raw silk, cotton, or a combination of the two. Originally from Shantung, China, it is commonly used for suiting and window treatments.

shaving mirror
A popular 18th-century framed and tiltable stand-mounted mirror, often fitted with drawers to hold shaving equipment and commonly placed on the top of chests. See also *standing mirror*.

shaving tables
Clever tables of the Chippendale period designed for dressing and shaving, commonly equipped with folding tops that open to reveal spring-loaded mirrors, a basin, and various drawers and compartments for soap, razors, and bottles. Also called a reflecting dressing table. See also *Rudd's dressing table*.

shawabty (SHAW aab tee)
Funerary figures used in Egyptian tombs that substituted for the deceased in the afterlife if called upon to do work. Also called ushabti or shabti.

sheaf back
A late 18th-century French chair with a caned or rush seat and a chair back featuring a bundle of stylized wheat.

shed ceiling
A sloped ceiling similar to a cathedral ceiling, but not as steep and often with attic space above for insulation and ventilation purposes. See also *cathedral ceiling*.

sheer
General term for a lightweight, gauzy fabric of natural or synthetic fibers that is semitransparent.

sheet glass
Glass drawn from a molten state into long sheets commonly used for windows.

Sheldon's tapestries
Tapestries of the 16th century created by Flemish weavers in England under the guidance of William Sheldon.

shell or cockleshell
A decorative motif, commonly in the shape of a scallop shell. Also, the basic structure or framework for furniture. See also *cockleshell, rocaille,* and *scallop shell*. See *illustration in the Motifs/Ornaments Appendix*.

shell chairs
An iconic 1960s chair with an ergonomically designed molded fiberglass body and metal legs, originally designed by Charles Eames and produced by Herman Miller. See *Charles Ormond Eames, 1907–1978 in the Architects, Artists, and Designers Appendix*.

shell keep
A circular stone wall constructed at the top of a moat as a castle stronghold during medieval times.

shellac
An alcohol soluble resin that produces a shiny surface when applied to wood.

shepherd's bed
A raised shelf designed for sleeping, often incorporated into the fireplace surround in Spanish Colonial architecture.

sheveret (she VUR ay)

A writing table, originally from the Louis XVI period, designed with a small bookshelf in the back. The front half of the top is hinged, opening to extend the width of the writing surface, supported by the front legs and framing that pull forward. See also *cheveret*.

shibayama (shee BAH yah mah)

Japanese decorative lacquerwork made for the export market in the early 19th century, characterized by fine inlays of ivory, mother of pearl, tortoiseshell, horn, etc., into gold-lacquered wood or ivory grounds.

shibi (shee BEE)

A Japanese ornamental roof tile accenting the ends of a roof ridgepole, often in the form of a sachihoko, a mystical animal with the head of a dragon and the body of a carp.

shibui (shee BOO ee)

A Japanese design aestheticly reflected in the use of natural materials and simple, unobtrusive beauty with subtle details suffused with inner meaning.

shield-back side chair

See *George Hepplewhite shield-back side chair*. See *George Hepplewhite, d. 1786, in the Architects, Artists, and Designers Appendix.*

shikibuton (shee KEE boo tohn)

The bottom mattress of a Japanese futon, the traditional bedding that is folded and stored during the day.

shikifu (SHEE kee foo)

Sheets used to wrap a shikibuton. See also *shikibuton*.

shikinen-sengu (shee KEE nen sen GOO)

A Japanese reconstruction ceremony preformed after the tradition of rebuilding a shrine every 20 years.

shimashira (shee MAH shee rah)

A central pillar placed over buried sacred relics within a Buddhist shrine.

Shinden Style (SHIN den STIYL)

A Japanese style of aristocratic domestic architecture from the Heian period (794–1185) featuring a main central building, or shinden, with covered walkways that lead to flanking rectangular pavilions that sit at right angles to the main structure.

shingle

Thin, flat rectangle forms laid in overlapping rows as a facing for exterior walls and roofs. Originally made of wood; however, various other materials have been used including slate, asbestos-cement, fiberglass-based asphalt, composite, ceramic, and metal.

Shingle Style

A late 19th-century American domestic style of architecture, based on the Queen Anne Style, Colonial American architecture, and Japanese forms, all sheathed in shingles. Other features include asymmetrical forms, wide porches, and short stubby columns.

shin-kabe (SHEEN kah BEE)

Literally translated as honest wall. A traditional Japanese plaster wall with an exposed structure like timber framing.

shiro (SHEE roh)

In architecture, Japanese for a castle.

shirring

An effect created by gathering fabric on a thread or rod to create fullness, such as in window treatments.

shitomido (shee TOH mee doh)

Reticulated shutters traditionally used as exterior partitions that allow ample light and air into Japanese houses. They may also be swung upward to open the wall.

shodana (shoh DAH nah)

A Japanese cabinet outfitted with various doors, drawers, and shelves, typically set in an asymmetrical arrangement.

shoe

A wedge foot used mostly on Early American tables. Also a convex molding. See also *quarter-round*.

shoin (SHOH een)

Originally a lecture hall within a Japanese temple, developed during the Muromachi period. Later used to simply signify a drawing room or study alcove, often overlooking a garden or view.

Shoin Style (SHOH een STIYL)

A Japanese style of residential architecture, centered on the *shoin*, that developed out of the Shinden Style from the 14th to the 16th centuries during the Muromachi and Azuchi-Momoyama periods. The style is characterized by square pillars, tatami-mat flooring, and sliding doors (fusuma, shoji, and sugito).

shoji (SHOH jee)

A translucent sliding screen used as an exterior or interior partition, door, or window covering in Japan. Frames of the screen are generally made of black lacquered wood backed by translucent rice paper.

shouldered architrave

A decorative door or window surround whose header extends past the vertical posts, creating shoulders.

show-frame

A 19th-century term for seating with an exposed wood frame.

show wood

Industry term for exposed and finished wood of upholstered furnishings.

shronk

A large German storage cupboard, usually composed of two to three stacking units similar to a Dutch kas.

shu gui (SHOO GWAY)

A two-doored Chinese wardrobe cabinet designed with interior shelves and drawers.

shutter

A moveable window or door panel used to protect, provide security, block views, and control light. Often utilized as a purely decorative element today.

shutter dog

A decorative iron bracket used to hold a shutter in place.

siamoise (sim WAH)

A mid 19th-century S-shaped seating device that seats two people in opposite directions, named after the famous Siamese twins, Chang and Eng. See also *tête-à-tête*.

side chair

A chair without arms, usually part of a dining room set, that replaced the stools or benches previously used by people other than nobility and heads of family in the 17th century. See also *hall chair* and *light chair*.

side table

Originally a term used to signify an ornate 18th-century serving table, flanked by two pedestals, often seen in the work of the English Adam brothers and William Kent. Today, a general term for a small table used at the side of a chair or sofa. Also called an end table.

sideboard

A piece of dining room furniture used for serving and display. The carcass is generally composed of a set of cabinets or cupboards and one or more drawers for storing linens and tableware, all capped by a long flat surface. It developed out of a medieval shelf used to store food before serving, which was followed by the crédence. The present form was perfected by George Hepplewhite and Thomas Sheraton in the late 18th century. See also *buffet*, *crédence*, and *credenza*.

sideboard

sidelights
A pair of narrow, vertical windows flanking a door.

siding
A material used to cover the outside of exterior walls such as shingles, boards, or aluminum panels.

siège courant (SEE ej COR ahn)
French furniture designed to be moveable and used in the middle of a room.

siège meublant (SEE ej mu BLAHNT)
French furniture designed to be used against a wall, often remaining in the same location.

sigma
A semi-circular-shaped couch, occasionally used to replace the triclinium in Roman banquets.

siheyuan (sz HU y wahn)
An historical type of Chinese residence, dating back as early as the Western Zhou period, based on four buildings connected by pathways that surrounded a courtyard. The layout was also used for palaces, temples, monasteries, businesses, and government offices.

silent valet
A frame, often of wood or metal, designed to hold a suit and other articles of men's clothing. When a pant press is added to the stand, it is called a clothes press. Also called a valet stand or clothes valet.

silhouette (sil oo ET)
The outline of an object or form. Also, a popular style of 18th- and 19th-century artwork created from various media such as painting and cutting silhouetted portraits out of black cards and setting them on white grounds.

silhouette mirror
An 18th-century mirror, designed by Thomas Chippendale, with a scrolled mahogany frame that is often carved and highlighted with gilding and usually containing a decorative ornament within the crest. Also called a fretwork mirror.

silk
A fine, natural fiber produced by silkworms as they make cocoons; known for its strength, softness, luster, and temperature-regulating properties. Silk fabric was developed in ancient China before 3500 B.C.E. and is commonly used today for clothing, window treatments, upholstery, rugs, bedding, and wall hangings.

silk-screening
A printing technique, original to China, that involves forcing ink through a fine silk screen treated with an ink blocking stencil. Each color in the design requires a separate screen.

sill
The bottom horizontal member of a structure such as a door or window frame, commonly made of stone, wood, metal, or brick. A door sill is also called a saddle.

silla (SEE yah)
Spanish for chair.

sillon de cadera (see YOHN DAY kah DAYR u)
A folding x-framed chair, similar to the Italian Dante and Savonarola chair, used by the Moors as a seat of dignity. Also called the hip-joint armchair. See also *Dante chair* and *Savonorola chair*.

sillon de cajun (see YOHN DAY CAY jahn)
A Spanish chair with a gondola back.

silver plate
A surface coating of silver over a base metal.

silvering glass
A late 17th-century process used to create looking glass by applying tin followed by a layer of quicksilver to the back of glass.

simianping (sz MEE en ping)
Chinese for flush-sided. A furniture construction technique using long tenons to set legs flush with the frame, popular from the Song to Ming dynasties.

singerie (SAAN ju ree)

French for monkey trick. A popular 18th-century French and English decorative motif portraying monkeys mimicking human activities, often in fashionable attire. See also *chinoiserie*.

single arch molding

A narrow half-round molding commonly used around furniture drawer fronts or door edges of the late 18th century in England and American. See also *cock bead molding*.

singerie

single bed

A bed designed to hold one person while sleeping, commonly sized at 39" × 75". Also called a twin bed.

single gate table

A table designed with a single swinging leg to support one drop leaf. Also called a tuckaway table.

sisal

A strong durable fiber with a rough texture from the Mexican agave plant, generally used to make rugs and twine.

sistrum

An ancient Egyptian musical instrument of the percussion family that resembles a rattle, often used in religious ceremonies.

Sitzmachine

See *Josef Hoffmann sitzmachine model no. 670*. See *Josef Hoffman, 1870–1956*, in the Architects, Artists, and Designers Appendix.

six-legged brass cat

A six-legged stand designed to hold a tray, usually made of brass. See also *cat*.

six-legged highboy

A highboy of the William and Mary period with six turned legs.

skene (SKEE nee)

A theater backdrop of ancient Greece.

skew arch

An arch, often used in the construction of bridges, with an axis other than 90 degrees. Also known as an oblique arch.

skirting

A strip of wood positioned below a window sill, shelf, or tabletop. Also, a fabric face, often pleated, used to hide the legs around the base of a piece of upholstered furniture. See also *apron* or *frieze*.

skylight

A roof window, of glass or Plexiglas, used to admit daylight into the space below without affecting privacy.

slant-front desk

A desk with an angled drop-front used for writing, supported on a base containing several drawers. Much like a secretary without the bookcase. Also called a slope-front desk or slant-top desk.

slat

A flattened horizontal bar connecting the vertical uprights of a chair back. Sometimes called a horizontal splat. Also, a thin, flat piece of wood, plastic, or metal used in in a window blind.

slat-back chair

See *ladder-back chair*.

slate

A fine-grained metamorphic rock of compressed clay or shale, commonly used as roof shingles and floor or wall tiles. Available in a variety of shades of grey, green, purple, brown, or cyan.

slatted bed frame

A mattress foundation without box springs, made entirely of wood slats.

slaw bed

A Dutch bed off the main room built into small cubicles.

abcdefghijklmnopqrStuvwxyz

sleep/sleeping chair

A chair with a hidden mattress inside that can be opened to form a bed. See also *ratchet chair*.

sleeper sofa

A sofa with a concealed spring frame and mattress that can be pulled out to form a bed.

Sleepy Hollow chair

A mid 19th-century American armchair with a high upholstered back that curves to form the chair's seat.

sleigh bed

A bed originating from the 19th-century French Empire period with a scrolled headboard and footboard that mimics the curves of a horse-drawn sleigh. Also seen in the American Empire period.

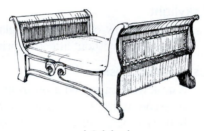

sleigh bed

slide

A shelf that pulls out from the body of a desk, secretary, or table. Also, a device that guides drawers on the inside of a drawer cavity.

sliding casement

A window style that opens by sliding one sash horizontally over the other. Also called a sliding sash window or slider.

sling chair

See Hardoy chair. See *Jorge Ferrari-Hardoy, 1914–1977, in the Architects, Artists, and Designers Appendix.*

sling sofa

See *George Nelson sling sofa*. See *George Nelson, 1908–1986, in the Architects, Artists, and Designers Appendix.*

slip

A thin mixture of clay and water, used in the production and decoration of ceramics. Slip is often used to join unfired pieces, to adhere figures and motifs, or to create decorative designs by dipping, painting, or splashing onto a clay body.

slip cover

A removable fitted cover designed to protect, change, or conceal the upholstery of furniture, popular during the Louis XV period.

slip match

A veneer pattern created by joining pieces of veneer in sequence without flipping. Often used with quarter-sliced and rift-sliced veneers.

slip seat

A chair seat that can be lifted up out of the frame and easily reupholstered. See also *drop-in seat*.

slipper chair

A short armless upholstered chair with a low seat, generally sitting only 12" to 14" off the ground and originally made for bedroom use.

slipper foot

A club foot with a pointed toe resembling a ladies slipper, popular during the English Queen Anne period. See *illustration in the Feet Appendix*.

slipper chair

slope

See *writing box*.

slope-front desk

See *slant-front desk*.

smalti

Opaque colored glass tesserae, often backed with gold or silver leaf, used in mosaic work of the Byzantine era.

smoker's chair

See *writing armchair* and *tablet chair*.

snack table

See *TV tray table*.

snake foot

A furniture foot designed to look like a snake's head, often terminating a cabriolet leg on tripod based tables and stands of English and American Queen Anne and Chippendale Styles.

snap table

See *tilt-top table*.

socketing

A woodworking joint created by shaping the end of a piece of wood to tightly fit a cavity cut into a second piece of wood. Often used to attach legs to a wooden chair seat.

socle (SAH kul)

A low unadorned block or plinth used to support a statue, column, urn, etc. Also, a wall base commonly used in ancient Greece.

sofa

A long upholstered seating unit containing a back and arms, designed for two or more people. First seen in 18th-century France, the term is derived from the Arabic word suffah. See also *canapé*.

sofa bed

A sofa whose seat contains a folded metal frame and thin mattress that opens to form a bed. Also called a hide-a-bed or sleeper sofa.

sofa table

A long narrow table commonly used behind a sofa and originally designed during the late 18th century with drop leaves at each short end and drawers within the frame of a long side.

soffit (SAHF fit)

The underside of a construction element such as an arch, flight of stairs, projecting cornice, or the ceiling space filled above kitchen cabinets. From the French word soffite, meaning formed as a ceiling.

soffit

soft-paste

A type of porcelain made by mixing white clay with frit, a glasslike substance. Originally created to mimic Chinese hard-paste porcelain. Sometimes called artificial porcelain.

softwood

Wood from conifers such as a pine, fir, or spruce. See also *hardwood*.

solar (SOH lur)

The private chamber of a lord and lady found in a medieval castle or manor house. Originally partitioned from the end of the Great Hall, the solar was a place for the family to retreat. Also called the great chamber.

solarium (su LAYR ee um)

A room constructed primarily of glass, originating during the Victorian era.

soldier

A brick laid vertically, exposing the narrow face.

soldier arch

A flat arch composed of vertically laid bricks, generally used to cover lintels and joists.

solium (soh LEE um)

A high-backed, solid-armed chair of ancient Rome, similar to the Greek thronos, used by a ruler or head of household. See also *Roman throne chair*.

solomonic column (SAHL u mah nik KAHL um)
A column with a spiraling twisted shaft, commonly seen in Byzantine architecture and decoration, purportedly of Eastern origin.

soportales (SOH por tah lays)
Spanish for an arcade, a covered passageway with shops on one or both sides.

sotto in sù (SOHT toh)
A Renaissance and Baroque Style of trompe l'oeil painting utilized on ceilings, often pictorializing the heavens opening up. Literally translated from Italian as "seen from below."

soutache (soo TAHSH)
A narrow, flat decorative braid, often in a herringbone pattern, commonly used to trim upholstery and drapery. It is also used on military uniforms to signify the wearer's rank.

spade/thimble foot
A tapered rectangular furniture foot resembling the blade of a garden shovel or spade, popular in the 18th-century English designs of George Hepplewhite and Thomas Sheraton. See also *sabot foot, tapered leg, therm leg,* and *thimble foot.* See *illustration in the Feet Appendix.*

spallière (SPAH lee ayr)
Italian painted or intarsiated wainscot panels, often created for the nuptial chamber of newly married couples during the 15th century.

span
The amount of space that a bridge, arch, or other structure covers.

spandrel
The triangular space created between adjacent arches. Also, a triangular piece between a vertical and horizontal member in architecture and furniture.

spandrel

spandrel steps
Steps with triangular-shaped treads.

spandrel wall
A wall constructed above the exterior curve of an arch to fill the spandrel. Also, a term used with curtain walls signifying the wall portion above a window in one story and below the windowsill of the next story.

Spanish chair
A high-backed chair with an upholstered seat and back of Spanish leather, turned legs, carved under-brace, and Spanish feet of the English Carolean period of the late 16th century.

Spanish chair
See *Børge Mogensen Spanish chair.* See *Børge Morgensen, 1914–1972, in the Architects, Artists, and Designers Appendix.*

Spanish Colonial furniture
Provincial furniture of the American Southwest, originating in the early 19th century and loosely based on Spanish styles. The furniture is simple, massive, and rectilinear in form, often accentuated with naive carvings and made of local woods finished with a dark stain or layers of paint.

Spanish elm
See *princewood.*

Spanish foot, Spanish scroll foot
An inwardly scrolled furniture foot featuring vertical grooves and a flared base, commonly seen on English furniture of the William and Mary and Queen Anne Styles. The foot originated in Portugal during the mid 17th century. Also called a Braganza foot, knurled foot, or paintbrush foot. See *illustration in the Feet Appendix.*

Spanish furniture
The most prominent periods of Spanish furniture are the 16th, 17th, and 18th centuries. Furniture during this time pulled heavily from the French and Italian Renaissance and was commonly infused with Moorish influences such as tooled cordovan leather and geometric motifs as well as inlay, brilliant colors, and gilding. Walnut was the wood of choice, often combined with structural or ornamental iron to create heavy, rectangular forms.

Spanish roof tile

A barrel or S-shaped clay tile, typically used on the roofs of Spanish or Southwestern style architecture.

sparking lamps

A small early 19th-century whale oil lamp favored by sparking (slang for courting) couples.

sparver

On old English term for a bed's canopy or tester.

specifications

A written guide to the details of a design project including measurements, materials, furniture, etc.

spectral colors

The colors generated when white light is refracted by a prism, traditionally including red, orange, yellow, green, blue, and violet.

speculum

An ancient Estruscan hand mirror, circular or oval in shape, made of cast bronze.

speed stripe

A trio of horizontal lines suggesting motion, commonly found on Streamlined Moderne or Art Deco architecture.

sphinx (SFINGKS)

A mythical creature with the body of a lion and the head of a human, originally used as a motif in ancient Egypt and repopularized during the Renaissance, Adam, Empire, and Regency periods.

spider-leg table

An 18th-century gate-leg table with eight slim straight legs, designed by Thomas Sheraton. Also, a late 18th and early 19th century candlestand, tea table, card table, etc., with delicate, thin curved legs.

spina

A short central barrier or wall at the center of a Roman circus.

spinapesce (SPIN ah pays ay)

A spiral herringbone brick pattern used to form a dome, commonly used in Italian Renaissance architecture, possibly stemming from earlier Persian domes.

spindle

A cylindrical wooden rod created on a lathe and typically decorated with various sized turnings, used in furniture design since the 17th century.

spindle and bead

A decorative molding with alternating split spindles and half spherical forms.

spindled panels

An interior shutter constructed of delicate spindles, commonly used as a Spanish window treatment that allows breezes to enter while maintaining privacy.

spinet (SPIN it)

A popular 17th- and 18th-century small harpsichord with strings set at an acute angle to the keyboard. Period spinet cases were generally highly decorated with paintings, carvings, gilding, and inlay. The term is also used contemporarily to denote a small upright piano approximately 5'L × 2'W × 4'H.

spinet

spiral

A curve beginning from a central point and gradually winding outward away from it.

spiral staircase

A stairway constructed around a central shaft

spiral turned leg

A furniture leg with a rope-like twist or descending flute, popular during the English Restoration, but original to Portugal and India. See also *barley twist*. See *illustration in the Legs Appendix*.

spiral whorl

See *paper scroll*.

spire

A tapered conical, polygonal, or pyramidal structure that terminates in a point at the top of a building, especially a church.

splanch

In residential architecture, a combination split-level and ranch-style house designed on three levels within a two-level skin, popular during the 1950s to 1970s in the United States. See also *ranch-style house* and *split-level house*.

splat

The central vertical member of a chair back, possibly shaped, carved, pierced, inlaid, or otherwise embellished, often used as a determinant of a chair's style.

splay

A component that is spread out or slanted.

splayed leg

A furniture leg that flares outward in a concave shape, used since ancient Greece and during the 18th-century Empire and Regency periods. See also *saber leg*. See *illustration in the Legs Appendix*.

splined joint

A small strip of wood inserted between and into two adjoining pieces of wood to create a stronger joint. See *illustration in the Joints Appendix*.

splint

Thin, flat strips of wood woven in a plain basket weave into a furniture seat, commonly found on rustic or provincial furniture. Coarser than rush or caning.

split baluster turning

A turned baluster split vertically in half to provide a flat surface, commonly applied as decoration to chests, dressers, and other furniture.

split spindle

A long, slender turned spindle that has been cut in half lengthwise, commonly applied as ornament to furniture and cabinetry of 17th-century England and America.

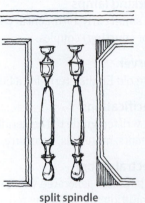

split spindle

split entry

An entry between floors, usually containing two short sets of stairs leading occupants to each floor.

split-level house

A house constructed with the floor level of one part of the house separated by a half story from another part of the house.

sponge painting

A decorative painting technique using sponges to produce a splotchy faux texture, popular in early American interiors.

spool furniture

American furniture of the mid to late 18th century, characterized by turnings resembling a series of stacked spools. Close-grained woods such as maple, birch, and black walnut were commonly used because of their strength with such turnings. See also *Jenny Lind bed*.

spoon back

American term for a chair back whose uprights are slightly concave to conform to the human body. The back was originally introduced by the Dutch. It first appeared in England during the William and Mary period, but was most popular during the Queen Anne period.

spoon foot

A furniture foot that often projects out at the base of a cabriole leg, with a simple, oval-shaped back that resembles the back of a spoon. Commonly seen on English Queen Anne furniture. See also *Dutch foot* or *pad foot*. See *illustration in the Feet Appendix*.

spoon-back chair

A chair originating in the 19th-century English Regency period with low set arms that commence at the front legs and uninterruptedly rise and sweep inward to form the back of the chair. Similar to the American Mme. Jumel chair. See also *Madame Jumel chair*.

spot or spotlight

A lamp with a narrow, focused beam spread.

sprig

A small, low relief ceramic ornament, created in a mold and attached to an unfired ceramic body with slip. Also, an ornamental motif representing a small stemmed flower or leaf.

spring line

The implied line between two spring points of an arch.

springpoint

The place at which an arch starts to curve.

spruce

An ornamental evergreen that is actually a type of pine closely related to fir with soft, light wood that is straight grained and strong, used for interior and exterior construction.

spun silk

Silk yarn made from waste fibers and damaged silk worm cocoons. The end product is heavier and less lustrous than the first-grade reeled silk.

spur

A projecting ornament often used at the foot of a Gothic column's shaft and a square plinth base. Also, a masonry buttress used as reinforcement in a fortification.

spur stone

A projecting stone set at the corner of a structure to protect it from damage by passing vehicles.

squab (SKWAHB)

Loose flat cushions, originally used to protect expensive hand-carved and caned seats of chairs, settees, and long stools. Replaced by upholstery in the late 17th century. See also *carreau*.

squinch (SKWINCH)

A method used to connect a dome to a square base via pendentive arches that project upward and inward from a corner. Also, an old English term for a corner cupboard.

S-scroll

A curved decorative ornament in the shape of an S, developed during the Louis XV period and also popular in the designs of Thomas Chippendale.

S-scroll legs

An S-shaped furniture support originally developed during the 17th-century Flemish Renaissance, also popular in the English Charles I and II and William and Mary periods, and the French Renaissance and Louis XIV periods. Also called a Flemish scroll. See *illustration in the Legs Appendix*.

stabadium (stah BAHD ee um)

An outdoor reclining sofa, constructed of stone or concrete, used for dining in ancient Rome.

stacking chairs

Chairs designed to stack one on top of another for easy storage, generally utilized for temporary seating arrangements for auditoriums, churches, dining, etc.

Staffordshire

Pottery made in Staffordshire, the center of the English pottery industry since the 17th century due to locally available clay, salt, lead, and coal. Notable 19th-century manufacturers in the area included Doulton, Minton, Moorcroft, Spode, and Wedgwood. Products from the area are often called Staffordshire ware.

abcdefghijklmnopqrStuvwxyz

stain

A wood finishing product with pigment or dye suspended or dissolved in a solvent, used to enhance and add color to the outer pores of wood. Available in transparent, semitransparent, and opaque applications that accentuate or obscure the wood grain.

stained glass

Glass that has been colored or stained with metallic oxides while molten. Invented during the Byzantine era to create designs, often for churches, that are held together by strips of lead.

staining

The process of applying a dye to wood in order to enhance surface characteristics such as grain, produce a uniform color, or match to surrounding wood.

stair brackets

Brackets applied to the exposed sides of an open stringer staircase, under the tread nosing, to add architectural detail.

stair rod

A metal rod, usually brass, used to hold carpet at the bottom of a riser between two steps of a staircase.

stalactite work

A 12th-century invention commonly seen in Islamic buildings, composed of a complex arrangement of small vertical prisms resembling stalactites. The designs are thought to possibly be a symbolic representation of the cave where Mohammed received the Koran. Also called mocárabe or honeycomb work.

Stam model 533 chair

See *Mart Stam model 533 chair*. See *Mart Stam, 1899–1986*, in the *Architects, Artists, and Designers Appendix*.

stamnos

A pottery jar with a wide mouth, short body, and two handles set on the shoulder, used for storing wine and water by the ancient Greeks.

stamping

A method of forming metal by pounding it into a desired shape. Also, a term associated with pottery when a stamp is used to imprint a design into the soft body of unfired clay.

stanchion (STAAN shun)

A vertical metal post, usually of rolled steel, employed as a weight-bearing support.

stand

In furniture design, a frame designed to hold a chest, cabinet, or other piece of furniture.

standard-size bed

Also known as a full-size bed or double bed. See *double bed*.

standing mirror

A framed mirror attached to a stand, often containing a drawer, designed to be placed on top of a chest or table to use while shaving in the 18th and 19th century. Also called a shaving mirror.

star molding

A molding containing a linear relief of stars, popular in Romanesque architecture.

starburst

A series of radiating lines surrounding a central object or light source, designed to resemble an exploding star.

stationary curtains

A curtain, such as shears used beneath draperies, designed to be fixed rather than moveable. Also called under curtains or glass curtains.

statuary bronze

A bronze alloy composed of bronze and tin, used for casting statues, generally treated with acid to achieve a dark brown color.

Steamboat Gothic

A late 19th-century architectural style with houses designed to mimic steamboats. The style was characterized by shingle structures and profuse jig-sawn details and was primarily seen in the Mississippi and Ohio river valleys. The term itself was popularized by Frances Parkinson Keyes's novel of the same name. See also *jigsaw*.

steel engraving

A early 19th-century method for reproducing art, in which a design is etched into a thin layer of steel over a soft copper plate, which is in turn inked and pressed onto paper.

steel furniture

Furniture predominantly of the Directoire and Early Empire Styles, produced from steel into strong folding pieces that could be easily transported during the campaigns of Napoleon Bonaparte. Designs included chairs, beds, tables, and desks.

steinzeug (STIYN soig)

German for stoneware.

stele (STEE lee)

An upright stone slab or pillar with an inscribed or sculpted face, designed as a monument or to commemorate significant events within the face of an architectural structure.

stellar vault

A vault that uses lierne, tertiary ribs that span main ribs, dividing the space to form a star shape. Also called a lierne vault.

stemware

A late 19th-century invention describing drinking glasses mounted on a stem.

stencil

A device created when a design is cut out of an impervious material in order that paint, ink, etc., can be applied through the openings to produce a repeatable design. Also, the process of painting with a stencil.

step table

A short occasional table, generally rectangular in form, with a shelf mounted on top of the main surface, creating a step-like design.

stepped curve

A device often used on the uprights of Queen Anne and Early Georgian furniture and chair backs of Hepplewhite designs, comprised of a curve with a sudden break or straight line inserted.

stereobate (STER ee oh BAYT)

The steps above the foundation, excluding the top level, in the crepidoma of an ancient Greek building. See also *stylobate*.

stereochromy (STER ee oh kroh mee)

A method used to permanently paint plastered walls, stone, and marble by sprinkling pigments with a mixture of water and sodium silicate, called water glass.

sterling

A silver alloy containing 92.5% silver and 7.5% other metals, creating a material hard enough to use for functional items.

Stick Style

A late 19th-century American Victorian architectural style characterized by a grid of decorative trim boards, called sticks, that alluded to medieval half-timbering.

stick table

A combination table and floor lamp, with a lamp shade topped columnar shaft that extends through a table top and continues down to form a base.

stick-back

A chair or bench with a back composed predominately of thin vertical spindles, such as a Windsor chair.

Stickley reclining armchair

See *Gustav Stickley reclining armchair*. See *Gustav Stickley, 1858–1942, in the Architects, Artists, and Designers Appendix*.

stile

In woodworking, one of the vertical members composing a frame surrounding a panel in rail and stile construction. Also, a series of steps utilized to traverse a fence or wall.

still life

A painting or drawing composed of inanimate, motionless objects, such as flowers and fruit.

stilted arch

An arch whose spring line is raised above the impost, i.e., it moves up vertically before beginning to curve.

stinkwood

A South African wood resembling walnut with an unpleasant odor when freshly cut, commonly used during the 17th and 18th centuries by local craftsmen employed by the Dutch East India Company to make furniture.

stipple engraving

A 16th-century engraving technique creating various tones through a pattern of dots instead of lines. The process was popularized in the 18th century for reproducing portrait drawings of famous people. See also *crayon engraving, intaglio,* and *intaglio engraving.*

stippling

The process of drawing, painting, or engraving using small dots to create solidity and shading.

stippone (STEE poh nay)

Large Italian Baroque cabinet with numerous drawers and compartments, sumptuously decorated with materials such as gilt bronze, ebony, and pietra dura. See also *pietra dura.*

stitched up

A 17th-century French upholstery technique comprised of pulling the seat upholstery over the rails and securing it underneath them. Also called a stuffover seat.

stoa (STOH u)

In Greek architecture, a covered walkway or portico lining the side of a building, generally with a row of columns on the outside edge and the wall of the building on the other. See also *colonnade.*

stoep (STOHP)

Dutch for a raised covered porch, commonly found at the entry of rural domestic architecture.

stoneware

A strong, opaque ceramic ware composed of clay and fusible stone, which gives it a nonporous quality, first produced by the Chinese in 500 B.C. and developed in the Western world around 100 to 1200 C.E.

stool

A seat with no arms and back, supported by legs or a central pedestal.

stopped channel fluting

Fluting with straight or rounded ends, commonly seen in classical architecture and 18th-century cabinet and furniture friezes.

straddle chair

A chair designed to be straddled when used. See also *cockfight chair, voyelle,* and *voyeuse.*

straddle chair

straight bracket foot

A furniture foot composed of two straight-sided brackets joined to form a mitered corner, especially found on 18th-century case pieces designed by George Hepplewhite and Thomas Sheraton.

straight leg

A quadrangular furniture leg with straight sides. See also *marlborough leg.* See *illustration in the Legs Appendix.*

strap hinge

A surface-mounted hinge with long leaves or flaps on each side.

strapwork

A popular decorative motif of the 16th and early 17th centuries, composed of flat, carved intertwining bands that resemble leather straps, often used in ceilings, panels, screens, and furniture. See *illustration in the Motifs/Ornaments Appendix.*

stretcher

A horizontal brace extending between the legs of a table or chair that provides additional support.

stretcher bond

A brick bond with only the stretchers showing.

strie (STREE u)

A fabric with an uneven striped effect created by warp yarns of varying tones. Also, a striped texture in faux painting.

string course

A projecting horizontal course of brick, stone, or other masonry unit, often used to separate building stories.

stringing

A narrow, contrasting band of inlay, commonly used to outline drawers, tabletops, legs, and other furniture parts.

strings

The side of a step, either open or closed, generally supporting the riser and tread.

strip window

A series of windows creating a horizontal band across a building façade. See also *ranch window*.

Stuart Style

The 17th-century English style associated with the reign of the house of Stuart, including the stylistic movements of Jacobean, Carolean, Restoration, and William and Mary, popularized in the work of Inigo Jones and Sir Christopher Wren. See *Inigo Jones, 1573–1652, and Sir Christopher Wren, 1632–1723, in the Architects, Artists, and Designers Appendix.*

stube (SHTOO be)

German for a room, parlor, or study. Commonly an all-purpose living room within a Pennsylvania German house, generally heated by a stove.

stucco

An exterior and interior wall finish, usually composed of portland cement, lime, sand, and water. The material is applied wet in a variety of smooth and textured finishes.

stuck molding

A molding that sits flush with the surface it adorns, instead of being applied on top. See also *planted molding*.

stud

A vertical framing member of a wall, generally a 2" × 4" of wood or metal, employed to support joists and receive laths or sheet material to finish a wall. Also, a decorative nailhead, often made of copper or brass, used to secure upholstery or ornament the face of cabinets, doors, etc. The nailheads originated as a functional device in medieval Spain, Portugal, and Italy. They were also popular in 17th-century England and France.

student lamp

A 19th-century oil lamp, usually of brass, designed with an oil reservoir that sits higher than the burner, a tole shade that partially covers its glass chimney, and often a ring on top that allowed portability.

studio apartment

A compact apartment, usually containing one main living space, a small kitchen, and a bathroom.

studio couch

A couch that contains a sliding cot beneath it, enabling the unit to convert into a pair of twin beds when cushions are removed.

Studio 65 capitello chair

A whimsical chair of polyurethane foam designed to look like an Ionic column capital, created in 1971 by Studio 65, a design studio founded by Piero Gaatti, Cesare Paolini, and Franco Teodoro in 1965.

Studio 65 capitello chair

studiolo (STOO dee oh loh)

A study found in wealthy Italian Renaissance homes.

study

In art, a practice drawing or painting, often part of a larger composition. In interior design, a room dedicated to scholarly work, also called a library.

stuffover seat

See *stitched up.*

stump

See *buttwood veneer.*

stump bed

A bed without tall posts that were originally designed to carry a cornice or tester.

stump foot

The foot of a furniture leg that is generally square and continues to the floor without any noticeable change in shape.

stumpwork or stump embroidery

A 17th-century embroidery style created on a ground padded with wool or horse hair, which produced designs in relief.

stupa (STOO pu)

A domed-shaped structure made to house Buddhist relics, symbolizing the primeval mound.

stylized

To reduce an element to its basic essence or restrict it to a particular style.

stylobate

In classical Greek architecture, a continuous base, plinth, or pedestal on which a row of columns rest, the upper part of a stereobate. Also, the top step of a crepidoma. See also *stereobate* and *podium.*

su gui (SU GWAY)

An enclosed Chinese bookcase with a wide base.

subfloor

A base floor constructed of a rough material, typically plywood, upon which a finished floor is laid.

subsellium (sub SEL ee um)

A little-known term for a misericord. See also *misericord.*

sudare (SOO dah re)

Japanese for screens or shades constructed of thin horizontal slats of wood or bamboo that can be easily rolled up or folded for storing. Also called misu.

suffah (SUF fu)

An Arabic platform used as a seat, out of which the modern term sofa originates.

sugar pine (white pine)

A soft, close-grained wood indigenous to California and southern Oregon with a creamy white to pale brown with faint pink tinted color, commonly used to make lumber, doors, windows, moldings, and piano keys.

sugi finish (SOO gee FIN ish)

A Japanese finishing technique for woodwork.

Sui Dynasty (SWAY DIYN us tee)

An Imperial Chinese dynasty from 581 to 618 C.E. known for the reunification of the north and south and as the "Golden Age" of Chinese art. The period is preceded by the Tang Dynasty.

suite

In furniture, a matched set of items designed to be used together.

summer beam

In English and Early American timber frame construction, the main ceiling support beam, often with one end resting on an exterior wall and the other on a central chimney.

summer bed

Two single beds placed side by side under a shared canopy.

sunburst

A decorative motif comprised of a central disk and radiating rays, commonly seen in the steep gable ends of Victorian architecture, decorative arts, jewelry, etc.

Sung Dynasty (SUNG DIYN us tee)

The imperial dynasty of China from 960 to 1279 C.E., known for art, literature, and philosophy.

sunk panel

A panel that is sunken below the surrounding surface. See also *panel*.

sunk top

A tabletop with the main surface sunken below a surrounding rim or edge. See also *piecrust table*.

supergraphics

Large-scale graphics, usually executed in vibrant colors and bold geometric forms, placed on walls, ceiling, and floors to give the appearance of expanded or altered space. Commonly seen in the 1960s and 1970s.

superimposed order

In architecture, the stacking of orders, one over the other, in several stories of a structure. The Doric is generally used on the first story, Ionic on the second, and Corinthian on the third; commonly seen in Ancient Greece and Rome and during the Renaissance.

supermullions

In Gothic architecture, the vertical bars or bands of stone found above the starting point of foliation within a tracery window.

supporting column

In furniture, a column supporting an overhanging frieze drawer on the front of a cabinet or chest, common during the Empire, Regency, and Biedermeier Styles.

surbase molding

Molding located above a base, such as on a piece of furniture where it is often carved, inlaid, or otherwise decorated.

Surrealism

A 20th-century avant-garde art movement that sought to free the unconscious mind from the exercise of reason, aesthetics, and moral preoccupation. Leading proponents of the style include Salvador Dali, Paul Klee, and Pablo Picasso.

suspended fixture

A lighting fixture that hangs from a ceiling.

Sussex chair

A provincial chair with a rush seat, named after the area in which it was originally made, popular during the English Arts and Crafts Era.

Sussex chair

sustainable design

A design philosophy that strives to maintain a balance between nature and the built environment. Also called environmental design, environmentally sustainable design, and environmentally conscious design.

suzani (SOOZ ah nee)

From the Persian word for needle. A decorative silk embroidered wall hanging or fabric covering from Uzbekistan, generally on a cotton or silk ground. Also known as suizane.

swag

An ornamental window treatment of fabric that is draped in a curved fashion. Also, a carved or painted festoon or garland of leaves, flowers, or fruit, often adorned with ribbons. See also *catenary, festoon,* and *garland*.

swag light

A suspended light fixture that avoids installation of electrical boxes within the ceiling. The fixture is suspended from a hook by a chain that is carried to the nearest wall, allowing the electric cord to run down the wall to an outlet where it is plugged in.

swan bed

A French Empire bed with carved swans flanking the headboard and carved cornucopia-like legs on the front or footboard; originally created by Pierre-Antoine Bellangé, a French cabinetmaker, for Joséphine Bonaparte.

Swan chair

See *Arne Jacobsen Swan chair*. See *Arne Jacobsen, 1902–1971, in the Architects, Artists, and Designers Appendix*.

swan neck

A general term used for moldings or handrails with an ogee curve that is shaped like a swan's neck. See also *ogee*.

swan neck pediment

A broken pediment with two opposing S curves with scrolled upper ends forming the raking lines, usually featuring a small central pedestal, sometimes topped with a vase, pineapple, or finial at its center. See *illustration in the Pediments Appendix*.

Swansea (SWAHN zee)

A 19th-century Welsh manufacturer of Staffordshire-type pottery. See also *Staffordshire*.

swastika (SWAHS ti ku)

An ancient cross form that dates back to the Bronze Age with four arms of equal length terminated by right angles that face in the same direction.

Swatow ware (SWAH tow WAYR)

Chinese export porcelain of the late Ming Dynasty, named for the port of Swatow from where it shipped.

Swedish Modern Style

A Swedish style of furniture featuring simple, clean lines and light woods devoid of carved, applied, or painted decoration. See also *Scandinavian Modern*.

sweep front

A furniture front with a slight bow or curve.

swell front

A furniture front with a segmental or bow front. Also called a kettle front. See also *bow front*.

swing glass

See *cheval glass* or *mirror*.

swing-leg table

A table constructed with a single leg attached to a hinged rail that swings out at a right angle to support a raised leaf. See also *flap table, eight-legged table, gate-leg table, thousand-leg table*, and *tuckaway table*.

swirl

An irregular wood grain effect with a spiral or twisted growth pattern, usually developing in a knot, wart, or tumor of a tree trunk or branch. See also *burl*.

Swiss fabric

A very fine, sheer cotton fabric first made in Switzerland. It may be plain, embroidered, or decorated with dots, which is called dotted Swiss.

swivel

A mechanism used below the seat of a chair, the top of a table, or other surface, that allows the face to rotate in an arc up to 360.°

Swivel chair

See *Frank L. Wright Swivel chair*. See *Frank L. Wright, 1867–1959, in the Architects, Artists, and Designers Appendix*.

sycamore

A heavy wood with a white to light brown color, native to North America, predominantly used for furniture, interior finish work, and butcher blocks.

symbol

In design, a graphic used to represent an organization, person, group, idea, virtue, etc.; generally seen as a carved, painted, or appliqued decoration.

symmetrical balance

A type of formal balance involving mirror images on either side of a central point or line.

symmetrical knot

One of two basic knots used to weave Islamic rugs.

ta (TAH)

A Chinese term for a platform designed for sitting or a daybed.

tabako-bon (TAH bah koh-bahn)

A Japanese term for tobacco box.

tabaret (Tab a ray)

A sturdy, satin-striped silk upholstery fabric.

tabby

A primitive type of concrete consisting of lime mortar, sand, water, and ground or loose shells, used by the Spanish in Colonial America. Commonly seen in Florida. Also, a fabric with a watered silk or moiré effect. Also used for an 18th-century English wallpaper with the same ground effect.

tabernacle frame

An early 18th-century term defined by Robert Adam in his *Works of Architecture* for the framing trim of a door, window, niche, or chimney with columns or pilasters and a pediment at the top.

tabernacle mirror

See *constitution mirror*.

tabernae (Tab ur nay)

Small shops located along the front of a Roman domus.

taberray

See *tabaret*.

tabernacle frame

tablas (TAH blahs)

A Spanish term for planks or boards.

table

A modern-day term for a flat horizontal surface placed on top of legs, trestles, or a pedestal base whose size and shape is determined by its use. In the 14th century, the same word was used in conjunction with religious carvings and paintings in churches; then again in the 16th century to designate an index, pocketbook, or tablet.

table à coiffer (TAY bul AH KWE fay)

A dressing table first introduced in the Louis XV period that had a center panel with a mirror and a single drawer below and two deep spaces on either side.

table à déjeuner (TAY bul AH DAY je nay)

The French term for a small table used for serving small meals or cocktails. It is often portable and typically has a gallery rail around the rim of the top.

table à coiffer

table à écran (TAY bul AH Ay krahn)

French for a table with a sliding screen.

table à écrire (TAY bul AH Ay kreer)

French term for a small desk with a single drawer. Typically the writing surface is covered with leather.

table à gradin (TAY bul AH GRAH dahn)

French for an 18th-century tiered desk composed of a flat writing surface and a tier of compartments or boxes.

table à jeu (TAY bul AH jheu)

French term for a card or game table.

table à gradin

table à l'Anglaise (TAY bul AH LAHN glayz)

Literally in the English manner or style, French for a dining room extension table popular during the Louis XVI period.

table à l'architecte (TAY bul AH LAR shee tekt)

French for a table with a hinged top. See also *architect's table*.

table à jeu

275

table à l'Italienna (TAY bul LEE tah lee-en ah)
A large rectangular French Renaissance table with wood or marble top and a base composed of massive carved figural ends, joined by a complex stretcher.

table à l'Italienna

table à milieu (TAY bul AH MIL yu)
From old French meaning middle or midst, a center table.

table à ouvrage (TAY bul AH OOV rahj)
French for worktable. See also *bag table* and *pouch table.*

table à rognon (TAY bul AH ROHN yohn)
Also known as a rognon table, this kidney-shaped table was popular in the Louis XV period and generally composed with a galleried top and a shelf beneath. See also *haricot, kidney desk,* and *kidney table.*

table chair
From the 16th and 17th centuries, an armchair that converts into a table. The back of the chair is a hinged table-top that when tilted forward over the arms forms a table. See also *chair table.*

table à rognon

table de chevet (TAY bul DE SHE vay)
A French term for a bedside or night table, most likely originating in the Louis XV period to hold a chamber pot, pitcher, and wash basin. Also called a table de nuit. See also *chevet.*

table de dame (TAY bul DE DAHM)
A small 18th-century lady's dressing or powder table, especially popular during the Louis XV period. See also *poudreuse* and *tricoteuse.*

table de nuit (TAY bul DE NOO ee)
French for a night or bedside table designed to hold a chamber pot, pitcher, and washbasin. Also called a table de chevet.

table dormant
A medieval English term for a stationary table that replaced the moveable boards on trestles previously used for meals.

table jardinière (TAY bul JAR dee nar)
French for a table with a well or pierced top designed to hold a plant container.

table rug
A rug used to drape a table.

tableaux (TA bloh)
From the French diminutive table or picture, tableaux are graphic representations such as pictures, paintings, or scenes.

tableaux tentures (TA bloh THAN tyur)
A set of wallpaper panels designed to compose a large panoramic scene or coordinated series when hung together.

tablero (TA blur oh)
Part of the Mesoamerican architectural style of stepped pyramids consisting of a framed stone panel and platform structure on top of an inward sloping surface.

tablet chair
A chair with a broad flat arm that serves a writing surface. First seen in the 18th century on Windsor chairs and today in many school-rooms. See also *comb-back writing chair, corner chair, roundabout chair, smoker's chair,* and *writing chair.*

tablinum (te BLIY num)
In an ancient Roman house, a room opposite the entrance, off of the atrium, serving as an office and for storing genealogy and other important records.

tabonuco (Ta boh noo ho)
A beautifully grained, light-colored West Indian hardwood, commonly used in furniture making.

tabouret (Ta boo ret)

A low upholstered stool in the shape of a drum. Also known as a taboret.

Tabriz Rugs (tah BREEZ RUGZ)

A Persian carpet from the city of Tabriz with a dense wool pile, often in tones of red and blue with contrasting cream, with a central medallion design. Occasionally incorporating stylized hunters, animals, flowers, or birds.

tabularium (TAb yoo lar ee-um)

In ancient Rome, a place within the Forum where official records were housed, and often the offices of many city officials.

taenia (TEE nee-ah)

In Greek architecture, a flat horizontal band in the Doric order that separates the frieze from the architrave.

taffeta

A fine lustrous silk or similar synthetic fabric with a crisp texture and warp and weft threads of equal size, resulting in a fabric that is smooth on both sides.

taffeta, antique

A stiff, plain-woven fabric designed to simulate 18th-century taffeta. One side looks like shantung and the other satin.

taffeta, faille (TA fe tah, FIY ul)

A taffeta with a pronounced crosswise rib weave.

taffeta, moire (TA fe tah, MOI-ur)

Silk or rayon taffeta with a wavy or watered appearance.

taffeta, paper

A lightweight taffeta treated to create a crisp, paper-like finish.

taffeta, tissue

A very lightweight taffeta with a fine cross-rib that is almost transparent.

taille douce (TIY DOOS)

The French term for a line engraving.

tailpiece

An extension on the back of certain Windsor chairs that supports the spindle braces.

tainoya (TAY noi-ah)

Literally translated as opposed halls. The subsidiary living quarters of Japanese houses in the Heian period (794–1185).

Talavera de la Reina (TAH lah var ah DE LAH RAY nah)

A city in the western part of the province of Toledo, Spain, famous for pottery factories and majolica earthenware tiles, especially the blue and yellow designs of the Renaissance, commonly known as talavera tiles.

Taliesin

The summer home of American architect Frank Lloyd Wright in Spring Green, Wisconsin, with low slung lines that appear to be growing out of the surrounding terrain. It was here that Wright designed Fallingwater, the Guggenheim, the Johnson Wax headquarters, and the first home of Herbert and Katherine Jacobs. See *Frank Lloyd Wright, 1867–1959, in the Architects, Artists, and Designers Appendix.*

tallboy

An English 18th-century chest composed of one chest of drawers sitting on top of another somewhat wider chest of drawers; in America, it is called a highboy. See also *chest-on-chest* and *highboy.*

tall case clock

See *grandfather clock.*

talon and ball foot

A furniture foot designed to resemble a bird's foot with talons grasping a ball. See also *claw and ball foot.*

talud (ta LOOD)

The inward-sloping surface above a tablero on each layer of a stepped pyramid in pre-Columbian Mesoamerican architecture.

tamagaki (TAH mah gah kee)

A fence that surrounds a sacred area such as a shrine or imperial palace in Japan.

tambour (TAM bur)
French term for a drum. In furniture, a rolling top constructed of narrow strips of wood glued to a canvas back, commonly seen on desks.

tambour curtain (TAM bor KUR ten)
A sheer cotton panel, generally with an embroidered border or allover pattern.

tambour embroidery (TAM bor im BROI du ree)
A continuously worked chain stitch introduced to the Western world by France, but originally from China. The technique was popular during the late 18th and 19th centuries and commonly used on curtain panels of cotton, muslin, etc.

Tamo (Ta moh)
A uniquely figured ash wood with a peanut-shaped grain native to Manchuria, but transplanted centuries ago to Japan where it was reserved for centuries for items made for Japanese royalty or shoguns. Also known as damo, shioji, yachidama, and Japanese ash.

tana (TAH nah)
A generic term for types of shelving designed for Japanese tea ceremonies. There are three basic categories of tana: shitsukedana or built-in shelving, tsuridana or suspended shelving, and oikidana or portable shelving.

tang hua an (TAYNG HOO-ah AHN)
A long Japanese table used underneath a painting, frequently with another table in front of it

tanguile (THAN gee)
A dark reddish-brown Philippine hardwood that resembles mahogany. Sometimes called Philippine mahogany.

T'ang Dynasty
Ancient Chinese dynasty of 618–907 C.E. generally regarded, when combined with the preceding Sui Dynasty, as the golden age of China. Known for the development of literature, pottery, sculpture, music, dance, art, and the invention of woodblock printing.

tang xiang (TAYNG SHUNG)
A long Chinese chest designed to hold fur-lined garments flat without folding.

tansu (THAN soo)
A general term for a Japanese chest. Offered in a wide variety since ancient times, but developing into more specialized forms in the Edo period. See also *katana-dansu.*

tapa cloth (TAH pah KLAWTH)
A cloth from the Pacific Islands constructed from the bark of trees, particularly the mulberry, and typically block printed with bright native patterns produced from natural animal and vegetable dyes.

tapered leg
A rectangular furniture leg that gradually narrows as it approaches the foot. Also called a quadrangular tapered leg.

tapestry
From the French term tappisser, meaning to line. A heavy hand-woven fabric with rich multicolored scenes or designs woven into the ribbed surface, originally used to line the walls of drafty medieval castles. Now produced by machine with a Jacquard attachment.

tapestry carpet
A carpet with a design produced by printing onto the warp threads before weaving.

tapestry knot
A general term for a knot of various forms such as a Persian, Turkish, or Spanish knot, used in the weaving tapestries.

tapet
A Renaissance term for a carpet, which was used as a table covering instead of a floor covering.

tapisseries (TAH pee su ree)
French term for tapestries.

taquillon (TA kee-on)
A Spanish chest of drawers used to support a vargueno. See also *vargueno.*

taquillon

tarsia

See *intarsia*.

taruki (TAH roo kee)

The rafters of traditional wood-framed Japanese architecture such as pagodas.

task seating

A work or desk chair designed to accommodate a user and increase productivity.

tassel

Threads or cords bound at one end to form a pendant used to ornament window treatments, pillows, etc.

tatami (tah TAH mee)

A woven straw mat of uniform size, three by six feet, used as flooring in traditional Japanese houses.

tateana (TAH tee-ah nah)

A New Stone Age (10,000 B.C.E.) Japanese pit dwelling approximately 2 feet deep and 15 feet in diameter covered with thatch.

taupe

French term for mole or moleskin. A dark, brown-grey hue, sometimes incorporating a tint of purple.

tavern table

A 17th- and 18th-century table used for dining within a tavern, characterized by simple construction and a short rectangular shape, often with legs connected by a box stretcher. See also *box stretcher*.

tavern table

tazar (TAH zar)

The main reception area of an Islamic residence, located within a winter or summer hall. It is the most elaborately decorated area within the house and is often distinguished by an archway and a couple of steps.

tazza (THAT sah)

Italian for a footed ornamental cup or salver with a large shallow bowl, often with handles. See also *salver*.

T-cushion

An upholstered chair or sofa cushion in the form of a "T" designed with a wider front than back in order to accommodate the arms, which do not extend to the seat front.

tea caddy

An elegant container for tea, commonly made of wood, china, pottery, pewter, or silver, especially popular during the 18th-century English Georgian period. Also known as tea canisters. See also *teapoy*.

tea kettle stand

A base designed to hold a tea kettle. During the 18th-century Chippendale Style, the stand took the form of a small pedestal table with a tripod base and a gallery rimming the tabletop.

tea table

A small 18th-century table, generally rectangular or circular in form, designed for serving tea.

tea tray

A tray used for serving tea, often round or oval in shape and with handles and a gallery rail.

tea trolley

A small serving cart with wheels used to serve tea and other light refreshments. Also called a tea wagon.

tea trolley

tea wagon

See *tea trolley*.

teak

A hardwood indigenous to Burma and other tropical areas with a light brown color, often streaked with black, and a durable naturally oily finish that is water resistant.

279

teapoy

A large tea chest with a hinged top that opens to reveal tea caddies; it generally has a pedestal base, but is sometimes seen with four legs. Also, the Hindustani term for a tripod.

teardrop brasses

Furniture pulls with a teardrop shape commonly seen during the English William and Mary period.

tejas (TAY hahs)

Spanish for curved clay roof tiles.

telamon (Te le mahn)

A male figure used as a column support in ancient Greece, similar to a caryatid. See also *caryatid*.

temenos (Te me nohs)

In ancient Egypt, the sacred space enclosed by a wall surrounding a temple. In Greece, the term was extended to cover the sacred ground bordering a temple or other holy site since many rituals were performed at an outside alter, often in front of the church.

tempera (TEM pu rah)

A painting medium composed of powdered pigment mixed with a water-soluble binder, frequently egg yolks, commonly used during the 16th century. Also known as egg tempera.

template

A pattern created of wood, metal, plastic, etc., used to guide work. A variant is templet.

temple front

An exterior façade that mimics the column supports, entablature, and pediment of a classical temple.

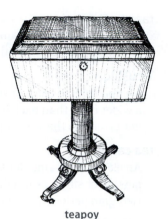

teapoy

telamon

templum

An area set apart for religious purposes in ancient Rome, generally enclosed by a wall and entered through a monumental gateway. The word temple is later derived from this Latin term.

tenia

In classical architecture, the flat, narrow band crowning a Doric architrave, directly below the frieze.

tenjo (TEN joh)

Japanese for ceiling. A bamboo ceiling would be a sunoko tenjo.

tenon

In carpentry, a projecting tongue of wood shaped to fit into an opening or mortise in another piece of wood, hence forming a mortise and tenon joint. See also *mortise and tenon joint*. See *illustration in the Joints Appendix*.

tenshu (TEN shoo)

The main defensive keep or tower of a Japanese castle. Also called a donjon or tenshukaku.

tensile strength

The maximum force a material can stand before breaking.

tent bed

A four-poster bed with an arched tester or canopy resembling a military campaign tent. Although originating in Europe, the tent bed reached the height of popularity during the late 18th and early 19th centuries in America. Also called a field bed.

tent-pole column

An Egyptian column with an unadorned capital in the form of an inverted bell.

tenture

General French term for wall hangings, especially wallpaper.

tepidarium (tep ee DAR ee-um)

The warm room of an ancient Roman bath heated by a radiant system under the floor.

term

A quadrangular tapered support topped by the bust of a human, animal, or mythological creature, popular during the Renaissance and French Rococo periods. Also known as a terminal figure. See also *herma*.

terminal figure

See *term*.

tern foot

A furniture foot formed of three scrolls.

terne

An alloy historically composed of lead and tin, used to plate steel to limit corrosion.

terra-cotta

Italian term for baked earth. Glazed or unglazed ceramics with a red body, commonly used to make building materials and decorative arts.

terra sigillata (TER ah SIJ yoo lah tah)

In ceramics, ancient Roman pottery of fine red clay with glossy slip decorations.

terrace

(1) A level area of earth with vertical or sloping sides. (2) In architecture a porch or balcony. (3) Also, a form of housing, original to late 17th-century England, produced by a row of identical houses sharing side walls. Alternately known as a row house.

terrazzo

A flooring material composed of marble or granite chips in a concrete mixture.

terre-cuite

French for terra-cotta.

tertiary colors

A color produced by combining a primary and secondary color.

tessellated (TES u lay ted)

A surface, such as a wall or floor, decorated with mosaic tesserae. See also *tesserae*.

tesserae (plural for tessera) (Te se ray)

Small, square mosaic tiles commonly made of glass, marble, bone, concrete, and other materials.

tester (TES ter)

The canopy of a four poster bed, often seen in full, half, or three-quarter lengths. The term is derived from the French term testiere meaning headpiece. See also *angel bed* and *canopy*.

testudo (tes TOO doh)

Latin for tortoise. A formation used by soldiers during battle, created by holding shields over their head so that they overlapped. Also, a large ancient Roman screen on wheels with an arched roof designed to protect troops below.

tête de nègre (TET DE NEG re)

Literally translated from French as the head of a black man. Also, a term no longer acceptable for a dark blackish-brown hue.

tête-à-tête

An S-shaped 19th-century double-backed chair with seats facing in opposite directions. Also called a courting chair. See also *canapé* and *marquise chair*.

tête-à-tête

têtes d'anges (TET DAHNJ)

French for heads of angels. Angel heads, often with wings, were a popular motif during the Renaissance and late 18th-century France and England. See also *cherub head*.

têtes d'anges

281

tetraconch
Greek for four shells. Originally a church or other religious building with a Greek cross plan containing an apse in each direction.

tetrapylon
Greek for four gates. An ancient Roman monumental gateway opening to all four sides.

tetrastyle
A style of portico with four columns across the front, originally from classical times.

texture
Element of design describing the tactile quality and appearance of a material's surface.

thakos (THAY kohs)
Greek for seat or chair, generally a boxlike unit.

thalamos (THA le mus)
The nuptial chamber of the oecus of an ancient Greek home. See also *oecus*.

thatch
Dry vegetation such as straw, reeds, rush, etc., used as a roof covering.

therm foot
A furniture foot with a rectangular tapered base. See also *spade foot*.

therm leg
A quadrangular tapered leg popular among 18th-century English designers such as George Hepplewhite and Thomas Sheraton.

thermae (THUR mee)
Large public baths of ancient Rome designed with various rooms for bathing such as a caldarium (hot bath), tepidarium (warm bath), and frigidarium (cold bath).

thermae window (THUR mee WIN doh)
See *Diocletian window*.

thimble foot
A cylindrical tapering foot commonly used on the tables and chairs of George Hepplewhite and Thomas Sheraton. See also *spade foot*. See *illustration in the Feet Appendix*.

third style painting
The third of four periods distinguished in wall murals of ancient Rome, employed between 20 B.C.E. and 50 C.E. and characterized by more figurative, colorful, and ornate decoration. Also known as the Ornate Style. See also *Ornate Style*.

thirteen-state tracery
Furniture fretwork of the late 18th century made of thirteen elements and commonly used to decorate secrétaire and bookcase doors.

tholos (THAHL ohs)
A small circular building lined with columns, sometimes in place of the walls.

Thonet (TOH nit)
Austrian furniture company known for bentwood furniture, established in 1849 by Michael Thonet. See *Michael Thonet, 1796–1871, in the Architects, Artists, and Designers Appendix*.

thousand-leg table
See *gate-leg table*.

three-back Winsor chair
See *comb-back Windsor chair*.

three-color ware
Chinese pottery of the Tang Dynasty known for its distinctive blue, green, and yellow glazes.

three-ply carpet
An early 19th-century flat woven carpet composed of three interwoven layers. Also called imperial carpet.

threshold
A strip or molding attached to the floor beneath a door.

throne chair

A solid-sided chair of stone that was used for official functions, generally with a rounded or rectangular back and a solid base displaying various carved designs such as a sphinx, griffin, or winged chimera. See also *Roman throne chair.*

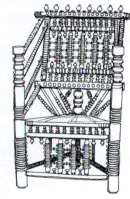

throne chair

thronos (THROH nohs)

An ancient Greek chair, often with arms, designed for a person of honor.

through cutting

The cutting of logs in parallel slices.

throw

A small blanket or coverlet.

throw pillow

A decorative pillow often used on a sofa, chair, or bed.

thrown chair

A common 17th-century armchair composed of turned frame members, spindles, stretchers, etc., often with only three legs and a triangular seat.

thrown chair

thrust

In architecture, the lateral force exerted from an arch or vault that is countered by support such as the buttress or flying buttress. See also *buttress* and *flying buttress.*

Thru-vu vertical blinds

The trademark name for a vertical strip window blind originally designed by George Nelson and Henry Wright in the 1960s. See *George Nelson, 1908–1986, in the Architects, Artists, and Designers Appendix.*

thumb molding

See *gadroon.*

thuya (THWEE yah)

A hard, reddish-brown wood indigenous to North Africa, often exhibiting a bird's eye figure, commonly used by the ancient Greeks and Chinese, and popular in 18th-century English cabinetwork as a veneer.

thyron (THIY rahn)

The ancient Greek term for a door.

tiama (TEE-ah mah)

See *sapeli.*

ticking

A twill or satin weave fabric that is woven of cotton and typically striped.

tidy

See *antimacassar* and *Macassar.*

tie beam

The horizontal beam connecting the rafters of a triangular truss, used to counter the outward thrust.

tieback

A device such as a cord or loop of fabric used to hold draperies or curtains at a window's side.

tie-dyeing

A method of resist dyeing textiles by gathering areas of the fabric to prevent dye penetration.

tielimu (TEEL ee moo)

A wood indigenous to China with an open grain, coarse texture, and greyish-black color. Tielimu is one of the oldest and firmest of hardwoods in China, literally translating as "strength of iron wood" and noted as a desirable furniture wood during the late Ming Dynasty.

tierceron rib (TEER se run RIB)

A rib that rises from a supporting pier to the primary ridge rib in a Gothic vault system.

tier curtain

A short curtain hung over the bottom half of a window, commonly used in kitchens and often complimented with a valence or other top treatment. Also called a café curtain.

tie rod or tie bar

In architecture, a metal rod used to provide additional tensile support against the outward thrust of an arch, vault, etc.

tierra amarillo (tee AYR ah ah mah REE yoh)

Literally translated from Spanish as yellow earth. A clay with a slight yellow color found along the Chama River Valley in Northern New Mexico and commonly used by Native Americans.

tierra blanca (tee AYR ah BLAHN kah)

Spanish for white earth. A light grey-colored clay with a composition of lime and reflective mica chips found in a cave near Taos, New Mexico.

tier table

A small round pedestal table with several shelves set one over the other, gradually getting larger in size as they move downward.

Tiffany lamp

Art Nouveau lamps produced by Tiffany & Co. with various glass shades, particularly known for the intricate leaded stained glass variety with natural designs depicting dragonflies, flowers, spiders, peacock feathers, etc. See *Louis Comfort Tiffany, 1848–1933, in the Architects, Artists, and Designers Appendix.*

tigerwood

A West African wood with a grayish to golden brown color, often accentuated with black streaks and ribbon striping and commonly used for cabinetwork and paneling. Also known as African walnut and Nigerian golden walnut.

ti hong (TEE HONG)

A type of Chinese cinnabar (red) lacquer that uses multiple layers of different colored lacquer underneath the surface, which when carved reveals a multicolored design. Also known as Peking lacquer.

t'iao (TEE-ow)

In Chinese architecture, the tiers of bracket sets supporting the roof.

tile

A thin slab of baked clay, stone, metal, or glass used as a roof, floor, or wall covering.

till

A small compartment or drawer, often hidden and accessed by secret springs or locks and generally found in chests, designed to hold money, jewelry, or important documents.

tilt-top table

A pedestal table with a hinged top that could be positioned vertically when not in use, popular in 18th-century England and America. When horizontal, the top was held in place by a spring catch. Also called a tip-top table or snap table.

tilt-top table

tin glaze

In ceramics, a lead and tin oxide glaze with a glossy, white, opaque finish.

tint

In color theory, a hue with white added to it. The opposite of a shade. See also *shade.*

tipi (TEE pee)

A Plains Indian tent structure with a conical shape traditionally made from wooden poles and animal skins. Also seen as tepee or teepee.

tip-up table

A pedestal table with two hinged leaves that hang from a central spine.

tirette (TEER et)

French for a table extension or slide that increases a table top's usable surface.

toddy table

A small 18th-century English Georgian table designed to hold drinks.

toile (TWAHL)

French term for a linen cloth or canvas. Also, an abbreviated version of toile de Jouy, a pastoral themed French fabric. See also *toile de Jouy*.

toile de Jouy (TWAHL DE ZHOI)

A white or cream cotton, linen, or silk fabric printed with a monochromatic pastoral theme in red, green, blue, black, or purple. Originally produced at Jouy, France, by Philippe Oberkampf in the mid 18th century. See *Christophe-Philippe Oberkampf, 1738–1815, in the Architects, Artists, and Designers Appendix*.

toiles d'indy (TWAHL DAHN dee)

Printed cotton and linen fabric with floral and traditional Indian motifs imported into France, commonly from India and Persia, during the late 17th century. See also *indienne fabrics*.

toiles imprintés

French for printed cloths.

toiles peintes (TWAAL PAANT)

French for painted cloth.

toilet mirror

A swing frame mirror mounted on a stand fitted with dressing table compartments, popular on chests and table tops during the 18th and early 20th centuries.

toilet mirror

tokonoma (TOH koh noh mah)

An alcove in traditional-style reception rooms of Japanese houses used to display flowers, scrolls, etc. Also called a toko.

tole (TOHL)

French for sheet metal. Painted metal or tin decorative objects, such as trays, boxes, etc., originally produced in 18th century.

tole shade (TOHL SHAYD)

A decoratively painted metal lampshade, often associated with early American design.

tonal value

The degree of lightness or darkness associated with a color.

tondo

A Renaissance term for a circular picture, painting, or other form of art used since classical Greece, but revived in the 15th century.

tongue and groove joint

A joint used to lay objects edge to edge, created by cutting a channel in the side of one object and a long narrow projection on the side of another. Used mainly with wood, the joint is commonly seen on flooring, paneling, etc. See *illustration in the Joints Appendix*.

top color

The color or colors applied over the ground of printed or screened fabrics, paper, etc., to create a design.

top rail

See *crest rail*.

tope (TOHP)

A dome-shaped Buddhist shrine or monument. Also called a stupa.

topiary art

The horticultural practice of training and clipping shrubs, trees, and other plants into formal, ornamental, often fanciful shapes. Practiced since ancient Roman times in Europe and revived during the Renaissance. Topiary art has also been practiced in China and Japan, but with a more natural aesthetic.

torch

A flambeau or flame motif that originated in ancient Rome and was repopularized during the Renaissance, Directoire, and Empire periods.

torchère (tor SHAYR)

Originally a floor candlestand created during the Louis XV period in France. Later, used to denote a small table designed to hold a gueridon. Today, the term is used for a floor lamp with a shade directing the light upward.

torchiera (tor chee AY rah)

Italian for floor candlestand.

torii (TOR ee)

Traditional gate composed of two posts topped by a pair of horizontal beams found at the entrance of a Japanese Shinto shrine, serving as a transitional element between sacred and profane zones.

torii

toron (TOR ahn)

Projecting wooden stakes serving as fixed scaffolding in West African Islamic architecture composed of mud brick.

torreon (TOR ee-ahn)

Spanish for a large tower.

torsade (tor SAHD)

French for twist. In design, a twisted ropelike or cable molding. See also *cable molding* and *rope molding*.

torso

The central part of the human body excluding the head and limbs.

torus

A semicircular convex molding original to classical architecture. See also *astragal*. See *illustration in the Moldings Appendix*.

touchstone

A vein-free Belgium black marble frequently used for mantels, chimney pieces, and clocks, popular during the Renaissance and Victorian eras.

tou-kung (TOO-KUNG)

In Chinese architecture, the clusters of brackets that support the roof. Also known as dougong.

toupie (TOO pee)

A top-shaped furniture foot.

towel horse or towel rail

A wooden rack with multiple crossbars intended to hold towels, popular during the mid 18th century in England.

trabeated (TRAY bee-ay tid)

Same as post and lintel construction. See *post and lintel*.

tracery

Ornamental stone mullions commonly found in the stained glass of Gothic architecture.

tracery

tracery pattern

A design mimicking tracery in wood, textiles, and other materials.

trachelion (TRAY kee lee-on)

Literally translated from Greek as "neck." A term used to denote the neck of a Greek Doric column.

tracking lighting

Light fixtures that are moveable along an electrified track mounted on a ceiling, wall, or other surface to provide light where needed.

traditional

A general term used to denote architecture, interiors, furniture, or decorative arts that relate to historic styles as opposed to transitional and contemporary styles.

traforo (trah FOR oh)

Italian term for piercing such as in fretwork and tracery.

transept

In church architecture, the space that crosses the nave at a right angle. See also *apse* and *nave*.

transfer printing

A method of transferring a one-color design from a copperplate to paper and then to pottery, similar to a decal.

transitional

A general term used to denote interiors and furniture that combine traditional and contemporary elements.

transitional Tulbagh chair (TRAN zi shun ul TUL bah CHAYR)

A pared down wooden version of the Tulbagh chair. See also *Tulbagh chair.*

translucent

A semitransparent material that diffuses light entering a space so objects beyond are not seen clearly.

transom

A horizontal crosspiece of wood or stone over a window or door. Also, a window designed to provide ventilation above this crosspiece.

transverse arch

An arch that crosses a vault to the opposite side, dividing the bays.

transverse rib

A main rib delineating a transverse arch within a rib vault.

trapeza (TRA peez ah)

Greek for a table.

trapezophoron (TRAH peez oh for en)

The marble legs or pedestal base of a small round table composed of three monopodiums set back to back. Alternate spellings include trapezophore and trapezophorum. See also *monopodium.*

trapunto

Literally translated from Italian as "to embroider." A quilting technique that outlines designs with stitches, then fills the quilted areas from behind. Also called stuffed technique.

trastero (TRAHS tar oh)

A Spanish cupboard that is freestanding.

travertine

A form of limestone with a light cream, tan, or white color formed by deposits of mineral springs and commonly used as building materials by the Romans and also in modern architecture.

travois (TRAH vwah)

A type of sled composed of an arrangement of poles covered by animal skins; commonly used by North American Indians to carry goods. Generally hauled by horses or dogs.

tray table

A collapsible table composed of a tray mounted on a folding stand. Also, any table designed to hold a tray as a tabletop.

tray table

trayle (TRAY ul)

A decorative motif composed of a continuous leafy vine with grape clusters, popular during the Tudor Style in England.

tray-top table

A small table with a low gallery rimming three or four sides of the tabletop, popular during the 18th century.

tray-top table

tread

In stair construction, the flat horizontal surface of a step.

trecento (TRE chen toh)

Italian term referring to the 14th century, literally translated as "three hundred."

"tree of life" pattern
A common Persian, Indian, and English Renaissance motif depicting a branching tree or vine thought to be a metaphor for how all life on earth is related. See also *horn*.

trefoil (tre FOI)
A three-lobed ornament common in Gothic architecture. See *illustration in the Motifs/Ornaments Appendix*.

trelliage (TREE-ahj)
A 19th-century term for decorative trelliswork or latticework. See also *trelliswork*.

trelliswork
A decorative framework or structure formed from interwoven wood, metal, or bamboo, generally designed as a support for climbing plants. See also *arbor*.

tremido (TRE mee doh)
A Portuguese wave ornament with wavy parallel lines.

trenail (TRE niy)
Literally translated as "tree nails." A rounded, tapered wooden peg commonly used to fasten wood components in covered bridges, fine 18th-century cabinetwork, etc. Also spelled as trenail or trunnel.

trencadis (TRAHN kah dee)
A type of mosaic using broken tile shards, first seen in the work of Antoni Gaudi. Also called pique assiette. See *Antonio Gaudi, 1852–1926, in the Architects, Artists, and Designers Appendix*.

trencher
A wooden plate or platter, commonly used for food during medieval times.

trespoli (TRES poh lee)
A small 18th-century Italian table with a tripod base designed to hold a candelabrum.

trestle
A furniture support composed of a horizontal member with two pairs of sloping legs, originally seen on tables of the Middle Ages. See also *trestle table*.

trestle table
A table supported by two or more trestles and a long horizontal stretcher, popular throughout history, especially in ancient Rome, the Middle Ages, the Renaissance, and Colonial America.

trestle table

triangle seat
Sometimes known as a corner chair or a boffet or buffet chair. See also *boffet chair* and *corner chair*.

triangular pediment
The triangular space formed by the raking cornices of a gable roof and the horizontal cornice above the entablature. Also used as a decorative element over windows, doors, and furniture.

tribunal (TRI byoo nul)
In ancient Roman basilica architecture, the elevated seating area for judges and other advocates of the court, generally located opposite the entrance.

triclinium (triy KLI nee-um)
The formal dining room of an ancient Roman home, generally lined with three couches (lectus) on three walls.

tricoteuse (TREE koh tuuz)
See *poudreuse* and *table de dame*.

trictrac table
French for a backgammon table.

tridarn

A 17th- and 18th-century Welsh piece of furniture with cupboards below and an open, spindle-sided dresser above that was used for display. See also *Dutch dresser* and *Welsh dresser*.

tri-fold mirror

A mirror with a central panel and two hinged mirrored side panels, designed to hang or sit on top of a chest or dresser.

trifid foot (TRIY fid FUUT)

A ribbed, three-toed furniture foot resembling a drake foot, commonly used on 18th-century English and American furniture. See also *drake foot*. See *illustration in the Feet Appendix*.

trifoil

Anglo-Norman name for a trefoil. See *trefoil*.

triforium (triy FOR ee um)

In a Gothic church, a shallow arcaded gallery located above the nave and below the clerestory.

triglyph

In a Doric frieze, a rectangular block with three vertical grooves that fills the space between two metopes.

trim

A general term for added decoration generally around the edges of an object.

tripartite plan

A three-part plan designed in a linear arrangement that moves from public to private, generally composed of an entryway, hypostyle hall, and sanctuary or living quarters, often seen in buildings of Ancient Egypt.

tripartite plan

tripod stand

A three-legged stand.

tripod table

A table supported by a three-legged columnar shaft.

tripos

Metal tripods used to support trays, kraters, and pots in ancient Rome.

tripteral

A classical building with three colonnades surrounding it. See also *colonnade*.

triptych (TRIP tiyk)

A hinged threefold artwork, screen, or mirror often used as an altarpiece.

triquetra (TRI ket rah)

An ornamental design composed of three interlaced vesica piscis or arced lobes.

triumphal arch

A monumental arch built to commemorate a notable campaign victory. See also *Arc de Triumphe*.

trivet

An iron tripod used to support a pot or kettle over a fire. Also, a short-footed metal stand used on a table under a hot dish.

trompe l'oeil (TRAHMP LOI)

French for "fool the eye." A painting technique using extremely realistic depictions that create three-dimensional illusions. Also called illusionism.

troneca (TROH nek ah)

Spanish for arrow loops, vertical slits in a parapet wall from which arrows could be fired at attackers.

trophy

A prize of war marking victories since ancient times. As early as the Baroque era, trophies have generally featured symbols of battle: weapons, horns, banners, spears, shields, or laurel leaves either carved or painted on a panel or a pilaster.

trumeau (tru MOH)

The French term for the decorative treatment of the space between windows and doors, particularly a central post dividing a large doorway in a church. Also, the decorative treatments above windows, doors, and mantles.

trumeau mirror (tru MOH MEER ur)

A tall, framed mirror of the late 18th century with a painted or carved panel above or below the glass yet within the frame. A trumeau usually hung over a mantel and was highly ornate and often gilded.

trumpet leg

A turned conical leg of the late 1600s and early 1700s that resembles an upturned trumpet often terminating with a ball, bun, or Spanish foot; typically seen on Baroque furniture, especially pieces of the English Restoration and William and Mary styles. See *illustration in the Legs Appendix.*

trundle bed or truckle bed

Originally Gothic in design, a child's or servant's bed on rollers that could be rolled under a full-size bed when not in use. See also *hide-a-bed* and *murphy bed.*

truss

A triangular support element providing stability and strength when spanning a space, often used for roofs.

trussing bed

A medieval portable bed that could be taken apart and tied up for traveling.

trussing chest

A small medieval traveling chest or coffer, usually carried in pairs on pack horses.

tsuitate (soo TAH tay)

A small, single-panel screen of paper, wood, or silk used to control drafts, sunlight, or views in traditional Japanese interiors.

tub chair

A late 18th-century easy chair with a low rounded back that continues to form the arms or wings, similar to the barrel chair.

tub chair

tub front

An alternate British term for a blockfront. See *blockfront.*

tub sofa

A fully upholstered French sofa with sweeping curved ends, like an extended tub chair.

tube chair

See *Joe Colombo tube chair.* See *Joe Cesare Colombo, 1930–1971, in the Architects, Artists, and Designers Appendix.*

tubular furniture

Contemporary furniture with a frame of bent tubular steel, especially popular in the first half of the 20th century.

tubular steel

Hollow steel tubing used in the manufacture of 20th-century modern furniture.

tuckaway table

A space-saving table with crossed or scissored legs that drop the top leaves close together or one in which the top tilts to vertical when not in use.

Tudor arch

A flat pointed arch, usually drawn from four centers, popular during the Tudor reigns of Henry VII, Henry VIII, Edward VI, Mary I, and Elizabeth I.

Tudor-Elizabethan period

The Tudor period in which Elizabeth I reigned, often treated separately as the Elizabethan period. It is referred to as the golden age in English history and the height of the English Renaissance.

Tudor rose

Heraldic emblem of the Tudor dynasty and later a decorative motif that consisted of one five-petaled rose superimposed on a larger one.

Tudor Style

A 16th-century English style marked by the reign of the Tudor monarchs, beginning with Henry VII in 1485 until the death of Elizabeth I in 1603. Also a phase of England's Early Renaissance. The architecture of the period is often characterized by decorative half timbers, tall narrow doors and windows, leaded glass, and Tudor arches.

Tudor Style, Great Bed of Ware

tufa

A lightweight, porous rock formed as a deposit from springs or streams; sometimes referred to as travertine.

tuft

In carpet construction, clusters of yarn fibers that are drawn through a medium to produce a surface of raised loops or cut pile.

tufting

An upholstery technique created when buttons placed between springs create a deep indention and excess fabric gathers into pleats beneath the buttons.

Tugendhat chair   (too JEND hat CHAYR)

See *Mies van der Rohe Tugendhat chair.* See *Ludwig Mies van der Rohe, 1886–1969, in the Architects, Artists, and Designers Appendix.*

Tulbagh chair

Tulbagh chair   (TUL bah CHAYR)

A South African chair, based on a Queen Anne chair and Dutch box chair, with a vase-shaped splat, box stretcher, and caned seat.

tulip pedestal chair

See *Eero Saarinen tulip pedestal chair.* See *Eero Saarinen, 1910–1961, in the Architects, Artists, and Designers Appendix.*

tulip pedestal table

See Eero Saarinen tulip pedestal table. See *Eero Saarinen, 1910–1961, in the Architects, Artists, and Designers Appendix.*

tulip wood

A wood indigenous to Brazil with a light yellow color streaked with red and purple, commonly used for ornamental inlay. The small tree is a member of the rosewood family.

tulipiere   (TOO li pee-ar)

A 17th-century vase designed to hold tulips and commonly made of Delftware. See also *Delft.*

tumulus

A mound of earth formed above a grave or graves, often with a domed or vaulted roof.

Tunbridge Ware

An 18th- and 19th-century type of veneer work composed of multiple small rods or dowels of wood arranged in a design. The work was typically used to cover decorative wares, primarily boxes, and was originally made at Tunbridge Wells in England.

tupelo   (TOO pe loh)

A black gumwood of light grey color, commonly used by wood carvers and for interior furniture parts, veneers, and cross banding. Unless properly dried, the wood has a tendency to warp.

Turkey rocker

A liberally tufted, overstuffed chair mounted on a spring base, popular in the late Victorian era.

Turkey work or Norwich work

A popular English Renaissance textile that imitates Oriental rugs, commonly used for upholstery and table covers, produced by knotting worsted yarn pulled through canvas or other coarse fabric.

Turkish corner

A nook or small room in late Victorian homes of the Exotic Revival Style, containing a multitude of pillows, ruffles, flowers, drapes, and often a hanging brass lamp designed to imitate Turkish interiors.

Turkish or Ghirdes knot (TUR kish NAWT)

A symmetrical hand-tied knot used in rug weaving, created by encircling two warp threads with wool; the loose ends emerge between the two warps. The knot is easier to produce than a Persian knot, but yields a coarser rug.

Turkish rug

A durable wool rug of geometric designs made with a short, close pile by nomadic tribes in Turkestan and Central Asia. The dominant color is blood red, often combined with cream, black, brown, and blue, produced by natural dyes such as vegetable. See also *prayer rug*.

Turkoman rugs (TUR koh men RUGZ)

Same as Turkish rugs. Also spelled Turkman.

turned chair

A Jacobean chair composed of elaborately turned frame members, often bobbin turnings, that evolved from a medieval triangular stool. Also called a thrown chair. See also *bobbin turning*.

turned construction

Construction using wood pieces that have been carved on a lathe.

turning

In furniture, an ornamental or structural element produced by shaping wood on a rotating lathe to create a series of bulbous forms, disks, nodules, or swellings.

turnip dome

A dome or cupola resembling a gracefully pointed inverted turnip that overlaps a turret or drum below. The shape most often appears in Near Eastern, Russian, or Arabic architecture and ornament.

turnip foot

A 17th-century variation of the ball foot resembling an inverted turnip with a flattened end, often incorporating a collar that separates it from the floor.

turpentine

A solvent and drying agent created from pine resin used in paint mixing.

turquoise

Developed from the old French term for Turkish. A daybed or settee developed during the Louis XV period with a mattress-like cushion, no back, and equally high ends, based on the Oriental divan.

turret

A small tower on top of a larger tower or at the corner of a building or wall.

Tuscan Order

A simple Roman variation of the Doric column with an unfluted shaft and a capital composed of only an abacus and echinus. The column height is seven times the diameter. See *illustration in the Architectural Orders Appendix*.

tussah silk

Silk with a light brown color made from wild silkworm cocoons.

tuxedo sofa

A clean-lined sofa with thin, squared-off sides that is slightly flared and meets the height of the sofa back, creating a continuous line. The design originated in the 1920s.

tuxedo sofa

TV tray table

A small, portable folding table, usually sold in sets of four, designed as a surface to eat from while watching TV. Also called a TV table, TV dinner table, personal table, or snack table.

tweed

A rough textured homespun originally made in Scotland, generally woven in two or more colors in a plaid, twill, check, or herringbone weave.

twill

In textiles, a term for basic weave. The fabric produced has a distinct diagonal line created by the weft yarn passing over one or more warp yarns, then under two or more.

twin bed

A bed designed for one person with a width of 39" and length of 75."

twining stem molding

A molding resembling a stylized tendril coiled around a long, thin stem, commonly used during the English Norman Style.

twist turning

A turning used in France and Holland in the late 16th and early 17th centuries that is spiral in form.

twisted column

A decorative, supporting pillar that appears to be twisted or spiraled around its vertical axis. See also *wreathed column.*

two-chair-back settee

See *courting chair.*

tyg (TIG)

A popular 16th- and 17th-century large English drinking mug with several handles or with two closely spaced handles.

tympanum (tim PAN ee-um)

The triangular space bound within a pediment or within an archway above a door.

tympanum

type

A domed roof commonly used to let light into interior staircases of English Renaissance houses.

T'zu-chou (SE-CHOO)

Northern Chinese stoneware, most examples of which make use of black and white decoration.

Tzu-tan (SE-TAN)

A red sandalwood used to make Chinese furniture, particularly popular during the Ming and Qing dynasties.

abcdefghijklmnopqrstuvwxyz

U

udjat (ud JAAT)
A motif depicting a human eye with markings of a falcon's eye, used in ancient Egypt.

ukiyo-e (oo kee OH yay)
Developed in Japan during the 16th century, these popular colored woodblock prints denote "pictures of the floating world" and commonly depict people, landscapes, and myths.

umbrella stand
A conspicuous piece of hall furniture developed in England in the mid 19th century that held umbrellas.

Umbrian furniture
Rustic provincial Italian furniture from a region of central Italy in the Apennines.

Umbrian furniture

underbracing
The array of stretchers found on tables, chairs, and other pieces of furniture. See also *box stretcher*.

underdrapery
A generally lightweight drapery panel found beneath an outer drape.

under eave bed
In American colonial times, a bed with short posts designed to fit beneath angled roof space.

underframe
In furniture, the lower part of the frame that is supported by the legs or feet. See also *skirt* or *apron*.

underglaze
The mineral pigment or pattern applied to pottery before the final glaze.

underlayment
The backing or padding found underneath a floor covering.

unicorn
A mythological creature resembling a horse with a single horn. Symbolizing chastity, the unicorn was often depicted in art of the Middle Ages.

universal design
Designs that accommodate all users, regardless of age or abilities.

universal joint
A joint capable of allowing both connected units to move independent of each other in all directions.

universal table
An 18th-century table of Sheraton design used as a dining table or breakfast table; also used to store condiments. Generally equipped with two sliding leaves and a drawer at one side that contains twelve storage bins and a writing shelf.

universal table

upholder
A term used during the 18th century for an upholsterer.

upholstered wall
A wall that is covered with batting and finished off with fabric that provides a soft, giving surface that adds sound absorption to the space. Walls of this type can be button tufted or sectioned into panels or squares.

upholstery
Materials, such as textiles and leathers, stretched across a span or frame to make a soft padded surface.

uplight
Light cast up into a room, often onto the ceiling, where it is reflected back into the room. Sometimes called indirect lighting.

uprights

Stiles that continue up from the back legs of a chair to support the chair back and connect to the top rail.

upson board

See *fiberboard*.

uraeus (yoo REE us)

In ancient Egypt, a spitting cobra motif used to symbolize royalty.

urn

A vase shape popular in Greco-Roman carving and seen again in the Renaissance and subsequent styles such as Louis XVI and Adam. Often used as finials or at the crossing of stretchers.

urn stand; urn table

Small tables designed for tea service that were popular in the late 18th century, especially with designs of Thomas Chippendale.

urn-shaped splat

A central, upright wooden member of a chair back that is shaped in the form of an urn or vase.

Utrecht velvet (yoo TREKT VEL vit)

A patterned mohair velvet created by flattening selected parts of the pile.

urn stand

V

vaisselier (vay sel YAY)

French for a dining room cabinet and shelves.

valance

A soft fabric window treatment used as a heading at the top of windows. See also *cantonniere, lambrequin,* and *pelmet.*

valet chair

See *Hans Wegner valet chair.* See *Hans Wegner, 1914–2007, in the Architects, Artists, and Designers Appendix.*

vanity

A modern 20th-century term for a dressing table that often has an attached mirror. See also *dressing table.*

varangian

A medieval turned three-legged chair with a triangular wooden seat. See also *thrown chair.*

vargueño (var GAY nyoh)

A Spanish drop-front cabinet on a base, typical of the 16th, 17th, and early 18th centuries. Decorations on the front of the cabinet are generally of wrought iron with rings or loops on the sides that permitted mobility. In contrast, the interior contains elaborately inlayed small drawers and doors. The cabinet sits on a base that typically displays splayed legs with iron braces.

Varigian

A Medieval turned three-legged chair with a triangular wooden seat.

vaisselier

vanity

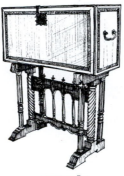

vargueño

varnish

A transparent protective finish used primarily on wood that is usually glossy and traditionally made from a combination of resin and solvent such as shellac and alcohol or gum and linseed oil.

vase

An open container used for ornamentation or holding flowers. These vessels are commonly shaped after classic sources and used extensively in the Louis XVI and Adam periods.

vase splat

The central, upright member of a chair back suggesting a vase form, common in the Renaissance and highly developed during the Queen Anne period.

vase turning

A profile in wood turning that resembles a vase shape with bulbous base and tapering neck. Commonly found in the turned legs of Windsor chairs.

vault

An arched form used as a ceiling or roof. See also *barrel vault, cross vault, fan vault, groin vault,* and *rib vault.*

veduta (ve DOO tah)

Italian for "view" and applied to detailed, large-scale paintings of cityscapes or scenic views.

veilleuse (vay-yuuz)

A French chaise longue of the Louis XV period.

velarium (ve LAYR ee-um)

A fabric covering or awning on a Roman amphitheater.

velour

A plush fabric made of cotton, wool, or spun rayon with a close nap resembling velvet.

vellum

Originally a fine-grained lambskin used as a writing surface or in book binding. In modern times, a heavy, translucent, cellulose-based paper used as a surface for architectural drawings and in the Art Deco period as wallpaper.

velvet

A short pile fabric usually made of silk or rayon.

veneer

A thin sheet of wood or other material applied to another surface, generally chosen for its color and markings to create a decorative effect.

Venetian blind(s)

A window treatment thought to have been invented near Venice that is made up of horizontal wooden slats (or other material later) connected by tapes that raise or lower the slats to control sunlight and views. They appeared in the mid 18th century in Italy, then moved into France, England, and the United States.

Venetian carpet

A reversible, flat-woven carpet in which the woolen warp conceals the weft, creating a striped effect.

Venetian chinoiserie

Louis XV Style furniture produced in Venice during the 18th century and characterized by embossed designs and a satin lacquer finish garnered from their direct trade with the Orient.

Venetian door

A door that includes glass side panels within the frame.

Venetian enamel

Enameled copper from the late 15th and 16th centuries, mostly in deep blues and white with repeated flower motifs of white and gold.

Venetian furniture

Late Renaissance furniture of Baroque and Rococo influence, produced in Italy with extravagant curves and ornamentation.

Venetian glass

A term given to glass made on the island of Murano, near Venice, since the 12th century.

Venetian gold or gilt

A gilt finish developed by craftsmen of Venice and Florence during the early Italian Renaissance where gold leaf was applied over red paint. The red under coat of the process partially shows through to create a finish with added brilliance and richness.

Venetian lace

A type of needlepoint lace that embroiders a pattern over base threads.

Venetian shutter (vu NEE shun)

A shutter with louvers.

Venetian window

Another name for a Palladian window. See *Palladian window*.

Venturi Art Deco and Sheraton chair

See *Robert Venturi Art Deco and Sheraton chair*. See *Robert Venturi, 1925– , in the Architects, Artists, and Designers Appendix.*

veranda, verandah

A gallery or walkway covered by a sloping shed roof and supported by columns or piers, which may be found on one or more side of a house.

verdigris (VUR di grees)

A patina that forms on metals with a greyed blue-green color. Common metals are copper, brass, and bronze.

verditer paper (VUR di tur PAY pur)

A term used for wallpaper found in 18th-century France that had a blue-green color derived from chalk and weathered copper.

verdure tapestry (ver DOOR Ta pe stree)

A tapestry design containing figures derived from foliage, trees, and flowers.

vermeil (vur MEEL)

A French term used for gilded silver or occasionally copper or bronze.

vermicular (ve MI kyoo lur)
Stonework of Renaissance buildings carved with irregular, squiggly, wormlike lines.

vermiculation (ve MI kyoo lay shun)
In masonry, the carving of blocks with irregular lines that imitate worm tracks. See also *vermicular*.

vermilion (vur MIL yun)
An Indian wood with a luminous red-orange color with pink tinted ground. See also *padouk*.

vernacular (vur NA kyoo lur)
In architecture, a term used for the methods of construction that use locally available materials and traditions.

vernacular furniture (vur NA kyoo lur FUR ni chur)
A style of furniture made in local traditions that is often simpler than furniture made in urban centers. It is generally made for everyday use.

Verner Panton chair
An icon of chair design, designed by one of the most influential Denmark designers, Verner Panton, and released in 1967 as a worldwide award winner; one of the first prototypes of a one-piece molded plastic chair that is practical, beautiful, and with ergonomic shape. It is made of rigid expanded plastic and has a lacquered finish in black, white, or red. See *Verner Panton, 1926–1996, in the Architects, Artists, and Designers Appendix*.

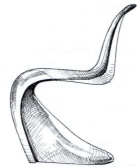

Vernor Panton chair

vernis de Gobelins
(vur NEE DE GOH be lin)
A method of Japanese lacquer introduced into France and used at the Gobelins factory in the late 17th century.

vernis Martin (VUR nee MAR ten)
A French term used to describe the shiny lacquerwork developed in the early 18th century, the latter part of the Louis XIV period, by the Martin brothers that imitated the lacquered relief work of the Far East. See also *japanning*.

verre de fongére (VAYR DE FAHN zhayr)
French for waldglas.

verre doublé (VAYR DOHBLE)
French for cased glass.

verre églomisé (VAYR ay gloh mee ZAY)
Decorative painting or gilding on the reverse side of glass. The technique was invented by the Romans, but made fashionable during the Neoclassical period.

verrerie (ve REE)
French for glass factory.

verrier (ve REE ay)
French for glassware cabinet or glass display with shelves. See also *vitrine*.

vertical blinds
Blinds made of vertical strips of metal, vinyl, or wood slats, used as window coverings.

vertical butt-and-horizontal book-leaf match
Pieces of veneer taken from a small log and arranged both vertically and horizontally in a vertical butt design and horizontal book-leaf match to form a series of rectangles.

vertical circulation
A term used to describe elements in architecture that lead from one level to another such as stairs, ramps, elevators, or escalators.

vertical files
A multitiered office file cabinet that is either letter (15") or legal (18") size in width, used to organize papers and records usually in a front to back order.

vertu/virtu (VUR too)

A term used to describe a love or taste for fine objects of art or curios.

vesica piscis (vi SIY kah PIY sus)

See *mandorla*.

vestal lamp

A paraffin lamp of the mid to late 19th century designed like an antique oil lamp with a base on stand.

vestibule

An entrance, passage, or room between the outer door and interior of a home or office.

Victorian

The general term for the style period pertaining to the reign of Queen Victoria in England from 1837 to 1901. The term also extends a decade later to include work in America. It can be broken down into the numerous styles.

Victorian Classic Style

This late 1860s sub style of Victorian covers the revival of French Louis XVI (Louis Seize) in Europe and America with its delicate lines and restrained Neoclassic decoration.

Victorian Gothic Style

An 1830s to 1850s sub style of American and English Victorian furniture characterized by pointed arches, tracery, and other Gothic motifs.

Victorian Jacobean Style

An 1870s wave of nostalgia for English Jacobean furniture brought strapwork and multiple turnings into vogue during the Victorian era.

Victorian Oriental Style

Renewed interest in Chinese and Japanese designs appeared in the later part of the 19th century bringing fretwork, bamboo turnings, and moldings to Victorian styling.

Victorian Renaissance Style

An 1850s to 1860s Victorian sub style inspired by the massive scale of the Italian Renaissance.

Victorian Rococo Style

This popular sub style of Victorian furniture recalled the French Rococo Style of Louis XV (Louis Quinze) from about 1840 to 1860. Marble tops, curves, and heavy carvings of birds, flowers, and fruit abounded on furniture often executed in rosewood, mahogany, or black walnut. Perhaps the most prominent American designer of the style was John Henry Belter. See *John Henry Belter, 1804–1863, in the Architects, Artists, and Designers Appendix.*

vieil (vi AY)

A silk brocade. Literally translated, the French term for old or old fashioned.

Vienna Secession (vee EN ah se SE shun)

A Viennese movement in art and architecture of the late 19th and early 20th centuries that rejected the prevailing academic styles in lieu of the free-flowing lines of Art Nouveau. The name is also tied to the association for artists founded within the movement in 1897 by Josef Hoffmann (later the founder of Wiener Werkstätte), Koloman Moser, and Joseph Maria Olbrich, whose first president was Gustav Klimt. See *Josef Hoffman, 1870–1956; Koloman Moser, 1868–1918;* and *Josef Maria Olbrich, 1867–1908, in the Architects, Artists, and Designers Appendix.*

vigas (VEE gahs)

The term given to heavy rafters, beams, or logs supporting the flat roofs of Spanish and Spanish Colonial architecture in the Southwest.

Vignelli Associates

A famous American firm of multiple disciplines founded in 1971 by Italian-born Massimo and Lella Vignelli. See *Massimo Vignelli, 1931– ,* and *Lella Vignelli, 1934– , in the Architects, Artists, and Designers Appendix.*

vignette (vi NET)

A running ornamental design consisting of leaves and tendrils, commonly seen in Gothic architecture. In French, it literally translates as "little vine."

villa

In Roman times, a country estate that included both house and grounds; from the Renaissance on, the term is used for an Italian country house.

Villa Savoye

See *Le Corbusier Villa Savoye.* See *Le Corbusier, 1887–1965, in the Architects, Artists, and Designers Appendix.*

vine

A popular classical motif associated with grapes, wine, and the god Bacchus. When used in ecclesiastical art, along with ears of corn, the motif symbolizes Christ.

vine motif

A conventional ornamental band motif of vines, originally used on Greek and Roman vases. The motif appeared as a well-known carved decoration during the Gothic period and as painted bands during the 18th century in classical French and English work.

vinette

An ornamental motif of the Gothic period that resembles vines and tendrils.

vinyl tile

A nonporous, resilient flooring tile that resists grease and oil as well as moisture and mild acids, has excellent wear resistance, and is produced in a wide variety of colors, sizes, and gauges.

violet wood

Another name for a purplish-colored Brazilian wood commonly used for inlay work in the 18th century. See also *amaranth* or *purpleheart.*

virginal (VUR ji nul)

Another name for a spinet. See also *spinet.*

vis-á-vis (VEEZ AH VEE)

See *tête-a-tête.*

vise, vice

An ancient term for a spiral staircase, usually constructed of stone, that wound around a newel.

vitreous enamel (vi tree US ee NA mul)

A glossy porcelain enamel on metal.

vitrification (vi tri fi KAY shun)

The process of converting to glass under intense heat.

vitrified (vi tri FIYD)

Clay goods that are impervious to water because they have been fired until the pores are closed.

vitrine (vi TREEN)

French term for a glass-fronted curio cabinet for the display of china, curios, or objects of art.

Vitrolite

A structural, pigmented opaque glass used in Art Deco buildings.

vitromania

The 19th-century practice of decorating a window to look like stained glass.

Vitruvian scroll

A band of continuous wavelike scrolls named after the classical Roman architect, Vitruvius. See also *running dog.*

vofet

Medieval term for buffet. See also *buffet* and *desserte.*

voider

A term from 18th-century England for a tray used to carry dishes and utensils back and forth from a table.

voile (VWAHL)

A plain-woven fabric that is light and transparent and generally made of cotton, wool, silk, or some synthetic fiber. See also *sheer.*

volute

A spiral, scroll-like form used extensively in classical capitals of the Ionic, Corinthian, and Composite orders.

Voysey two hearts chair

See *Charles Voysey two hearts chair*. See *Charles Francis Annesley Voysey, 1857–1941, in the Architects, Artists, and Designers Appendix*.

voussoir (voo ZWAHR)

A wedge-shaped block used to construct an arch. The central voussoir is called a *keystone*. See also *intrados* and *keystone*.

volute

voyelle (VOIel)

A French cockfight chair, commonly seen during the Louis XVI period. See also *cockfight chair*.

voyeuse (VOI yuz)

A low French chair with a padded back rail, designed for users to straddle and rest their arms on the back. Called a conversation chair in England.

vulture

A stylized vulture motif used to represent the Egyptian goddess Nekhbet, protectress of Upper Egypt.

vyse (VIYS)

See *vise* or *vice*.

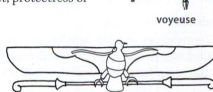

voyeuse

vulture

wachseinlegen (vahk SIYN lay gen)

A 17th-century decorative technique used on Dutch furniture of incised lines filled with a yellow mixture of sulfur and wax or putty.

wachstuchtapete or Wachstuch Tapete (VAHK stuk tah PEE tu)

An 18th-century German wall covering. See also *arras, hangings,* and *guadamicil.*

wag-on-wall

One of the earliest American hanging wall clocks with exposed weights and pendulum, usually with thirty-hour movement and known colloquially as wag-on-wall.

wainscot (WAYN skot)

Term defines wooden paneling applied to the lower part of an interior wall and treated differently from the remaining wall above.

wainscot chair

A 16th- and 17th-century English, French, and American rectilinear armchair with a carved paneled back and a hinged seat that covered a storage box. See also *bible chair, chancel chair, panel-back chair,* and *scrowled chair.*

wainscot chair

wainscot cupboard

Commonly known as a press cupboard. See *press cupboard.*

waisted leg (WAYST ed LEG)

Chinese furniture leg used on ceremonial furniture by attaching the leg to the apron and recessing it from the edges.

waldgas (VIYLD gahs)

A green- or brown-tinted rustic glass popular in Germany during the medieval times, often referred to as forest glass.

wall bed

See *Murphy bed.*

wall hutch

A ventilated wall-mounted livery cupboard.

wall lights

See *sconce.*

wall mirror

See *pier glass.*

wall pillar

German Baroque churches found in German-speaking areas that had a series of open chapels separated by pillars flanking the nave.

wall plate

Horizontal wooden piece at the top of the wall to which the rafters are attached.

wall treatment

Treatments or decoration for the wall, including fabric, paint, mirrors, graphics, tiles, etc., in different arrangements.

wall units

Wall-hung or freestanding compartmentalized cabinets with shelves, drawers, desks, etc., used for storage.

wallpaper

Decorative paper printed with designs by either hand or machine in a variety of colors, patterns, and textures, with the earliest decorative paper imported from the Far East in the 17th century. Also, a computer background picture or pattern.

walnut

A light brown hardwood native to Europe and America with great strength and excellent adaptability in color, texture, and figures. See also *Age of Walnut.*

walnut, black

A dark brown wood with a fine grain from eastern North America, known as Juglan nigra or Eastern black walnut; expensive due to limited supply; used especially for furniture, veneer, cabinets, and rifle stocks. Same as English walnut.

walnut, Circassian

A type of walnut wood from the eastern part of Turkey in the valley of Circassian mountains and from Russian's Caucasus Mountains, which gives the wood beautiful patterns of swirls and curves in shades of brown similar to American black walnut; used for furniture, veneer, cabinetwork, and interior paneling.

walnut, oiled

An oil treatment used especially on floors; it gives the wood a dull satin finish that is resistant to heat and stains.

walnut, Oriental

A sturdy wood known as Eucalyptus wood, which is durable with excellent weathering properties and a pinkish-brown color that turns reddish-brown with age and exposure. It is used in making furniture, especially garden style furniture.

Walnut period

See *Age of Walnut.*

walnut, white

A walnut wood (Juglans cinerea), known as butternut, native to the eastern United States and southeast Canada, light in weight, highly resistant to rot; used in millwork, furniture, paneling, and carving curios, but limited in use.

wardrobe

A large cabinet or cupboard with doors designed for hanging clothes. See also *armoire, garderobe,* and *kas.*

warp

Threads that run lengthwise on a loom, whereas the weft runs crosswise. See also *weave.*

Warren Platner model 1725A chair

A classic chair designed in the 1960s during the modern movement by Warren Platner that transformed steel wire into a unique sculptural piece with its unmistakable frame and choice of upholstery. See *Warren Platner, 1919–2006, in the Architects, Artists, and Designers Appendix.*

Warren Platner model 1725A chair

washstand

Small table or cabinet containing a basin for washing developed in the 18th century in many forms by designers in England, America, and on the Continent.

Wassily chair   (WAHS i lee CHAYR)

See *Marcel Breuer Wassily chair.* See *Marcel Breuer, 1902–1981, in the Architects, Artists, and Designers Appendix.*

watadono   (wah tu DOH noh)

A wide corridor in Japanese design.

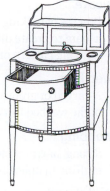

washstand

water gilding

A surface prepared by applying successive layers of white gesso, then faced with iron oxide, allowed to dry, and then dampened with sized water before the gold leaf is adhered.

Waterford

Glass factory put into operation in Ireland during the late 18th century.

waterleaf or water leaf

An 18th-century decorative motif derived from Greek architecture that resembles an elongated laurel leaf pattern used to enrich the cyma reversa molding.

wattle and daub   (WAH tul AND DAWB)

A construction technique of interwoven twigs or sticks called wattle with plastered mud, clay, or dung between the supports called daub.

wave pattern or wave scroll

A decorative wavelike series of carved, inlaid, and painted scrolls in a horizontal band, found in Roman architecture and also called Vitruvian scroll or "running dog." See also *Vitruvian scroll.* See *illustration in the Motifs/Ornaments Appendix.*

weatherboard

Sawn boards used on ships and houses referred to as clapboard siding.

abcdefghijklmnopqrstuv**w**xyz

weave

Process of making fabrics by interlacing warp and weft threads on a loom to create different patterns and textures depending on the weaving pattern of the yarns used.

web foot

A carved or grooved foot used on a cabriole leg that has the appearance of the webbed feet of animals.

webbing

Strong, narrow, linen or jute bands used as a support for springs and stuffing in upholstery seats.

wedding chest

See *cassone* and *cedar chest*.

Wedgewood

A pottery produced near Stoke-on-Trent in Staffordshire, England, especially during the late 18th and early 19th centuries. See also *Jasperware*.

weft

Threads that run crosswise on a loom and are often referred to as filler threads. See also *filling* and *woof*.

Wegner peacock chair

See *Hans Wegner peacock chair*. See *Hans J. Wegner, 1914–2007, in the Architects, Artists, and Designers Appendix*.

Wellington chest

A tall, narrow, plain chest introduced in the 19th century and named after the Duke of Wellington. It was commonly made of rosewood or mahogany, solidly constructed, but aesthetically pleasing with its soft, natural texture. It had a locking device designed with the right-hand side of the frame overlapping the drawers that bolted above and below to the projecting cornice and base, thus preventing the drawers from being opened.

Wellington chest

Welsh dresser

Often referred to as a sideboard with drawers and/or door compartments below, while the upper part receded with open shelves to display china. See also *Dutch dresser* and *tri-darn*.

Welsh dresser

welting (WEL ting)

Cord covered in fabric used to trim upholstery seams, tiebacks, valances, curtains, etc., to give a finished appearance.

Wendell Castle chair

A 1963 masterpiece by Wendell Castle of a sculpted chair with a hard leather sling seat. See *Wendell Castle, 1932– , in the Architects, Artists, and Designers Appendix*.

Wendell Castle chair

Werkbund (VARK bunt)

A German association of artists, designers, architects, and industrialists, active from 1907 to 1937, founded by Hermann Muthesius, Peter Behrens, Heinrich Tessenow, Fritz Schumacher, and Theodor Fischer, for the development of modern architecture and very instrumental in the later creation of the Bauhaus.

westwerk (WEST werk)

A monumental west entrance to a medieval church consisting of a tall façade with two towers or turrets.

Wethersfield chest

See *Connecticut chest* and *Hadley chest*.

whatnot

A 19th-century Victorian shelving unit designed to display decorative ornaments. See also *encoignure*.

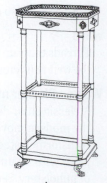

whatnot

wheat ear

A symbol or decorative motif, carved, painted, or inlaid, found on Hepplewhite Style furniture in the late 1700s.

wheel-back chair or wheelback chair

A chair with a circular back and radiating spokes, found mostly on 18th-century English chairs.

wheel window

A circular window used during the Gothic period.

whiplash

Flowing lines that curved back on themselves and were very popular during the Art Nouveau period.

white copper

A term referring to a whitish alloy of copper. See also *paktong*.

whitewood

A trade name used by woodworker's for pale woods such as yellow poplar, cottonwood, basswood, and magnolia. Due to its uniform grain of little interest, it is used more for interior parts of furniture, shelving, and cores for veneer work. See also *poplar*.

whorl (WORL)

A spiral scroll decoration typically used on the feet or ends of chair arms in the late 17th century in England. See also *knurl foot* and *paintbrush foot*. See *illustration in the Feet Appendix*.

wicker

Interwoven flexible twigs used to construct woven furniture and baskets, and often called wickerware.

widow's walk

An observation platform with an elaborate rail built on the roof of a house accessible from the interior of the house by stairs or a ladder, originally designed to observe vessels at sea. The name came from the wives of the mariners who, often in vain, would watch for their husbands' return, many being left widows.

Wiener Werkstätte (VEE nur vark SHAHT)

A Viennese workshop on the European Continent founded in 1903 by Josef Hoffmann and Koloman Moser for the purpose of promoting the design and manufacture of applied arts in the modern style. See *Josef Hoffmann, 1870–1956, and Koloman Moser, 1868–1918, in the Architects, Artists, and Designers Appendix.*

wig stand

A small 17th- and 18th-century English tripod stand fitted with small drawers and a small basin for wig dressing, and a dummy to hold the wig. It was sometimes referred to as demoiselle.

Wiggle chair

See *Frank O. Gehry Wiggle chair*. See *Frank O. Gehry, 1929– , in the Architects, Artists, and Designers Appendix.*

wigwam

Huts built of grass and thatch by the native American tribes on the eastern American Continent.

William and Mary Style, 1689–1702

A Baroque Style that evolved in England and America during the reigns of King William (1689–1702) and Queen Mary (1689–1694).

William and Mary Style

William Morris chair

An early recliner named for William Morris, founder of Morris & Co., probably reproduced from a prototype version by Ephraim Colfax of Sussex, England; its main features were its reclining back, hand-dyed fabrics, and hand-carved woods. See *William Morris, 1834–1896, in the Architects, Artists, and Designers Appendix.*

William Morris chair

William Morris settle

A settee from Morris & Co., founded by William Morris, characterized by its honest design and better standards, which intended to mimic the art of the Middle Ages. See *William Morris, 1834–1896, in the Architects, Artists, and Designers Appendix.*

William Morris settle

Williamsburg

A historic, reconstructed, and restored colonial city dating from 1699 to 1780, which became colonial Virginia's capital. The re-creation of the entire colonial town by the Rockefeller Foundation from 1928 to 1934 was to provide Americans with the atmosphere and the ideals of an 18th-century colonial city and revolutionary leaders.

willow brasses

A popular 18th-century Chippendale period hardware referred to as "willow" brasses, sometimes plain and sometimes intricate with cutout designs.

willow pattern

A popular scenic pattern, Chinese in character, for porcelain and ceramic ware that originated in England in the 18th century. Commonly called Blue Willow.

Wilton carpet

Woven carpet produced at Wilton in Wilshire, England, with multileveled surfaces, a variety of patterns, and a limited number of colors per pattern.

winder or winding stair

A wedge-shape tread located at the turn in a stairway.

window breast

A thin screen wall below a window, particularly in Gothic architecture.

window crown

A general term for a decorative molding at the top or over a window, for instance, a decorative pediment.

window of appearance

A window with a balcony, a balustrade, and a baldachin located on an upper floor from which one can make an appearance to the public.

window seat

A seat unit made to fit into the bottom of a window recess or alcove, sometimes upholstered and made to open for storage.

window shade

A covering for a window made of heavy fabric or a piece of stiffened cloth or paper sometimes attached to a spring roller that can be pulled or raised or constructed of cloth with cords that are used to raise or lower. See also *Austrian shade.*

window stool

A sash or opening in a wall or roof that admits light and air and is often framed and fitted with glass. Also, an upholstered bench fitted into a window recess, as defined by Hepplewhite. See also *window seat.*

Windsor chair

A popular 18th- and 19th-century chair in England and America made of wood and having a spindle back shaped in fans, hoops, or combs and sometimes spindle legs named for Windsor Castle. It is also called a stickback. See also *arrow-back chair, comb-back writing chair, fiddle-string back, Philadelphia chair,* and *stick-back.* See *illustration for comb-back Windsor chair.*

Windsor chair, American

A version of the Windsor chair introduced into Philadelphia from England in the 1730s, with many types being produced in the 18th and 19th centuries and still being made today. Commonly known as the stick chair.

wine cooler

A vessel or bucket used to chill a bottle of wine. See also *cellarette* and *sarcophagus.*

wine table

See *horseshoe table* and *hunt table.*

wing

A structure attached to and projecting from the side of a main building. Also, a piece of furniture with projecting sides.

wine cooler

wing bookcase

See *block front* and *broken front*.

wing chair

A tall upholstered lounge chair with wings or earpieces on either side of the back to shield users; evolving in England and America after 1750. See also *forty-wink chair*.

winged claw

A foot used on Empire sofas and heavy pieces.

wishbone or Y chair

See *Hans Wegner Y chair or wishbone chair*. See *Hans J. Wegner, 1914–2007, in the Architects, Artists, and Designers Appendix*.

Womb chair

See *Eero Saarinen Womb chair*. See *Eero Saarinen, 1910–1961, in the Architects, Artists, and Designers Appendix*.

wood engraving

The process of engraving on wood using a wooden block that has a design cut in the end grain.

woodcut

A design carved and incised into a block of wood in such a way that the image of the design is left raised so it can be transferred to paper by ink.

woof (WUUF)

See *weave* and *woof*.

work table

Late in the 17th century various forms of small tables appeared for needlework, painting, reading, games, etc. See also *pouch table* and *bag table*.

wormholes

Small to large holes in wood caused by bugs such as beetles or the worms of beetles, eating into the wood. Wormholes are often created artificially to fake antiques; however, they go

wing chair

work table

straight through the wood rather than the more organic pattern made by worms.

wormy chestnut

A type of wood from insect-damaged trees that became fashionable in the United States, where it was used for a variety of purposes, such as for paneling, cabinets, and some furniture due to its light-brown color and rough texture.

WPA style (Works Progress Administration)

A stripped classical architectural style of the 1930s projects of the American government agency, the WPA.

wreath

A circular shape of an assortment of various materials constructed as a ring or circlet and hung as a decorative arrangement or placed on a memorial; also worn as a mark of honor or victory.

wreathed column

A column with a twisted or spiral appearance. See also *twisted column*.

Wright Peacock chair

See *Frank L. Wright Peacock chair*. See *Frank Lloyd Wright, 1867–1959, in the Architects, Artists, and Designers Appendix*.

writing arm

Wide writing tablet suitable for the arm of a Windsor chair.

writing armchair

An antique armchair known as the writing armchair in the United States and as the tablet chair in the United Kingdom, resembling a Windsor-style armchair but with an oval pad or tablet replacing the right arm. See also *corner chair, roundabout chair, smoker's chair,* and *tablet chair*.

writing desk; writing table

Any type of table or desk with a slanted or flat top fitted with drawers or compartments and used for writing. See also *Carlton table* and *escritoire*.

wrought iron (RAHT IY urn)

A welded and forged iron that is worked, bent, and twisted until it is suitable for use as decoration and for parts of furniture.

X-chair

Ancient transportable folding chair found in Egypt and Rome and reappears in the Middle Ages. Same as X-frame chair.

X-frame

A supporting frame, shaped like the letter X, used in furniture, especially chairs.

X-shaped chair

Chairs, including the curule, the Dante, and the Savonarola, that have legs with the supporting framework shaped like the letter X. See also *curule, Dante chair,* and *Savonarola.*

X-stool

A folding stool with a leather seat that is supported by an X-shaped underframe, found in ancient Egypt; later other variations of the structural principle can be found in Rome, Middle Ages, Renaissance, and Empire. See also *curule.*

X-stool

X-stretcher

Crossed stretchers that connect diagonally the four legs on chairs, tables, and other pieces of furniture. See also *cross stretcher* and *saltire.*

xiang qian   (SHAHNG KEE-on)

A Chinese lacquer technique where recesses were made in dried lacquer and spaces were filled with ivory, metals, mother of pearl, and other materials.

xystus   (ZIY stus)

Roman garden found in a villa with trees and flower beds, surrounded by a colonnaded ambulatory or portico. Also, in ancient Greek architecture, a covered portico or ambulatory used by athletes for exercising.

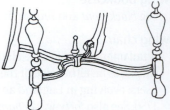

X-stretcher

Y chair or wishbone chair

See *Hans Wegner Y chair or wishbone chair.* See *Hans Wegner, 1914–2007, in the Architects, Artists, and Designers Appendix.*

yagura (YAH gur ah)

Tower in Japanese architecture.

yan ji (YAHN JEE)

A draw-leaf table used by the Chinese.

yang ci (YANG CHEE)

Metal plaques, called Canton enamel, painted with enamels in Chinese designs.

yarn

The basic strand of textile fiber from which thread, twine, or cloth is made. Yarn can be either spun yarn or continuous filament yarn.

yarn dyeing

The process of dyeing before the yarn is woven into a textile.

yellow wood

A wood native to South Africa, light in color, and used for veneer.

yeoman furniture

A picturesque term invented in the early years of the 20th century and loosely applied to furniture made in the countryside, which perpetuates the character and ornament of that period.

yeseria (ye ser EE yah)

Spanish term for elaborately carved lacelike patterns of plaster, used extensively on walls of Moorish rooms.

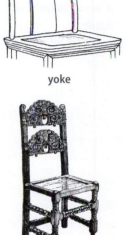

yeseria

yew, English

A very hard, elastic, red-brown wood, resistant to wear and decay, native to England and used on English furniture in the 17th and 18th centuries, either as a veneer or in solid form.

Yi (YEE)

The Chŏson period of the Korean Dynasty (1392–1910). See also *Chos-n.*

yin ping tuo (YIN PING TOO-oh)

A lacquer technique used in China in which materials such as metals or ivory are applied before the lacquer dries; then the entire piece is lacquered again and burnished to reveal the design.

yoke

yoke or yoke-back

A top rail typically found on the chair back of English Georgian or Queen Anne chairs, named for the shape of the back, derived from its resemblance of a milkmaid's yoke or ox-yoke. See also *Chippendale* and *Queen Anne Style.*

Yorkshire/Derbyshire chair

A regional chair from Yorkshire, England, and similar to a Derbyshire chair.

Yorkshire/Derbyshire chair

Yorkshire ladder-back chair

A provincial chair from the 18th century, characterized by its rush seat and ladder back composed of five slats curved to fit one's back, very plain in style.

yosemune-zukuri (YOH su mee oo na)

Hipped roof associated with Japanese architecture.

Yrjö Kukkapuro Karuselli chair (eer EE oh koo KAH paw roh KAH roo sel ay)

A classic Finnish swivel and rocking armchair with leather upholstery and a shell and base of fiberglass; designed in 1964 by Yrjö Kukkapuro. See *Yrjö Kukkapuro, 1933– , in the Architects, Artists, and Designers Appendix.*

Yrjö Kukkapuro
Karuselli chair

abcdefghijklmnopqrstuvwxyz

Yuan Dynasty (YOO un DIY nus tee)
Mongol Dynasty of China (1260–1368 C.E.) ruled by Emperor Kublai Khan.

yuba (YOO bah)
A wood, defined as Tasmanian oak, with dense texture and curly figure.

yurt (YURT)
A movable circular tent of felt, skins, etc., used by nomads in Mongolia and Siberia. See also *ger*.

yurt

zabutons (zah BOO tohn)
Japanese square floor cushions used for seating.

zaguan (ZAH gwahn)
A Spanish covered passageway that leads to large double doors through which carriages and livestock can be driven.

zakomara, pl. zakomary (ZAH ku mur ah/ZAH ku ma ree)
Semicircular gables often with a shell design, traditionally used on Russian buildings.

zanjas (SAHN has)
An aqueduct made of fired clay tiles found in Spain.

zapata (sah PAH tah)
A Spanish Colonial architectural bracket or corbel (often chip carved).

zapata

Zapotec (ZAH pu tek)
An early civilization living in the Oaxada highlands of Mexico, a flourishing society from about 200 B.C.E. through 1000 C.E. known for its distinctive gray pottery. By 950 C.E. the Zapotec society abandoned Monte Alban and later was absorbed by the Aztecs.

zarf (ZARF)
A footed holder for a cup without a handle.

zebrawood
A light brown tropical wood with dark brown strips used as a veneer on cabinetwork for inlays and bandings.

zelkowa serrata (ZEL koh wah)
Known as Keyaki, a Japanese hardwood used for making furniture.

zhedievi (zhe DEE yi)
An X-shaped folding chair made in China.

zhedievi

zhuan lun hing chang (zoo AHN LUN HING CHUNG)
A Chinese octagonal bookcase with a central shaft and two doors that conceal interior shelves and pigeonholes.

zhuo table (ZOW TAY bul)
A Chinese rectangular table with corner legs, not inset. See also *kan'g table*.

zhuo table

ziggurat
An ancient large Mesopotamian pyramid temple. See also *Babylonia*.

zigzag
Chevron motif. See *chevron* and *dancette*. See *illustration in the Motifs/Ornaments Appendix*.

zitan (si TAHN)
Wood for Chinese furniture.

ziggurat

zoomorphic (zohu MOR fik)
Certain design elements relating to animals and/or animal parts.

zoophorus (zoh AHF er us)
A medieval sculptural frieze with animals, beasts, sea monsters, Zodiac signs, and other creatures.

zuiwengyi (zoo WENG yee)
A Chinese chair with an adjustable back and often referred to as the "drunken Lord's chair." See also *chanyi chair*.

zwiebelmuster (ZWEE bul mus tur)
A popular pattern found in Meissen porcelain, wallcoverings, and fabric and often referred to as "onion pattern" by the Germans.

zwischengoldglas (ZWISH un gohld glas)
A technique used in ancient Rome and later in 18th-century Germany where a glass vessel ornamented with gold was protected by another layer of glass.

Appendix

Appendix

Architects, Artists, and Designers

Aalto, Aino (1894–1949) A Finnish architect and designer and the wife of Alvar Aalto who collaborated with him on many projects.

Aalto, Alvar (1898–1976) Architect and designer from Finland and founder of the furniture design company Artek with Harry and Marie Gullichshen. He was also a leader in Scandinavian Modern design and became famous in the 20th century for his furniture creations of laminated wood. Even though he is considered an architect, his work spans beyond architecture to furniture, textiles, and glassware.

Aarnio, Eero (1932–) A contemporary Finnish architect and furniture designer known for his molded fiberglass furniture. Some of his best known works are the globe or ball chair, 1966, and the gyro or pastille chair which received the A.I.D. award in 1968.

Adam, Robert (1728–1792) A famous and influential architect and designer of buildings, furniture, and interiors in the Neoclassical Style of the 1760s through the 1780s that left a mark on England's architecture and design.

Affleck, Thomas (1740–1795) A Scottish born cabinetmaker who came to Philadelphia in 1763 and became well-known for his Georgian and Chippendale Style furniture.

Albers, Anni Fleischmann, b. Annelise Else Frieda Fleischmann (1899–1994) German Bauhaus teacher, textile designer, and artist. She was the wife of Josef Albers, another teacher and painter at the Bauhaus. Both fled Germany in 1933 and ended up at Black Mountain College in North Carolina. She also designed textiles for Knoll from 1959 in abstract geometric patterns.

Albers, Josef (1888–1976) German Bauhaus teacher, painter, sculptor, and designer who was dedicated to the study of color. He fled Germany in 1933 with his wife Anni Albers and ended up at Black Mountain College in North Carolina where he taught for 16 years before transferring to Yale University in 1950. He also headed the Department of Design at Yale from 1950 to 1958.

Alberti, Leone Battista (1404–1472) A renowned Italian Renaissance architect, sculptor, painter, poet, musician, and scholar who wrote several books on architecture, perspective, and painting that influenced later artisans, architects, and craftsmen. His work had a powerful influence on future generations moving toward a stronger conceptual direction.

Albertollii, Giocondo (1742–1839) An Italian Neoclassical Style decorative designer and interior decorator who was greatly responsible through his elaborate ornamentation for the spread of the Neoclassic Style in Italy.

Alexander the Great (356–323 B.C.E.) From 336–323 B.C.E. he was a Greek ruler who conquered the Persian Empire and extended the territories of the Greek Empire. As a result the art and architecture of the Hellenistic period were in great demand and the influence spread eastward. He created one of the largest empires in ancient history.

Antoinette, Marie, baptisted Maria Antonia Josephina Johanna, (1755–1793) The Archduchess of Austria who married Louis XVI in 1770 at age 15 and became Queen of France at 19 when her husband ascended to the throne in 1774. After the French Revolution, she was imprisoned, convicted of treason, and executed in 1793.

Arp, Jean Hans (1886–1966) A French sculptor, painter, poet and abstract artist who was one of the pioneers of abstract art. He was also a founder of the Dada group in 1916, abandoning the Cubist movement; later in 1922 he joined the Surrealist movement.

Ash, Gilbert (1717–1785) An American furniture maker from New York, whose son, Thomas Ash, became known as the established maker of Windsor chairs.

Ashbee, Charles Robert (1863–1942) An English designer, author, and architect who founded the Guild and School of Handicraft in 1888 and who believed that the constructive and decorative arts are foundational in any artistic culture.

Asplund, Erik Gunnar (1885–1940) A well-known Swedish architect of the 20th century whose principal work was the Stockholm City Library, 1920–1928; an example of restrained and classically based modernism.

Audran, Claude III (1658–1734) A foremost French decorator, painter, and designer who first worked for Louis XIV as a decorative painter at both Versailles and Fontainebleau palaces. He also created wall murals and tapestries, but was especially known for the decoration of the Luxembourg Palace during the Regénce period.

Aulenti, Gae b. Gaetana Aulenti (1927–) An Italian architect, designer, and teacher who is best known for her furniture designs and other objects such as lamps. In the late 1950s she gained recognition when she became a supporter of the controversial Neo-Liberty Style.

Avisse, Jean (1723–1796) A French furniture designer appointed maître ébéniste in 1745 during the Rococo and Neoclassical Style. He produced chairs, sofas, chaises, etc., characterized by elaborate decorations with shells, flowers, and leaves. His work was stamped with his signature IAVISSE.

Baccetti, Andrea (n.d.) Italian manufacturer of Renaissance Revival Style furniture that reflected 15th- and 16th-century Italian design and was especially ornate and heavy. He also created pieces with references to Moorish designs.

Bach, Richard F. (1887–1968) Director of the Department of Industrial Relations at the Metropolitan Museum of Art from 1917 to 1940. He was responsible for multiple exhibitions of American industrial arts that were instrumental in the manufacture and consumption of good design.

Badlam, Stephen (1715–1815) American cabinetmaker from Dorchester, Massachusetts working during the American Federal period.

Baillie Scott, Mackay Hugh (1865–1945) Prominent British architect and furniture designer of the English Arts and Crafts movement. Notable works include: Red House, Majestic Hotel, Onchan Village Hall, Evidence, and Oakleigh.

Baldwin, Benjamin (1913–1983) American interior designer of the 1960s and 1970s noted for his minimalist interiors. Also a distinguished designer of furniture and textiles.

Baldwin, William (1903–1984) American post-World War II designer and decorator known for his fresh, clean approach to color and form and mastery of scale and proportion. Commonly known as Billy Baldwin.

Ballin, Claude (1614–1678) French metal worker of vases and urns during the Louis XIII and Louis XIV periods.

Bardi, Lina Bo (1914–1992) Modern Italian architect known for her design of the Sao Paulo Museum of Art and her revolutionary "Glass House" in Brazil.

Barnsley, Sidney (1865–1926) English Arts and Crafts furniture designer and member of the Cotswald School along with associate Ernest Grimson.

Barragán, Luis (1902–1988) A 20th-century Mexican architect known for his quiet minimal aesthetic in architecture and landscapes, and for his use of adobe, stucco, cobblestones, and unfinished wood. His most prominent work is the residence San Cristobal, 1967–1968, in Mexico City. He received the internationally renowned Pritkzer Prize for architecture in 1979.

Bartelemy, Jean Simon (1743–1811) French painter and decorator famous for his panel series called "Love Assisting at the Toilet of Grace" created for Marie Antoinette's bedroom during the Louis XVI period.

Baughman, Milo (1925–2003) A 20th-century furniture designer known for his interesting use of colors and textures, material combinations of steel, chrome, and wood and fine craftsmanship partnered with mass production.

Beardsley, Aubrey (1872–1898) Prominent English illustrator and author of the Art Nouveau period and Aesthetic movement. He was also co-founder of the magazine called *Yellow Book* for which he served as art director and produced multiple cover designs and illustrations. His illustrations for Oscar Wilde's *Salome* are also a notable accomplishment.

Behrens, Peter (1868–1940) German architect influential in the beginning of the modern movement and known for his utilitarian style and clarity of form. Le Corbusier, Walter Gropius, and Mies van der Rohe were well-known students of Behrens. His most notable works include the AEG Factory and the Deutscher Werkbund.

Belanger, Grancois–Joseph (1744–1818) French architect and designer of the Neoclassic Style; he was known for the design of many private houses and gardens.

Bellini, Mario (1935–) Influential Italian architect, furniture designer, and product designer and former editor-in-chief of *Domus*.

Belter, John Henry (1804–1863) A 19th-century Victorian American cabinetmaker known for his laminated woodwork that was highly pierced and carved. He worked primarily in the Rococo Style to produce sinuous frames with heavy rolled moldings and flower carvings out of rosewood, walnut, and oak.

Beneman, Guillaume (1750–1811) French cabinetmaker who first worked for Marie Antoinette at St. Cloud, then as a master cabinetmaker for Louis XVI, and later executed the Empire Style designs of Percier and Fontaine.

Benjamin, Asher (1773–1845) An American architect and author of the Federal and Greek Revival Styles whose multiple publications heavily influenced design in New England. Notable buildings include: Leavitt-Hovey House, Charles Street Meeting House, Old West Church, African Meeting House, Headquarters House, and Charles Playhouse.

Bennett, Ward (1917–2003) Noted self-taught interior designer who worked early on as design consultant for Skidmore, Owings & Merrill. He later opened his own design practice in New York and completed notable projects such as the interior of Chase Manhattan Bank in New York and homes for the Rockefellers and other high profile clients. He also designed furniture for Geiger International and Brickel Associates, as well as tableware, cutlery, glass objects, and jewelry for Tiffany & Co.

Berain, Jean (1636–1711) Famous French designer of furniture, tapestries, and wood and metal accessories during the Louis XIV period. Especially known for his arabesque forms and for creating inlay designs for André Charles Boulle.

Bernini, Gian (Giovanni) Lorenzo (1598–1680) Architect and sculptor from Italy who had a great influence on the 17th-century art of Rome. His most renowned work is the great colonnade at St. Peter's.

Bertoia, Harry (1915–1978) An Italian-born modern furniture designer, artist, and sculptor who studied at the Cranbrook Academy of Art. He worked for Charles and Ray Eames, then opened his own studio in the 1950s. He is known for the design of the Bertoia Collection for Knoll which contains five wire pieces, including the famous diamond chair.

Bewick, Thomas (1753–1828) An English engraver who introduced white line engraving. He is often called the "Father of Modern Wood Engravings."

Biennais, Martin Guillaume (1764–1843) French cabinetmaker and personal silversmith of Napoleon.

Bijvoet, Bernard (1889–1979) A 20th-century Dutch architect and business partner of Johannes Duiker. The partnership was known for their avant-garde style. They achieved early acclaim as students for their competition winning design for the Fine Art State Academy, but their most noted works are the Aalsmeer House and the Maison de Verre.

Bindesboll, Thorvald (1846–1908) Danish painter and designer known for his modern Art Nouveau Style and the development of modern Danish arts and crafts.

Bing, Samuel (1838–1905) A German art dealer in Paris whose Maison de l'Art Nouveau introduced Japanese art to the western world. This became a major factor in the development of the Art Nouveau Style.

Blondel, Jacques Francois (1705–1774) A French architect of the Louis XV period renowned for his refined Rococo Style and boiserie of elegantly straight sided, Rococo cornered, lined panels.

Boffrand, Germain (1667–1754) Gifted French architect working in the Late Baroque and Rococo Style and one of the creators of the Régence Style. Noted works include: Hôtel de Soubise, Hôtel Le Brun, Château de Lunéville, and Château de Commercy.

Botta, Mario (1943–) Modern Swiss architect known for his strong use of basic geometry to create unique volumes. Noted buildings include: National Bank of Greece, Athens; San Francisco Museum of Modern Art; Bechtler Museum of Modern Art, Charlotte, NC; and Santa Maria degli Angeli, Mote Tamaro, Switzerland.

Boucher, Francois (1703–1770) A Famous 18th-century French decorative artist and painter instrumental in the Rococo Style of Louis XV. He was a favorite of Madame de Pompadour and served as an inspector at the Gobelins factory.

Boucher, Jules Francois (1736–1781) French painter of the Neoclassic Louis XVI Style. He was the son of renowned artist Francis Boucher.

Boulard, Jean–Babtiste (1725–1789) Ébéniste and sculptor of the Louis XVI period who was best known for the creation of the famous Fontainebleau bedstead.

Boulle, Andre Charles (1642–1732) A famous French cabinetmaker who worked for Louis XIV and was highly regarded for his design work and scrolling furniture inlay of beautiful metals and tortoiseshell called boulle-work.

Brandt, Edgarn (1880–1960) French designer of the Art Deco Style who specialized in iron furnishings and some bronze work.

Braque, Georges (1882–1963) French painter and sculptor of Cubism and Fauvism. He is widely considered the developer of Cubism with Pablo Picasso.

Breuer, Marcel (1902–1981) A 20th-century modern architect and furniture designer, who studied and taught at the Bauhaus. Later he moved to the United States where he taught at Harvard University and continued his practice until his death. Some of his most well-known designs include: The Geller House, UNESCO Headquarters, Whitney Museum of Art, Pirelli Tire Building, Ameritrust Tower, laccio tables, cesca chair, and the wassily chair.

Briseaux, Charles Etienne (1680–1754) French Rococo architect and interior designer known for his straight sided boiserie with moderately curved tops.

Brown, Eleanor McMillen (1890–1991) A 20th-century American interior decorator known for opening the first full-service interior decoration firm, McMillen, Inc. in 1924, and also known for her seamless mix of classical revival styles with properly scaled architectural detail.

Brunelleschi, Filippo (1377–1446) One of the most prominent architects and engineers of the Italian Renaissance; he also invented linear perspective. His most notable works include: dome of the Florence Cathedral, Basilica di San Lorenzo di Firenze, Santo Spirito de Firenze, and the Pazzi Chapel.

Buckland, William (1734–1774) A prominent Colonial English-American architect who worked primarily in Maryland and Virginia. His most notable works include: Gunston Hall, 1755–1759, and the Hammond-Harwood House, 1774.

Bugatti, Carlo (1855–1940) Italian Art Nouveau interior decorator, furniture designer, and furniture manufacturer known for his quirky forms. His son constructed the well-known Bugatti racing car.

Bulfinch, Charles (1763–1844) An American architect of the Federal and Republic periods who was revered by many as the first native-born American architect. He is known for his designs of the Boston Statehouse, 1799; Harvard's University Hall, 1815; Massachusetts General Hospital, 1820; Beacon Hill's memorial column, 1789; and Boston's Franklin Crescent, 1793.

Bullock, George (1777–1818) The most influential English cabinetmaker of the 19th century, renowned for his high quality work and refined and elegant inlay. He worked primarily in the Neoclassical Style and was also a noted artist.

Burne-Jones, Edward (1833–1898) A British artist and designer of the Pre-Raphaelite Brotherhood, Aesthetic movement, and Arts and Crafts movement. Particularly known for his Pre-Raphaelite paintings and stained glass, Burnes-Jones was also a founding partner in Morris, Faulkner, and Company with William Morris.

Burnham, Daniel H. (1846–1912) A prolific American architect and urban planner known for the designs of the Flatiron Building in New York, the Reliance Building, Marshall Field and Company Building, and Rookery Building in Chicago, as well as Union Station in Washington DC. Burnham was also responsible for the master plans for numerous cities including downtown Washington DC and Chicago. He also served as Director of Works for the 1893 World's Columbian Exposition in Chicago.

Caffieri, Jean-Jacques (1725–1792) A French sculptor, son of Jacques Caffieri who was also a sculptor. He was appointed sculptor du Roi to Louis XV, and became known for his portrait busts, in terracotta or marble.

Caffieri, Philippe (1714–1774) A French sculptor and bronze caster, son of Jacques Caffieri, who became sculpteur-ciseleur ordinaire du roi (sculptor and bronze caster to the king) replacing his father after his death. Philippe worked in the early Neoclassical Style known as goût grec.

Calder, Alexander (1898–1976) An American sculptor, painter, and designer, best known for his "mobiles" hanging abstract sculptures whose forms inspired many designers in the 1950s.

Campbell, Colen (d. 1729) A Scottish architect who published three folio volumes, 1715, 1717, 1725, entitled *Vitruvius Britannicus*, a survey of English classical architecture of the 17th and 18th centuries, giving him recognition as one of the initiators of the Neo-Palladian movement.

Canabas, Joseph, b. Joseph Gengenbach (1712–1797) A French cabinetmaker who, during the 18th century in Paris, was probably one of the first craftsman to specialize in the production of solid mahogany.

Caravaggio, Michelangelo Merisi da (1573–1610) A early 17th-century Italian Baroque painter best known for scenes from everyday life and his dramatic use of streaming light, as seen in his well-known painting "The Calling of Saint Matthew."

Carlin, Martin (ca.1730–1785) An 18th-century French cabinetmaker who was appointed maître ébéniste by Louis XVI. He was known for his delicate, charming Neoclassical furniture using rosewood and Sevres porcelain.

Carrere and Hastings Architects, John Carrere (1858–1911) and Thomas Hastings (1860–1929) A New York architectural firm from the late 19th century to the early 20th century who specialized in Beaux-Arts designs. One of the firm's earliest works is the Ponce de Leon Hotel in St. Augustine, Florida.

Castle, Wendell (1932–) An American furniture craftsman from Emporia, Kansas who graduated from the University of Kansas in 1961 and became a leader of the Craft Revival in the USA, pioneering a technique using laminated wood in stacks and carving these into amorphic shapes used for seating. In 1980 he started his own craftsman school. More recently his work has been mainly historical using exotic materials to produce exquisite work.

Cauvet, Gilles-Paul (1731–1788) A prominent French designer, architect, and sculptor during the Louis XVI period of furniture and interiors, who designed carved boiserie (wood paneling) for many Paris houses. In addition, he influenced many wood carvers with a book he published in 1777 of engraved designs for furniture and interiors.

Cellini, Benvenuto (1500–1571) Considered a great Italian Renaissance goldsmith and sculptor he was also an important artist of the Mannerist Style.

Chadwick, Don (1936–) An American industrial designer who studied at the University of California Los Angeles in the 1950s and opened his own design practice in 1964. In 1994 he and Bill Stumpf developed the Aeron office chair. His most recent design was the Chadwick chair for Knoll.

Chambers, Sir William (1723–1796) An English architect, author, and the first treasurer of the Royal Academy, whose style was based on English Palladianism. After a trip to China, he published a book on China entitled *Designs of Chinese Building, Furniture, etc.*, which strongly influenced chinoiserie in England. One of his more spectacular works is the Pagoda in Kew Gardens.

Charles I (1600–1649) The King of England from 1624–1649, until his execution in 1649 due to the many religious conflicts permeating his reign. The style of furniture and interiors at this time was Jacobean.

Charles II (1630–1685) King of the three kingdoms of England from 1660–1685. He was residing in Holland when his father, Charles I, was beheaded, at which point he returned to England to take the throne in 1660. The style of furniture produced during his reign is referred to as Restoration or Carolean.

Chippendale, Thomas I (n.d.) An English cabinetmaker from the early 18th century and father of Thomas II, who was the best known of the Chippendales.

Chippendale, Thomas II (1718–1779) An English cabinetmaker, the best known and most noted of the Chippendales, who published the *Gentleman and Cabinet-Maker's Director* in 1754, that depicted the refined Georgian Style. Other editions in 1759 and 1762 depicted the French Rococo, Chinese, and Gothic Styles.

Chippendale, Thomas III (1749–1822) An English cabinetmaker and son of the most noted Chippendale, Thomas II, who continued his father's business with Thomas Haig, and designed mostly in the Regency Style. He declared bankruptcy in 1804.

Churriguera, Jose Benito de (1665–1725) A Spanish architect and sculptor who influenced the Baroque and Rococo Styles in Spain, later known as the Churrigueresco Style. When he died, his obituary hailed him as "the Spanish Michelangelo." His most outstanding work was the altarpiece in the church of S. Esteban, Salamance, Spain, 1693.

Cimabue, Giovanni, also known as Biencivieni di Pepo (c. 1240–1302) An Italian painter from Florence, who designed mosaics and frescoes, known as a master painter and forerunner of Italian Renaissance. Many works are attributed to him but only one is dated and credited to his name, the mosaic of St. John the Evangelist in the Pisa Cathedral.

Cipriani, Giovanni (1727–1785) A Florentine decorative painter and draftsman who worked mostly in England under Sir William Chambers and Joseph Wilton, painting and decorating public and private buildings as well as furniture.

Clerisseau, Charles-Louis (1721–1820) A French architect and draftsman during the French Empire period, who influenced many architects and designers, such as Robert Adam, William Chambers and Thomas Jefferson.

Clodion, Claude Michel (1738–1814) A French sculptor noted for his terra-cotta statuettes of mythological subjects and similar themes for decorative friezes. He won the grand prize for sculpture at the Académie Royale. Some of his works are among public collections at the Getty Museum, the Art Institute of Chicago, and the Metropolitan Museum of Art.

Cobb, John (c. 1715–1778) English cabinetmaker and upholsterer of the 18th century who formed a partnership with William Vile. He designed furniture of high quality in satinwood, a material often used on Neoclassical pieces of this period.

Cochin, Charles Nicholas (1715–1790) A mid 18th-century French designer, art critic, engraver, and writer, son of Charles-Nicolas Cochin, artist, and winner of numerous awards as an engraver. He was referred to as Charles-Nicolas Cochin le Jeune (the Younger) to distinguish him from his father who had the same name.

Cochois, Jean-Baptiste' (n.d.) An 18th-century French cabinetmaker and inventor of change-about or dual-purpose furniture; one example was a chiffonier that became a night stand.

Cole, Sir Henry (1808–1882) An English civil servant, inventor and author that was a prime mover in the "Great Exhibition of 1851" which was a huge success due to his successful financial planning. He supposedly designed the world's first postage stamp, the Penny Black, and the first commercial Christmas card. In 1875 he was knighted by Queen Victoria.

Colombo, Cesare Joe, b. Cesare Columbo (1930–1971) An Italian painter, sculptor, architect, and industrial designer who created more efficient spaces with greater flexibility for different functions. As an industrial designer he designed pottery, furniture, and lighting. His furniture, such as the tube chair, was framed with various sizes of tubing so it could be clamped together to make seat furniture of different shapes. His interiors were futuristic in shape, color, and arrangement. He died very young at the age of 41.

Columbani, Placido (1744–1801) Even though Placido Columbani worked chiefly in England during the latter part of the 18th century, he was actually an Italian architectural designer who, like the Adam Brothers and Pergolesi, designed the enrichments for furniture. He was also a prolific designer of chimney pieces.

Coney, John (1656–1722) An important Bostonian silversmith, goldsmith, and engraver, noted for his engraving of the first bank notes printed in the Massachusetts Bay Colony in 1690 and again those in 1702. His work exhibited excellent craftsmanship in all aspects of gold and silversmithing.

Copeland, Henry or Copland, H. (n.d.) An 18th-century English cabinetmaker, who worked for Thomas Chippendale the elder and who in partnership with Matthias Locke in the mid 18th century produced furniture designs in the Rococo Style. In 1746 he also published, with Matthias Lock, *A New Book of Ornaments,* and between 1752 and 1769 other collections were published by Copeland in collaboration with Matthais Lock. Most of his work is credited to Thomas Chippendale.

Corbusier, Le, b. Charles-Édouard Jeanneret (1887–1965) An internationally influential Swiss architect and designer who worked in August Perret's office in France and with Peter Behrens in Germany in the early 20th century. With an interest in Greek architecture, Le Corbusier launched Purism in 1917 and was the first generation of the labeled International School of Architecture. He also was the first architect to study rough-cast concrete for sculptural forms as found in one of his outstanding architectural designs, Ronchamp in France.

Cotte, Robert De' (1656–1735) A French architect who was a leader of the Régence and who brought leadership in architecture to France from Italy. He worked on the royal buildings of France as a pupil of Jules Hardouin-Mansart, and he completed Mansart's projects on the royal chapel at Versailles and the Grand Trianon after Mansart's death.

Crane, Walter (1845–1915) An English painter, writer, artist, and book illustrator who was considered to be one of the most popular disciples of William Morris and an important designer of the Arts and Crafts movement. He produced influential childrens' books, decorative arts, illustrations, and paintings.

Cressent, Charles (1685–1768) A leading French cabinetmaker, sculptor and fondeur-ciseleur of the late Régence and early Rococo Styles, and a pupil of Boulle. His work was characterized by plain veneer of satinwood or amaranth in parquetry patterns, but he is better known for the sculptural gilt bronze mounts decorating his furniture.

Cresson, Louis I (1706–1761) An 18th-century cabinetmaker, and the son of Jean Cresson. He established Rue de Clery and became a carpenter of the Prince de Conde and the Duke of Orleans. His designs were manufactured in the Louis XV Style and signed with "L-Cresson" to distinguish himself from others using the same last name.

Cret, Paul Philippe (1876–1945) A French architect and industrial designer who graduated from the École des Beaux-Arts in Paris, and studied at the Atelier of Jean-Louis Pascal before coming to the United States in 1903, where he taught at the University of Pennsylvania and later became head of the Department of Architecture. He designed several buildings in New York, Philadelphia, and Washington D.C., as well as designing many war memorials. The University of Texas commissioned him to build the Beaux-Arts signature tower in 1934; he also created a master plan for the campus and collaborated on about twenty other campus buildings.

Cucci, Domenico (1635–c. 1705) A cabinetmaker, bronze worker, and carver born in Italy and trained in Rome. He went to France in c. 1660 to work at the Gobelins for Cardinal Mazarin during the Louis XIV period.

da Vignola, Giacomo Barozzi (1507–1573) A 16th-century Italian Renaissance architect responsible for a Treatise on the Five Orders of Architecture which revitalized the Vitruvian standards of proportions.

Daedalus The Greek architect associated with the legends of the infamous labyrinth of Crete, who made wings for himself and his son Icarus in order that they may escape imprisonment within the maze.

Dagly, Gerard (1653–c. 1714) A French craftsman who introduced Japanese lacquer into France during the 17th century. The process was employed at the Gobelins factory and was termed Vernis de Gobelins.

Dali, Savador (1904–1989) Prominent and versatile Catalan-Spanish artist best known for his work in the Surrealist movement. Noted works include the Mae West Lips Sofa, 1937; Lobster Telephone, 1936; and his most famous painting "The Persistence of Memory," 1931.

Darly, Matthias (1741–1778) An 18th-century English designer, engraver, and print seller known to have engraved many plates for Thomas Chippendale as well as for his own designs of furniture, ceilings, chimney pieces, decorative panels, girandoles, etc.

Daum A French glass making family who worked in the Art Nouveau Style.

David, Jacques Louis (1748–1825) A French painter considered to be a leader in the Empire Style, and given the title of Court painter for Louis XVI.

d'Aviler, Augustin-Charles (1653–1701) A 17th-century architect and designer to Louis XIV.

da Vinci, Leonardo (1452–1519) Illustrious Florentine painter, sculptor, architect, scientist, engineer, writer, and musician considered to be one of the most creative figures of the Italian Renaissance.

Day, Lewis F. (1845–1910) An English industrial designer of the late 19th century.

Delanois, Louis (1731–1792) A French cabinetmaker and maître ébéniste of Louis XV who designed most of the furniture at Versailles.

Della Robbia family: Luca, Andrea, Giovanni, Girolamo (1400–1566) A family of Italian Renaissance sculptors famous for the creation of Della Robia faience.

Delorme, Philibert (1515–1570) A French architect given the title of court architect to Francis I, Henry II, and Charles IX.

Deskey, Donald (1894–1989) American interior, furniture and textile designer of the Art Deco and Streamline Moderne Styles. His most prominent project was the interior of New York City's Radio City Music Hall.

DeWolfe, Elsie (1865–1950) American interior designer often credited with the invention of modern professional interior design.

Diffrient, Niels (1928–) American industrial and furniture designer whose varied projects include the design of exhibits, computers, trucks, tractors, and a sewing machine. Most know for his designs of ergonomic task chairs such as the Diffrient chair, 1979, for Knoll and the freedom chair, 1999; and liberty chair, 2004, for Humanscale.

Dinkeloo, John (1918–1981) The 20th-century American architect who designed the Oakland Art Museum and the Ford Foundation Headquarters, and extensions to the Metropolitan Museum of Art with partner Kevin Roche.

Ditzel, Nana (1923–2005) Danish furniture designer of the postwar era who relished designing with new materials and techniques, producing furniture for well-known manufacturers such as Frederica, Kvist, and Getama. Also known for her jewelry designs for Georg Jensen and textile designs for Kvadrat. Noted works include the Bench for Two and the Trinidad stacking chair.

Dollman, George von (1830–1895) A 19th-century German Romantic and Gothic Revival architect known for his design of two palaces for King Ludwig II of Bavaria, the Schloss Linderhoff, 1881; and Schloss Neuschwanstein, 1886.

Domenlg, Gunther (1934–) Austrian architect first noted for his expressionistic and counter-modern design of Z-bank in Vienna, Austria, 1979. His later work followed a more modeled and flowing vein. Notable works include: Zentralparkasse bank, Vienna; RESOWi-Zentrum, Graz; T-Center, Vienna; and the Steinhaus, Steindorf.

Downing, Andrew Jackson (1815–1852) A 19th-century American landscape designer and advocate of the Gothic Revival Style. Downing published multiple journal articles and books on gardening, as well as an influential pattern book, *The Architecture of Country Houses*. He also collaborated with Jackson Davis on the pattern book *Cottage Residences*.

Draper, Dorothy (1889–1969) Renowned American interior decorator and nationally syndicated columnist known for her use of bold, dramatic colors, prints and creative, affordable design solutions for the WWII era. She designed many townhomes of New York City's Gramercy Park and directed Good Housekeeping magazine's *Architectural Building* and *Furnishing Studio* in 1941.

Dresser, Christopher (1834–1904) An important multi-faceted English designer and theorist of the Aesthetic movement. Dresser contributed designs to Owen Jone's *Grammer of Ornament* and published *The Art of Decorative Design*, 1862, *The Development of Ornamental Art in the International Exhibition*, 1862, and *Principles of Design*, 1873.

Dreyfuss, Henry (1904–1972) Leading 20th-century American industrial designer known for the design of the Western Electric tabletop telephone, Hoover vacuum cleaner, Big Ben alarm clock, Princess phone, Polaroid SX-70 Land camera and many other products.

Drummer, Jeremiah (1645–1718) An early American silversmith of Boston, Massachusetts. Also known to have engraved the first paper currency plates in 1710.

du Cerceau, Jacques Androuet (1510–1584) A popular French Renaissance architect and designer who studied under Bramante in Italy and published one of the earliest known Renaissance furniture pattern books as well as engraved furniture, silver, and textile designs. He was also patriarch of the Androuet du Cerceau family of architects.

Dubois, Jacques (1693–1763) A French Régence and Louis XV cabinetmaker.

Dubois, Rene (1737–1799) Parisian cabinetmaker for Louis XV and Louis XVI who was appointed the title of maître ébéniste in 1755.

Dugourc, Jean-Démosthène (1749–1825) An 18th-century French designer known for his Pompeii inspired furniture and favored use of the quiver and arrow motif.

D'Urso, Joe (1943–) Influential and widely known American interior designer known for his minimalist style, innovation, and bold forms. He also developed a collection of tables and seating for Knoll in the 1980s.

Eames, Charles (1907–1978) An American furniture, product and exhibition designer of the mid 20th century, who is most known for designing side and arm chairs of molded laminated plywood bent into compound curves that are formed to the human body. His use of rubber shock mounts between the chair seat and base, added flexibility and a way to unite two varied materials. His most famous design, the Eames Lounge Chair, is one of Herman Miller's most successful pieces. Many of his designs were created in conjunction with his wife, Ray Eames.

Eames, Ray Kaiser (1912–1988) An American painter and designer of the mid 20th century and major contributor to the modern movement especially with her textile designs. Wife of Charles Eames.

Eastlake, Charles Locke (1836–1906) An English Victorian architect and furniture designer of the Gothic Revival Style. His linear furniture forms were decorated with incised ornaments and were so popular that the style became known as Eastlake Style. He also published the influential *Hints on Household Tastes* in 1868.

Egas, Enrique de (1455–1534) A Plateresco architect of the Spanish Renaissance known for his design of Santiago de Compostela and Holy Cross Hospital.

Elliott, John (1813–1791) An 18th-century American Quaker cabinetmaker based in Philadelphia who created many notable wall mirrors and dressing cases.

Evalde, Maurice (n.d.) A Franco-German cabinetmaker and maître ébéniste of Louis XVI who was known for his design of a famous jewel cabinet for Marie Antoinette.

Fay, Jean Baptiste (n.d.) A well-known French textile and wallpaper designer of the Louis XVI period.

Fenton, Christopher (1806–1865) Bennington pottery manufacturer. Also known for handcrafted Fenton Glass.

Ferrari-Hardoy, Jorge (1914–1977) Active Argentinian architect, designer, and city planner best known for his collaboration in the design of the sling chair, manufactured by Knoll.

Folwell, John (n.d.) Premier cabinetmaker of the Philadelphia-Chippendale school often called the "Chippendale of America." Known for his creation of the furniture for the Continental Congress.

Fontaine, Pierre Francois Leonard (1762–1853) Neoclassical French architect and designer who, with Charles Percier, created Directoire and Empire Styles. Major works include the furniture and interiors of Malmaison, St-Cloud, the Tuileries, and the Louvre.

Fornasetti, Piero (1913–1988) A 20th-century Italian painter, sculptor, interior decorator, engraver, and product designer known for his witty, whimsical use of images and color.

Fortuny, Mariano (1871–1949) A 20th-century Spanish fashion, fabric, and lighting designer famous for his silks and stenciled cottons. He worked from his couture house in Venice, Italy from 1906–1946.

Forty, Jean Francois (n.d.) French designer, engraver, and metal worker of the Louis XVI period known for his furniture mounts, metal accessories and published works of designs.

Foster, Norman Robert (1935–) British architect who together with his international firm, Foster + Partners, created such notable buildings as the Willis Building, Wembley Stadium, and the Hearst Tower.

Fragonard, Jean-Honoré (1732–1806) French painter of the Louis XV and Louis XVI periods known for his wall decorations and murals for boudoirs. Mme. Du Barry was one of his well-known clients.

Frank, Jean-Michel (1895–1941) Parisian interior and furniture designer of the 1930s known for his haut-monde interiors and furniture made with materials such as shagreen and mica.

Frankl, Paul T. (1886–1958) Austrian-American architect, furniture designer, and textile designer of the Art Deco Style who helped shape American modernism with his celebrated skyscraper style. Also known for his metal furnishing, textiles, and wallpapers.

Fuller, Richard Buckminster (1895–1983) American architect, engineer, and designer responsible for the invention of the geodesic dome and for coining or popularizing terms such as Dymaxion, ephemeralization, and synergetic.

Furness, Frank (1839–1912) American architect of the Victorian era working predominately around Philadelphia and known for his eclectic, boldly scaled structures.

Gabriel, Ange-Jacques (1698–1782) Premier French architect during the reign of Louis XV whose major work included the Petit Trianon, Place de la Concorde, Pavilion Butard, Place de la Bourse, and the Opera at the Chateau de Versailles.

Gallé, Émile (1846–1904) Famed French glassmaker and furniture designer of the Art Nouveau era.

Garnier, Jean Louise Charles (1825–1898) A 19th-century French architect working in the Neo-Baroque Style of the French Beaux Arts period. Known for the Paris Opera House and the Casino at Monte Carlo.

Gaudi, Antonio (1852–1926) Spanish architect and furniture designer who worked in his own unique version of the Art Nouveau Style with added color, unusual materials, and abstract techniques. His most well-known works include: La Sagrada Familia, Casa Battló, Casa Milá, and structures in the Park Güel.

Gaudreau, Antoine Robert (1680–1751) An 18th-century cabinetmaker who worked on the Tuileries and Bibliotheque Nationale for the French court.

Gehry, Frank O. (1929–) Prolific American architect and furniture designer known for his deconstructed architectural style in buildings like the Guggenheim Museum in Bilbao, Spain; Walt Disney Concert Hall in Los Angeles, CA; Vitra Design Museum in Germany. Iconic furniture includes his Experimental Edges line out of corrugated cardboard and the basket woven Cross Check Series for Knoll International.

Gibbons, Grinling (1648–1721) English Baroque wood carver and sculptor most known for his beautifully detailed carvings of foliage, flowers, birds, animals, fruit, and shells for such buildings as St. Paul's Cathedral, Blenheim Palace, and Hampton Court Palace.

Gibbs, James (1682–1754) Influential 18th-century English architect and furniture designer influenced by the work of Sir Christopher Wren. His most noted designs include St. Martin-in-the-Fields in London and Radcliffe Camera at Oxford University. Also known for publishing many architecture and design folios.

Gilbert, Cass (1859–1934) Prominent American architect of the Beaux Arts Style and early advocate of the skyscraper. Noted structures include the Woolworth Building, Supreme Court Building, and West Virginia State Capitol.

Gillow, Robert (1702–1772) English furniture maker and founder of Gillows of Lancashire, 1730, a furniture company that exported furniture to the British Colonies of the West Indies.

Gimson, Ernest (1864–1919) An influential English architect and furniture designer of the English Arts and Crafts movement.

Girard, Alexander (1907–1993) American architect and designer largely known for his mid-century modern textile designs for Herman Miller.

Girardon, Francois (1628–1715) An 18th-century French sculptor known for his work at Versailles and the Louvre, as well as his bronze equestrian statue of Louis XIV.

Goddard, John (1724–1785) Prominent Newport, Rhode Island cabinetmaker of the 18th century known for his block fronts topped by a carved shell in a convex-concave pattern.

Goodhue, Bertram Grosvenor (1869–1924) American architect noted for his work in the Neo-Gothic Style. Projects include: Saint Thomas Church, New York City; St. Bartholomew's Church, New York City; chapel and original campus of the United States Military Academy, West Point, New York; Nebraska State Capitol, Lincoln, NE; and Virginia Military Institute, Lexington, VA.

Goodison, Benjamin (ca. 1700–1767) London cabinetmaker of the early Georgian period who often supplied furniture to the royal palaces.

Gostelowe, Jonathan (1744–1795) An 18th-century Swedish-American cabinetmaker working out of Philadelphia in the Chippendale Style.

Goujon, Jean (1510–1565) French architectural sculptor of the Renaissance. He is most known for: the allegories for the facade of the Louvre, caryatids for the musician's platform of the Louvre, six relief nymph figures for the Foutaine des Innocents, and The Four Seasons panels for the hotel of Jacques de Ligeris.

Graves, Michael (1934–) American architect, furniture designer and product designer of the Postmodern Style. Several important buildings include the Portland Building, Oregon; Walt Disney World Dolphin Resort, Orlando, FL; NCAA Hall of Champions, Indianapolis, IN; Walt Disney World Swan Resort, Orlando, FL; and the Humana Building, Louisville, KY.

Gray, Eileen (1878–1976) Irish architect and furniture designer who inspired modernism and Art Deco. She worked mainly in Paris and designed some of the 20th century's most recognizable pieces of furniture: the Bibendum Chair, the Transat Armchair, and the E-1027 Table.

Greene, Charles Sumner (1868–1957) and Henry Mather Greene (1870–1954) Brothers and influential 20th-century American architects of the American Arts and Crafts movement. Primarily working in California and known for their ultimate bungalows that stressed the importance of structure. Their most well-known residences include the Gamble House and Blacker House, both located in Pasadena, CA.

Grendy, Giles (1693–1780) London furniture maker and prolific exporter of the English Georgian Style, especially japanned furniture.

Gropius, Walter (1883–1969) German architect considered to be one of the pioneers of modern architecture and founder of the Bauhaus.

Guillemart, Francois (d. 1742) French cabinetmaker appointed maître ébéniste under Louis XIV; also active during the Regency period.

Guimard, Hector (1867–1942) French architect and furniture designer of the Art Nouveau Style. His most notable works include: Castel Béranger, Hotel Guimard, and his famous entrances to the Paris Metro stations.

Gwathmey, Charles (1938–2009) Noted American architect and principal in the New York based firm of Gwathmey, Siegel & Associates Architects. Completed projects include: Guggenheim Museum addition, 1992, and the American Museum of the Moving Image, 1988.

Haig, Thomas (n.d.) An English cabinetmaker and partner of Thomas Chippendale; probably in charge of the business finances.

Halfpenney, William (before 1723–1755) An 18th-century English architect who identified himself as an "architect and carpenter," very influential in promoting the Chinese taste in decoration and architecture. Most of the buildings he designed are in and near Bristol, England, with only one surviving building attributed as his work, the Cooper's Hall built in 1743–1744.

Hardouin-Mansart, Jules (1646–1708) A 17th-century French architect who served as Louis XIV's chief architect and superintendent, representing the power of Louis XIV through the grandiose French Baroque architecture at Versailles from 1675 where he designed all the extensions and renovations, including the Royal Chapel, the celebrated Hall of Mirrors, the Grand Trianon and the Orangerie.

Harrison, Peter (1716–1775) An English born and trained architect who emigrated to Rhode Island in 1740 with his brother to become a merchant and captain, but returned to England in 1743–1745 for formal training as an architect. Returning to America, he is considered the first professionally trained architect and many buildings are attributed to him, such as his best-known building, the Redwood Library in Newport, Rhode Island.

Hawksmoor, Nicholas (1661–1736) A leading late 17th-century English architect who entered the service of Christopher Wren at the early age of 18. He was involved heavily in the building of Wren's City of London churches during the 1680s, characterized by the Baroque sense of mass and monumentality. He was also commissioned to work on Castle Howard, Yorkshire, in 1699 and on Blenheim Palace in 1705, with the decorative details attributed to his design.

Henri VIII (1491–1547) The King of England and second monarch of the House of Tudor. He succeeded his father in 1509 until 1547, during which time he imported the Renaissance into England but retained Gothic shapes. He broke with the Pope and lead a reformation of the Anglican Church by divorcing his wife Catherine so he could marry Anne Boleyn. He had six wives and ordered several beheaded on the grounds of adultery. He was 56 years old at his death.

Hepplewhite, George (d. 1786) An English furniture designer and cabinetmaker whose work is identified with classical revival, known for his heart, shield and oval-shaped chair backs. He collaborated with the Adam Brothers producing simple and more rational designs of their taste. His wife, after his death, published *The Cabinet Maker and Upholsterer's Guide*, a volume of 300 designs from A. Hepplewhite and Co. drawings. Following the success of this publication, a second and third edition were produced.

Herrara, Juan de (ca. 1530–1597) An outstanding 16th-century Spanish architect, mathematician, and geometrician, representing the peak of the Renaissance in Spain. The Monastery of San Lorenzo de El Escorial is one of his fully developed sober style buildings.

Heurtaut, Nicholas (1720–1771) A 18th-century French master sculptor and cabinetmaker who trained at St Luc Academy and was instrumental in the movement against the Rococo Style with his symmetrical, classical pieces. Display of his work can be found at the Louves, Versailles and other museums internationally.

Hitchcock, Lambert (1795–1852) An American cabinetmaker from Litchfield, Connecticut who made a Sheraton Style chair titled the "Hitchcock" chair, characterized by a "pillow back" or oval-turned top rail, painted black with a rush or caned seat, straight-turned front legs, and fruit and flower powdered-gold stenciled decoration on the top rail. He applied mass-production methods to his hand-turned chairs in the 1820s, 30s, and 40s, and was probably one of the first Americans to use labor saving technology in his cabinetmaking.

Hoffmann, Josef (1870–1956) A gifted Austrian architect, interior designer, and designer of furniture, textiles, wallpaper, clothing, etc.; influenced by the Arts and Crafts movement and its followers, John Ruskin, William Morris, Charles Robert Ashbee, and Otto Wagner. He is credited as the founder of the Wiener Werkstätte with Koloman Moser and was a proponent of the Gesamtkunstwek, or "total work of art." In addition to being a gifted architect, he was also one of the pioneers of the modern style.

Hogarth, William (1697–1764) An 18th-century English-born painter, social critic, editorial cartoonist, and printmaker whose work ranged from realistic portraiture to comic strip-like scenes, such as *A Rake's Progress*, which depicts the reckless life of Tom Rakewell, a rich merchant's son wasting his money on an immoral lifestyle.

Holland, Henry (1745–1806) An 18th-century English architect and interior designer of nobility, and contemporary of James Wyatt, George Dance, and Joan Soane, who was a primary leader of the early phase of the Regency Style in England.

Hope, Thomas (1769–1831) Leading English furniture designer of the Empire Style (also termed English Regency Style) and author of the furniture design book entitled *Household Furniture and Interior Decorations*, an 1807 publication that epitomizes and moderates the pseudo classical style of the period.

Horta, Victor (1861–1947) A Belgium Art Nouveau architect, interior designer, and furniture designer, described by John Julius Norwich as "undoubtedly the key European Art Nouveau architect." From 1893 he designed private houses, such as the Hotel Tassel, Hotel Solvay, Hotel van Eetvelde, and Maison Horta, now a museum.

Huet, Christophe (1700–1759) An 18th-century French painter who depicted animals doing human activities and dressed in human clothing. In addition, he was an engraver that worked in the Rococo Style, having apprenticed under Charles Dagomer, an animal painter and member of the painters' guild, and the Académie de Saint-Luc, Paris.

Huet, Jean-Baptiste (1745–1811) A French painter, engraver, and designer of wallpaper for Reveillon and toiles de Jouy for Oberkampf.

Hunt, Richard Morris (1827–1895) A 19th-century American architect and major contributor of the eclectic style of architecture. Hunt was educated in Paris at the Ecole des Beaux-Arts, traveled throughout Europe, and spent several years as an architect in Paris before returning to the United States to open his own office in 1858. Known for building the Tribune Building, one of New York's first skyscrapers, 1873–1875, and the Biltmore mansion, 1890–1895, in Ashville, N.C.

Hunt, Thomas F. (1791–1831) English architect and author of several books, best known for the pattern book entitled *Exemplars of Tudor Architecture and Furniture* (1829–1830), that exemplified his fondness for the Tudor Style. As an architect, Hunt was responsible for the repairs at St. James's Palace and Kensington Palace.

Ictinus (n.d.) Greek architect during the second half of the 5th century B.C.E. and chief designer, along with Callicrates, of the Parthenon in Athens, Greece.

Ince, William (d. 1804) English cabinetmaker and furniture designer known as one of the best imitators of Thomas Chippendale's work and for his book entitled *The Universal System of Household Furniture* that was published in 1762 with his partner John Mayhew.

Iribe, Paul (1883–1935) A French-born multi-faceted designer who gained an international reputation as a fashion illustrator. He was also a well-known designer of wallpaper, fabrics, and furniture used by Parisian fashion houses. After coming to Hollywood in 1920, he worked with Cecil B. DeMille, a producer/director, designing sets and costumes for melodramas.

Isozaki, Arate (b. 1931–) A Japanese Architect and designer who studied at the University of Tokyo, known for his traditional Japanese designs with strong geometric forms reflecting post-modern and mannerist influences.

Itten, Johannes (1888–1967) A color theorist and design educator at the Bauhaus from 1919 to 1922 and later at Yale University, where he taught elements of design, including shape, texture, rhythm, color, line, pattern, and density. His books such as *The Art of Color* and *The Elements of Color* are still used today, and cosmetologists use Itten's work to forecast seasonal color.

Jacob, Georges (1739–1814) A leading furniture maker of the Louis XVI, Directoire, and Empire periods noted for his wide variety of chairs and appointed maître ébéniste in 1784.

Jacob-Desmalter, Francois Honore Georges (1770–1841) The son of George Jacobs and a French cabinetmaker during Louis XVI and Directoire periods; also a furniture designer for Napoleon.

Jacobsen, Arne (1902–1971) An internationally successful Danish architect and designer known for his furniture of laminated plywood and steel, particularly the creation of the Egg chair. In addition, he is remembered for his contributions to architectural and design functionalism and for Danish Modern design.

Jacquard, Joseph-Marie (1752–1834) French inventor of the early 19th-century Jacquard loom, which enabled multicolored, patterned textiles to be woven less expensively. The invention also led to the development of programmable textile looms, and an adapted loom, for the carpet industry.

Jeanneret, Charles Édouard (1887–1965) See Corbusier, Le.

Jefferson, Thomas (1743–1826) A man of many talents, he was the author of the Declaration of Independence, President of the United States, leading architect of his home, Monticello, architect of the Virginia Capitol and the University of Virginia, a leading statesman, and a scientist. He is also noted as the father of the United States Classical Revival Style.

Jencks, Charles (1939–) A Baltimore architect, architectural theorist, landscape architect, and designer, well-known for his book entitled *The Language of Post-Modern Architecture*, 1977, which extended the concept of Postmodernism in architectural discourse.

Jensen, Georg (1866–1935) An early 20th-century silversmith and sculptor from Denmark. He produced his first complete set of flatware in 1906 called "Continental," and continued to produce more pieces until 1918.

Johnson, Philip (1906–2005) An influential architect born in Cleveland, Ohio who played an important role in defining 20th century architecture, particularly the international style, which was a part of American architecture for fifty years, and the Postmodern Style where historic styles were incorporated into contemporary building designs. He was also the founder of the Department of Architecture within New York's Museum of Modern Art. His glass home in New Canaan, Connecticut is one of his best known buildings, along with the Seagram Building in New York City designed in association with Mies van der Rohe, and the Four Seasons restaurant within the Seagram Building.

Johnson, Thomas (1714–1778) An English woodworker and carver of the mid 18th century. As a contemporary of Thomas Chippendale, he worked in several styles, including Gothic, Chinese, and Rococo. He became an author after the 1750s, the first book was entitled *Twelve Girandoles*, then he penned a *Collection of Designs*, and finally *A New Book of Ornaments*. His designs were considered fanciful and eccentric.

Jones, Inigo (1573–1652) An influential 17th-century English architect and leader of the early English Renaissance. Labeled the most significant architect of the modern period, he introduced the Palladian Style in his design for the Queen's House, at Greenwich and the Banqueting House at Whitehall. He also designed furniture in the Italian Baroque Style.

Jones, Owen (1809–1874) A talented 19th-century English architect, designer, and author of the *Grammar of Ornament* (1856) and another book first labeled *Examples of Chinese Ornament*, then later called *The Grammar of Chinese Ornament* (1867). Also a designer of wallpapers, carpets, and silks exclusively for Jackson & Graham.

Jones, William (1746–1794) An 18th-century English architect and furniture designer, influenced by French design, who published a book entitled *Gentleman and Builder's Companion*, 1739, which was filled with plates of ceilings, tabernacles frames, chimneypieces, etc.

Joubert, Gilles (1689–1775) An 18th-century French cabinetmaker, appointed as maître ébéniste for the Garde-Meuble of Louis XV, who produced case furniture in the Rococo Style. He was known for his small furniture, tables and secretaries, and for grand commodes with gilt-bronze mounts integrated into the shape and form of the furniture.

Juhl, Finn (1912–1989) One of the first Danish architects and furniture designers recognized internationally in the mid 20th century for his sculptured wood elements and his ability to produce beautiful and quality craftsmanship that modernized Danish designs.

Juvarra, Felipe (1678–1736) An 18th-century Italian architect and prolific designer, who also worked as a imaginative stage designer for Cardinal Ottoboni in Rome. He worked in the late Baroque and early Rococo periods, designing ornament and decoration in an flamboyant style. One of his most recognized works is La Superga, 1716/1717–1731, a church and monastery.

Kahn, Louis Isadore (1901–1974) A 20th-century American educator, architect, and philosopher, born on the Estonian island of Saaremaa. He emigrated with his family to Philadelphia where he trained in the Beaux-Arts at the University of Pennsylvania, and later became a design critic and professor at Yale University from 1947 to 1957; also a professor in the School of Design at the University of Pennsylvania. During the last two decades of his life he produced most of his work which was characterized by a concern for structure, light, materials, and humanistic values.

Kakiemon, Sakaida, born Sakaida Kiizaemon (ca. 1596–1666) A Japanese painter and pottery artist from the 17th century, well-known for decorations done by his development of colored enamel designs on porcelain.

Kauffmann, Angelica (1741–1807) Born in Switzerland, she became a decorative painter in England from 1766 to 1781, and worked for the Adam Brothers decorating and painting plaques, medallions, and panels. She also worked for Hepplewhite and Sheraton, painting in the Neo-classical Style. At the age of 23, she was accepted in the L'Accademia di San Luca and later became the founder-member of the Royal Academy in London. She was also a specialist in subject pictures, which brought her international patronage by many noble families.

Kaufmann, Edgar, Jr. (1910–1989) A curator and scholar of architectural history and decorative arts, he studied painting in Florence, Vienna, London and New York, and apprenticed at Taliesin under Frank L. Wright from 1933–1934. He was the heir to Fallingwater and was a devoted preservationist. He also became an adjunct professor at Columbia University, teaching architecture and art history, and the curator of the Good Design exhibition at the Museum of Modern Art, New York, in the 1950s.

Kent, William (1685–1748) English early 18th-century architect, landscape designer, furniture designer, and artist, and a leader in promoting the Palladian Style of architecture in England. He retained the Baroque Style for his interiors in such places as Hayden Hall and for furniture designs with heavy classical details. He is well-known for Palladian architectural works, including the English Treasury, Whitehall, and Cheswick House.

Kjaerholm, Poul (1929–1980) A 20th-century Danish furniture designer, who created modern functional furniture with elegant and clean lines. In 1952 he graduated from the Copenhagen School of Arts and Crafts, after which he designed a variety of chairs, including the PK22 and the PK20 swing chair. In the last few years of his life, from 1976 until his death in 1980, he was professor and director of the Copenhagen Art Academy.

Klee, Paul (1879–1940) A distinguish teacher, painter, and graphic artist born in Switzerland, but considered both a German and a Swiss artist of the early 20th century. A master of modern art in the Expressionist, Bauhaus, and Surrealist movements, with extraordinary sophistication. He was also a well-known writer on formal and aesthetic problems.

Klint, Kaare (1888–1954) An early 20th-century architect, furniture designer, and teacher from Denmark who promoted the Danish Modern Style internationally.

Knoll Bassett, Florence (1917–) Known simply as "Shu," Florence Knoll graduated from Kingswood School then studied at Cranbrook Academy of Art under Mies van der Rohe and Eliel Saarinen. An architect and furniture designer, who in 1947 married Hans Knoll (1914–1955), the son of a furniture manufacturer from Germany who moved to America. She became Hans Knoll's business and design partner, revolutionizing interior space planning by developing the Knoll Planning Unit. She believes in the "total work of design," through integration of architecture, interior design, textiles, graphics, manufacturing, advertising, and presentation.

Kukkapuro, Yrjo (1933–) Born in 1933 in Finland, he graduated in 1958 as an interior designer from the Institute of Industrial Arts in Helsinki. He is best known for his furniture designs, building comfortable chairs and sofas based on the human form, reducing his design to the simplest, graceful, beautiful lines. The Karuselli (Finnish for Carousel) chair, with a fiberglass seat and leather upholstery on a single leg support, is one of his earliest pieces that received lots of acclaim internationally. Regarded as an outstanding 20th-century furniture designer, he is President of the University of Art and Design, Helsinki.

Kuramata, Shiro (1934–1991) Influential Japanese designer who studied at Tokyo Polytechnic until 1953. He later went on to study interior decoration at the Kuwazawa Institute and founded his own design practice that designed furniture, over 300 bars, and multiple restaurants. Miss Blanche and Glass Chair are two of his original pieces of furniture.

Le Corbusier (1887–1965) *See* Corbusier, Le.

Lignereux, Martin-Éloi (1750–1809) Noted French Empire cabinetmaker of the late 18th and early 19th century.

Mackintosh, Charles Rennie (1868–1928) Scottish architect and designer noted for his highly distinct version of the Art Nouveau Style. Also a member of the Glasgow Four. He created notable designs including: the Glasgow School of Art, 1897–1909; Hill House, 1902–1903; and the Willow Tea Room, 1902–1904.

Mackmurdo, Arthur H. (1851–1942) English architect, designer and social reformer considered to be a pioneer of the Arts and Crafts movement. He founded the Century Guild for craftsmen and began publishing *The Hobby Horse*, an art magazine, in 1882.

Majorelle, Louis (1859–1926) Prominent French designer and manufacturer in the Art Nouveau Style. His factory was located in Nancy, France where he also served as one of the vice-presidents of the École de Nancy.

Mallet-Stevens, Robert (1886–1945) Influential French architect and designer of shops, factories, apartment buildings, and private residences who is recognized for his work between the two world wars. Notable buildings include the Villa Cavrois, Villa Noailes, and Villa Paul Poiret.

Mansart, François (1598–1666) Early 17th-century French architect credited with bringing classicism into the French Baroque. His extensive use of a four sided, double sloped roof led to the mansard roof being named after him. Noted works include the Orleans wings of the Chateau de Blois and the church of Val-de-Grace in France.

Manwaring, Robert (n.d.) An 18th-century English furniture designer and cabinetmaker noted for the introduction of small brackets between a chair's front seat rail and leg as well as the following publications: *Carpenter's Complete Guide to the Whole System of Gothic Railing; The Cabinet and Chair-maker's Real Friend and Companion*, 1765; *Whole System of Chair Making Made Plain and Easy*, 1765 and *The Chair Makers' Guide*, 1766.

Marot, Daniel (1661–1752) French architect, furniture designer and engraver of the Louis XIV period, and son of Jean Marot. After the revocation of the Edict of Nantes, Marot fled France for Holland where he introduced the French Baroque Style. Later, he also introduced the style to England and became chief designer to William III.

Marot, Jean (c. 1619–1679) A 17th-century French architect, designer and engraver primarily known for two important series of engravings instrumental in the study of 17th-century French architecture: *La Petit Marot* and *Le Grand Marot*.

Martin brothers 1) French brothers named Guillaume and Etienne-Simon Martin who worked as cabinetmakers during the 18th century reign of Louis XV and were known for their Chinese style of lacquer finish called Vernis Martin. 2) Four brothers named Wallace, Walter, Charles and Edwin who were pottery manufacturers working the transition from Victorian to studio pottery in late 19th century and early 20th century in England.

Mathsson, Bruno (1907–1988) A 20th-century Swedish furniture designer and architect known for his functional modern pieces combined with the Swedish craft tradition. Notable works include: Grasshopper, 1921; Mimat, 1932; Eva chair, 1935; and swivel chair, 1939.

Mayhew, John (1736–1811) An 18th-century English cabinetmaker and founding partner of Ince and Mayhew, a firm that published a volume of engraved designs called *The Universal System of Household Furniture* to rival Thomas Chippendale.

McCobb, Paul (1917–1969) American furniture and industrial designer of the Modern Style, perhaps best known for his modulor furniture.

McComb Jr., John (1763–1853) American architect known for many landmark designs of the 18th and 19th centuries including: New York City Hall, Montauk Lighthouse, and Gracie Mansion.

McIntyre, Samuel (1757–1811) Noted American woodcarver, cabinetmaker, and architect of the Federal Style, who worked primarily in Salem, Massachusetts.

Meier, Richard (1934–) American contemporary architect and furniture designer known for his rational designs and use of the color white. Awarded the Pritzker Prize for architecture in 1984, his most famous design is the Getty Center, an art museum in Los Angeles. Other selected works include: Barcelona Museum of Contemporary Art, Barcelona; Ara Pacis Museum, Rome; Meier House, Essex Fells, New Jersey; and the High Museum of Art, Atlanta, GA.

Meissonier, Juste-Aurèle (1695–1750) Popular French architect, goldsmith, sculptor, painter, and furniture designer of the Rococo Style, known for his extravagant designs. He was appointed as a designer to Louis XV in 1725.

Mendelsohn, Erich (1887–1953) German architect working in the expressionist style and one of the founding partners of Der Ring, a liberal-minded architectural group. Important works include: Einstein Tower, Potsdam; Schocken Department Store, Stuttgart; De La Warr Pavilion, Bexhill-on-Sea, Sussex, England; and Mossehaus offices, Berlin.

Michelangelo Buonarroti (1474–1564) Major Italian Renaissance painter, sculptor, and architect, commonly known as Michelangelo, who had an unparalleled influence on the development of art in the western world. Some of his best known works include: the Statue of David, the Pietà, and the scenes from Genesis and The Last Judgement in the Sistine Chapel in Rome, Italy.

Mies van der Rohe, Ludwig (1886–1969) Noted German architect and furniture designer of the Modern Style that served as the last director of the Bauhaus and as the director of the School of Architecture at the Illinois Institute of Technology. His most well-known pieces of furniture are the Barcelona Chair, 1929; Brno chair, 1930; and tugendhat chair, 1929. Some of his iconic structures include: Barcelona Pavilion, Barcelona, Spain, 1929; Farnsworth House, Plano, Ill, 1946; Lake Shore Drive Apartments, Chicago, Ill, 1948; Seagram Building, New York, NY, 1954; and Tugendhat House, Brno, Czech Republic, 1930.

Milton, Thomas (n.d.) An 18th-century English designer known for his chimney-piece designs.

Mogensen, Børge (1914–1972) A 20th-century Danish furniture designer whose use of simple functional forms and natural materials helped bring the Danish Modern Style to the international stage. Notable works include: Spanish chair, 1959; hunting chair, 1950; sleigh chair, 1953; Spoke-back Sofa, 1945; and shell chair, 1949.

Mondrian, Piet (1872–1944) A 20th-century Dutch abstract painter known for his compositions of non-representational gridded forms filled with primary colors on a white ground, and his contributions to the De Stijl art movement.

Monnoyer, Jean-Baptiste (1636–1699) Franco-Flemish painter known for his floral decorations during the Louis XIV period and his cartoon designs for tapestries produced in the Gobelins and Beauvais tapestry workshops.

Montigny, Philippe-Claude (1734–1800) Late 18th-century French maître ébéniste known for his high quality boulle cabinetwork with inlays of tortoise, silver, ebony, or brass and his restoration of original boulle furniture.

Morris, William (1834–1896) Founder and leader of the British Arts and Crafts movement and noted theorist associated with the Pre-Raphaelite Brotherhood. In partnership with the artist Edward Burnes-Jones and the poet Dante Gabrielle Rossetti, he formed Morris and Co., a design firm that that influenced the decoration of homes and churches of the time with offerings of wallpapers, furniture, tapestries, carpets, stained glass, and home accessories.

Moser, Koloman (1868–1918) Famous Austrian artist of the Vienna Secession and co-founder of the Wiener Werkstätte, whose designs had considerable influence on 20th-century graphic art.

Nash, John (1752–1835) Prolific English architect of the Regency period whose well-known work includes: the Royal Pavilion, Buckingham Palace, and Carlton House Terrace.

Natoire, Charles-Joseph (1700–1777) French painter whose Rococo Style work was incorporated into boiserie panels, overdoors, and overmantels of many salons and boudoirs of the 18th century.

Nelson, George (1908–1986) American industrial designer and architect considered to be one of the founders of American Modernism. As founding partner of George Nelson Associates and Director of Design for Herman Miller furniture company, Nelson created numerous 20th century modern pieces. Some of his most iconic works include: ball clock, 1950; coconut chair, 1955; sling sofa, 1964.

Neutra, Richard (1892–1970) A 20th-century American naturalized Austrian architect of the International Style, noted for his airy yet geometrically rigorous structures of light steel framing with cantilevered walls and balconies. Notable works include: Miller House, Palm Springs, CA; Lovell House, Los Angeles, CA; Kaufman House, Palm Spring, CA.

Noguchi, Isamu (1904–1988) Acclaimed 20th-century Japanese American artist-designer noted for his sculpture, furniture, lighting, ceramics, architecture, set designs, and gardens. His most influential works include: the Japanese Garden, UNESCO Headquarters, Paris; Red Cube, HSBC Building, New York; Sky Gate, Honolulu Hale, Honolulu, Hawaii; Akari lanterns; and the Noguchi table manufactured by Herman Miller.

Norman, Charles Pierre Joseph (1765–1840) French architect, designer, and engraver that produced numerous engraved plates of the Empire Style, most notably for the influential publications of Percier and Fontaine.

Oberkampf, Christophe-Philippe (1738–1815) French naturalized German founder of Jouy, France manufacturer of printed cottons and creator of toile de Jouy.

Oeben, Jean Francois (1721–1763) An 18th-century French master cabinetmaker for Louis XV. The famous roll-top bureau du roi, signed by Jean Henri Reisner, was begun by Oeben in 1760, although it remained unfinished at his death in 1763. The piece was later finished by John Henri Reisner in 1769.

Olbrich, Josef Maria (1867–1908) Austrian architect, designer, and co-founder of the Vienna Secession in 1897. He was responsible for the design of the movement's iconic exhibition building, the Secession Hall, located in Vienna, Austria.

Oppenord, Alexandre-Jean (1639–1713) Menuisier en ebène (furniture-maker in ebony) and later ébéniste du roi of Louis XIV. Father of Gilles Marie Oppenord.

Oppenord Gilles Marie (1672–1742) French architect and designer of the Régence period and an initiator of the Rococo Style.

Oudry, Jean Baptiste (1686–1755) French Rococo painter, engraver, and tapestry designer known for his naturalistic animal and hunt paintings and a series of tapestries based on the fables of La Fontiane. He was later the director of the Beauvais and Gobelins tapestry manufactories.

Pabst, Daniel (1826–1910) A 19th-century German immigrant to America in 1849 who became one of Philadelphia's master cabinetmakers. Working with Frank Furness, he created pieces with high relief in the Renaissance Revival, Modern Gothic, Colonial Revival and Neo-Grec Styles. He also worked at cameo-carving (intaglio) in wood. Even though he produced thousands of pieces over fifty years, there are only two signed pieces.

Pafrat, Jean-Jacque (n.d.) An 18th-century master cabinetmaker for Louis XVI who worked with Martin Carlin and created pieces for Marie Antoinette for which he received fame.

Pain, William (c. 1730–c. 1790) An 18th-century architect, joiner, carpenter and author of several architectural pattern books, his first being *The Builder's Companion* or *Workman's General Assistant*, containing many plates depicting construction of brick and stone arches, chimneys, columns, ceiling, etc.

Paine, James (1717–1789) An 18th-century English architect and Palladian designer, responsible for the central block of Kedleston Hall, Derbyshire, where he suggested the colonnaded hall. Robert Adam altered the design after he displaced him. He was also a known bridge builder and held several positions in the Office of Works, but lost his job during the reorganization of 1780.

Palladio, Andrea, b. Andrea di Pietro della Gondola but known as "Palladio" (1508–1580) A 16th-century Italian Renaissance architect, mannerist in his approach, with an extraordinary interest in the composition of the interior in terms of spatial effects. His architecture was modeled after classical Greek and Roman forms, which he used in domestic architecture in northern Italy. He was also commissioned to do churches in Venice, with three magnificent churches remaining today: S. Giorgio Maggiore, II Redentore, and "Le Zitelle" (S.M. della Presentazions). In 1570 his book entitled *I Quattro Libri dell Architettura (The Four Books of Architecture)* influenced architecture in England and America and made a place for him in architectural history.

Panton, Verner (1926–1998) Born in Odensee, Denmark, Panton became an architect and furniture designer and follower of Arne Jacobsen, having worked for him from 1950–1952 before opening his own office in Switzerland in 1955. He was known for his experimentation with form and materials, inflatable furniture, sculptural designs, many playful and futuristic, and vivid colors. He experimented with housing, the 1957 Cardboard House and the 1960 Spherical House. During the years 1958–1960, he designed the Cone chair, Heart chair, Wire Cone chair and the Panton Chair. He is well-known as one of the most innovative of the 20th-century designers.

Papillon, Jean-Michel (1661–1723) A French wallpaper designer, who in 1688 produced printed sheets that would form matching consecutive designs when pasted on a wall. Often attributed as being the inventor of wallpaper.

Parish, Mrs. Henry II, b. Dorothy May Kinnicutt but known as "sister Parish" (1910–1994) Leading American interior designer during the 20th century and design partner of Albert Hadley, a designer from Tennessee. She was the first interior designer to decorate the White House for the Kennedys. While her partner, Albert Hadley, was a modernist, she was a designer of homey, traditional interiors with a love for painted furniture and patchwork quilts.

Paulin, Pierre (1927–) A 20th-century French designer of furniture, characterized by a steel frame with a sculptural appearance, covered with polyurethane foam and stretched upholstery. The ribbon chair, 1966, is one of his famous productions. He also received the commission to design furniture for the Louvre Museum in 1968.

Paxton, Sir Joseph (1803–1865) English architect and landscape gardener, who in 1837 designed the Great Conservatory, a huge cast-iron heated green house which became the test structure for his greatest masterpiece, the prefabricated glass and iron Crystal Palace of the Great Exhibition of 1851.

Percier, Charles (1764–1838) French architect of the early 19th century, commissioned by Napoleon I as one of the official architects, along with Pierre Fontaine. Both helped create the Empire Style. Collaborating with Pierre Fontaine, he published a pattern book in 1801 entitled *Recueil de décorations intérieures* which included a set of engraved designs for interiors and furniture. The book inspired designers, including Duncan Phyfe and Thomas Hope, and it also helped promote the development of the Empire Style.

Pergolesi, Michael Angelo (n.d.) An 18th-century Italian decorative painter, architect, and furniture designer who worked extensively in England for Robert Adam. In addition to designing furniture, mantelpieces, doors, chandeliers, ceilings, etc., he authored a book between 1777 and 1801 entitled *Designs for Various Ornaments on Seventy Plates*.

Perriand, Charlotte (1903–1999) French furniture designer and interior designer who worked on creating functional spaces and furniture made from chromed steel and anodized aluminum, then during the 1930s she began using more traditional materials that were affordable. Perriand went on to work for Le Corbusier in the 1970s. She collaborated with him on many successful pieces and was later contracted by Cassina to produce new editions of Le Corbusier furniture.

Phyfe, Duncan (1768–1854) A Scottish furniture maker who moved to Albany, New York in the late 18th century where he became one of the most well-known furniture designers of the Neoclassical Style by the mid 19th century. Influenced by Sheraton, Thomas Hope, and the French Empire, he headed a very successful furniture design business.

Picasso, Pablo Ruiz, b. Pablo Diego José Francisco de Paula Juan Ne pomuceno Maria de los Remedios Cipriano de la Santisima Trinidad Ruiz y Picasso (1881–1973) An extremely influential 20th-century painter, sculptor, stage designer, and ceramicist, well-known for his involvement as co-founder of the Cubist movement. He was a prolific artist creating more than 50,000 works done in a variety of media. At the time of his death, he was still in possession of his life's work, which was left to his heirs and the French state. His work lives on with famous works, such as *Les Demoiselles d'Avignon*, 1907. He will forever be known as one of the greatest modern artists who worked in a variety of media and styles.

Pillement, Jean-Baptiste (1728–1808) A painter and textile designer, creating textiles in the Rococo Style with winding stripes, interlacing ribbons, and particularly noted for his chinoiseries. He painted exquisite landscapes and engravings. He also designed textiles during both the Louis XV and Louis XVI periods.

Piranesi, Giambattista, also Giovanni Battista Piranesi (1720 –1778) An 18th-century Italian architect, printmaker, and art theorist, well-known for his etchings of Rome. He did measurements of many of the ancient edifices in Rome and published a book entitled *Antichita Romane de' tempo della prima Repubblica e dei primi imperatori (Roman Antiquities of the Time of the First Republic and the First Emperors)*. Later in 1769 he published some bizarre designs of chimneypieces and a range of furniture pieces. One of his best known works as a restorer of ancient sculpture is the Piranesi Vase. In 1777–1778 he published *Avanzi deli Edifici di Pesto* (*Remains of the Edifices of Paestum*), which is a collection of views of Paestum, Italy.

Platner, Warren (1919–2006) An American architect, interior designer, and furniture designer born in Baltimore who earned a degree in architecture from Cornell University School of Architecture and worked for Eero Saarinen in the 1960s. He opened his own office in Connecticut in 1967 under the title Platner and Associates. He was the designer and developer of the Knoll "Platner Collection," a major contribution to the furniture industry. He often was involved in large architectural and interior design commissions and believed in designing the details, even as minute as dishes and textiles.

Ponti, Gio (1891–1979) An important 20th-century Italian architect, industrial designer, furniture designer, and artist. He was also founding editor of Domus magazine where he published his designs and work. Even though he played many roles, his greatest role was that of a writer, where he was an advocate for design excellence. Words of his daughter describe his career: "Sixty years of work, buildings in 13 countries, lectures in 24, 25 years of teaching, 50 years of editing, articles in every one of the 560 issues of his magazines, 2500 letters dictated, 2000 letters drawn, designs for a 120 enterprises, and 1000 architectural sketches."

Prud'hon, Pierre-Paul (1758–1823) A celebrated French Romantic painter from the late 18th and early 19th centuries, known for his allegorical paintings and portraits. As a painter and designer of the Empire period, he is best known for his painting of Empress Josephine, which hangs in the Louvre. He was influenced by both Neo-classicism and Romanticism.

Pugin, Augustus Welby Northmore (1812–1852) An early 19th-century English architect, designer, theorist, and author who was one of the most influential ecclesiastical architects of mid-19th-century English architecture and design and one of the principal theoreticians of the Gothic revival. He wrote and published *The True Principles of Pointed or Christian Architecture*, 1841, advocating a correct Gothic Style for buildings and describing Gothic as a utilitarian architecture. Two other publications by Pugin influenced monastic and institutional buildings: *Apology for the Revival of Christian Architecture in England*, 1843, and *The Present State of Ecclesiastical Architecture in England*, 1843.

Pullman, George Mortimer (1831–1897) A 19th-century American industrialist and developer of the railroad sleeping car in 1864; one of Chicago's most influential persons but also a very controversial figure. He was buried in a Pullman Sleeper with criss-crossed steel rails placed on top. To insure the body would not be exhumed or desecrated, several tons of cement were poured on top.

Quervelle, Anthony Gabriel (1789–1856) A French furniture designer who came to Philadelphia in 1817. He designed exquisite furniture with unique architectural motifs and foliage in the American Empire Style.

Raffaello Sanzio da Urbino, known simply as Raphael (1483–1520) A High Renaissance architect and painter from Italy, who succeeded Bramante as architect of St.Peter's. He was a leading painter, who decorated rooms with frescoes and paintings for Popes Julius III and Leo X. He was one of the three great masters, together with Michelangelo and Leonardo da Vinci. The Apostolic Palace of The Vatican has many of his works, including some of the largest work of his career.

Randolph, Benjamin (1721–1791) A leading Philadelphia cabinetmaker in the latter part of the 18th century who made highboys and chairs in the Chippendale Style. He worked for Thomas Jefferson, who roomed at his home in 1775 and 1776 while in Philadelphia. It is rumored that Jefferson composed the Declaration of Independence on a desk made by Randolph.

Rateau, Armand-Albert (1882–1938) Having studied at the Ecole, this French architect and designer first worked with the famous decorator Georges Hoentschel, then he started his own business in 1919.

His work became known in America when he was named the interior designer of the wealthy New York Blumentahl family's ballroom and indoor pool in 1920, and in the following years he continued to work for them. His workshop was in Neuilly-Levallois where he employed two hundred and twelve craftsmen.

Reich, Lilly (1885–1947) A German designer known for her association with Ludwig Mies van der Rohe in designing both the Brno chair, a chromed steel frame chair, and the Pavillion, an x-shaped design with the finest upholstery. She also worked in Vienna for the Wiener Werkstätte before she met Mies van der Rohe. In 1929, Reich and Mies organized Germany's contribution to the World Exposition in Barcelona. In 1921 she was asked by Mies to head the interior design workshop at the Bauhaus, but the appointment was only for a limited time due to the closing of the Bauhaus.

Réveilon, Jean Baptiste (1725–1811) Wallpaper designer in France in the 18th century, with strong Neoclassical influence. He opened his own paper mill and shop in 1775 and provided the colored wallpaper for the first hot-air balloon in 1783. The Revolution destroyed his mansion, all of his furniture, and all the wallpaper, etc. Fleeing from France, he and his family moved to England. He rented his wallpaper factory to Jacquemart & Bénard.

Revere, Paul (1735–1818) Well-known for his ability to watch the British military and for the famous ride warning of British arrival in Boston, he was also an outstanding American silversmith and engraver who decorated his own work. Documentation shows that he crafted more than 5,000 products during his lifetime.

Richardson, Henry Hobson (1838–1886) A 19th-century American architect, and one of the most influential leaders of the Romanesque Revival Style. Having studied at the Ecole des Beaux-Arts and graduating from Harvard, he did some of his finest work in Boston, using a Romanesque design for Trinity Church, 1872–1877. Other very successful buildings designed by Richardson were Albany City Hall, Sever Hall at Harvard University, and the New York State Capital. Richardsonian Romanesque was a term used vaguely to identify most structures from the mid-1870s to the 1900s, particularly those with arches faced with ashlar granite, and other features identified with Richardson, such as

eyebrow windows, short heavy columns, and dormers referred to as "Loire dormers."

Riemerschmidt, Richard (1868–1957) A late 19th-century through early 20th-century German architect, product designer, and city planner, who studied at the Academy of Fine Arts, Munich, then worked as an artist and architect independently. He is credited with being an influential figure in Jugendstil, which is the German form of Art Nouveau. He was also the founder of architecture using that style. During the 1920s and early 1930s he was professor and director of Kolner Wekschulen (a college of art and design, a forerunner of the Academy of Media Arts Cologne). In addition to being a leader of the Jugendstil Style of architecture in Germany, he also worked as a product designer involved in furniture, glass, porcelain, textiles, and wallpaper.

Riesener, Jean-Henri (1734–1806) A French cabinetmaker that began his career with and succeeded Jean Francois Oeben, a master cabinetmaker to Louis XV. He continued to work into the next regime for Marie Antoinette and was named ebenistre ordinaire du roi (cabinetmaker to the king) in 1774. He survived the French Revolution by removing royal emblems from furniture for the new regime. Also known for his ingenious design of mechanical fittings for desk and tabletops that allowed them to be raised or lowered with a single button.

Rietveld, Gerrit Thomas (1888–1964) Born in Utrecht, he became a Dutch architect and furniture designer and a leader of the De Stijl movement. He is known for his famous Red-Blue chair, constructed in 1918. Even though the chair is uncomfortable and lacked stability, Rietveld used it to express a doctrine of sculptural form. The Schroeder house, one of his De Stijl architectural designs of 1924, is an excellent example of his use of primary colors and his allegiance to the De Stijl movement.

Risom, Jens (1916–) A 20th-century Danish born interior designer and furniture designer, who came to the United States and became an influential designer and producer of modern furniture with high standards. He worked under the tutelage of Kaare Klint and Ole Wanscher. At the beginning of his career, he was a textile designer. He became the Director of Interior Design for Dan Cooper, Inc. and then he joined Hans Knoll to help with the New York World's Fair exhibition. Collier's magazine invited him to design the interior for the "House of Ideas" in Rockefeller Center. After the war, he started his own business, received numerous awards, and was knighted by Queen Margrethe with the Danish Knight's Cross.

Robsjohn-Gibbings, Terence Harold (1905–1976) Born in England, he studied architecture at London University and became a naval architect, designing interiors for ocean liners, and then became a set director for motion pictures. By the 1930s he was well-known as a decorator of American houses, characterized by the use of classical Ancient Greek design mixed with the elegant Art Deco Style. After working for many wealthy and famous clients in New York, he worked in Grand Rapids for the Widdicomb furniture company as a designer, then he decided to relocate to Greece where he became a decorator for Aristotle Onassis. He designed the Klismos chair in 1960 with Greek cabinetmakers, Susan and Eleftherios Saridis. Several books on antiques and decoration were published under his name.

Rodriquez, Ventura (1717–1785) Spanish 18th-century architect and leader of the developing Rococo in a Spanish form, which is evident in his design of the Chapel of Our Lady of Pilar in the cathedral of Saragoosa.

Roentgen, David (1743–1807) An 18th-century German cabinet-maker, known throughout Europe for his mechanical designs. He was appointed maître ébéniste by Marie Antoinette. He held a position of high distinction for his marquetry, which was bold and embraced the late Rococo and Neoclassical Styles.

Rubens, Peter Paul (1577–1640) A major influence as a late 16th and early 17th-century Flemish painter, etcher, and draughtsman, producing tapestry cartoons for the monarch. He worked as a painter for Marie de Medici in Paris at the Luxembourg Palace. As a painter, he was a proponent of the extravagant, emphasizing color and movement, and is known for his portraits, landscapes, altarpieces, and paintings of allegorical subjects and mythological scenes produced during the Counter-Reformation.

Ruhlmann, Emile-Jacques (1879–1933) A French interior designer and furniture designer who in the 1920s in Paris created luxury Art Deco designs. He used luxurious and exotic materials such as ebony intarsia inlay, tortoise shell, and expensive woods. Town houses and other Paris interiors designed by Ruhlmann were fashionable and extravagant. He also designed several rooms in the Élysée Palace.

Ruskin, John (1819–1900) Leading 19th-century English writer, art critic, and historian exerting an influence on the Arts and Crafts movement through his writings of *The Seven Lamps of Architecture*, 1849, and *The Stones of Venice*, 1851–1853. One of his statements, "all noble ornamentation is the expression of man's delight in God's work" depicts the Gothic idea formulated in his writings.

Saarinen, Eero (1910–1961) Innovative Finnish-American architect and furniture designer of the International Style. Prominent work includes TWA's futuristic terminal at New York's JFK Airport and collaborations with furniture designer, Charles Eames. He was the son of celebrated Finnish architect, Eliel Saarinen.

Saarinen, Eliel (1873–1950) Finnish architect who moved to the United Sates in 1923 and became the first president of the celebrated Cranbrook Academy of Art. Projects include: the Helsinki railway station, National Museum of Finland, and the Finnish pavilion of the World Fair of 1900. He was the father of Eero Saarinen.

Sanderson, Robert (1608–1693) One of the earliest known New England silversmiths. He was a partner in the firm of Hull & Sanderson (ca. 1652 to 1683) in Boston, MA.

Saunier, Claude Charles (1735–1807) French maître ébéniste (master cabinetmaker) for Louis XV and Lois XVI.

Sauvage, Piat Joseph (1744–1818) An 18th-century Belgian painter who worked for a time under the Hapsburg rule and later in France for Louis XVI, where he painted a portrait of Marie-Antoinette and several paintings for the chapel of Saint-Cloud. Known for his simulated sculptured bas-relief in grisaille.

Savery, William (c. 1721–1787) Prominent Philadelphia based American chair and cabinetmaker of the Colonial period, working in the Chippendale Style.

Seddon, George (c. 1727–1801) Successful 18th-century English Georgian cabinetmaker who founded a large furniture making firm in London in the early 1750s, at its height employing over four hundred craftsmen.

Soane, Sir John (1753–1837) An English architect, specializing in Neoclassical architecture, which was characterized by clean lines, excellent proportions, simple massing of form, and dedication to detail. His most outstanding work was the Bank of England.

Spode, Josiah (1733–1797) English potter and founder of the Stoke-on-Trent pottery works, Spode, famous for stoneware, bone china, and the introduction of transfer-printed earthenware.

Stam, Mart (1899–1986) Dutch-born leader of 20th-century modern architecture, pioneer furniture designer, and Bauhaus teacher, perhaps best known for his furniture design experiments with tubular steel, especially his revolutionary design of canilevered chairs such as the model 533 chair.

Starck, Philippe (1940–) Prolific French interior, furniture, and product designer of the New Design Style. Some noted interiors include: the Felix restaurant bar at the Peninsula Hotel in Hong Kong, the Cafe Costes in Paris, the Royalton Hotel in New York, the Delano Hotel in South Beach, and the Mondrian Hotel in Los Angeles. Many of Starck's furniture designs are of poly carbonate plastic for Kartell, an Italian manufacturer. His most well-known pieces include: the transparent ghost chair, ErolSi chair, bubble club sofa and armchair, and the La Bohème stool.

Stern, Robert Arthur Morton (1939–) American Postmodern architect and author, founder of Robert A. M. Stern Architects in New York, NY and Dean of the Yale University School of Architecture. His noted works include: Federal Reserve Bank, Atlanta, GA; Gerald R. Ford School of Public Policy at the University of Michigan; Museum for African American Art, New York, NY; Norman Rockwell Museum, Stockbridge, MA; and the planning for the Disney Town of Celebration, Orlando, FL. Generally credited as Robert A.M. Stern.

Stickley, Gustav (1858–1942) American cabinetmaker known for his fumed quartersawn oak furniture in simple geometric shapes. Stickley was founder of the periodical *The Craftsman* and generally considered the "Father" of the American Arts and Crafts movement.

Stiegel, Henry William (1729–1785) Noted Pre-Revolutionary German-American glassmaker and founder of American Flint Glassworks, 1762, in Manheim, Pennsylvania.

Stumpf, Bill (1936–2006) An American industrial designer who studied at the University of Illinois, after which he studied environmental design at the University of Wisconsin until 1968. He worked with Don Chadwick to design the Aeron chair; he also helped design the Ergon chair. Working with specialists he conducted extensive research into the ways people sit in chairs.

Sullivan, Louis (1856–1924) American architect generally considered to be America's first truly modern architect. A famed member of the "Chicago School" known for his beautiful naturalistic terra cotta designs over masonry. Famous Buildings include: Carson Pirie Scott Store, Guaranty Building, and the Wainwright Building.

Summers, Gerald (1899–1967) A 20th-century English furniture designer who used modern materials such as laminated wood to express geometrically simple designs.

Swan, Abraham (c. 1720–1765) Influential 18th-century English architect, designer, and author known for his architectural details of the English Rococo Style popular in residences of Georgian England and Colonial America.

Talbert, Bruce (1838–1881) A 19th-century Scottish designer best known for his furniture designs. His work for the Holland & Sons' stall at the 1867 Paris Exhibition was award winning, but his most notable piece was the Pet sideboard, 1873, which he designed for Gillows of Lancaster. Talbert also designed metalwork for Cox & Sons, cast iron for the Colebrookdale Co., textiles for Warners, Barbone & Miller and Cowlishaw, Nichols & Co. and wallpapers for Jeffrey & Co.

Tatlin, Vladimir (1885–1953) Russian architect and designer often called the father of Constructivism. Noted for his design of the monument of the Third Communist International.

Terry Sr., Eli (1772–1852) Early 19th-century Connecticut inventor and clockmaker who introduced mass production to clock making.

Thomas, Seth (1785–1859) An American clockmaker, pioneer of mass production in the art of clock making, and founder of the Seth Thomas Clock Company.

Thomire, Pierre-Philippe (1751–1843) Prominent French sculptor who produced gilt-bronze objects and mounts in the Neoclassical and Empire Styles. His most prestigious work was a cradle designed for Napoleon's infant son. Thomire also won a gold medal for his work in the 1806 Exposition Publique des Products del'Industrie.

Thonet, Michael (1796–1871) German-Austrian cabinetmaker known for his Austrian furniture company, Thonet, which used his patented process of bending laminated wood under heat to mass produce curvilinear bentwood furniture.

Thornton, Dr. William (1759–1828) British-American architect, inventor, painter, and physician of the Federal period known for his design of the United States Capitol.

Tiepolo, Giovanni Battista (1696–1770) An 18th-century Venetian painter and printmaker known for his brilliantly colored frescoes filled with light and extraordinary perspectives.

Tiffany, Louis Comfort (1848–1933) Prominent American artist and designer of the Art Nouveau and Aesthetics movements renowned for his stained glass work that took the form of windows and lamps. He also created glass mosaics and blown glass and was founder of Tiffany and Company.

Tilliard, Jean Baptiste (1685–1766) French maker of chairs during the Louis XV period.

Tintoretto, Jacopo Comin (1518–1594) Late Renaissance Venetian painter known for his energetically robust work, masculine figures, and bold use of perspectives in the Mannerist Style. His paintings covered religious, mythological and historical subjects. Some noted works include: Saint George and the Dragon, Allegory of Prudence, Angelica and the Hermit, and Baptism of Christ.

Titian (1477–1576) Born as Tiziano Vecellio, but better known as Titian. The leading painter of the 16th-century Late Renaissance Venetian School. Known for his versatility, sensuous quality, and deep interest in color. Important works include: Sacred and Profane Love, The Assumption of the Virgin, Bacchanal of the Andrians, and Rape of Europa.

Townsend, Job (1699–1765) An 18th-century Quaker cabinetmaker of Newport, Rhode Island, often thought of as the dean of Newport furniture makers.

Townsend, John (1732–1809) Celebrated 18th-century American cabinetmaker of the American Colonial period known for his use of the block-and-shell motif. Based out of Newport, Rhode Island, John was the son of Christopher Townsend, who was the brother of Job Townsend.

Tufft, Thomas (1842–1893) Late 18th-century Philadelphia cabinetmaker, known for his simple lowboys.

Utzon, John (1918–2008) A Danish architect known for his self termed "Additive Architecture" that forms naturally like the growth patterns of nature. His most prominent designs include the Sydney Opera House, 1956–1973; and Bagsværd Church, 1968–1976. He was the winner of the Pritzker Prize for architecture in 2003.

Van Briggle, Artus (1869–1904) American potter of Art Nouveau Style who first established himself as a potter at Rookwood Pottery and later founded the Van Briggle Pottery company in Colorado Springs, Colorado in 1901.

Vanbrugh, Sir John (1664–1726) Influential English architect, designer, and dramatist of the Early Georgian Style. Best known for his work on Blenheim Castle and Castle Howard.

van de Velde, Henry (1863–1957) A Belgium architect, designer, and originator of the Art Nouveau Style. Known for such works as: van de Velde House in Brussels, Belgium; Havana Company Store in Berlin, Germany; and the interiors and furniture of Samuel Bing's Paris art gallery L'Art Nouveau.

Vandergoten, Jacobo (d. 1724) A Brussels tapestry maker called to Madrid by Phillip V to direct Spain's royal manufactory of tapestries and rugs in Madrid from 1720 until his death in 1724.

van Doesburg, Theo (1883–1931) Dutch painter and art theorist instrumental in establishing the De Stijl movement with architect J.J.P. Oud and lecturer at the Bauhaus from 1921 to 1923.

van Risamburgh, Bernard II (ca. 1696–1766) One of a family of French cabinetmakers who served as a maître ébéniste to Louis XV. His Rococo Style furniture is stamped with the initials "B.V.R.B."

Venturi, Robert (1925–) Postmodern American architect, designer, theorist, author, and founding principal of the firm Venturi, Scott, Brown and Associates and regarded as one of the most influential architects of the 20th century. Known for coining the maxim "less is a bore" and for works such as the Sainesbury Wing of the National Gallery in London, Dumbarton Oaks Library in Washington, D.C., Freedom Plaza in Washington, D.C., and the Seattle Art Museum.

Vignelli, Lella (1934–) Italian designer and architect. Co-founder of the prominent design firm, Vignelli Associates with her husband, Massimo Vignelli in 1971. Leilla and Massimo received the National Lifetime Achievement Award from the National Museum of Design in 2003.

Vignelli, Massimo (1931–) Italian designer, married to Lella Vignelli, with whom he co-founded Vignelli Associates, a prominent firm that works primarily in the Modernist tradition on a range of products from packaging to furniture design. Vignelli was inducted into the Interior Design Hall of Fame in 1988, received the Visionary Award from the Museum of Art and Design in 2005, and with his wife the National Lifetime Achievement Award from the National Museum of Design in 2003.

Vignola, Giacomo Da (1507–1573) Italian architect noted for the classification of the "Orders of Architecture" based on Vitruvian proportions.

Vile, William (1700–1767) One of the best English cabinetmakers of the Georgian age and partner of John Cobb, known for his fine Rococo Style furniture during the early reign of George III.

Viollet-le-duc, Eugene-Emanuel (1814–1879) A 19th-century French architect and theorist who served as a key figure in the Gothic Revival Style.

Vitruvius Pollio, Marcus (n.d.) Popular architect and architectural theorist of the Roman empire (46–30 B.C.E.) whose work served as inspiration for designers of the Renaissance era.

Voysey, Charles Francis Annesley (1857–1941) English architect and designer of furniture, wallpaper, and textiles of the Arts & Crafts period in Great Britain. Influenced by the works of Arthur Mackmurdo and Charles Rennie Mackintosh. He is best known as C.F.A. Vosey.

Wagner, Otto (1841–1918) An Austrian architect who admired the machine and understood its essential character. He became one of the most influential figures in the development of 20th-century European architecture as a designer of the Secession movement.

Ware, Issacs (1704–1766) An 18th-century architect-designer of buildings and furnishings, as well as interior decorator who collaborated with William Kent on Holkham Hall in Norfolk. He also published the *Complete Book of Architecture*.

Warhola, Andrew, Jr. known as Warhol, Andy (1928–1987) An inspiring artist and major figure in the Pop Art movement during the 1960s and identified by the media as the "Prince of Pop." He is known for painting daily objects such as "Campbell's Soup" cans and Coke bottles and for his silkscreen prints of famous personalities like Marilyn Monroe and Elizabeth Taylor. He continued to work through the 1970s and 1980s until his death in 1987.

Watteau, Jean-Antoine (1684–1721) A well-known painter of the French Regénce period, who depicted balls, pastoral scenes, musical parties, etc. and whose art was graceful and full of idyllic shepherdesses, and attenuated decorative borders.

Webb, Philip Speakman (1831–1915) An important English architect who was a friend of William Morris and designer of the Red House at Bexleyheath in southeast London, England, 1859.

Wedgewood, Josiah (1730–1795) A distinguished English potter that established the Wedgewood factory in England in 1769 and is famous for his Jasperware and other pottery pieces.

Wegner, Hans (1914–2007) An outstanding Danish furniture designer who became an assistant to Arne Jacobsen from 1939–1943 before opening his own design shop. His designs of modern furniture are known for comfort and exquisite craftsmanship.

Weisweiler, Adam (1744–1820) Cabinetmaker during the Louis XVI period and early French Empire who strongly influenced the Egyptian classical designs in furniture he made for Marie Antoinette.

Whieldon, Thomas (1719–1795) An 18th-century potter at Fenton, Staffordshire, England, and an early partner of Josiah Wedgwood. He was the designer of a speckled earthenware called "Whieldon" ware (also called "Tortoiseshell").

Whistler, James Abbott McNeill (1834–1903) An American painter, etcher, and decorator who traveled the world and eventually settled in London where he became famous for his work in etching, lithography, pastels, and watercolor. He was the author of many essays on art theory.

White, Stanford (1853–1906) A 19th-century American architect and founding partner in the New York architecture firm McKim, Mead, and White who specialized in interior design, furnishings, and decorative elements of buildings.

Wolfe, Elsie de (1865–1950) A leading American designer of the early 20th century who had great influence in America and Europe on 18th-century elegance especially the French versions. She was the first female professional interior designer in the United States, a socialite, and prominent figure in New York.

Wormley, Edward (1907–1995) American furniture designer in the 1930s known for his conservative forms of modern furniture with Dunbar as his exclusive client.

Wren, Sir Christopher (1632–1723) Renowned classic English architect-designer noted for his design of St. Paul's Cathedral and many other churches in London. An interior decorator of mantels, fireplaces, wall treatments, and pews.

Wright, Frank Lloyd (1867–1959) A prolific American architect, designer, historian, author, and critic who had significant influence on the 20th-century building design. He promoted organic architecture. Later he opened architecture schools at Taliesin East and West where he personally trained many architects.

Wright, Russel (1904–1976) American industrial designer who in the 1930s and 1940s designed popular ceramic dinnerware. He was successful at designing for home use including the use of modern functional forms, simplified shapes, and cheerful colors in furniture, appliances, ceramics, fabrics, and many other daily life products.

Wyatt, James (1747–1813) Successful English architect who spent time in Venice in the mid 17th century and whose designs were Neo-Gothic and Neoclassical.

Zucchi, Antonio Pietro (1726–1795) An acclaimed Venetian artist/painter who worked in England with Robert Adam, decorating interiors, and making panels, plaques, and medallions for furniture. He married Angelica Kauffman, who also was a painter.

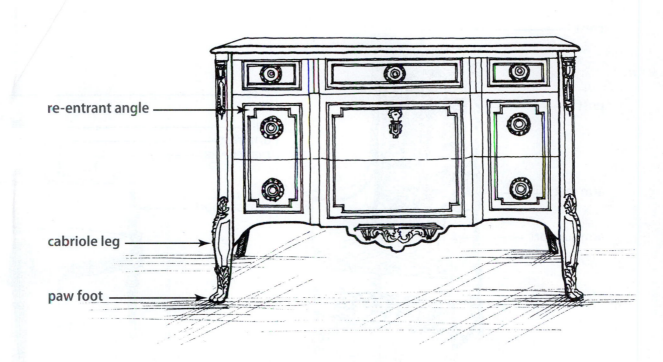

re-entrant angle

cabriole leg

paw foot

Chair Vocabulary

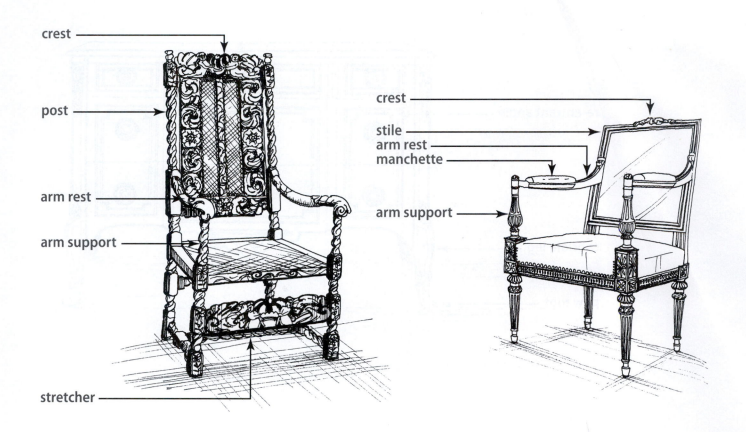

crest

post

arm rest

arm support

stretcher

crest

stile

arm rest

manchette

arm support

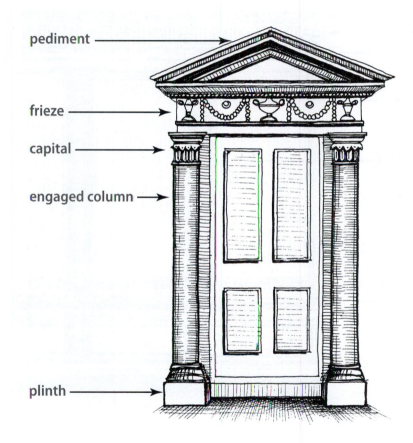

pediment

frieze

capital

engaged column

plinth

Wall Design

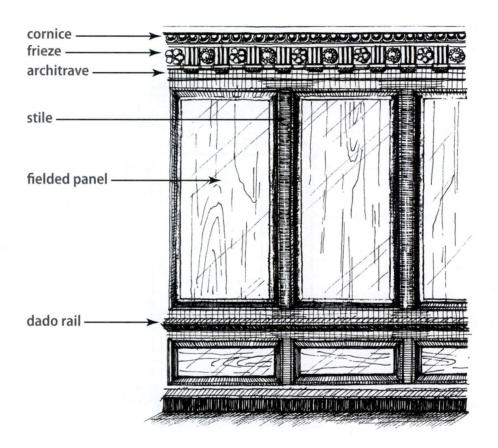

cornice

frieze

architrave

stile

fielded panel

dado rail

Doric Order   Ionic Order   Corinthian Order

Tuscan Order   Composite Order

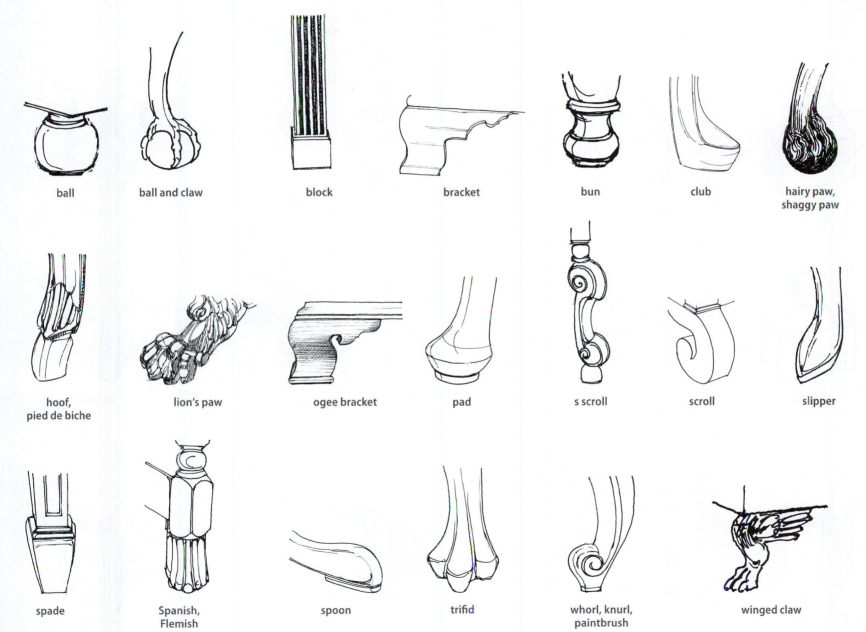

ball

ball and claw

block

bracket

bun

club

hairy paw,
shaggy paw

hoof,
pied de biche

lion's paw

ogee bracket

pad

s scroll

scroll

slipper

spade

Spanish,
Flemish

spoon

trifid

whorl, knurl,
paintbrush

winged claw

Joints

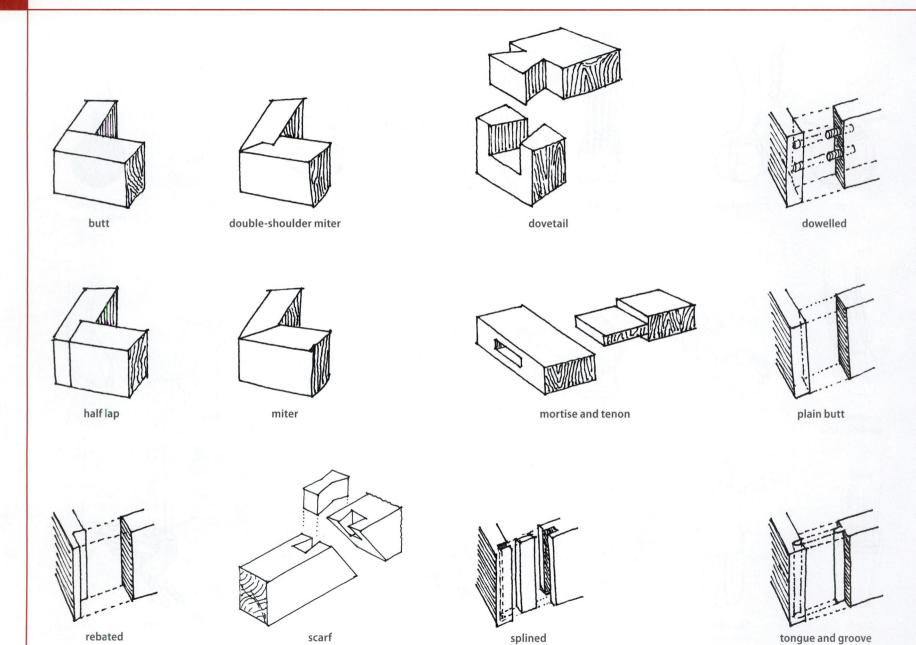

butt

double-shoulder miter

dovetail

dowelled

half lap

miter

mortise and tenon

plain butt

rebated

scarf

splined

tongue and groove

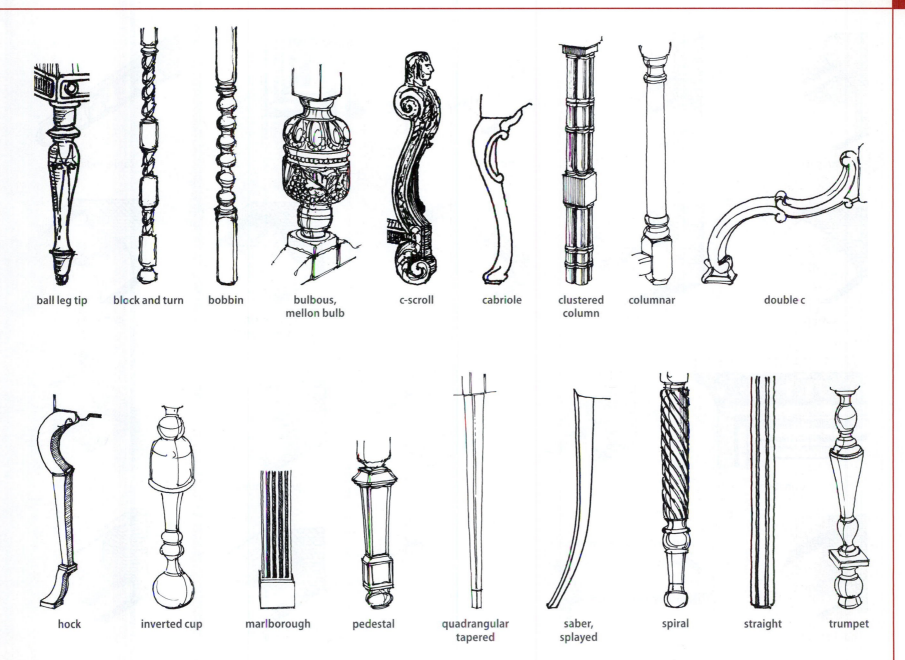

ball leg tip   block and turn   bobbin   bulbous, mellon bulb   c-scroll   cabriole   clustered column   columnar   double c

hock   inverted cup   marlborough   pedestal   quadrangular tapered   saber, splayed   spiral   straight   trumpet

Moldings

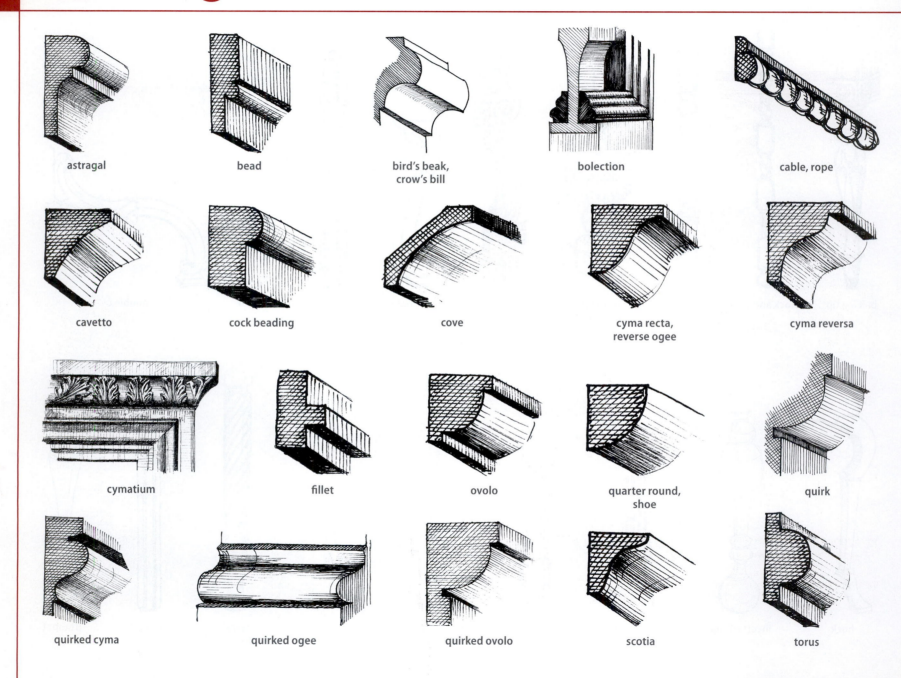

astragal

bead

bird's beak,
crow's bill

bolection

cable, rope

cavetto

cock beading

cove

cyma recta,
reverse ogee

cyma reversa

cymatium

fillet

ovolo

quarter round,
shoe

quirk

quirked cyma

quirked ogee

quirked ovolo

scotia

torus

acanthus

anthemion

arabesque

bead and reel

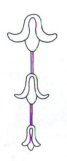

bellflower,
husk

c scroll

cobochon

cartouche

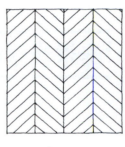

chevron,
herringbone

cinquefoil

dentil

diapering

egg and dart

fleur di lis

foliated scroll

gadrooning

Greek fret, key,
meander

griffin

grotesque

guilloche

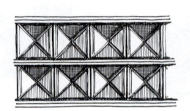

heraldic device

honeysuckle,
palmette border

lotus bud

lozenge

lunette, fan

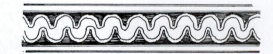

palmette

patera

quadruple spiral

quatrefoil

raies de couer

appendix

rinceau

rosette

s scroll

shell

sphinx

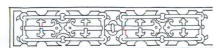

strapwork

trefoil

wave

zigzag

Pediments

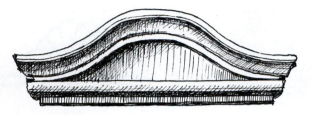

bonnet

broken scroll, swan's neck

broken triangular

double bonnet

open

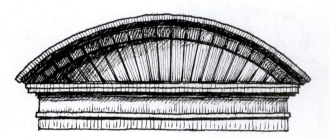

segmental

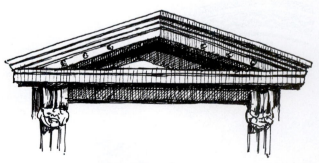

triangular